OXFORD HISTORICAL MONOGRAPHS

BENJAMIN COLLINS AND THE PROVINCIAL NEWSPAPER TRADE IN THE EIGHTEENTH CENTURY

C. Y. FERDINAND

CLARENDON PRESS · OXFORD

1997

Oxford University Press, Great Clarendon Street, Oxford OX2 6DP

Oxford New York

Athens Auckland Bangkok Bogota Bombay
Buenos Aires Calcutta Cape Town Dar es Salaam
Delhi Florence Hong Kong Istanbul Karachi
Kuala Lumpur Madras Madrid Melbourne
Mexico City Nairobi Paris Singapore
Taipei Tokyo Toronto

and associated companies in
Berlin Ibadan

Oxford is a trade mark of Oxford University Press

Published in the United States
by Oxford University Press Inc., New York

British Library Cataloguing in Publication Data
Data available

Library of Congress Cataloging in Publication Data
Data applied for

ISBN 0–19–820652–6

1 3 5 7 9 10 8 6 4 2

Typeset by Graphicraft Typesetters Ltd., Hong Kong
Printed in Great Britain
on acid-free paper by
Biddles Ltd., Guildford & King's Lynn

For MMF *and* LAF

PREFACE

THIS history of the eighteenth-century provincial newspaper press began
as a more narrowly focused bibliographical study. Indeed, I first became
interested in the *Salisbury Journal*, the most important of the Wessex
regional papers, when I was trying to discover the precise relationship
between the Salisbury printer, bookseller, and banker, Benjamin Collins
and the printing of the first edition of Smollett's *Humphry Clinker* (1771).
As the topic developed I became equally concerned to place the *Salisbury
Journal*, which was the keystone in Collins's complex and successful business structure, into the broader context of the history of the whole inter-
connected book and newspaper trade in England, already long established
when country newspapers came on the scene. The evidence of the *Salisbury
Journal* itself, and of the other regional Wessex papers, plus significant
new documentary material, provided the basis for a new construction of
the provincial newspaper, including discussion of the levels of management, the areas of distribution, the numbers circulated, and the geography
and make-up of readership. The simple mechanics of production can be
considered in the light of this practical evidence; so can the editorial
policy that governed the presentation of news and advertising, and the
dual role of the newspaper in both describing and instructing the times.

Any eighteenth-century newspaper can provide useful evidence for the
history of education, of literacy, of advertising, of leisure, even of literature. There are countless ways in which the evidence of serials can be made
to serve different interests: from projects that trawl through the papers to
extract specific information, like certain genres of advertisement, to others
that take a more comprehensive approach. Yet they remain a relatively
underused resource in social, cultural, and commercial history.

One of the mysteries of this project remains the whereabouts of Collins's
correspondence. There is no question that Benjamin Collins played a
central, vital role in the regional book and newspaper trade through much
of the eighteenth century. Likewise he had an important role to play, too,
in the London trade. His name appears in hundreds of book imprints. Yet
he spent most of his life in Salisbury, which would have meant that much
of his business must have been conducted by post. Only a few letters and
documents in his hand have been located, despite searches through all
the obvious repositories. The Public Record Office, the British Library,

the Bodleian Library, the Beinecke Library at Yale, Duke University Library, local record offices, the East India Office, Gosling's Bank, and private collections all hold other evidence of his business dealings. It is true that Collins's account books were around early this century and Charles Welsh was able to include tantalizing extracts in his book about Collins's colleague John Newbery, but it seems certain that they were later destroyed. Perhaps the publication of this fuller account of Benjamin Collins and his newspapers will assist in locating other evidence, not just about him, but about the wider newspaper trade in the eighteenth century.

C.Y.F.

ACKNOWLEDGEMENTS

RECOVERING the history of Benjamin Collins and the *Salisbury Journal* has taken me into archives and libraries in England and the United States and has in fact put me in touch with an active community of scholarship that includes academics, family descendants, historians, librarians, and newspapermen. Among those who have helped me along the way I would like to thank John Bidwell, Jeremy Black, Matthew Brack, Colin Brodie, Michael Crump, Norman Evans, Derek Gladwyn, Michael Harris, Gerald Harriss, Charles Hind, Clive Hurst, Andrea Immel, Joanna Innes, M. J. Jannetta, Graham Jefcoate, Paul Langford, Geoffrey Martin, Ian Maxted, Robin Myers, Roy Porter, Esther Potter, The Earl of Radnor, James Raven, R. H. Reed, K. H. Rogers, Jenny Ruthven, Margaret Smith, Nancy Steel, John Styles, Michael Treadwell, Michael Turner, Gareth Weekes, Ian Willison, Joseph Wisdom, and Marjorie Wynne.

This work owes something to every scholar cited in the footnotes here, especially to the late Graham Cranfield and Roy M. Wiles for their pioneering work on the eighteenth-century provincial newspaper trade in England, and to the late Albert H. Smith, for his pioneering work on Benjamin Collins.

Particular thanks are due to O M Brack, Jr. for his generous encouragement and his readiness to share a comprehensive knowledge of eighteenth-century English literature and history.

I owe a special debt to D. F. McKenzie for his constant and painstaking attention to this work throughout its preparation.

CONTENTS

LIST OF MAPS

LIST OF TABLES

ABBREVIATIONS

BL	British Library
Bodl	Bodleian Library
BRO	Berkshire Record Office
DRO	Dorset Record Office
ESTC	*Eighteenth-Century Short Title Catalogue*
GM	*Gentleman's Magazine*
HC	*Hampshire Chronicle*
HRO	Hampshire Record Office
LM	*London Magazine*
PRO	Public Record Office
SJ	*Salisbury Journal*
VCH	*Victoria County History*
WRO	Wiltshire Record Office

Eighteenth-century punctuation and spellings—including *stationary* and *distributer*—have been retained in quotations.

Introduction

IN 1772 James Linden had every reason to believe that his latest project, a newspaper published from the southern port areas to serve a Hampshire readership, would surely succeed. Hampshire had never really had its own newspaper, except for short-lived local editions of the Salisbury and Reading papers. Readers could always subscribe to the London papers, and for that matter to any other paper, but it was not unreasonable to believe that there would be a market for a locally published newspaper that followed what was by then an established provincial format: an inexpensive four-page weekly made up of news from the London and Continental papers, combined with local reports and advertising. In a way Benjamin Collins had already proved that point with the *Salisbury Journal*, which drew much of Hampshire into its catchment area. But that was published from Wiltshire. Many would have agreed that Southampton had the advantage over Salisbury in its ready access to news of shipping, the colonies, and the armed forces.

Linden himself had done his part to promote a growing readership: for almost fifteen years he had been educating 'young Gentlemen' at his Southampton school. The course of study he originally offered—arithmetic, 'MERCHANTS-ACCOMPTS, by double Entry', navigation, and astronomy—produced potential newspaper readers of course, but was also sensitive to the specific needs of his neighbours in the mercantile and naval business.[1] His was a small educational establishment to begin with, one that he could run more or less singlehandedly, but as he began to see more possibilities in the book trade and his school became more popular, he had to take on an assistant who was 'capable, occasionally, to take the whole Care of the same'.[2]

James Linden's association with the book trade began in the mid-1760s. Three books advertised in the *Salisbury Journal* in 1766, a geography, an accounting manual, and Perrault's *Mother Goose*, might readily have formed part of Linden's school curriculum, and he was listed as one of the booksellers who could provide copies. A number of the books Linden sold were ones in which Benjamin Collins had an interest as printer, shareholder in the copyright, or joint bookseller, a sure sign that

---

[1] *SJ*, 25 June 1759.   [2] *SJ*, 29 Aug. 1768.

Linden then could be included in Collins's trade network. Stationery, second-hand books, the lottery, and a circulating library were later added to Linden's business near the Southampton market-house.[3] He had set up his own printing office by 1768 and was able to print and publish the popular *Southampton Guide* as well as take on jobbing work—printed forms, broadside advertisements, and so on—for the neighbourhood; by early 1770 Linden was also the Southampton agent for the *Salisbury Journal*, a post he was to abandon when he set up his own paper.

James Linden was in his mid-40s when the first number of the *Hampshire Chronicle* appeared in August 1772. His various other enterprises were stable, and indeed his school was so successful that it is still running today.[4] He knew accounting well enough to teach it, had a sound sense of local requirements, knew and was himself part of the provincial distribution networks, and must have learned something else of the newspaper trade from his association with Benjamin Collins. The expense of the initial outlay for a newspaper might have deterred a newcomer to the trade, but Linden had already invested in a printing press, and had some type. He had still to organize a constant large supply of stamped paper, sharpen his editorial skills, perhaps engage an express service to get the London news quickly to Southampton, and find his subscribers, but that would not have been difficult for a man in his position. In fact a move into the newspaper line made good business sense for someone such as Linden, for a periodical, once established, formed and extended trade contacts and brought in consistent work and income. Book and jobbing work were not nearly so steady.

James Linden's big mistake was to underestimate the competition from Salisbury. The advent of this new Southampton paper went unremarked in the *Sherborne Mercury* and the *Reading Mercury*; in fact the ports-area agent for the Reading paper, William Dawkins in Gosport, had been dropped from the Reading paper's list of agents a few months before, almost as if to make way for the addition of Linden's agency. However, Linden's most formidable opponent was Benjamin Collins, the entrepreneur owner of the *Salisbury Journal*, not much more than 20 miles from Southampton. In setting up a rival paper within the area staked out as the *Journal*'s, and by actively poaching some of its subscribers, Linden not only antagonized another newspaper proprietor, but, more serious,

---

[3] Used books were advertised for sale by his catalogue in 1768 (*SJ*, 7 March); the first notice in the *Journal* for Linden's circulating library was 27 June 1768.

[4] A. Temple Patterson, *A History of Southampton 1700–1914*, i. *An Oligarchy in Decline 1700–1835* (Southampton: University Press, 1966), 41–2, 58 n., 65, 85, 115.

he undermined his own communications with Collins's trade network, which was the most extensive and important in the region. Linden had other contacts that enabled him to circumvent some of the consequent problems however, and the *Hampshire Chronicle* started life with a plausible system of agencies: Benjamin Law, the Chapter and London coffee houses in the capital, Edward Easton II just around the corner from Collins in Salisbury, and fourteen others scattered around the county.

That Linden and Collins recognized each other as particular enemies is evident from the direction of their opening shots: Collins warned his Hampshire readers in print that they would scarcely have need to turn over the pages of a paper published in a town handicapped by its location, 'hemmed in by the sea'. Linden responded. His 'card' to the editor of the Salisbury paper thanks him 'for the very polite and unsolicited manner in which he has advertised the HAMPSHIRE CHRONICLE, and also for exercising his friendship and good will, in pointing out those *weighty* particulars which may be opposed to his success'. Irony was not one of Linden's strong points. Nor, it turns out, was running a newspaper.

The *Chronicle*'s early years were not easy on Linden. He was able to employ an apprentice printer, Robert Draper,[5] in 1774, and he seems to have been in financial control for at least the first year, until he became 'J. Linden and Co.', bringing in various partners in an effort to secure stronger backing. The 'company' included first Linden and J. Webber (August 1773–October 1774); then Linden, Webber, and John Wise for a couple of years; then Linden, Wise, and John Ward until October 1776;[6] at that same time Linden and James Hodson announced that they were 'sole Proprietors and Publishers' of the *Hampshire Chronicle*; this last partnership was dissolved Michaelmas 1777 and Linden was alone again.

The *Gentleman's Magazine* announced James Linden's bankruptcy in February 1778.[7] It may be unfair to suggest that Benjamin Collins had anything directly to do with Linden's failure, but there is no doubt that Collins was a keen businessman, who made a great deal of money and many enemies. Certainly Linden had much less experience in the book and newspaper trade than his rival. He also had a large family: he had

---

[5] PRO IR. 1/59/96; see Ian Maxted, *The British Book Trades, 1710–1777: An Index of Masters and Apprentices recorded in the Inland Revenue Registers at the Public Record Office, Kew* (Exeter: Ian Maxted, 1983), no. 0979a.

[6] The announcement of the dissolution of this partnership appeared in the *Hampshire Chronicle*, 7 Oct. 1776.

[7] Certificate, 16 Mar. 1779; dividend, 15 Oct. 1781 (Ian Maxted, *The British Book Trades, 1731–1806: A Checklist of Bankrupts*, Exeter Working Papers in British Book Trade History, 4 (Exeter: I. Maxted, 1985), 16).

married Margaretta Martin in 1750 and had at least seven children.[8] His son James, who was to take up the printing business in the 1780s, was only 10 years old in 1772, 16 when his father's bankruptcy was made public. Linden may simply have taken on more than he could handle.

At any rate, Linden's creditors sold the *Hampshire Chronicle* in May 1778, ostensibly to a consortium headed by the Southampton bookseller-printer Thomas Baker, but in fact one in which Benjamin Collins held the controlling interest. The whole operation was shifted to a more central location in Winchester and placed under the management of John Wilkes, whose inexperience was overcome with a crash course in newspaper work directed by the *Salisbury Journal*'s manager, John Johnson, and a few of his workmen.

Despite his published agreement to have nothing further to do with newspapers, Linden was able to disrupt the Collins *Hampshire Chronicle*'s circulation by publishing another paper, for which he retained the old name, the *Hampshire Chronicle*.[9] But this was a short-lived episode. His son James and son-in-law Alexander Cunningham took up Linden's book and printing concern in the 1780s. He eventually returned to better success in his old trade, education, but never fully recovered from this disappointment. When James Linden wrote his will in 1804, he still had outstanding debts from 'prior to my Failure' and despite his hopes of providing for the surviving members of his family his estate amounting to less than £100 was wholly inadequate.

Meanwhile the new *Chronicle* partners—Benjamin Collins, his son and apprentice Benjamin Charles, and employee John Johnson, along with John Wilkes, and John Breadhower—soon ran into difficulties. A profit reported at their first meeting proved to be illusory; Wilkes, against the advice of Collins, attempted to push the paper's catchment area beyond

---

[8] The marriage in June 1750 is noted in William J. C. Moens, *Hampshire Allegations for Marriage Licences Granted by the Bishop of Winchester 1689–1837* (London: Harleian Society, 1893), xxxv. 481. Christenings for Rosamond (26 Dec. 1751), Daniel (26 Nov. 1754), Margaret (25 Jan. 1760), James (31 May 1762), and Charlotte-Martin (15 Feb. 1767) are recorded in the parish registers for Holyrood, Southampton. Two other children, Elizabeth and Dinah, are mentioned in Linden's will, dated 7 July 1804 (HRO 1806/A/56).

[9] No copies of Linden's later *Chronicle* have been traced, but there is evidence of it in a half-sheet list 'of all the country news-papers throughout England' produced by the London agent William Tayler, where he notes a *Hampshire Chronicle* printed by Wilkes and published on Mondays, and a *Hampshire Chronicle* printed by Mowbray, published on Saturdays (a single copy of Tayler's notice is recorded by the *ESTC* at the Royal Society of Arts Library, London, dated [1786]). The printer was possibly Walter Mowbray, whom *ESTC* records as working in Portsmouth in the 1780s and 1790s. A. Temple Patterson suggests that it was James Linden's son who was behind the unsuccessful *Chronicle* (*History of Southampton*, i. 42).

practical limits; Collins came to believe that Wilkes was a poor manager; Wilkes accused the other partners of carelessness; Linden's rival paper, the partners claimed, reduced their circulation to about 500. (However, they looked to Linden's 'very indigent and necessitous Circumstances' to solve this last problem without the troublesome inconvenience of hiring a lawyer.) The issue of losses and responsibilty became so contentious that the partnership was dissolved in March 1783 and later that year Wilkes attempted to sue his former co-proprietors in the Court of Exchequer.

Bills and answers were prepared on both sides. The account books covering the duration of the Collins partnership, along with cash books, minutes, and the office copy of the newspaper were presented in evidence. Benjamin Collins died not long after this, leaving an estate of at least £85,000, and the case seems to have been dropped. Fortunately no one remembered to collect the exhibitions, and they remain in the Public Record Office to this day.[10]

In describing both sides of the problem, the partners detailed every step that brought them to the point of lawsuit. They did not disagree about the make-up of the proprietorship, nor the motives each partner had in joining. Their stories chime when they talk about distribution, circulation, agencies, fees for journalism, delivering copy to the editorial office, the duties of the editor: in short, how the newspaper was run. Their disagreements lay elsewhere and concerned management style and accountability. The account books speak for circulation figures, precise edition sizes, routes of distribution, the price of a local newspaper. The records left behind by the *Chronicle* disputants document a newspaper press that had by then been established in the provinces some fifty or sixty years. But the model they construct is naturally derived from precedents set down in the longer course of the history of the English newspaper.

The story of the English provincial newspaper press is closely associated with the book trade and really begins in London, for until the final lapse of the 1662 Licensing (or Printing) Act in 1695, printing was illegal in the provinces.[11] The situation was shaped to a great extent by

---

[10] PRO E. 140/90–1; E. 112/1959/147. I am grateful to G. H. Martin for his help, which led to their discovery in the Court of Exchequer papers, PRO.

[11] The lapse of the Licensing Act has been widely discussed. See e.g. Raymond Astbury, 'The Renewal of the Licensing Act in 1693 and Its Lapse in 1695', *Library*, 5th ser., 38 (1978), 296–322; John Feather, 'From Censorship to Copyright: Aspects of the Government's Role in the English Book Trade 1695–1775', in Kenneth E. Carpenter (ed.), *Books and Society in History* (New York: Bowker, 1983), 173–98; and Frederick S. Siebert, *Freedom of the Press in England, 1476–1776: The Rise and Decline of Government Controls* (Urbana: University of Illinois Press, 1952), 237–63.

the Stationers' Company's monopolistic tendencies and Star Chamber Decrees of 1586 and 1637 that restricted printing to London and the two university towns. True, the 1662 Act, which renewed the monopoly and all its restrictions, placed limits that were largely theoretical on personnel within the book trade—in practice there were never so few as the prescribed twenty master printers in the capital when the Licensing Act was in force for example[12]—but there is little evidence of any large-scale attempts to circumvent the Act by setting up clandestine presses in the provinces.[13] This was due as much to economic factors as to any rigid enforcement of the law. Books, news, indeed most commodities, were readily supplied from London to anyone in the country who wanted and could afford them. The distribution system through which these goods were channelled was one that had been laid down in Roman times.[14]

'London, as in all other articles of commerce, is likewise the grand emporium of Great Britain for books, engrossing nearly the whole of what is valuable in that very extensive, beneficial, and . . . lucrative branch of trade.'[15] James Lackington was writing in the late eighteenth century, but any of his predecessors for centuries past would have recognized the truth of his observation. Provincial booksellers in the later seventeenth century were retailers for the most part, who sold London imprints to their customers, and supplied them with stationery, medicines, and other goods. While an extensive wholesale and retail distribution network for the book trade was an early development, printing itself—of books, ephemera, or of newspapers—was not a substantial part of the provincial trade until the eighteenth century. London lost its relative monopoly on important sections of the book trade (that is on copyholding, printing, and publishing; the distribution and binding side had always been shared) in the

[12] Michael Treadwell, 'Lists of Master Printers: The Size of the London Printing Trade, 1637–1723', in Robin Myers and Michael Harris (eds.), *Aspects of Printing from 1600* (Oxford: Oxford Polytechnic Press, 1987), 141–70.

[13] James Raven suggests that 'Certain country jobbing printing apparently predated the lapse of the licensing laws', citing as evidence the fact that the Act of 1662 specifically mentioned books of blank bills ('Print and Trade in Eighteenth-Century Britain', Thirlwall Essay, Cambridge, 1985). Such printing would have been legal, but small-scale.

[14] John Feather discusses the relationship between the eighteenth-century book trade in London and in the provinces in the first chapter of *The Provincial Book Trade in Eighteenth-Century England* (Cambridge: Cambridge University Press, 1985). The 17th-cent. distribution network for chapbooks is discussed in Margaret Spufford's *Small Books and Pleasant Histories: Popular Fiction and Its Readership in Seventeenth-Century England* (Cambridge: Cambridge University Press, 1981), 111–28.

[15] James Lackington, *Memoirs of the First Forty-Five Years of the Life of James Lackington*, new edn. (London: printed for the author, 1792), 416.

first decade of that century, but it nevertheless continued to dominate the trade. Further developments in an already efficient, comprehensive national distribution system meant that provincial printers and publishers had always to contend with their London-based counterparts in the market for books.

News was available in the provinces before 1700 in several forms, which all derived from London in one way or another. From about 1640 news was regularly supplied in the newsbooks.[16] By the later seventeenth century the most accessible form was the printed newspaper. An official version of the news was provided by the *London Gazette* (founded in 1665 as the *Oxford Gazette*), the only paper published with any regularity during the second half of the century.[17] Much of its content was of Continental origin and would have been of great interest to English readers, especially in times of Continental war, when the *Gazette* had the first authorized accounts. At other times it was considerably less engaging. 'Domestic intelligence' was circumscribed by the Licensing Act, by privilege, and by mutable definitions of treason and libel. Other London newspapers were founded both before and after the *Gazette*, particularly when there was a newsworthy crisis. The temporary lapse of the Licensing Act between 1679 and 1685 saw a plethora of new papers, but few of those survived for long.[18]

All the London and the Continental newspapers could be posted to country customers by London agents.[19] News that was thought not fit to print, or rather news of a different nature, was available to them in the manuscript newsletters. These were communications copied by teams of professional scribes and posted to subscribers up to three times a week. The labour that went into producing them was intensive, so they were expensive: Henry Muddiman's normal charge was about £5 annually,

---

[16] Joad Raymond (ed.), *Making the News: An Anthology of the Newsbooks of Revolutionary England 1641–1660* (Moreton-in-Marsh: Windrush Press, 1993), introduction.

[17] P. M. Handover, *A History of* The London Gazette *1665–1965* (London: HMSO, 1965).

[18] James Sutherland pays particular attention to these unlicensed newspapers in *The Restoration Newspaper and Its Development* (Cambridge: Cambridge University Press, 1986). He lists the 'more important London newspapers from 1660 to 1720', 250–3. See also Carolyn Nelson and Matthew Seccombe (comps.), *British Newspapers and Periodicals 1641–1700: A Short-Title Catalogue of Serials Printed in England, Scotland, Ireland, and British America* (New York: Modern Language Association, 1987).

[19] Printers and proprietors organized country distribution, and sometimes Government officers acted as agents. See Michael Harris, 'Newspaper Distribution during Queen Anne's Reign', in R. W. Hunt, I. G. Philip, and R. J. Roberts (eds.), *Studies in the Book Trade in Honour of Graham Pollard* (Oxford: Oxford Bibliographical Society, 1975), 139–51.

another's was recorded at £4 in 1689.[20] Because only the well-off (who after all were unlikely to be inflamed to commit rash acts) could afford them, because they were circulated privately, and because they were handwritten, these newsletters were exempt from many of, if not all, the restrictions placed on printed material. Indeed John Toland, discussing the enforcement of the Stamp Act in about 1717, thought that the 'printed are preferable to written News-papers, as being more open to the Law'.[21] The House of Commons's prohibition against printing its votes and proceedings did not apply, for example, so a newsletter reader could expect to be reasonably well informed on parliamentary matters. The most successful newsletter author-proprietors were naturally those who were best placed to discover domestic intelligence. Henry Muddiman, whom Pepys described as a good scholar, but an 'arch rogue', had access to the correspondence of the two Secretaries of State. In addition, he was able to receive and send letters, including his own newsletters, postage free.[22] The manuscript newsletter remained an important source of information, both for the private reader and for the commercial printed newspaper, well into the eighteenth century.[23]

We should not, for this time, underestimate the role of the local town crier in disseminating news. In fact some of the most solid evidence we have of the eighteenth-century crier's effectiveness is to be found in the newspapers themselves, for example in notices that lost property had been recovered after it had been locally advertised in this manner.[24]

---

[20] J. G. Muddiman, *The King's Journalist, 1659–1689: Studies in the Reign of Charles II* (London: John Lane, 1923), 166; Henry L. Snyder, 'Newsletters in England, 1689–1715 with Special Reference to John Dyer—a Byway in the History of England', in Donovan H. Bond and W. Reynolds McLeod (eds.), *Newsletters to Newspapers: Eighteenth-Century Journalism* (Morgantown: West Virginia University Press, 1977), 8; and Sutherland, *Restoration Newspaper*, 7.

[21] John Toland, 'Proposal for Regulating the News-Papers', BL Add. MS 4295, fo. 49ʳ.

[22] Muddiman, *King's Journalist*, 130–1; and Sutherland, *Restoration Newspaper*, 5–10.

[23] There seems little question that newsletters survived past 1750. William Tayler, the London newspaper agent, was concerned in the newsletter business in the 1780s for example: he advertised in 1786 that he supplied manuscript minutes of the House of Commons. Lady Newton described the Legh Family collection of newsletters that covered 'a period of some hundred and fifty years'—'the first preserved . . . is of April 8, 1679' (*Lyme Letters, 1660–1760* (London: Heinemann, 1925)). When Joseph Fox of Westminster died in 1746, his obituary said he was 'eminent for sending written News Letters to most parts of the Three Kingdoms'. He was succeeded in this business by his son (*General Advertiser*, 25 Nov. 1746). See Michael Turner, 'The Syndication of Fiction in Provincial Newspapers 1870–1939: The Example of the Tillotson "Fiction Bureau" ', B.Litt. thesis (Oxford University, 1968).

[24] A horse that had been cried at Salisbury, Warminster, and Hindon was thereby discovered according to the *Salisbury Journal* of 29 May 1758 for example. John Styles has

The oral mode, however, continued as a vivid and, in certain contexts, the preferred medium for certain other public communications. This vibrant printed account in the *Salisbury Journal*, with a Salisbury date line, just manages to convey a sense of how the oral tradition overlapped with the printed:

Tuesday and Wednesday last, was held here the *Michaelmas Fair*, as 'tis call'd; on which Occasion there was (as usual) much Cheese, much Concourse, and much Fun; abundance of Hops, abundance of Onions, and several Squadrons of Pigs. The Music of the Latter served as Symphonies, Accompanyments, and Chorusses to two itinerant, florid *Orators*, who held forth near the inchanting Sounds abovemention'd. The first of these Orators appear'd in the Shape of a *Doctor*; and requir'd nothing to complete him, but a spotted Horse; He drawing Teeth as fast as other People shell Pease. The second Orator (a great Scholard,) who harangued over Books, wou'd have made the Emperor of Auctioneers, had He but learnt to read; He having Lungs of Brass and Cheeks of the same Metal. In another Part of the Fair, were two learned, ingenious Gentlemen, between whom, and a Monkey (with a couple of Parrots,) a most Pathetic Dialogue was carried on, which (unhappily,) cou'd not be well heard, for the Vociferation of the Crouds gaping round. Nothing was regretted but the want of a Fiddle or Bagpipe.

> Where were Ye? ye *Bagpipers!* ye *Crowdero's!*—
> At some blind Alehouse, in a paltry Village,
> There scraping, squeaking; propt on wooden Legs,
> Why rather not come forth, and in the City,
> Exert your melting Talents and receive
> The *Chaplet*, due to high, harmonious Merit?
>
> (*SJ*, 16 October 1749)

But such reflections suggest the possibility that in the burgeoning provincial newspaper press we have some of the most striking evidence —if only it could be quantified—of another significant step in the spread of literacy beyond the metropolis. Although estimates of literacy rates in the late seventeenth and early eighteenth centuries are currently being re-evaluated, it is certain that much of the population, at least in the lower ranks, could not read at this time. It has been argued that the greater output of book titles in the eighteenth century is merely evidence of the greater book-buying power of the privileged literate classes (the same few buying more stock for their libraries), and not an indication of a growing

investigated the effectiveness of various modes of advertising in 'Print and Policing: Crime Advertising in Eighteenth-Century Provincial England', in Douglas Hay and Francis Snyder (eds.), *Policing and Prosecution in Britain 1750–1850* (Oxford: Clarendon Press, 1989), 55–111.

rate of literacy.[25] But the spread of printing into the country after the lapse of the Licensing Act, especially in the development of the provincial newspaper press, is a more reliable gauge of changing levels of literacy: the provincial papers themselves, produced in more titles, and larger and larger editions, surely represent more people who could read. With all their advertisements for books published in such variety—in parts, in large expensive folios, by subscription, in pamphlet-format, in boards, bound, unbound—the newspapers bear further proof of the growing popularity of reading through the eighteenth century.

While it was still possible to be prosecuted for printing offensive material in the early eighteenth century (just as it is today), after 1695 printing presses were allowed to operate anywhere and the restrictions on the numbers of printers were thereby removed. The effect on the newspaper press was, curiously, an almost immediate upsurge of papers in London itself—there were new titles and some of those appeared more frequently.[26] Londoners who were printers, with established homes and shops, in 1695 might well have seen greater opportunity and security in a move into the expanding metropolitan newspaper trade, rather than out into the provinces. Certainly the newspaper was a commodity with a tried and proven national market. The London papers, both the printed ones and the handwritten newsletters, had of course been widely available from their beginning earlier in the century; indeed their presence in the provinces may well have inhibited the early growth of the country news-paper, especially immediately after 1695 when the market saw so many new London-based periodicals.

When printers and booksellers began to migrate to the provinces after 1695, they found that book work was practically limited to the occa-sional edition of a sermon or poem with specific local appeal. The new share-book system, whereby the ownership of copyrights was increasingly subsidized, and more and smaller shares in copies were offered for sale, theoretically made it easier for the provincial bookseller to establish an interest in important or best-selling books; yet the London establish-ment, organized more or less in still-effective congers, managed to retain its common-law monopoly on the most profitable titles until the middle of the eighteenth century. Besides, most established or aspiring authors

[25] James Raven, *Judging New Wealth: Popular Publishing and Responses to Commerce in England, 1750–1800* (Oxford: Clarendon Press, 1992), 56–7.
[26] There were eleven new serials in 1695, ten in 1696, thirteen in 1698; by comparison 1693 and 1694 saw six and four new serials respectively, including the *Scottish Mercury* (see Nelson and Seccombe, *British Newspapers and Periodicals*, Chronological Index).

would naturally seek out London agents for both printing and publishing. On the other hand, if job-printing of advertisements, notices, warrants, and forms brought less prestige, it still meant useful, if irregular, income.

The principal effect of this lapse of the Licensing Act, however, was one that followed almost by default and was virtually unperceived at the time: the freedom to set up a press anywhere in the kingdom, to serve local communities through the locally printed word, gave to printing an immediacy quite unprecedented in England. Considering the far-reaching significance of this event, its consequences seem to have been only slowly realized. Printers first migrated to the provinces soon after 1695, but it was not until at least 1701 that the first provincial newspaper made its appearance. News for the provinces was still filtered through London and in fact was usually selected from the London papers, but now at least it could be printed in and distributed from a local office, along with an expanding bulk of ephemera, in the immediate service of local needs.

It is uncertain who first perceived and acted upon the need for an inexpensive medium for local advertisements and for news extracted from the London papers and, much less often, from regional sources. Most probably it was either the London printer Francis Burges (ST2:0908)[27] who moved to the country to establish the *Norwich Post*, or another Londoner, William Bonny, with his *Bristol Post-Boy*, both of them in business about 1701.[28] As R. M. Wiles notes, it is significant that the homes of England's very first provincial newspapers, Norwich and Bristol, were 'progressive cities over a hundred miles from London', an attitude and geography that seemed to enhance an early country paper's chances of survival.[29] Bristol booksellers had already developed strong links with London, particularly in the provision of a well-established outlet for the increasing volume of Nonconformist publications. While it may not have been the first provincial newspaper, the earliest issue to survive in fact is a copy of the *Bristol Post-Boy*, no. 91, for 12 August 1704, printed and

---

[27] The ST numbers cited throughout refer to the *Biographies of the London Book Trade*, a database recording information about Stationers' Company personnel from its incorporation in the mid-16th cent. through to the 1830s. Most of the numbers follow those in D. F. McKenzie's 3 vols. of *Stationers' Company Apprentices*. An index and name-authority file is forthcoming.

[28] Francis Burges, son of a London clerk, was apprenticed to Freeman Collins from July 1692 to Dec. 1699 (D. F. McKenzie, *Stationers' Company Apprentices 1641–1700* (Oxford: Oxford Bibliographical Society, 1974), 35); no record is found of Bonny's apprenticeship. Discussion of the question of priority may be found in R. M. Wiles, *Freshest Advices: Early Provincial Newspapers in England* (Columbus: Ohio State University Press, 1965), 14–16, and in G. A. Cranfield, *The Development of the Provincial Newspaper 1700–1760* (Oxford: Clarendon Press, 1962), 13–15.   [29] Wiles, *Freshest Advices*, 16.

published by William Bonny who, as a London printer, had been used extensively by John Dunton (ST2:3420). Dunton was himself an experienced publisher of serials, including the successful *Athenian Mercury* and another periodical designed for women readers.[30] Bonny left London for Bristol in 1695 because, Dunton suggests, he had financial problems, and Plomer records that 'the Chamber of the City coming to the conclusion that a printing press might be useful in several respects, but not being disposed to allow a "foreigner" to compete with local booksellers in their special business, granted him the freedom on condition that he dwelt in the city and exercised no trade save that of a printer.'[31] The *Norwich Post* possibly preceded the Bristol newspaper by about a year. A local newspaper, managed with some skill, could bring certain advantages to proprietor and subscriber: the best news culled from a number of London and Continental papers for less than the cost of a single London paper; a reliable vehicle for advertisements; steady presswork for the printer; and a 'constant Introduction' to booksellers in London and the country.

Not all provincial towns could provide the progressive, large-scale context of a Bristol or a Norwich, however, and many were unable to sustain a local newspaper early in the eighteenth century. At least fifteen provincial newspapers were begun before 1712 but only four of those remained in business after the Stamp Act of that year (10 Anne, c. 19). It has to be said that the Government's intentions in imposing this new tax—and indeed any of the other newspaper stamp taxes—were not primarily to oppress or censor; rather the Government hoped to raise revenue by taxing an established and popular commodity.[32] Nevertheless the issue

[30] John Dunton, *Life and Errors*, ed. John Bowyer Nichols (1705; new edn. London, 1818), 2 vols.; and Gilbert D. McEwen, *The Oracle of the Coffee House: John Dunton's Athenian Mercury* (San Marino, Calif.: Huntington Library, 1972).

[31] Henry R. Plomer, *Dictionary of the Printers and Booksellers Who Were at Work in England, Scotland and Ireland from 1668 to 1725* (London: The Bibliographical Society, 1922), 41. Dunton discusses Bonny's career in *Life and Errors*, i. 247–8.

[32] Toland wondered 'Whether the Duties laid upon News-papers were intended as a fund for the public service, or a restraint upon the swarming of such papers, or for both of these ends' ('Proposal for Regulating the News-Papers', fo. 49ʳ). More recently, the legislation has been described as a repressive measure. Cranfield discusses the measure in those terms in *Development of the Provincial Newspaper*, 17–18, as does Michael Harris in 'The Structure, Ownership and Control of the Press, 1620–1780', in George Boyce, James Curran, and Pauline Wingate (eds.), *Newspaper History from the Seventeenth Century to the Present Day* (London: Constable, 1978), 84. Or as a measure with a dual purpose: first to restrict offensive ephemeral publications, and second to raise revenue. Siebert adopts this view (*Freedom of the Press*, 309). D. Nichol Smith is noncommittal ('The Newspaper', in A. S. Turberville (ed.), *Johnson's England: An Account of the Life & Manners of His Age* (Oxford: Clarendon Press, 1933), ii. 362–3). In his discussion of the Stamp Act, Jeremy

was not a clear-cut one for contemporaries. Many of the papers that failed did so long before the effects of the new law were felt. The commercial incentives to develop a successful newspaper were powerful however, and other proprietors were undeterred: 135 new papers were started between 1713 and 1760. Thirty-nine (a little over 25 per cent) of the total 150 managed to remain in business past 1760.

Since many of the printers who established the first provincial presses came from London, they naturally printed their newspapers after the London models they knew. Most of their provincial readers were already familiar with London publications too, and any new competitors would have had to observe the physical conventions of the genre. Stanley Morison described two traditions of news reading at the end of the seventeenth century, that of the hand-written newsletter with its comparatively unrestricted reports read by the well-to-do, and that of the less expensive printed newspaper, which was hampered to a certain extent by the libel laws and restrictions on parliamentary coverage. The physical format and layout of the two were obviously different, and readers naturally came to associate content and style with a specific appearance.[33] It is not surprising that Bonny's *Bristol Post-Boy* should have started out as a weekly, printed in double columns on both sides of a single half-sheet, in the style of the *London Gazette*. Other printers imitated aspects of the intimate style of the handwritten newsletter, some going so far as to employ a special script type, or opening with a salutation, in much the same way as the first Western letterpress printers had incorporated the conventions of the familiar manuscript book.[34] Until the Stamp Act of 1712 there were no external restrictions on the newspaper trade that might have affected

---

Black notes both the fiscal aspects and the problems the Government had experienced with pre-publication censorship (*The English Press in the Eighteenth Century* (Philadelphia: University of Pennsylvania Press, 1987), 10–11). But D. F. Foxon, in the fullest discussion of the Stamp Act, has convincing evidence to support the view that the Government intended to raise money by taxing well-established commodities, including soap and newspapers (Foxon, 'The Origins of the Tax on Printed Works', 'Technical Problems and Solutions', 'The Application of the Act, and Its Effects', and 'Evasion of Duty', unpublished Sandars Lectures (University of Cambridge, 1978)). J. A. Downie and R. M. Wiles are of similar opinion (*Robert Harley and the Press: Propaganda and Public Opinion in the Age of Swift and Defoe* (Cambridge: Cambridge University Press, 1979), 149–61, and *Freshest Advices*, 18–22).

[33] Stanley Morison, *The English Newspaper: Some Account of the Physical Development of Journals Printed in London between 1622 & the Present Day* (Cambridge: Cambridge University Press, 1932), 47–8.
[34] Principally *Dawks's News-Letter*, but also *Sam. Farley's Bristol Post Man* began 'Sir'. Stanley Morison, *Ichabod Dawks and His News-Letter, with an Account of the Dawks Family of Booksellers and Stationers, 1635–1731* (Cambridge: Cambridge University Press, 1931).

physical appearance. Proprietors were free to develop a more market-able format and both four- and six-page papers evolved in the first decade of the century, although the older four-page newspaper was still more popular.

In 1712 a $\frac{1}{2}d$. duty was imposed on *every* copy of a newspaper or pamphlet printed on a half-sheet or less; there was a 1*d*. duty on *every* copy of a newspaper or pamphlet larger than a half-sheet, but not exceeding a whole sheet; and a 2*s*. duty was required on only *one* copy of a pamphlet larger than one sheet, and not exceeding six sheets octavo (or twelve sheets quarto, or twenty sheets folio), no matter how large the edition. Tax of 1*s*. was to be paid on each advertisement in papers published weekly or more often. The new regulations required that stamped sheets had to be purchased through the London Stamp Office in advance of printing, an inconvenience felt most by those in the country.

The new Act had an indirect but marked effect on the appearance of English newspapers. There was a loophole. The first to notice, as Toland reports, was an enterprising Londoner:

But it haveing been the design of the Parliament, that all News-papers shou'd pay a duty of one halfpenny for each half-sheet, this end is manifestly defeated by printing of news-papers on a sheet and a half (as other papers in long slips) wherby they become not lyable to be stampt, and so pay nothing. This contriveance, first set on foot by a paper call'd the Daily Benefactor since dropt, was straight imitated by St James's Evening Post, printing a running Title of half a sheet, which serves for all the year round, and a sheet of small paper every postnight, which they sell with it. This is likewise the practise of Mist in his London-post . . . as also of all the other weekly Journals, Medleys, and such other papers, most of 'em written by Papists, Nonjurors, or other disaffected persons.[35]

The provinces were not far behind, and within a month or two of 1 August 1712, when the Act had come into effect, John White was publishing his *Newcastle Courant* in six pages on one and a half sheets of unstamped paper.[36] Not only was he able to evade the newspaper tax by publishing what could be legally defined as a pamphlet (newspapers were uniformly printed on either whole or half-sheets according to the law), but he was able to avoid the real inconvenience of arranging for the purchase and delivery of pre-stamped paper from London and then organizing return and credit for unsold copies. Others all over the country followed suit; by 1714 even the Government-supported press, including the

---

[35] Toland, 'Proposal for Regulating the Newspapers', fo. 49^r.
[36] Wiles, *Freshest Advices*, 47–8.

London Gazette, was issued in a practically duty-free, six-page format.[37] It could be said that the new legislation allowed newspaper printers even more freedom; certainly these new conditions showed that proprietors paid greater respect to economic forces than to the conservative reading habits of their subscribers.

Printers who switched from two or four pages to six or twelve sometimes found that the change meant a surfeit of space. The plain-style newspaper, its title undecorated or flanked perhaps by modest woodcuts and followed directly by the date and news, gave way to elaborate title-pages and plenty of white space. The average newspaper sheet size, limited by the technology, did not change significantly with the new law, so the six-page paper printed on a sheet and a half retained a familiar folio page size, while the twelve-page paper's extra fold meant a smaller page (about 15 to 16.5 cm. × 20 to 21.5 cm.; 6 to $6\frac{1}{2}$ inches × 8 to $8\frac{1}{2}$ inches).

The Government closed the loophole when the Stamp Act was reimposed in 1725. The term *newspaper* was more strictly defined this time, so that each sheet or half-sheet of every copy was liable for duty. The number of sheets or half-sheets making up a newspaper was strictly regulated; however *size* of sheet for newspapers and pamphlets was never legally defined, not even in 1757 when the tax was doubled. This proved an incentive to papermakers to produce sheets as large as eighteenth-century technology and manpower would allow. The six- and twelve-page papers vanished, replaced immediately by the four-page newspaper printed on a larger half-sheet.

The layout of the weekly provincials was largely governed by the arrival of the three London posts each week. Layout too was limited by the nature of hand-press production. Since most of the main news was gathered from the metropolitan and Continental newspapers and news-letters (supplemented with other 'articles of intelligence' submitted by local correspondents), the compositor had to wait for the last post with the last batch of newspapers before he could finish setting his final page. To save time most provincial newspaper printers adopted the practice of composing, correcting, and printing the outer forme, that is pages 1 and 4 of a four-page paper, early in the work week. However, some printers composed their newspapers one page at a time, in order from page 1 to page 4, a practice in fact adopted in the early years of the *Salisbury Journal*. It would still have been common to *print* two pages (one forme) at a time, but at least one number of the *Journal* seems actually to have

---

[37] Handover, *London Gazette*, 46.

been *printed* one page at a time. This was obviously an inefficient means of production, and may have been dictated by a shortage of type. Other printers collected the news from all three posts into one section, which meant that non-commercial material could not be composed until after the arrival of the last post.[38]

In any event some type—that of the headline, recurrent advertisements, or the colophon for example—could be left standing for long periods. This represented a further saving in time, for it meant that less copy had to be set up in type during the week, and less type had to be distributed at the end of the week. The most common practice in the country was to fill page 1 with old news from the first post and page 4 with advertisements, allowing that side of the sheet to be printed early. This meant that the 'freshest advices' usually appeared on page three. Sometimes the printer miscalculated the amount of space required for information brought by the final post, and there are plenty of examples of the latest news squeezed in, set in type smaller than the rest, reported more concisely than the original story would seem to warrant, or even spilling into the margins. Occasionally an item on one page would be contradicted on another, or a story on page 4 might continue on page 3. None of this would have surprised an eighteenth-century newspaper reader.

Accurate circulation figures for the earliest weekly provincial newspapers do not exist, but an overall pattern of sporadic but definite growth can be detected from the available evidence. The accompanying development of literacy in the provinces, doubtless promoted by the greater accessibility of reading material as well as by a more extensive and concentrated educational system, is relevant. Developments in the metropolitan newspaper press naturally had an effect on the country market too, for the London papers had—indeed still have—a large national readership.

Another measure of newspaper growth is frequency of publication. James Sutherland describes the appearance of the thrice-weekly London *Post-Boy* in 1695 as 'a genuine advance' in the development of the newspaper.[39] The *Post-Boy*'s editor sometimes struggled to fill its two pages with news, but the new format was successful enough to inspire imitators: the *Flying-Post* and the *Post Man* were established before the end of the same year. The very first *Posts* were so called because they were published Monday, Thursday, and Saturday evenings in time for distribution to the

---

[38] See Wiles, *Freshest Advices*, 77–9.   [39] Sutherland, *Restoration Newspaper*, 26–8.

country by mail. Their commitment to the provincial market was evident in the name, and extended even to the provision of one blank page so that a purchaser could write letters to country correspondents without paying additional postage. The accessibility of these early London-based papers played a significant part in encouraging the country demand for newspapers in general.[40]

On 11 March 1702 England's first daily newspaper, the *Daily Courant*, was published by a young Samuel Buckley (ST2:4209) in London. The paper was successful, enjoying a Government subsidy and, probably because of that support, a circulation of over 2,000 after the fall of the Tories,[41] but it had no competition until almost two decades later when the *Daily Post* arrived on the scene in 1719. More and more London papers were reaching the provinces: 650 copies of the *London Journal* were sent into the country in 1722; by 1726 the total was 2,200.[42] The number of readers, as distinct from subscribers, might well have been from ten to twenty times that figure.[43] Newspapers found numerous country readers —and listeners—in private households, coffee-houses, inns, circulating libraries, and reading rooms.

Newspaper circulation figures naturally fluctuated during the eighteenth century. New papers sprang up in times of crisis when public interest was high; others failed for various reasons, including mismanagement, competition, and the remarkable dearth of marketable news in peaceful years; and through the century a significant part of the reading population regularly shifted from town to country and back again according to the season, a move that must have had an effect on local circulation figures. Unfortunately Stamp Office records that might have provided specific clues to newspaper circulation after 1712 in both London and the provinces were destroyed in the nineteenth century. Circulation figures for a number of London newspapers, however, can be deduced from other documents that have survived.

'A Proposall to encrease the Revenue of the Stamp Offices', discovered among the Treasury papers, contains an informed estimate of the circulation of nine London newspapers in about 1704.[44] Weekly reports on newspaper stamp-duty revenue eight years later in 1712, now included in the Harley Manuscripts Collection in the British Library, corroborate the

---

[40] Michael Harris, *London Newspapers in the Age of Walpole: A Study of the Origins of the Modern English Press* (London: Associated University Presses, 1987), 33–5.

[41] Handover, *London Gazette*, 49–50. [42] Feather, *Provincial Book Trade*, 37.

[43] James R. Sutherland, 'The Circulation of Newspapers and Literary Periodicals 1700– 1730', *Library*, 4th ser., 15 (1934), 124. [44] Ibid. 110–24.

1704 figures and provide further useful details.[45] For example an edition of 800 was estimated for the *Daily Courant* in 1704; similarly duty was paid on an average of 859 copies daily in 1712. The *London Gazette* (many copies of which were distributed gratis) was printed in very large editions of about 6,000 in 1704 and 5,143 in 1712; the *Post Man*, estimated 3,800 in 1704, up to 3,812 in 1712; while the *Flying-Post* experienced an upsurge from 400 in 1704 to 1,350 in 1712. The Treasury's reporter thought that about 43,800 copies of his nine newspapers circulated weekly in 1704. Arthur Aspinall has examined related Audit Office accounts of the advertisement duty revenue in Great Britain in the eighteenth century. While his statistics are employed in charting the steady growth of newspaper advertising, they also provide another indication of the increasing market for the newspapers in which they appeared.[46] At the same time it is of some comparable interest to note that a monthly journal such as the *London Magazine* had print runs of between 6,000 and 8,000 in the 1730s and 1740s.[47] Every one of these periodicals would have had a provincial component to their readership.

It appears that a relatively lower circulation could sustain a provincial newspaper early in the century, even in the face of competition from the metropolitan papers. Population was certainly lower and less concentrated in the country districts and cost-efficient modes of distribution from county capitals to outlying districts were being developed. Samuel Farley thought that 200 subscribers for the *Salisbury Post Man*—the town's very first newspaper—made it a viable proposition.[48] Likewise the Harley reports of about the same time include one *Bristol Post* with an average weekly edition of 288. These figures hardly suggest either large turnover or high profit margins, and it needs to be stressed therefore that a newspaper in the provinces was usually only part of a diverse business that involved job-printing, perhaps a little local book or pamphlet production, and the sale of a variety of other items, most often including quack medicines;[49]

---

[45] J. M. Price, 'A Note on the Circulation of the London Press 1700–1714', *Bulletin of the Institute of Historical Research*, 31 (1958), 215–24; see also Henry L. Snyder, 'The Circulation of Newspapers in the Reign of Queen Anne', *Library*, 5th ser., 23 (1968), 206–35.

[46] Arthur Aspinall, 'Statistical Accounts of the London Newspapers in the Eighteenth Century', *English Historical Review*, 63 (1948), 201–32.

[47] D. F. McKenzie and J. C. Ross, *A Ledger of Charles Ackers, Printer of* The London Magazine (Oxford: Oxford Bibliographical Society, 1968), 11.

[48] *Salisbury Post Man*, no. 1 (27 Sept. 1715).

[49] See Roy Porter's ch. on 'Medical Entrepreneurship in the Consumer Society' in his *Health for Sale: Quackery in England 1660–1850* (Manchester: Manchester University Press, 1989), and John Alden, 'Pills and Publishing: Some Notes on the English Book Trade, 1660–1715', *Library*, 5th ser., 7 (1952), 21–37.

such diversification allowed some of the initial losses in a new venture to be absorbed. An established newspaper with a stable readership could provide the advantage of a modest but steady income, a point Charles Spens was to make when considering a potential partnership in the 1750s— 'He proposes to keep on what he has to do with the News Paper, which will not take up three Hours of a Day, as it will be 50L. a Year clear Money, and a constant Introduction to the Booksellers.'[50]

When mid- to late eighteenth-century provincial newspapers described their circulation, it was usually in terms of 'vast Numbers' or 'several Thousands', something vaguely impressive. Wiles and Cranfield, however, both cite the editors of the *Newcastle Journal* of 14 July 1739, who claimed that they were then selling 'nearly 2000 of these Papers weekly'.[51] Therefore the evidence suggests that in the 1710s a regular sale of editions of about 200–300 country newspapers was respectable. By the late 1730s, 1,000 to 2,000 subscribers were probably not uncommon for the better established provincial papers. The *Salisbury Journal* may not have attained these numbers until after it had been in business for at least a few years, but by 1780 the *Journal* was one of the more successful of its kind and its editors were plausibly claiming a circulation of around 4,000.[52] The discovery of the account books for one period of the *Hampshire Chronicle* provides firm production and circulation figures for at least one provincial newspaper from the late 1770s through the early 1780s. The *Chronicle*, despite stormy management after a bankruptcy, and widespread competition for a share of the existing market with a rival paper of the same name, the Reading newspapers, and the *Salisbury Journal*, was printed at this time in editions of just over 1,000. The increases in the numbers of titles and subscribers for both the London and metropolitan newspapers demonstrates much more than growth and shift in actual population. It is testimony to the growth of literacy.

Early English newspapers reached their metropolitan readership through distribution systems involving the Post Office and a network of individual periodical publishers, mercuries, and hawkers. (In brief, seventeenth- and eighteenth-century periodical publishers were the backers and wholesalers; mercuries were distributors; hawkers sold the newspapers, pamphlets, or books in the streets.[53]) The *London Gazette*, for example, took over a

---

[50] Charles Spens and James Emmonson to William Bowyer [June 1754?], Bodl. MS Eng. Misc. C.141, fo. 21.

[51] Cranfield, *Development of the Provincial Newspaper*, 171; Wiles, *Freshest Advices*, 97.

[52] Printed receipt, Salisbury and S. Wiltshire Museum, Salisbury.

[53] See Michael Treadwell, 'London Trade Publishers 1675–1750', *Library*, 6th ser., 4 (1982), 99–134.

system of mercuries—'bookwomen'—who distributed and sold the paper in return for a percentage of the edition.[54] Casual readers could purchase or hire a newspaper from a hawker in the street, from the newspaper office itself, or from a newsagent, or they could read or listen to the news at local coffee-houses or other commercial gathering places. Subscribers on the other hand received their papers through the penny post or by the trade network of distributors, agents, and newsmen.[55] The same London papers reached provincial subscribers through the postal system for the most part. Normal postal rates in the late seventeenth, early eighteenth century could add considerably to the expense of a newspaper—2*d*. for the first eighty miles, 3*d*. for distances within the kingdom beyond eighty miles—but they might be reduced or eliminated altogether by an agent with franking privileges, as a Member of Parliament sending material to his constituents, or a clerk of the Post Office. Other modes of London-to-provinces distribution were by commercial and private carriers. Some country newspaper proprietors, including those in the Wessex area, paid for an express service from London, riders who brought back the latest news, including the newspapers, with as much expedition as money could buy. Metropolitan newspapers were thereby transformed into a national news service during the eighteenth century and that phenomenon can be attributed, in part, to the growing efficiency of their distribution.

Reaching the market was a more complicated problem outside London. Cost-efficient newspaper distribution in the provinces depended on an effective and reliable communications system among regional towns and villages. The network that gradually evolved during the eighteenth century naturally made use of the existing systems: bookselling had been a part of the provincial urban scene for centuries, even though few English books were actually *printed* outside London, York, and the two university towns until the 1700s, so some channels for the distribution of printed material were already in place. Related was a less formal, lower-level network of chapmen and pedlars who walked the country selling goods of all kinds, including ballads, pamphlets, and small books.[56] Carriers were another resource that provincial printers could exploit. In many respects the newspaper networks, centred on the printing office and dependent

[54] Thomas O'Malley, 'Religion and the Newspaper Press, 1660–1685: A Study of the *London Gazette*', in Michael Harris and Alan Lee (eds.), *The Press in English Society* (London: Associated University Presses, 1986), 31.

[55] Harris, 'Structure, Ownership and Control', 89–92.

[56] Tessa Watt, *Cheap Print and Popular Piety 1550–1640* (Cambridge: Cambridge University Press, 1991); Laurence Fontaine, *History of Pedlars in Europe*, tr. Vicki Whittaker (Oxford: Polity Press, 1996).

upon distributors, agents, and newsmen, were modelled on those established by the London trade. The main difference in the country was the greater distance that had to be covered to reach a more widely scattered population.

Country readers could always buy the newspaper at the printing office or from a newsagent in the larger towns, and by at least 1707 casual sales were also made by the hawkers who cried the local papers in country towns.[57] But other provincial distributors, the newsmen and carriers, regularly had to cover 35- and 40-mile routes often on foot, sometimes on horseback, to make their deliveries.[58] Indeed they were frequently called 'running Footmen' after their usual mode of travel. These men and boys were employed on a regular basis by the country newspaper proprietors expressly to convey papers, books, stationery, patent medicines, and whatever else their employers might sell. The carrier network was ideal for serving customers who lived out of the way of the dedicated newsmen. A slower, less specific method, it still had the advantage of almost daily deliveries along well-established circuits, as Felix Farley demonstrated: his *Bristol Journal* listed 162 locations served by 100 operators from twenty-five Bristol inns in 1754.[59] The post was employed as well. Samuel Farley informed potential subscribers that the *Salisbury Post Man* might be had 'by the Post, Coach, Carriers, or Market People; to whom they shall be carefully Deliver'd' and that the paper would by these means 'be made Publick in every Market Town forty Miles distant from this City; and several will be sent as far as Exeter'.[60] Large provincial catchment areas meant that agencies in outlying towns and villages developed as a necessary extension of an efficient delivery system. Newsagents were commonly recruited from the ranks of the business community and followed a variety of occupations—tailors, postmen, milliners, rum dealers, and bakers among them—but most often they were themselves members of the book trade, sometimes even the co-operative proprietors of other newspapers. Their job was to organize local distribution of the newspaper, including employing and training newsboys, soliciting advertising and news, and collecting on accounts.

The traffic in newspapers did not flow only away from London to the provinces and then from provincial centres to the outlying areas. London proprietors read the country papers, purchased by subscription or perhaps exchange, and they occasionally incorporated provincial material into their

---

[57] Cranfield, *Development of the Provincial Newspaper*, 190.   [58] Ibid. 192–3.
[59] Wiles, *Freshest Advices*, 118–19.   [60] *Salisbury Post Man*, no. 1 (27 Sept. 1715).

own newspapers. Some London coffee-houses later in the century made a point of providing back files of provincial newspapers for their clients. Provincial newspaper owners advertised in the national papers and took care to establish London business connections. The *Salisbury Journal*, the *Sherborne Mercury*, and the *Hampshire Chronicle*, among other successful eighteenth-century country papers, had at least one agent in London practically from the start, and their proprietors made sure that their papers could be read in the coffee-houses there.

The proliferation of London newspapers and their ready availability in the country at the beginning of the eighteenth century were factors the provincial printers had to take into account when planning new papers.[61] The presence of the London papers might have inhibited the establishment of country rivals in the very early years of legal provincial printing (that is from the lapse of the Printing Act in 1695 to the turn of the century), when the natural conservatism of the newspaper-reading market could have discouraged innovation. Yet in important ways metropolitan competition aided the growth of the provincial newspaper trade. Entrepreneurs recognized that country readers already accustomed to a regular supply of news could grow to appreciate a single, locally produced newspaper that included a digest of news selected from national and Continental sources, both printed and written—the common boast of the provincial press was that it always contained 'the most Material Occurrences both foreign and domestic'. Supplementing this central supply of news of course were the local advertisements and journalistic contributions that gave the country papers regional flavour and greater commercial value. That, and the important fact that each country editor edited a selection of news uniquely tailored to local needs, made each country paper substantially different from any other paper. Compared to the metropolitan newspaper, its country counterpart could be more accessible, contained a whole week's news, had a local business section, and was cheaper. All this helped to make the new provincial papers competitive, marketable, and viable.

G. A. Cranfield called his chapter on the content of the provincial newspaper 'Blood and Sex'[62] and indeed such topics have always helped to sell newspapers. War was particularly good for sales. Other components were court and Continental news, shipping information, lists of preferments, promotions, deaths, and bankrupts, stock reports, and advertisements. Literary and political essays as well as poetry, usually drawn from

---

[61] John Feather takes a somewhat different view of the spread of the early provincial newspaper press (*Provincial Book Trade*, 37).

[62] Cranfield, *Development of the Provincial Newspaper*, 65–92.

the monthly magazines and often of a high calibre, made up part of the non-commercial content, especially in times of peace. Readers generally welcomed these contributions, except when they appeared to pre-empt solid news.[63]

The seventeenth century had produced competent journalists such as Henry Muddiman,[64] and in the eighteenth century a number of literary figures—Defoe, Addison, Steele, Fielding, Johnson, Smollett, and Goldsmith among them—were associated with periodicals.[65] Yet journalism remained in an early stage into the eighteenth century, and much of what was reported was based on hearsay and contributed by various agents and correspondents anonymous, onymous, and pseudonymous. A story might begin 'We hear' in one week's paper and conclude with a retraction in the following week's. News culled from printed sources could be equally unreliable, and, to complicate matters further, it was relatively easy to purchase a place in a newspaper for practically any story, so long as it had an element of plausibility. Yet as communications became better editors could more credibly justify claims to accuracy and authenticity; journalism likewise became somewhat more professional with the regular employment of newsagents and others to send in news items, and as editors themselves came to be more aware of their editorial role. And, while a clear-cut editorial section was not to be found in the papers until the late eighteenth century,[66] recognizable editorial comments were published much earlier.

Advertising, already established in seventeenth-century English newspapers, grew in economic importance as proprietors—and the Government —realized its potential to produce revenue. Many newspapers, including

---

[63] In the late 1730s Robert Raikes had to abandon an essay section called 'Country Common Sense' in his *Gloucester Journal*, because readers objected (C. H. Timperley, *A Dictionary of Printers and Printing, with the Progress of Literature, Ancient and Modern* (London: H. Johnson, 1839), 664). There was some critical comment on this in the rival *Salisbury Journal*, while the *Gentleman's Magazine* in London praised the '*ingenious Essay*', attributing its downfall to the inferior sensibilities of its readers: '*the Crowd of his Customers, not approving of any Thing that required the use of Reflection, cry'd out. That these Essays, which were design'd for improving their Morals, encouraging Arts and Industry, and rectifying several Abuses, deprived them of a great many Relations of News, perhaps most of them false or insignificant*' (*GM*, Jan. 1739). [64] See Muddiman, *The King's Journalist*.
[65] See Alvin Sullivan (ed.), *British Literary Magazines: The Augustan Age and the Age of Johnson, 1698–1788* (Westport, Conn.: Greenwood Press, 1983).
[66] Lucyle Werkmeister suggests that the *Star* provided the first real editorials in 1789 (*The London Daily Press 1772–1792* (Lincoln: University of Nebraska Press, 1963)). Jeremy Black gives credit for the first provincial-press editorials to Benjamin Flower (*Cambridge Intelligencer*) and Joseph Gales (*Sheffield Register*), both late in the century. Black also notes that material found in these clear-cut editorials had forerunners in editorial comment earlier in the century (*English Press in the Eighteenth Century*, 281), a point confirmed in the *Salisbury Journal* as early as the 1730s.

the *Salisbury Journal*, changed their names to incorporate 'Advertiser' in the title, and a few new papers were established with advertising as the main focus. Books and medicines provided the text of most early advertising, a reflection of the newspaper owners' book-trade background and close connections with the pharmaceutical trade, but this commercial part of the newspaper soon developed local texture as notices for real estate, runaway apprentices, livestock, entertainments, and services were included in greater numbers. While the non-commercial section of the provincial paper was very rarely illustrated (there were probably fewer than a dozen news pictures in the *Salisbury Journal* during Benjamin Collins's lifetime for example), small woodcuts often accompanied advertisements. They usually depicted the authorized seal to be found on bottles and packets of patent medicines. Collins's own patented Cordial Cephalic Snuff, a remedy for practically any ailment of the head, was sometimes identified by a woman clutching a packet of the snuff in one hand, evidently confident that it will cure the migraine headache from which she is obviously suffering.[67]

The eighteenth-century English newspaper is unquestionably an impressive, but still underused source for the study of developments in the social, political, and economic life of the century. The newspaper has been called the engine that drove the book trade; the growth of literacy is linked to its evolution. This is particularly true in the provinces, where newspapers addressed and serviced a new readership. Twentieth-century scholarship, when it has turned to the newspaper press, has tended either to concentrate on a single topic illustrated with examples or to pull together extracts from different newspapers to build up an anecdotal history.[68] Students of both methods have amassed a substantial body of evidence.

---

[67] e.g. in the *Journal* of 13 Sept. 1756.

[68] The single-subject approach, in which provincial newspapers have proved their value as primary resources, has informed studies such as John Alden's 'Pills and Publishing'; J. Jefferson Looney's 'Advertising and Society in England 1720–1820: A Statistical Analysis of Yorkshire Newspaper Advertisements', Ph.D. diss. (Princeton University, 1983), and 'Cultural Life in the Provinces: Leeds and York, 1720–1820', in A. L. Beier, David Cannadine, and James W. Rosenheim (eds.), *The First Modern Society: Essays in English History in Honour of Lawrence Stone* (Cambridge: Cambridge University Press, 1989), 483–510; John Styles, 'Print and Policing'. The two classic general studies of the provincial newspaper press in the first half of the 18th cent. are Cranfield's *Development of the Provincial Newspaper* and Wiles's *Freshest Advices*; Jeremy Black's *English Press in the Eighteenth Century* includes the London newspaper press as well as the country. The study that probably comes closest to this one in dealing with a specific paper is K. G. Burton's *The Early Newspaper Press in Berkshire (1723–1855)* (Reading: published by the author, 1954).

This present account of the eighteenth-century provincial newspaper press, however, is derived primarily from a detailed case study of one newspaper, an approach that has not been attempted until now. It is a fruitful course, for the *Salisbury Journal* is representative of the many provincial newspapers that succeeded; it reached a varied population within a large and equally varied catchment area; and it is still available to be read in one long unbroken run, in person at the Beinecke Library, Yale University, or on microfilm anywhere. But the *Journal* was only part of the business empire (and 'empire' does seem the appropriate description here) controlled by Benjamin Collins of Salisbury, whose career is discussed in Chapter 1. Among his many enterprises were other newspapers, including London titles, and, more important to this investigation, a competing Wessex newspaper, the *Hampshire Chronicle*. The accounts for this paper, identified a few years ago in the Public Record Office, provide the sort of detailed information that was unavailable to Roy Wiles and Graham Cranfield when they were writing about the early provincial newspaper trade.[69] A commercial infrastructure, described in Chapter 2, that was only suggested to them in their sampling of numerous provincial papers is confirmed and enlarged in these documents, which are unique both for the region and in the extensive explanatory material accompanying them. Together with the newspapers themselves, they offer rare details of the network of communications that was deployed to serve Wessex readers in the eighteenth century. In Chapter 3 those readers are defined by geography and by the material they wrote and read. Chapter 4 looks at the physical body of the provincial newspaper, and how it got to be that way, from the limitations of paper size and hand-press production, to Government regulations that influenced the number of pages, the different networks that carried material to the editor for refashioning, and the decisions the editor made in setting up the weekly news and advertisements. At the same time the dual prescriptive–descriptive role

---

[69] Cranfield, *Development of the Provincial Newspaper*; Wiles, *Freshest Advices*. The *Hampshire Chronicle* account books were only the first to be rediscovered. Since then Hannah Barker of St Peter's College, Oxford, has found account books for two other country newspapers, the *Chelmsford Chronicle* and the *Salopian Journal*. The *Chelmsford Chronicle* records cover the period between 1777 and 1784 in detailed quarterly accounts (Essex Record Office, Acc. 5197, D/F/66/1) and those of the proprietors of the *Salopian Journal* document proceedings at shareholders' meeting between 1793 and 1799 and provide a thorough financial record of the paper from Dec. 1793 to Mar. 1795 (Shropshire Records and Research Unit, MS 1923); see Hannah Jane Barker, 'Press, Politics and Reform: 1779–1785', D.Phil. thesis (Oxford University, 1994, especially her ch. on 'The Economics of the Provincial Press', 133–64). However, they are outside the scope of this study and Benjamin Collins had nothing to do with either.

of the newspaper is made clearer. It is possible to see the country paper
both responding to and helping to shape the social, political, and economic changes within its evolving catchment area. The last two chapters
deal with the contents of the newspaper: the news itself, essays, and verse
in Chapter 5, the profitable part, advertisements, in Chapter 6. This
study, in its comprehensiveness and in its analysis of the construction
of the regional newspaper press and its relationship to the book trade
and to other commercial developments, usefully complements Wiles's
and Cranfield's work. In many respects this analysis of the Wessex press
may serve for other regions and other readers—infrastructure, networks,
and marketing at a basic level were similar through the provinces. But it
is more to be hoped that this volume will be a base for further investigation of the tremendous impact the newspaper press made on eighteenth-
century life.

I

Benjamin Collins: The Man behind the Newspapers

THE first number of Samuel Farley's thrice-weekly *Salisbury Post Man: or, Packet of Intelligence from France, Spain, Portugal, &c.* is dated 27 September 1715.[1] Farley did not find the 200 regular subscribers he felt were required to make his ambitious venture a profitable one and Salisbury's first newspaper failed within a matter of months.[2] Yet the times were not wholly unpropitious, for the same year saw the birth of Benjamin Collins, almost certainly one of the founders of the town's second newspaper, the *Salisbury Journal*. He went on to become a dominant figure in the regional book and newspaper trades and in banking.

Benjamin Collins was christened in the parish church at Great Faringdon, Berkshire, on 14 October 1715.[3] He left Faringdon as an adolescent, moved to the more alluring Salisbury, and became the motivating force behind the *Salisbury Journal* through most of its first fifty years. His concerns were multifarious, incorporating regional and London newspapers, real estate, money lending, banking, the sale and invention of medicines, the East and West India trade, lottery tickets, bookselling, printing, publishing, bookbinding—but all of it based on his exploitation of the opportunities and connections he found in the early provincial newspaper and book trade. The eighteenth century saw a remarkable transition in English newspaper marketing, from a solely London-produced commodity to one that was also constructed and published in and for the

---

[1] While the *Post Man* was dated 27 Sept. 1715, it was not issued until mid-November, when the first number contained news of two important battles of the 1715 Rebellion.

[2] 'If 200. Subscribe, it shall be Deliver'd to any Private or Publick House in Town, every *Munday, Thursday*, and *Saturday* Morning . . .' (*Salisbury Post Man*, 27 Sept. 1715, *Salisbury Journal* Office, Salisbury). The fullest discussion of the *Post Man* is in Norah Richardson, 'Wiltshire Newspapers—Past and Present. Part III. The Newspapers of South Wilts', *Wiltshire Archaeological Magazine*, 40 (1919), 318–51; the paper is also briefly discussed in R. M. Wiles, *Freshest Advices: Early Provincial Newspapers in England* (Columbus: Ohio State University Press, 1965), 71–2, 168–9, 413, 488–9.

[3] Faringdon Parish Register, Berkshire Record Office (BRO), D/P53/1/2. Apparently it was usual for healthy babies to be baptized about two weeks after birth.

provinces. There was also a further shift from the gentleman-author writing within the tradition of courtly patronage to the professional author who depended on the mass patronage of the reading public, a transition most famously documented in Samuel Johnson's letter to Lord Chesterfield, February 1755.[4] Collins's generation of booksellers was the first to take full advantage of these developments in the commercialization of literature.[5] The life of Benjamin Collins sheds light on the making of a successful provincial bookseller, newspaper proprietor, and entrepreneur. At the same time his biography naturally informs a study of the newspapers he controlled.

'The dregs of the people' was one hostile contemporary's description of Benjamin Collins's origins.[6] Certainly Collins's beginnings were not auspicious. He was the seventh son, the eighth of nine children of William Collins, a Faringdon tallow chandler, and his wife Margaret Pierce of Idstone in the nearby parish of Ashbury.[7] William Collins would never have written 'Esq.' after his signature, but he was probably one of the more successful of his generation of Collins brothers, for the evidence of other Berkshire records suggests that the Collinses were a long-established Faringdon family of illiterate labourers and yeomen.[8] William Collins at least was able to invest in a farm and mill at Shrivenham (Wiltshire) by 1727[9] and two years later his seven surviving children received modest

---

[4] James Boswell, *Life of Johnson*, ed. R. W. Chapman; new edn. corrected by J. D. Fleeman (Oxford: Oxford University Press, 1970), 183–8.

[5] One discussion of this phenomenon is in Alvin Kernan, *Printing Technology, Letters & Samuel Johnson* (Princeton, NJ: Princeton University Press, 1987).

[6] A letter 'To the Printer of S——Y' signed 'F. Gerard' in the *Detector*, no. 1 [1786?], 5. This scurrilous periodical appeared well after Collins's death in Feb. 1785, apparently established for the sole purpose of attacking (or exposing) Collins and his family, as well as a few other Salisbury notables. The Detector's identity remains a mystery, but among Collins's known enemies was James Linden, the Southampton printer who published his *Hampshire Chronicle* in direct competition to the *Salisbury Journal* from 1772. Then Benjamin Charles Collins's will mentions 'needy and artful Villains' who had attempted to garnish his father's estate. They were Maurice Lloyd, Viscount Newhaven, and Gregory Bateman. 'Rogues of lesser note' were also involved (PRO PROB. 11/1478/368). Only the first three numbers of the *Detector* seem to have survived—in single copies—in the collection of the Earl of Radnor at Longford Castle, Salisbury. Quotations from the *Detector* are given here with the Earl of Radnor's kind permission.

[7] The two were married in Faringdon parish church, 13 Dec. 1700 (Faringdon Parish Register, BRO D/P53/1/1). The marriage ended with Margaret's death in Oct. 1719 (Faringdon Parish Register, BRO D/P53/1/2). See Table 1: A Collins Genealogy.

[8] See e.g. the will and inventory of William Collins (d. 1631) (BRO D/A3/2/88), and the administrations for William Collins (d. 1700) (BRO D/A3/2/103).

[9] Indenture tripartite between Richard Byrchall and Robert and Susanne Young, all of Sevenhampton, Wiltshire, and William Collins, dated 6 Nov. 1727 (WRO 802/24). There may have been other real estate transactions for which the records have not survived.

inheritances.[10] It is possible too, though the documentary links have yet
to be established, that the Faringdon Collinses were related to the prosperous Collins family of East Lockinge, about 10 miles south-east of
Faringdon.[11]

Great Faringdon, the town in which Benjamin Collins spent his child-
hood, stands on the ridge between the Vale of the White Horse and the
River Thames, near the London–Cirencester–Gloucester road. The eighteenth-century population of Faringdon was probably just under 2,000,[12]
which would have made it a mid-sized rural town. Its most famous son was
George III's Poet Laureate Henry James Pye (1745–1813), who celebrated
the town in *Faringdon Hill* (1774). Oxford is its nearest large neighbour,
17 miles north-east; London is about 80 miles to the east; Salisbury, about
60 miles to the south. This part of the county was a productive one, known
for its sheep and cattle, and a good location for someone in the business
of making soap and candles. Relationships formed by the Faringdon Collins family in these early years of the eighteenth century—particularly
with the family of the local apothecary Robert Baldwin—were to prove of
great strategic value to the youngest Collins son's career.

Benjamin Collins was 4 years old when his mother Margaret died in
1719; his father William died in 1729.[13] By this time Benjamin's elder

[10] Margaret (1708–?) and Mary (1718–?) were bequeathed £250 each; Joseph (1710–90),
£100 plus his father's 'Implements and Utensils for Soap making'; Benjamin (1715–85) and
Francis (1713–82), £100 each; William (1705–40?), £5; Richard (1704–?), the option of purchasing the rights to the Faringdon property from Benjamin, Francis, and Joseph on payment
of £10 to each of them; the residue to be divided equally among the seven. The will, dated
12 May 1729, was proved 27 Sept. 1729 (PRO PROB. 11/632/243). Apparently there was
no inventory connected with the will. That William inherited only £5 and Richard an option
on payment was not necessarily a sign of any disapproval; more likely it suggests that these
two sons had already been provided for. It is difficult to estimate present-day equivalents for
18th-cent. sums, but Richard B. Schwartz, in his *Daily Life in Johnson's London* (Madison:
University of Wisconsin Press, 1983), 44–54, suggests a sensible comparative approach. For
example, a London labourer before 1765 might earn from 9s. to 12s. a week; ordinary claret
was 3s. to 10s. a gallon early in the century; a 4-lb. loaf of bread was 4d. to 5d.; and Johnson
paid about £18 p.a. rent (excluding tax and tithes) for his Gough Square residence.
[11] This Collins family lived for centuries in Betterton House; Ferdinando Collins became
Lord of Betterton Manor in 1876 (William Page and P. H. Ditchfield (eds.), *VCH Berkshire*
(London: St Catherine Press, 1924), iv. 307, 310). An 18th-cent. Ferdinando Collins has a
number of advertisements in the *Salisbury Journal*, mostly for cockfights.
[12] The 1801 census reported 1,928 in Great Faringdon (*VCH Berkshire*, ii. 237).
[13] Margaret Collins was buried on 9 Oct. 1719, William on 31 Aug. 1729. The latter was
a difficult year for the country as a whole; an unusually large number of burials is recorded
in Faringdon for the summer of 1729 (Faringdon Parish Register, BRO D/P53/1/2).
'Mortality crises', when the annual crude death rate is more than 10% above trend, are
recorded in England for 1728–9 in E. A. Wrigley and R. S. Schofield, *The Population
History of England 1541–1871* (Cambridge: Cambridge University Press, 1989), 332–6.

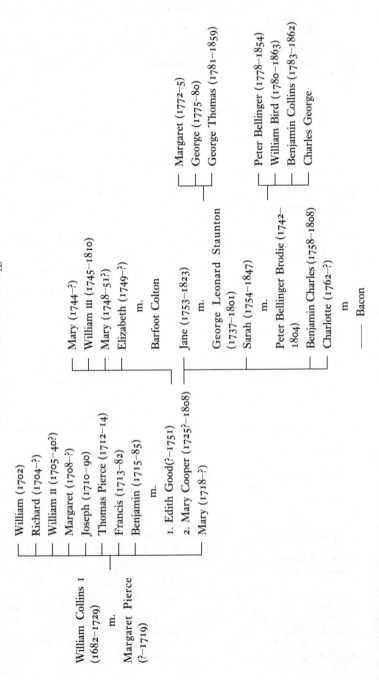

TABLE 1. *A Collins Genealogy*

William Collins I
(1682–1729)
m.
Margaret Pierce
(?–1719)

William (1702)
Richard (1704–?)
William II (1705–40?)
Margaret (1708–?)
Joseph (1710–90)
Thomas Pierce (1712–14)
Francis (1713–82)
Benjamin (1715–85)
  m.
  1. Edith Good(?–1751)
  2. Mary Cooper (1725?–1808)
Mary (1718–?)

Mary (1744–?)
William III (1745–1810)
Mary (1748–51?)
Elizabeth (1749–?)
  m.
  Barfoot Colton

Jane (1753–1823)
  m.
  George Leonard Staunton
  (1737–1801)
Sarah (1754–1847)
  m.
  Peter Bellinger Brodie (1742–1804)
Benjamin Charles (1758–1808)
Charlotte (1762–?)
  m
  —— Bacon

Margaret (1772–5)
George (1775–80)
George Thomas (1781–1859)

Peter Bellinger (1778–1854)
William Bird (1780–1863)
Benjamin Collins (1783–1862)
Charles George

brother William II (1705–40?) was beginning a book-trade career in Salisbury. The evidence of early Salisbury imprints suggests that William's
master had probably been Edward Easton, bookseller in Silver Street,[14] or
possibly but much less likely, Charles Hooten, printer and apothecary in
Milford Street.[15]

Salisbury booksellers had been selling books, first in manuscript and
then printed, for centuries when William began his training. A family of
booksellers called Hammond was working there and in London in the
sixteenth and early seventeenth centuries.[16] They were followed by John
Courtney, who is recorded in business from at least 1650 to 1675.[17] A
bookseller of that same name is recorded in Salisbury in 1715 and 1716,
and another bookseller there named Pope published Richard Eyre's
Oxford-printed sermon, *The Necessity of Grace*, in 1715. The pattern of
a few local booksellers retailing London-produced books, providing a
bookbinding service, and selling stationery and other goods is typical of
provincial towns before the eighteenth century. The situation was one
defined both by the restrictions on printing and the marketing requirements of the monopolistic London booksellers.

There was no printer in Salisbury until Samuel Farley arrived about
1715. Farley was no novice to the trade: he was almost certainly the
Samuel 'Farlow' (ST2:0913) who served an apprenticeship with Freeman
Collins (ST2:3217), and was freed in 1699,[18] exactly the same year that he
is found in partnership for the first time with Samuel Darker (ST2:3839)
in Exeter. Samuel Farley set up the *Exeter Post Man* about 1704, and a
printer of the same name established the *Bristol Post Man* in 1713. Whether
or not he was the same man, or another kinsman, it is certain that one

---

[14] It is just possible that he is the Edward 'Eaton' of Westminster who began, but did not
complete, a formal apprenticeship under William Phillips in Nov. 1689 (D. F. McKenzie,
Stationers' Company Apprentices 1641–1700 (Oxford: Oxford Bibliographical Society, 1974),
ST2:3527). If so, he would have been in his mid-40s in 1720.

[15] Plomer finds Hooten working in Salisbury 1729–30 (*A Dictionary of Printers and
Booksellers . . . 1726 to 1775* (London: The Bibliographical Society, 1932), 131). He is not
listed in McKenzie's *Apprentices*. The imprint of the newspaper suggests that Hooten was
working for William Collins rather than the other way round, and William Collins does not
take up printing until years after Hooten is no longer in evidence.

[16] R. B. McKerrow, *A Dictionary of Printers and Booksellers . . . 1557–1640* (London:
The Bibliographical Society, 1910), 122; A. W. Pollard and G. R. Redgrave, *A Short-Title
Catalogue of Books 1475–1640*, iii: Katharine F. Pantzer, *A Printers' & Publishers' Index*,
with a Chronological Index by Philip R. Rider (London: The Bibliographical Society,
1991), 75; E. Gordon Duff, *A Century of the English Book Trade* (London: The Bibliographical Society, 1905), 63.

[17] Plomer, *A Dictionary of the Printers and Booksellers . . . 1668 to 1725* (London: The
Bibliographical Society, 1922), 83.   [18] McKenzie, *Apprentices 1641–1700*.

Samuel Farley was printing in Salisbury in 1715.[19] He printed the *Salisbury Post Man* for a few months, and produced at least one local sermon.[20] But Farley stayed only long enough to test the market.

The next to set up a printing office in Salisbury was Charles Hooten, who is known to have printed a local sermon as well as the *Salisbury Journal* in 1729–30. Edward Easton had established himself as a bookseller in Salisbury by 1720 when his name appeared in the imprint of a local sermon.[21] The Collins family entered the picture when William Collins II arrived in the 1720s.

The money he inherited from his father (both the £5 mentioned in the will and any funds he may have received before this) may have enabled William to buy into a partnership with Easton after completing his training: 'E. Easton and W. Collins, booksellers in Silver Street' are linked as partners in the imprints of five books printed by Charles Hooten in 1730, three of them by the eccentric librarian and dissenting minister Samuel Fancourt. One sermon, John Price's on 'humanity and alms-giving', was printed for William Collins alone.[22] Collins, Hooten, and Easton were also connected with Salisbury's second newspaper, the *Salisbury Journal*, begun about this time. Wiltshire readers were evidently reluctant to give up or to supplement the London newspapers in numbers sufficient to support what amounted to a digest of London and foreign news with local advertisements, so Salisbury's second newspaper failed after a year. The *Salisbury Journal*, no. 58 for 6 July 1730, bears Charles Hooten's notice that 'This Paper not being encouraged according to Expectation, I shall from this time decline it; but all other Printing Business will be perform'd after the best Manner By Yours, &c., Charles Hooten'.[23] Hooten, Easton, and William Collins are named either in the advertisements or in

---

[19] Our knowledge of the provincial press would benefit from a close study of the numerous Farley family of Bristol, Exeter, and, for a short time, Salisbury. It is unclear if there were one or two Samuel Farleys at work in the early part of the century. See Plomer, *Dictionary 1668 to 1725*, 115, and Wiles, *Freshest Advices*, 383–4, 412–14.

[20] Daniel Whitby, *A Sermon Preach'd at the Cathedral Church of Sarum, November the 5th, 1715* (Sarum: printed and sold by Sam. Farley, and John Courtney: and to be had in the cities of London, Oxford, Bristol and Exeter).

[21] According to Plomer, Easton was working in Salisbury from perhaps 1725 until his death in 1753 (Plomer, *a Dictionary 1726 to 1775*, 81.) His will was proved 24 Dec. 1753 (PRO PROB. 11/805/314).

[22] Based on a search of the on-line *ESTC* Sept. 1995. The unusual career of Samuel Fancourt is charted in Monte Little, *Samuel Fancourt 1678–1768: Pioneer Librarian*, Wiltshire Monographs, 3 (Trowbridge: Wiltshire Library and Museum Service, 1984).

[23] A copy of this final number of the first *Salisbury Journal* is preserved in the office of the present *Salisbury Journal*. If the numbering is accurate and the paper was issued once a week this would give a commencement date of 25 May 1729.

the imprint of the newspaper; but the initials BC intertwined with WC in the monogram at the head of the first page suggest that by July 1730 at the latest another interested party was the young Benjamin Collins.

Benjamin apparently had left Faringdon about 1729 to learn the book trade from his brother in Salisbury; the large number of burials, including his father's, recorded in the Faringdon parish register for the summer of 1729 suggests reasons for the move south: a season of great economic hardship that affected much of the country may have been a factor or one of the many 'epidemics of fever' that occurred in 1729. Perhaps, with both his parents now dead, he entered apprenticeship under the guardianship of his elder brother. In his father's will Benjamin's portion of the estate was greater than William's, probably more than enough to buy a share in the copyright of the *Salisbury Journal*. Start-up costs for the paper would have been relatively modest. In the first place the partners did not have to invest in printing equipment, since Hooten, already a working printer, was involved as either a partner or a contract printer. As part-owner, however, Benjamin Collins would have been liable for a proportion of the expenses of running the newspaper (the many but constant expenses for stamped paper, type, composition, presswork, and so on, much of it payable in advance), and at the same time he would have been entitled to an equal proportion of the profits. In spite of his youth—he was not yet 15—it is likely that Benjamin Collins did buy into the venture at once and that his investment is reflected in the newspaper's monogram. Even though the *Salisbury Journal* was temporarily unsuccessful, investment in copies (that is, copyrights) was potentially the most lucrative aspect of the trade, a point Benjamin was quick to see, and one that was well borne out by his later career.

Evidence for his apprenticeship from 1729 or 1730 to William Collins II lies primarily in that *Salisbury Journal* monogram, which places Benjamin in Salisbury with his bookseller brother in 1730. There can be little doubt that the initials BC do in fact stand for Benjamin Collins. No other party with the same initials has been associated with the newspaper and Benjamin Collins himself later wrote that the business had 'been carried on by himself, and Brother before him' (*SJ*, 23 October 1775).[24] Benjamin may have been a partner in the newspaper—which after all required only money—but he had still to learn a trade and 14 years was the usual age

[24] Provincial apprenticeships are difficult, sometimes impossible, to document, and it is not surprising that no official record of Benjamin Collins's apprenticeship has been discovered. This suggests that the arrangement was an informal one, with no duty paid, since only those for which duty was payable are listed in the Inland Revenue records at the PRO.

to begin one. He was not yet a partner in the bookselling side of the business, for Benjamin's name does not figure in the imprints of any of the twelve books known to have been printed for William during the 1730s.[25] It is significant that the *Salisbury Journal* was successfully revived on 27 November 1736, just after Benjamin's 21st birthday, which was by then a common age to move up to journeyman status. Although the paper is 'Printed for *William Collins* Book-seller in *Silver-Street*', the BC/WC monogram of 1730 resumes its old place next to a woodcut view of Salisbury at the head of page one.

These years of training for Benjamin were the years in which his brother was establishing and then expanding his business. At first William was closely linked with Edward Easton. But he was evidently sole owner of the copyright for one minor 1730 publication, a sermon on humanity and alms-giving by John Price. Later imprints indicate that Easton and Collins continued to work together as booksellers, but were no longer sharing the same premises. (That Easton was probably first William's master and then his partner before William began business for himself helps to explain an otherwise puzzling spirit of co-operation that evidently existed between the Collinses and the Eastons, who must often have been competing for exactly the same market.)

Provincial bookselling in the eighteenth century included not just the distribution of any locally produced works and sometimes the buying and selling of copyrights in local book titles, but also the retailing of London imprints. Country booksellers had to demonstrate to their customers that it was more convenient—but not more costly—to make book purchases through their local bookshops. Therefore it was important for the provincial bookdealer to cultivate strong links with the big book-producers. London had a virtual monopoly on the most profitable titles, provided

---

[25] Albert H. Smith says that Benjamin Collins's name appears in 'an edition of the Bible, annotated by Samuel Humphreys, and printed and published in Salisbury in 1735' ('The Printing and Publication of Early Editions of the Novels of George Tobias Smollett', Ph.D. diss. (University of London, 1975), ii. 340). This must be the 3-vol. folio Bible annotated by Humphreys, issued in parts, and printed by R. Penny in London 1735–9 (T. H. Darlow and H. F. Moule, *Historical Catalogue of Printed Editions of the English Bible 1525–1961*, rev. A. S. Herbert (London: British and Foreign Bible Society, 1968), no. 1076). Although Collins's name does not actually appear on the title-page, Plomer (*Dictionary 1726 to 1775*, 197–8) notes that the first vol. was advertised in the *Craftsman*, 27 Dec. 1735—this advertisement includes 'a long list of predominantly west country booksellers by whom subscriptions were to be taken in and proposals issued—including "Mr Collins [almost certainly William] at Salisbury"'. Robert Penny apparently had Salisbury connections too, for his closest relative and one of his executors was Thomas Penny, son of Thomas Penny of White Parish near Salisbury (Plomer, *Dictionary 1726 to 1775*, 197–8; with thanks to M. J. Jannetta for tracking down both Bible and advertisement).

the largest concentrated market for printed material, was the entrepôt for foreign news and products (including good-quality Continental paper), and regulated stamp taxes on pamphlets and newspapers. On the other hand reciprocity could benefit the London booksellers who required provincial advertisers and distributors such as Collins and Easton to service the growing country market.[26] In 1730 William Collins and Edward Easton were therefore associated with Richard Hett (ST3:1771), Richard Ford (ST3:4881), and John Gray in the Poultry, and J. Noon in Cheapside. This partnership may have been founded in the nature of the Dissenting tracts they published, for the Londoners were closely associated with such works.[27] In the same year Stamford Wallace's little book on Stonehenge provides imprint evidence of Collins's first connections with the mainstream London book trade in John Knapton (ST3:4778) and fellow Berkshireman Thomas Astley (ST3:1822). By 1732 Richard Baldwin (ST3:8721), who was a brother of Robert Baldwin the Faringdon apothecary and partner with Thomas Astley, was working with William Collins.[28] Judging from imprints and advertisements, the arrangement was a co-operative one in the tradition by which the London partners provided most of the book production and an outlet to the London market, while the Wessex partners assisted London books to reach the more widespread country audience by acting as advertisers, retailers, and distributors.

The books and newspapers themselves provide most of the information we have on the early provincial trade. Much less durable is evidence for associated activities: account books have been disbound for waste paper or destroyed; miscellaneous products found in eighteenth-century booksellers' shops—the ink, the stationery, the medicines—have long since disappeared; job-printing is ephemeral for the most part; bookbindings

[26] John Feather discusses this symbiotic relationship in the first chapter of his *The Provincial Book Trade in Eighteenth-Century England* (Cambridge: Cambridge University Press, 1985), 1–11. Feather argues that the evolution of this relationship made the London booksellers' concern with enforcement of copyright more and more impracticable.

[27] Hett, Ford, and Gray had separate shops in the Poultry; John Gray himself became a Dissenting minister in Yorkshire after 1732 (Plomer, *Dictionary 1726 to 1775*, 95–6, 108, and 123).

[28] The first book recorded in *ESTC* to bear their joint imprint is William Diaper's *Brent a Poem* for which D. F. Foxon suggests a publication date of 1732 (*English Verse 1701–1750: A Catalogue of Separately Printed Poems* (Cambridge: Cambridge University Press, 1975), i. D291). It is 'Printed for William Collins at the Bible and Crown in Silver Street, and sold by T. Astley and R. Baldwin, London'. The wording of the imprint suggests that Collins was sole shareholder for this local production; Baldwin and Astley acted as retailers to the larger London market. *Brent*, a poem on a local subject and consisting of only seven leaves folio, is a typical product of the provincial press; the village of Brent, near Wells, is close enough to Salisbury to make Collins a logical choice for local publisher.

can no longer be traced to their craftsmen; other services have been for-
gotten. William Collins would have been unusual if he did not also incorporate stationery and patent medicines into his business at an early
stage. But it is not until 8 January 1736/7 that we have solid evidence of
any activity besides straightforward bookselling and newspaper publishing. The *Salisbury Journal* imprint for that date notes that not only does
William Collins offer 'Bibles, Common-Prayer Books, Shop Books, &c.',
but 'Advertisements are taken in . . . And Books Bound after the Neatest
Manner. And Money [may be had] for any Library or Parcel of Books'.
In March of the same year we find William Collins handling a reward for
a lost or stolen silver tankard (*SJ*, 12 March 1737); a month later he
began advertising Squire's Grand Elixir, Dr Bateman's Pectoral Drops,
and Daffy's Elixir, three durable and profitable quack medicines[29] (*SJ*,
18 April 1737). And within a couple of years he was advertising a varied
job-printing service:

> *At the Printing-Office in* Salisbury, *and by the Distributers of this Journal, Attorneys,
> and Justices Clerks may be supplied with* Copies of Writs, High-way Warrants,
> Warrants of Removal, Misdemeanour, and all Sorts of Blanks, and Receipts for
> the Land-Tax, Bills, Bonds, Certificates, &c. *neatly printed, and at the most reason-
> able Prices.* (*SJ*, 28 August 1739)

It is almost certain that the medicines, stationery, secondhand books,
and job-printing all predated the revived *Salisbury Journal*; indeed profits
from this side of the business probably subsidized the new paper. The
Journal is the primary source of information on that side of Collins's
trade.

When the *Journal* was re-established in November 1736, it was without the renewed assistance of Charles Hooten. Instead, typographical evidence indicates that the Collins brothers had their newspaper printed by
the Sherborne printer William Bettinson, although he was not named in
the imprint.[30] Less than two years later the *Journal* was an entirely independent Collins operation. The imprint for the *Salisbury Journal* of 27
February 1738/9 announces important developments: First, the paper is

[29] The term 'quack medicines' has been given a certain new legitimacy in Roy Porter's
definition (see *Health for Sale: Quackery in England 1660–1850* (Manchester: Manchester
University Press, 1989)).

[30] John Newbery, who was later to play an important part in Benjamin Collins's business
dealings, certainly owned a share in the *Sherborne Mercury*, but it is not known when he first
invested in that newspaper. He bequeathed a share in that and other papers to his wife Mary
in his will written in 1767 (Charles Welsh, *A Bookseller of the Last Century* (London:
Griffith, Farran, Okeden & Welsh; New York: E. P. Dutton, 1885), 160–7).

now 'Printed by WILLIAM COLLINS and Comp. at the PRINTING-OFFICE on the Ditch in SALISBURY'. Second, it is clear that 'Comp.' must have included Benjamin Collins, and the new imprint marks a change in his status. The new address suggests that printing and bookselling were carried on in two separate shops for a time: printing on the Ditch, bookselling remaining in nearby Silver Street. Finally, agents for the *Salisbury Journal*, vital if the country newspaper was to be distributed with any effectiveness, are listed for the first time.[31] They include Thomas Astley in London and N. Poole in Faringdon,[32] as well as five other provincial distributors as far away as Gloucester and Taunton. By the late 1730s the business in which Benjamin Collins was trained contained components of his later success: a network of professional contacts that extended to London as well as into the country, a newspaper that promoted the growth of that network, and experience in the sale of a variety of book-related products and services, including bookbinding and job-printing. William worked in Salisbury for at least ten years; in August 1740 he quietly disappeared from the *Journal*'s colophon (*SJ*, 12 August 1740), leaving the operation of the printing office on the Ditch and the bookshop in Silver Street in Benjamin Collins's hands.[33]

From 1740 the changes multiplied under the vigorous direction of the young bookseller-printer. One of the first was a decision to take an apprentice, Richard Baldwin II (ST3:0376), son of the London Richard Baldwin with whom William had been connected, and nephew of the Faringdon apothecary Robert Baldwin.[34] This was a wise decision, for

---

[31] J. Everard, a silk-dyer in Andover, was in fact the first agent noted (21 Nov. 1737). He is mentioned, however, in the context of his other business and without reference to other agents, which gives this very first notice an ambiguous quality.

[32] N. Poole is in neither Plomer, *Dictionary 1726 to 1775* nor McKenzie, *Apprentices 1701–1800*. He or she is possibly related to John Poole of Faringdon who sold lottery tickets in the *Salisbury Journal* in 1761 (3 Aug. 1761). A number of Pooles—related to the Collins family—are mentioned in Francis Collins's will (PRO PROB. 11/1091/274–5).

[33] Norah Richardson deduced from the change in imprint that William Collins died in Aug. 1740 ('Wiltshire Newspapers—Past and Present. Part III [Continued]', *Wiltshire Archaeological Magazine*, 41 (1920), 57). It is unlikely that he is the William Collins who was buried in Milford, just outside Salisbury on 14 Mar. 1739/40 (Laverstock Parish Register, WRO 1324/1). That William's disappearance passed without comment in the *Salisbury Journal* may be the only hint we have of the brothers' personal relationship. There is no comment in the *Sherborne Mercury* either (and I thank Gerald Harriss for verifying this).

[34] Richard Baldwin II was apprenticed 16 Sept. 1740, for a consideration of £25 (PRO IR. 1/50/133; see Ian Maxted, *The British Book Trades, 1710–1777: An Index of Masters and Apprentices Recorded in the Inland Revenue Registers at the Public Record Office, Kew* (Exeter: Ian Maxted, 1983), no. 0365a; and Christabel Dale, *Wiltshire Apprentices and Their Masters 1710–1760* (Devizes: Wiltshire Archaeological and Natural History Society, 1961)). Baldwin was made free of the Stationers' Company by patrimony 3 Feb. 1747 (D. F. McKenzie,

Richard brought direct experience of his father's London bookshop; he seems to have shared Benjamin Collins's good, intuitive business sense; and he went on from his training with Collins to become a successful member of the closed London book trade.[35] Indeed, it may well have been through his first apprentice that Benjamin Collins was better able to establish his own close connections with London. Two other apprentices joined Collins in the 1740s: Richard Holland in 1742 to learn bookselling and Edward Stevens in 1747 to learn printing. A total of nine apprentices in various book trades are documented for Benjamin Collins in the Inland Revenue records: Richard Baldwin, apprentice bookseller (1740); Richard Holland, bookseller (1742); Edward Stevens, printer (1747); Caleb Preston, bookbinder (1753); George Sealy (1755); Thomas Goodfellow (1766); Richard Wilkes (1766); James Robbins (1775); and his son Benjamin Charles Collins (1775). If the Inland Revenue documents accurately record all his apprentices, then this established Collins's pattern of formally employing only one or two apprentices at a time for the rest of his career.[36] This is a pattern that shows the versatility required for success in the provincial book trade.

A conspicuous page-one notice in the *Salisbury Journal*, 20 October 1741, advertised another move:

BENJAMIN COLLINS, Bookseller and Stationer, at the *Bible and Crown* in *Silver-street*, is remov'd higher up, into *the Corner Shop fronting the Poultry Cross* (late in the Occupation of Mr. *Thomas Smith*, Apothecary) by whom are sold Books in all Faculties, and Parts of Learning, as cheap as in *London*. Likewise *Stationary Wares* of all Kinds, both Wholesale and Retail. Also Books Bound, Letter'd, and Gilt, in the neatest Manner on easy Terms.[37]

Stationers' Company Apprentices 1701–1800 (Oxford: Oxford Bibliographical Society, 1978)). Richard Baldwin's career is discussed in C. Y. Ferdinand, 'Richard Baldwin Junior, Bookseller', *Studies in Bibliography*, 42 (1989), 254–64.

[35] The London book trade was closed in the sense that it practically monopolized shares in the best-selling printed works, even to the extent of excluding provincial and peripheral London booksellers from the trade sales at which shares in copies changed hands. Benjamin Collins was able to obtain his shares by purchasing them directly from colleagues, some of whom may have acted as his agent at the sales. Shares in pamphlets and books of purely local interest, however, were commonly owned by provincial booksellers. For trade sales, see Terry Belanger, 'Booksellers' Sales of Copyright: Aspects of the London Book Trade, 1718–1768', Ph.D. diss. (Columbia University, 1970), and 'Booksellers' Trade Sales, 1718–1768', *Library*, 5th ser., 30 (1975), 281–302.

[36] See Maxted, *British Book Trades: Masters and Apprentices*, nos. 0365a–0365i, and Dale, *Wiltshire Apprentices*.

[37] This notice ran for 14 weeks, indicating perhaps the extent to which the newspaper in 1741 depended on casual sales. Regular subscribers would have seen the notice within the first week or two.

Apparently the new premises were large enough to contain both the printing and the bookselling operations. And the location must have been a better one: any shop on Silver Street would have been accessible to traffic crossing the River Avon at Fisherton Bridge, the main route into Salisbury from the west. The Poultry Cross had an additional advantage in that it was a congregating point near the edge of the market square, not only on Tuesdays and Saturdays when the Cross was the site of the poultry, fruit, and vegetable market, but also on other days of the week.[38]

More provincial agents were added to the *Salisbury Journal* distribution network in the 1740s. Ten are named in the imprint for 23 March 1742, when the newspaper could be had in Reading, Oxford, Bristol, Bath, and the Isle of Wight, as well as throughout Wiltshire and its adjoining counties.[39] The geographical range of his network raises questions of how Collins transported copies of his *Journal*, as well as books, stationery supplies, and medicine, to his widely scattered provincial agents. He had several options, of course: the local carriers and waggon drivers who were slow, but relatively reliable; the post, usually prohibitively expensive; or his own network of newsmen. Although all three means were employed at one time or another, it was most efficient to send goods by a route specifically designed by Collins, and clearly such a system is in operation by April 1741 when he reminds his newspaper readers that a pamphlet describing the recent trial of Samuel Goodere could be purchased either at the Printing-Office, or 'by the News-Men' (*SJ*, 7 April 1741). Benjamin Collins's distribution system, well planned and well executed within the first few years of his career, helped ensure his later success.

Benjamin Collins saw early in his career, too, that investment in steady selling authors and titles was another key to successful bookselling. Pre-requisite, of course, was an ability to recognize those authors and titles, an ability which Collins demonstrably possessed. John Newbery (1713–67) of Reading, and later of London, was to prove the most important of

[38] An early 19th-cent. painting depicts a congested Poultry Cross on market day. See John Chandler, *Endless Street: A History of Salisbury and Its People* (Salisbury: Hobnob Press, 1987), pl. 19. A somewhat later print shows a less crowded, more comfortable meeting place. See David Burnett, *Salisbury: The History of an English Cathedral City* (Tisbury, Wilts.: Compton Press, n.d.), 35.

[39] The imprint for that date includes 'T. ASTLEY, Bookseller in St. *Paul*'s Church-yard, *London*; J. NEWBERY, Bookseller in *Reading, Berks*; J. FLETCHER, Bookseller in *Oxford*; W. FREDERICK, Bookseller in *Bath*; J. COLLET, at the Bible in *Castle-street, Bristol*; Mr. HARRIS, jun. Bookseller in *Gloucester*; T. SHERWOOD, in *Devizes*; R. WELCH, in *Lymington, Hants*; R. WOOLLRIDGE, Bookseller in *Shaftesbury, Dorset*; T. GEARE, Bookseller in the *Isle of Wight*; . . .'

Collins's new agents in this respect. The *Salisbury Journal* had advertised one of his books as early as 21 July 1741, but Newbery himself was not added to the list of *Journal* agents until March 1742. In 1745 Collins and John Newbery began a series of little books designed for children, *The Circle of the Sciences*, 'Digested in a Method entirely new, whereby each Branch of *Polite Literature* is render'd extreamly easy and instructive'. Royal Licence was granted to Collins and Newbery on 18 December 1744 (*SJ*, 8 January 1744/5). According to an advertisement in the *Salisbury Journal* of 12 November 1745, the first of at least seven volumes to be published was *An Easy Introduction to the English Language*, printed for John Newbery and sold by Benjamin Collins and others. An addition to the series was *The Royal Battledore* (1746? Roscoe J21), which Collins claimed was 'My own invention'.[40] This was an ingenious imitation hornbook, printed on card on one side, with Newbery's distinctive embossed, coloured paper pasted on the other.[41] Beginning readers were warned that 'He that ne'er learns his ABC, for ever will a Blockhead be', while 'he that learns these Letters fair, shall have a coach to take the Air', and presumably transport to the bookshop to buy lots of Collins/ Newbery books. The story of the *Circle of the Sciences* is a complicated one: the advertisement with the royal privilege that appeared in the *London Penny Post* ten days after the *Salisbury Journal* advertisement (18 January 1744/5) does not mention Benjamin Collins; some of the advertised volumes have not survived; others survive in different editions with different titles; and there were late additions—like the undated *Royal Battledore*—that capitalized on the popularity of the series. Sidney Roscoe thought that the *Circle* was composed of 'seven orthodox volumes' only, excluding the *Battledore* and other volumes; but other scholars accept the additions. In at least one sense, the *Battledore* was introductory to the *Circle*, even if it was first issued after other volumes

---

[40] A claim readily accepted by Andrew Tuer, *History of the Hornbook* (London: Leadenhall Press, 1897), 405–6. Roscoe numbers cited in the text are to be found in S. Roscoe, *John Newbery and His Successors 1740–1814* (Wormley, Herts.: Five Owls Press, 1973).

[41] Bodleian Library, Oxford, has a copy of this rare *Battledore* at Arch. AA. d. 8. Collins's account books, from which this claim to invention is taken, were destroyed earlier this century: 'In Salisbury I was just too late to secure the ledgers of B. Collins who printed *Roderick Random*. It is tragic to think that they were all destroyed within the last twenty years' (John Johnson to Arthur Rogers of Newcastle on Tyne, bookseller, 19 Feb. 1932, Oxford University Press file: OUP/PR/11/9/2/2). I am grateful to Esther Potter and Clive Hurst for bringing this letter to my attention. Charles Welsh transcribes portions of the account books in his biography of John Newbery, *Bookseller of the Last Century*. Most of the following information on copies is from Collins's 'Account of Books Printed, and Shares Therein. No. 3. 1770 to 1785', reproduced in part as Appendix 7 of Welsh's book.

in the series had already appeared, for children could learn to read by its means and then move on to other titles.[42] The series was extraordinarily successful: *The Royal Battledore* was still selling well in 1780, with nearly 100,000 copies sold between 1771 and 1780.

The Royal Primer (Roscoe J324), for which Collins also claimed credit, did even better, selling 20,000 copies between October 1771 and October 1772. In this case large sales did not necessarily mean large profits—the battledores sold wholesale for 1*d*. each and cost £3.10*s*. per thousand to produce—yet the children's books were steady sellers constantly advertised in the *Journal*, and, reaching a previously untapped segment of the reading population, they played a part in creating a more literate society and enlarging the market for yet more books. Collins's ingenuity in this area even extended to an instructive alphabet game: first advertised as a *Set of Fifty Squares* in mid-1743, it soon grew to *A Set of Fifty-Six Squares*, and went through many editions over the years.[43] Collins continued to be associated with juvenile literature and John Newbery, and obviously valued his shares in Newbery-related titles, only relinquishing them on his death to his son Benjamin Charles.[44]

Another copyright Benjamin Collins is known to have held ('of Mr John Newbery') in the 1740s is a one-quarter share in *The Evangelical History of Our Lord Jesus Christ* (Roscoe J174?), and a topical sermon by the Bishop of Salisbury is entered to him as sole proprietor in the Stationers' Company Register in 1745.[45] Imprints of other books provide evidence that, early in his career, Collins was fully aware of this lucrative

---

[42] Roscoe, *John Newbery*, J60–72. Elizabeth Eaton Kent (*Goldsmith and His Booksellers* (Ithaca, NY: Cornell University Press, 1933), 55) and Welsh (*Bookseller of the Last Century*, 186–8) both accept the claim printed above the *Battledore*'s imprint that it was 'the first Introductory Part of the *Circle of the Sciences*'.

[43] *Fifty Squares* was first advertised in the *SJ*, 28 June 1743; *Fifty-Six Squares*, 26 June 1744. A set of the *Fifty-Six Squares* was recently purchased by the private collector Lloyd Cotsen, who has now deposited his collection in the Princeton University Library.

[44] Bequeathed to Benjamin Charles were 'my Copyright or Right of Printing Publishing and vending the Salisbury Journal together with my Copyrights and Shares of Copyright of and in the following Books Viz my third Share of the Royal Battledore [Roscoe J21] Royal Primmer [Roscoe J324] Pretty Book for Children [Roscoe J307] Pretty Book of Pictures or the History of Tommy Trip [Roscoe J308] Museum or Private Tutor for Masters and Misses [Roscoe J253] Royal Psalter [Roscoe J326] Daily Journal or Gentlemans and Tradesmans compleat annual Pocket Book the eighth Part of Fennings Spelling Book and one third Part of the compleat Letter Writer [the last three not in Roscoe]...' (Benjamin Collins's will, PRO PROB. 11/1127/120; see Appendix).

[45] *A Sermon Preached at the Cathedral Church of Salisbury October 6th 1745. On Occasion of the Rebellion in Scotland*, entry dated 18 Oct. 1745 (Stationers' Company Register of Copies, 1710–1746, p. 606).

aspect of bookselling: he was printer, and presumably at least part-owner, of copies in a number of works with local interest or origin and he was gradually strengthening his links with the London book trade through joint shareholding. As ever, the *Salisbury Journal*, and later on his other newspapers, provided Collins with a convenient means of ensuring that any of his or his colleagues' books could be regularly promoted and widely distributed.

If the numerous notices for second-hand books in the *Salisbury Journal* are anything to go by, provincial booksellers, including Benjamin Collins, found buying and selling used books a good sideline. Collins, at the centre of a network of local newsagents and booksellers, was particularly well placed to learn of opportunities in this line. Used books formed part of a country bookshop's regular stock, but were commonly advertised when a large collection became available:

A CATALOGUE of the valuable LIBRARIES of GAUNTLET FRY, Esq; of Netherhampton . . . and the Rev. *Mr.* DERBY, of Poole . . . which will be Sold very cheap, according to the Prices printed in the Catalogue. *By* BENJAMIN COLLINS, . . . The Sale to begin *Monday* the 25th of *March*, 1751, and continue till all are sold. (*SJ*, 18 March 1751)

The Collins brothers were also able to offer their customers a supply of prints, including both competing versions of the different horse pictures published by Thomas Bakewell and John Bowles from London, and Benjamin was later able to print and publish what has become the best-known map of Salisbury in the eighteenth century.[46]

More than for books and prints, in which profits were limited by substantial production costs, the profit margin for medicines, often cheaply produced, could be very large. The medical part of a diversified business probably subsidized the book and newspaper side to some extent. The pseudonymous Detector, describing several means by which Collins made his fortune, wrote that 'the nostrums and quack medicines of his day . . . yield a profit of five and twenty per cent. If I am not misinformed, he has paid Dr. Norris alone 750*l* for his drops in the course of a year—'.[47] And Norah Richardson transcribes one receipt from Benjamin Charles Collins to Francis Newbery: 'Received of Francis Newbery, Esquire, fourteen hundred and seventy one pounds and six shillings, being the ballance of snuff stamps, and medicines account due December 31, 1796.'[48] Even

---

[46] *The City of Salisbury with the Adjacent Close, Church and River Accurately Surveyed by William Naish* (Sarum: Printed and Sold by Benj. Collins, 1751).
[47] *Detector*, no. 2 [1787?], 8–9.   [48] Richardson, 'Wiltshire Newspapers', 64.

though this records a transaction that took place a generation later, the large sum involved gives some idea of the profits that could be made from this other trading, and especially from medicine. Benjamin Collins continued to stock best-selling nostrums, adding to those names sold by his brother before him. However he did not limit himself to sales alone: On 27 December 1743 the Cordial Cephalic Snuff, 'an effectual Remedy for most Disorders of the Head', was advertised in the *Salisbury Journal* for the first time. The Cephalic Snuff was Collins's own invention, popular enough that he found it worth the trouble to secure Letters Patent for it in 1773.[49] The medicine was regularly advertised in Collins's newspapers, and elsewhere, sometimes as a sort of bonus to purchasers of Dr Henry's Chymical Nervous Medicine. Cephalic Snuff even appeared on stage, as part of Lord Ogleby's hypochondriacal repertoire, in the second act of Garrick and Colman's *The Clandestine Marriage* (1766).

Similar ingenuity was practised in his newspaper advertising. During his first decade as proprietor Collins was continually experimenting with advertisements in the *Salisbury Journal*, moving them from one part of the paper to another, changing the size and style of type, employing small woodcuts to advertise the 'name-brand' products, and disguising advertising as news. He was quick to see the possibilities of linking a current story with marketing: when the main news was from the ship *Ramilies*, 17 October 1757, the bottom margin of that page carried a message to 'All Merchants, Captains, of Ships, and others . . . That by BENJ. COLLINS, Bookseller and Stationer . . . are made and sold, Wholesale and Retail, all Sort of Books for Accompts, as Day-Books, Post-Books, and Leidger-Books . . .' The marked-up office copy of the newspaper, which has found its way to the Beinecke Library, Yale University,[50] suggests that Collins often placed small advertisements of his own at the end of longer, duty-paid notices, as a way of avoiding the expense of the duty on advertisements.[51] There was one final move for Collins's business, by now called 'THE PRINTING-OFFICE, STAMP-OFFICE, and BOOKSELLERS-SHOP', in May 1748. The new premises were on the New Canal (formerly

[49] Patent No. 1030, 18 May 1773 (Bennet Woodcroft, *Alphabetical List of Patentees of Inventions from March 2, 1617 (14 James I.) to October 1, 1852 (16 Victoriae)* (London: Queen's Printing Office, 1854), 120). One copy of a single-sheet advertisement entitled 'The Virtues and Uses of the Cordial Cephalic Snuff' (1775?) is located in the Francis A. Countway Library of Medicine, Harvard Medical Library, Boston.

[50] The copy in the *Salisbury Journal* office is clean, and begins in the mid-1750s.

[51] Each advertisement in the marked-up copies usually has a MS 'Entd.' or 'Pd.', probably referring to entries in Collins's office account books. The combined advertisements have only one notation.

called the Ditch) in 'the House late in the Possession of Messieurs *Tatum* and *Still*, Apothecaries; being the same which Mr. *Rawlins Hillman*, Apothecary, deceas'd, formerly liv'd in' (*SJ*, 9 May 1748). The location itself, across from Fisher Row and Butcher Row near the east end of the market, probably had little geographical advantage over Poultry Cross. But evidently this house/shop was bigger and better, previously advertised as 'A VERY large handsome commodious Dwelling-house, the Front new Built' (*SJ*, 31 August 1747). The inventory accompanying Collins's lease describes twenty-four rooms large and small, including a warehouse, a chocolate room, a study, and two parlours; William Naish's map of Salisbury shows that the printing office and living quarters were grouped round a courtyard reached by a passage from New Canal. The move proved to be a satisfactory one—Collins at first leased the house from the estate of Rawlins Hillman, and then bought it for £650 on 8 October 1756; the *Salisbury Journal* remained in this same position until 1962.[52]

While one can piece together a relatively complete picture of Benjamin Collins the businessman from 1740 on, little record of his personal life has survived. Shaftesbury Holy Trinity parish registers show that he was married to Edith Good of Shaftesbury on 1 June 1743 when he was 27 years old.[53] (It is possible that he had made a previous marriage, but no certain evidence of that, or of any other children, has been discovered: he may have been the Benjamin Collins who married Eleanor Young in Knook, about 17 miles north-west of Salisbury, on 27 January 1734. He would have been 18 years old then.) Benjamin and Edith Collins's first child Mary was born in July 1744. William Collins III was christened in the parish church of St Thomas, Salisbury, on 11 December 1745; another daughter, also named Mary (the first had probably died), was christened on 21 April 1748 and was buried less than three years later; their youngest child was Elizabeth, christened 9 June 1749. Edith Collins was buried at Holy Trinity Church, Shaftesbury, 27 February 1751.

Soon after Edith's death, Collins married Mary Cooper by whom he had four children: Jane, christened 5 July 1753; Sarah, 20 August 1754; Benjamin Charles, 27 December 1758; and Charlotte, 10 September 1762.[54]

---

[52] Leases and releases for the property, WRO 911/1.

[53] Shaftesbury Holy Trinity Parish Register, DRO.

[54] The baptisms of all Benjamin Collins's children are recorded in the Salisbury St Thomas Parish Register (WRO 1900/7). Edith Good Collins's burial is recorded in the Shaftesbury Holy Trinity Parish Register (DRO). I am grateful to the late Derek Gladwyn

Whatever Collins's other motives for marrying Mary Cooper, his choice had practical business implications—her brother-in-law Joseph Elderton was to assist Collins in several legal matters, and although Edith Good's family had a good reputation in Shaftesbury, Mary Cooper might have been even better placed in Salisbury society.

To soften the portrait of the single-minded man of business there is one sketch of the personal man that found its way into the local news section of the *Salisbury Journal,* 9 October 1749. Ignoring the political overtones, it is a report, probably firsthand, of an outing to Old Sarum, which gives the pleasant impression of a man who could appreciate a picnic:

a Cloth being spread upon the green Carpet, they brake Cakes, and pour'd forth a Libation of *Frank Collins*'s generous Wine out of respect to One of the right honourable Representatives of the Soil, and another no less worthy Patriot. After-wards a *Ballad*, writ for the joyous Occasion, (with a proper Chorus, which the Birds enliven'd,) being sung, the whole concluded with a Dance, three Huzza's, and a gracious Peep from the Sun.[55]

Collins was unusual in his inventiveness and clearly he was an exceptionally able business manager, but during the first part of his career only activities that have traditionally been associated with the provincial book trade are documented. In the 1740s Collins's business contained the components of any typical provincial bookselling concern: books and pamphlets (some of them locally produced, but most of them London-printed), a newspaper, job-printing, bookbinding, and medicines. Once he had established himself as a newspaper proprietor and bookseller and built up his capital, he was ready to extend himself further. Benjamin Collins's unusual financial success, the greater diversification that success allowed, and his close ties with London set him apart from most provincial booksellers later in his career.

Many of the developments of Collins's middle years can be charted in the pages of the *Salisbury Journal,* by this time claiming to be 'one of the most extensive Country Papers in the Kingdom' (*SJ,* 2 June 1755). For example as early as 1752 Collins was prepared to lend 'SUMS of

for directing me away from another Edith Collins who, by coincidence, was buried at Milford, 8 July 1751 (Laverstock Parish Register, WRO 1324/1). In spite of the fact that the Benjamin Collins family had a house in Milford, the Edith Collins buried in Shaftesbury in February is unquestionably the wife of Benjamin.

[55] Frank Collins was Francis, Benjamin Collins's older brother, a vintner who ran the Mitre and Crown Tavern, Silver Street, Salisbury.

MONEY, FROM One Hundred to Ten Thousand POUNDS . . . on Free-hold Estates, *or other good* Securities, AND ON MODERATE TERMS. None but PRINCIPALS will be treated with, and secrecy may be depended on' (*SJ*, 13 January 1752). This first evidence of serious banking activity on Collins's part places him in another tradition of the eighteenth-century book trade, that of the bookseller-turned-banker.[56] Francis Gosling, of Gosling's Bank, is the century's most famous example, and John Feather records a provincial example in William Jackson of Oxford, the news-paper proprietor/bookseller who founded the Old Bank at Oxford.[57] The Detector wrote with some bitterness about this aspect of Collins's business:

As we might justly be censured for branding Mr. C——ns with the name of *Userer*, without substantiating our charge, it is become necessary to premise, that this man carried on the business of a country banker, which he began with nothing, and finished with a very opulent fortune.—He had no connections at his outsetting, because he could form none; for no man of worth would risk his real property with a needy adventurer.—The laws have restrained the interest of money from exceeding five per cent. per annum, and so in proportion for any shorter or longer period—and this legal interest is always obtainable on real security, without trouble, without risk, and without expence.—Hence it is obvi-ous that our hero (perhaps like some other bankers) either made more of his capital (if he had any) than the lawful interest, or that he established himself from a lucky combination of fortuitous circumstances, without any capital at all—and the latter we are inclined to believe must have been the fact.—It is an erroneous opinion, that the paper in circulation leaves a banker with a large surplus of running cash; for, if there is no provision always kept in readiness for that paper, there is an end to his credit, and of course to banking and Mr. Collins himself has in his time experienced the inconveniency of a sudden *run*.[58]

---

[56] Collins's own bankers were Baron Dimsdale & Co. in their various 18th-cent. part-nerships. There is for example this notice in the *Salisbury Journal* of 12 Aug. 1765: 'LOST, At Eling, near Redbridge, Hants, on Wednesday last, the 7th Instant, in the Evening, A BILL of EXCHANGE for eighty Pounds, No. 1190, drawn by Benjamin Collins on Mess. Amyand, Staples, and Mercer, Bankers, in Cornhill, London, payable to Mr. John Staite, or Order, one Month after Date, dated Salisbury, August 3, 1765 . . .' John Wilkes's Bills of Complaint mention 'sundry Draughts or Bills drawn by . . . Benjamin Collins on Messieurs Staples Dimsdale and C°. Bankers in London' (*Wilkes* v. *Collins et al.*, PRO E. 112/1959/147). That bank was first established in 1760 as Amyand, Staples, & Mercer (see L. S. Pressnell and John Orbell, *A Guide to the Historical Records of British Banking* (New York: St Martin's Press, 1985), 36). Although the bank's 18th-cent. records are incomplete, R. H. Reed, Archivist for the National Westminster Bank where the Dimsdale archives are held, confirms that the two sons, William and Benjamin Charles, certainly had accounts in the 19th cent. [57] Feather, *Provincial Book Trade*, 22.

[58] *Detector*, no. 2 [1786?], 9–10.

While the Detector's ironic assessment is a biased one, there seems to be some truth in what he says, for Benjamin Collins certainly advertised his services as moneylender. Records of property-based loans have disappeared with Collins's account books, but a document in the Wiltshire Record Office demonstrates that he also, in effect, lent money on lives. 'With the privity and approbation of the . . . Earl of Suffolk and Berkshire' an annuity of £30 was purchased by Collins from the Honourable Charles Howard's £200 annuity for a single payment of £210. After seven years, Collins's annuity would have paid for itself.[59] In this case Collins's gamble paid off, but not to his great profit since Howard died just seven and a half years later. The large sums Benjamin Collins had at his disposal in the early 1750s must have been based—at least in part— on revenue generated during the first years of his career. Apparently moneylending produced even more income during this period. It is worth adding that Collins's banking activities in the 1750s came very early in the history of provincial banking.

A simultaneous enterprise was a 'publick register'. Modelled on the London Universal Register Office, which had been advertised in the *Salisbury Journal* in the late 1740s, this was a sort of clearing house for information

at the PRINTING-OFFICE On the NEW CANAL, in this City, [where] MASTERS and Mistresses may be informed of Servants of all Kinds; and such Servants as are out of Place, and can produce written Characters from their last Masters or Mistresses, may enter their Names, Characters, and Qualifications (paying only Six-pence) and be recommended to such Places as are suitable for them. Gentlemen may likewise be informed of Houses or Lodgings to be Lett . . . of Estates to be bought and sold . . . An Entry is likewise kept for Horses, Coaches, Chaises, Chairs, &c. for Sale . . . (*SJ*, 9 March 1752)

The population of Salisbury in the mid–eighteenth century was over 6,500;[60] its cathedral and close as well as its location at the hub of important roads from London, Southampton, Exeter, Oxford, Marlborough, and Poole

[59] Assignment, dated 8 Feb. 1766 (WRO 88/9/20).
[60] A parish census in June 1753 reported 2,125 in St Thomas parish, 2,965 in St Edmund's, and 1,496 in St Martin's, for a total of 6,586 (*SJ*, 2 July 1753). This is somewhat fewer than the three parishes recorded in May 1695: 2,364 in St Thomas's, 2,745 in St Edmund's, and 1,569 in St Martin's, with a total of 6,678. (The *Salisbury Journal* report links population with smallpox inoculations and deaths from that disease.) The 1801 Census records 7,668 in Salisbury. The 18th-cent. population seems to have fluctuated between about 6,500 and 7,500. See John Chandler's discussion in *Endless Street*, 33–47.

gave the town a relatively cosmopolitan flavour. The judgement that local readers would buy such a service was probably correct. Another venture was the Salisbury Lottery Office. During the 1740s Collins had often counselled against the dangers of playing the lottery, instructing his readers in odds and misguided optimism. That, however, was the *London* Lottery. By 1760 Collins's Lottery Office was in operation, channelling the proceeds into the account of a man whose own optimism was not without foundation.

Collins continued to advertise his services as a job-printer through these years, and solicited books to be 'Bound, Letter'd, and Gilt, in the neatest Manner on easy Terms' (*SJ*, 20 October 1741). The binder's job was not a prestigious one in the eighteenth century, and doubtless much of the hard binding work would have been allocated to one of his apprentices, but it was an integral part of Collins's book trade, one that he often advertised. Advice published in the middle of the Seven Years War adds an interesting footnote to that business:

The Purchasers of Books are desired to take Notice, that during the excessive high Price that Leather now bears, on Account of the great Quantities that are bought up for the Army, the Booksellers of Town and Country are obliged to advance the Price on every Volume in Duodecimo Three-pence, and on every Octavo Six-pence, and larger Books in Proportion. They therefore beg Leave to recommend it to all Gentlemen, &c. to take their Books for the present sew'd up in Boards, for the sewing each Volume in Boards, and binding it afterwards, when Leather is reduced to its usual Price, will amount to no more than the present Price of Binding only, and the Books will be much better; as, by this Means, the Print will be preserv'd distinct and clear, and the Letter not set off on the opposite Page, as is commonly the Case with all new Books that are bound up immediately after they are printed. (*SJ*, 11 August 1760)

In March 1753 he took on a young man to train as a binder, Caleb Preston;[61] in October 1754 Collins gave notice that books could be bound at his printing-office by 'One of the best BINDERS in England' (*SJ*, 14 October 1754). This might well have been Preston a year and a half into his apprenticeship. Collins also stocked a wide range of stationery goods: pens, ink in several varieties, sealing wax, slates, 'DODSLEY's curious new-invented Writing-Paper . . . Exceeding fine Quarto Paper, neatly ornamented with a Border of Flowers, and gilt at the Edges . . . Ditto, gilt at the Edges, without Ornaments . . . Ditto, in Octavo Size, ornamented

---

[61] Maxted, *British Book Trades: Masters and Apprentices*, no. 0365*d*, and Dale, *Wiltshire Apprentices*.

and gilt . . . Ditto, for Messages, ornamented and gilt, and folded up into a proper Size . . .' (*SJ*, 16 May 1757) and other plain, coloured, embossed, gilt, and Continental papers. It was a line that, in its detailed description, says something about the sophisticated market for stationery in eighteenth-century Wessex. He also cultivated business connections with some of the local gentry and at least one noble family: house books for Longford Castle, the Earl of Radnor's seat in Wiltshire, record small annual payments to 'M^r: Collins Bookseller' in the late 1760s.[62]

Other aspects of the book trade were by no means neglected during these years. The *Salisbury Journal*, by now a fully reliable source of income from subscriptions and advertisements, remained a mainstay of the Collins business. Benjamin Collins wrote in a terse style characteristic of businessmen to John Nourse, the London bookseller, on 2 January 1766 'that as Mr Harris's Books dont seem to move here I woud advise you to advertise em in the *Salisbury Journal*, otherwise twill be known but to few in these Parts that they are publishd You may see the Paper every week at the Chapter Coffee House Pauls Church Yard, or at Mr Newbery's'.[63] And greater free capital allowed Collins to add to his inventory of copyrights: Collins bought a number of copies from, or together with, John Newbery in the 1750s, among them Gordon's *Every Young Man's Companion* (one-eighth share, £5 5s.; Roscoe J148A), *The Muses' Banquet* (one-half share, £5 5s.; Roscoe A373A), *Poetical Tell-Tale* (one-half share, £2 2s.; Roscoe A415), John Reeves's *Art of Farriery* (one-third share, £10; Roscoe A434), and Richard Rolt's *Dictionary of Trade* (one-twelfth share, £88 10s.; Roscoe A453).[64] Other book investments included another Collins scheme, the *Daily Journal, or Gentleman and Tradesman's Annual Account Book for the Pocket* (one-fourth share, valued at £168 in 1768), the tenth edition of Richardson's *Pamela* (one-eighteenth share, £2 2s. in 1763; Roscoe A316), and Smollett's *Humphry Clinker* (one-half

---

[62] Payments ranged from £4 19s. 6d. in 1767 to £10 8s. 0d in 1769. Collins was not employed as sole agent to supply books: other booksellers with whom the estate had direct dealings at this time were Charles (ST3:2475) and Edward Dilly, John Whiston and Benjamin White, and Thomas Lowndes, all in London. No evidence has been discovered that Collins worked for the Earls of Pembroke at nearby Wilton House.

[63] Benjamin Collins to John Nourse, 2 Jan. 1766, *Salisbury Journal* office, Salisbury. 'Mr Harris' is James Harris (1709–80) of the Close in Salisbury whose books by this date included *Three Treatises: The First concerning Art; the Second concerning Music, Painting, and Poetry; the Third concerning Happiness* (1744); his most famous work *Hermes: Or a Philosophical Inquiry concerning Language and Universal Grammar* (1751); and *Upon the Rise and Progress of Criticism* (1752). See Clive T. Probyn, *The Sociable Humanist: The Life and Works of James Harris 1709–1780* (Oxford: Clarendon Press, 1991).

[64] Welsh, *Bookseller of the Last Century*, 355–6, 273, 286, 299, and 301.

share, £105). Various details of some forty-five copies can be garnered
from Welsh's incomplete transcriptions of Collins's account books, Collins's
will, and the Stationers' Company Register of Copies; that Collins had an
interest in other published titles can be deduced from their imprints.
Humphry Clinker was in fact one very profitable title—Collins's moiety of
profits for the first edition amounted to £46 6s. 6d., and for the second
edition to £120 6s., but most of his copies could be described as books
that generated small but steady revenue—the margin between production
costs and sales was simply too small for that to be otherwise. Some books
were altogether unprofitable. One of Collins's few bad investments was in
The Vicar of Wakefield (Roscoe A200). He, John Newbery, and William
Strahan (ST3:7992) purchased one-third shares from Oliver Goldsmith
in 1762 for £21 each. Collins sold his share after the third edition for only
5 guineas, a loss, in terms of share prices only, of 15 guineas.[65]

Periodicals, however, were Collins's real speciality. The successful conduct of a regional newspaper and his firm connections with the book-trade
establishment naturally drew him into the London newspaper market. He
took advantage of public interest in the Seven Years War to set up two
new papers. The first, the thrice-weekly *London Chronicle* (Roscoe A306A)
in 1757 was, Collins claimed in his account books, his 'own scheme at the
setting out'. It had an auspicious start with an Introduction by Samuel
Johnson, who was paid a guinea for writing it, and went on to enjoy
extensive circulation in England and on the Continent. Johnson called the
Chronicle his favourite newspaper; Robert Dodsley edited it.[66] The newspaper occasionally proved an embarrassment to Dodsley, who remained
nominal editor for some time. He complained to William Strahan, printer
and another partner in the venture, that the acting editor Charles Spens
exercised little caution in accepting copy.[67] Benjamin Franklin, himself a
printer who was conscious of typography's full range of meaning, was
irritated that his essay on the King of Prussia had been reprinted in the
Chronicle 'stripped of all the capitaling and italicing that intimate the
allusions and mark the emphasis of written discourse, to bring them as
near as possible to those spoken'.[68] Collins had both the *Chronicle* and the

---

[65] Welsh, *Bookseller of the Last Century*, 61.

[66] James Boswell, *Life of Johnson*, ed. George Birkbeck Hill, rev. L. F. Powell (Oxford:
Clarendon Press, 1934–50), i. 317; ii. 103.

[67] Robert Dodsley to William Strahan, 14 Jan. 1757 (James Tierney (ed.), *The Correspondence of Robert Dodsley 1733–1764* (Cambridge: Cambridge University Press, 1988),
258–9).   [68] Ibid. 55–6.

Salisbury Journal painted into his portrait in the 1770s, evidence of his pride in both these achievements.

Collins, with a large partnership—Benjamin Vaughan, Stanley Crowder (ST3:4021), John Wilkie (ST3:4287), John Newbery, John Hutchinson, Peter Fearon, Charles Walter, Dale Ingram, Thomas Maude, Thomas Jefferys, Sloper Forman, William Faden (sometimes McFaden, ST3:3636), John Coote, and Whiston Bristowe—established the daily London paper the *Public Ledger* (Roscoe A430) in 1760 'to serve the Purposes of Trade and Commerce in a better Manner than the other Daily Newspapers then in being'.[69] Collins took the opportunity offered by his interest in the *Ledger* to propose to his Wessex readership that 'For the future all Advertisements inserted in the SALISBURY JOURNAL, shall (if desired) be also mentioned the same week in the above Daily Ledger, and registered in the office in St. Paul's Church Yard London; an advantage by means of a settled Correspondence with the said office . . . without any additional expense to the Advertiser' (*SJ*, 21 January 1760)—an unusual arrangement potentially beneficial to all concerned. Goldsmith's *Citizen of the World* first appeared in the pages of the *Public Ledger* in 1760 as the *Chinese Letters* written by Altangi; some of Altangi's letters were also published in the *Salisbury Journal* about the same time. The pattern of Benjamin Collins's business dealings frequently included litigation, and a trawl through Chancery records in the Public Records Office is informative: one lawsuit was begun in 1779 over a question of the *Chronicle*'s ownership. The Answers of the printer William Faden and one of the publishers Thomas Brewman to Collins's Bills make it clear that Benjamin Collins was the main backer of the enterprise.[70]

And of course Collins was able to add another country paper to his repertoire in 1778, when James Linden's bankruptcy offered Collins the opportunity to improve his own situation. He secretly purchased the controlling interest in the *Hampshire Chronicle*, moved it from Southampton to Winchester, hired a new manager, and was able to increase his overall circulation figures. Buying up the competition was an effective way of dealing with it.

Benjamin Collins also owned shares in other types of periodicals: a one-sixteenth share in the *Rambler* (purchased for £22 2s. 6d. from William

---

[69] Articles of agreement, 3 Jan. 1760 (William Faden's Answers, *Collins v. Faden*, PRO CH. 12/104/32).

[70] William Faden's Answers, *Collins v. Faden*, PRO CH. 12/104/32; *Collins v. Brewman*, CH. 12/1254/11.

Strahan in 1757), a one-twelfth share in the *Gentleman's Magazine* (purchased from David Henry and R. Cave for £333 6s. 8d. in 1755, and later sold to Francis Newbery; Roscoe A179), and a one-quarter share of Ralph Griffiths's *Monthly Review* (£755 12s. 6d. in 1761).[71] Griffiths apparently sold the *Monthly Review* shares to avoid bankruptcy in 1761; he bought back Collins's share from his estate in 1789. The *Review* had prospered under its new managers—the one-quarter share was returned to Griffiths for £900, while Collins's share of the profits for the preceding seven years amounted to £957 7s., averaging nearly £140 a year.[72] This pattern of silent partnership in different periodicals is similarly evident in John Newbery's business. Newbery could bequeath to his wife 'all my Right Shares Benefit and advantage that I am anyways Interested or Intitled unto of in or to all and every the Newspapers or papers hereafter to be printed called as follows that is to say the London Chronicle Loyds Evening Post the publick Ledger Owens Chronicle or the Westminster Journal the Sherborn or Yeovill Mercury . . .'[73]

Collins continued to cultivate connections within the book trade. Testimony to the strength of his relationship with John Newbery lies in Newbery's will, by which only three men were to receive mourning rings: Robert James (1705–76, of Dr James's Fever Powder fame), Thomas Greenough (probably the man behind Greenough's Teeth Tinctures), and Benjamin Collins.[74] William Strahan (1715–85), a Scottish printer and publisher working with great success in London, was another important business partner, perhaps the most important for Collins. The partnership, in business by 1756, was based in book-trade activities but evidently extended well beyond that. Strahan's records with Gosling's Bank show that unusually large sums were transferred to Benjamin Collins of Salisbury—amongst numerous transactions of generally under £50 with other parties (many of them with important names in the trade), Strahan sent drafts to Collins for £100 (26 July 1756), £220 (26 August 1756), £250 (21 January 1760), £500 (1 August 1760), and £810 12s. 6d. (12 February 1772).[75] In all there are more than thirty entries for Benjamin

---

[71] Welsh, *Bookseller of the Last Century*, 19, 84, and 356. William Strahan bought another one-fourth share of the *Monthly Review* only two days after Collins did (Strahan Ledgers, BL, Add. MS 48800, opening 118).

[72] Two receipts from Benjamin Charles Collins to Ralph Griffiths (Bodl. MS Add. C.89, fos. 119* and 119**).

[73] Newbery's will is transcribed in Welsh, *Bookseller of the Last Century*, 160–7.

[74] Ibid. 163.

[75] Gosling Bank Records, Archives Dept., Barclay's Bank PLC, London. (References to the Gosling Bank records are cited with permission.)

Collins in the ledgers from 1756 to 1772, most of them recording sums well in excess of £50, most of them payments *by* Strahan *to* Collins, when one might reasonably expect to find Collins paying Strahan for printing work.[76] The bank ledgers reveal only figures and names; the nature of the transactions is not disclosed, although a few of the sums might be linked to entries in Strahan's account books. It is known that Strahan and Collins made a joint bid of £800, with £40,000 security, for the Cambridge University printing privileges in 1765.[77] The bid was unsuccessful, but it does demonstrate that the partnership was ready to deal in large sums. The two were joint shareholders, bought shares from each other, and sent printing jobs to each other.[78] William Collins III (ST3:7965), Benjamin's eldest son, was apprenticed to William Strahan in 1763.[79] The relationship was close enough that Collins could express mild irritation that his daughter Jane Collins Staunton had not paid visits to Mrs Strahan and her daughter immediately upon arrival in London in 1781: 'I see by Mrs Staunton's Letter to her Mother she has been paying many visits in Town, but not one, which I am sorry to hear, to Mrs Strahan, which I wish she had done immediately after her Arrival, however, tis better late than never and as you was daily in Expectation of receiving orders to be ready to embark [word illegible], twill be a good Apology for Mrs Staunton not waiting on Mrs Strahan before, which I desire she will do as soon as possible after the Receipt of this, also on Mrs Spotiswood (Miss Strahan that was) . . .'[80] Perhaps most suggestive of the scope of the Collins–Strahan connection is an entry in William Strahan's account books under Collins: 'To Mr Granger Boatswain of the Royal Charlotte India man for Freight of Silks . . . [£]3 15[s.]'.[81] It may be significant that two of Benjamin

---

[76] Only five are payments by Collins to Strahan, and three of those are in 1766, when William Collins III was apprenticed to Strahan.

[77] R. Rabicoff and D. J. McKitterick, 'John Nichols, William Bowyer, and Cambridge University Press in 1765', *Transactions of the Cambridge Bibliographical Society*, 6 (1976), 338.

[78] While the Strahan Ledgers usually record payments made by Benjamin Collins for his share of printing costs for different works, there is a record that Collins was paid 'for Matter composed by him at *Saly*' relating to *The History of the World* (BL, Add. MS 48899, fo. 18).

[79] William was apprenticed 6 Sept. 1763 at 17 and was freed 6 Nov. 1770; no premium was paid (McKenzie, *Apprentices 1701–1800*, 340). William's late apprenticeship to Strahan might be explained by an earlier false start in another trade.

[80] Benjamin Collins to George Leonard Staunton, 2 Jan. 1781, Sirs George Leonard and George Thomas Staunton Papers, Manuscript Dept., William R. Perkins Library, Duke University, North Carolina. Cited with permission.

[81] BL, Add. MS 48808, opening 5. That Collins was shipping silks from India does not mean he was a bona fide East India Co. trader. Each crew member was allotted a portion of cargo space for his own use, as a perquisite, and it was for this service that Collins was paying. The shipping contract would have been a private one, between the two individuals.

Collins's most important London connections had themselves been relative outsiders at the beginning of their careers, Newbery from Berkshire, Strahan from Scotland.

In the course of his career Collins is associated in recorded imprints with some forty provincial booksellers; by the same measure his associations with members of the London trade were nearly double that number. A further indication of his success in penetrating the London establishment may be found in an unresolved copyright case of 1758. Collins, the defendant, was charged 'by Mr. Tonson and some other of the London Booksellers' with selling Scottish-printed (that is, pirated) copies of the *Spectator*. When the court realized that both sides were in collusion—Collins as much as his London colleagues stood to gain from a decision supporting a London monopoly on the copyright—the case was referred 'to the Twelve Judges of England, and it has lain over ever since'.[82]

The year 1770 marked a transition in Benjamin Collins's career. For some thirty years he evidently maintained his sole proprietorship of the newspaper he had helped to establish; during the same period he also developed his other business concerns. The *Journal* imprint for 1 January 1770 tells part of the story: the paper is no longer 'Printed by B. Collins'; rather it is 'Printed by J. Alexander, sold by G. Sealy'. Imprints for the next five years suggest at least five other changes in management. An eighteenth-century solicitor's instructions book in the Wiltshire Record Office,[83] plus the Bills and Answers in the case of Wilkes *v.* Collins[84] tell most of the rest of the story. To state it briefly,[85] Collins sold half the copyright and stock of the *Salisbury Journal* to John Alexander and George Sealy in late 1769. He retained at least a half-share in the newspaper until mid-1773, when he sold his share of the copyright, but reserved for himself an annuity of £400 (that is about half the estimated annual profits),

[82] *Considerations of the Nature and Origin of Literary Property* (Edinburgh, 1767), 27. The essay has been attributed to John Maclaurin, Lord Dreghorn. More details of the case may be found in the Hardwicke Papers at the BL, particularly in an outline of the case at Add. MS 36193, fos. 109–21. Lord Mansfield wrote that as he did not 'know whether the Parties may not acquiesce under the Opinion that shall be given in this Court, I should be desirous of having it argued before the twelve Judges' (Add. MS 36201, fo. 53).

[83] WRO 761/1. The 'Instructions Book' was in the hands of J. J. Hammond, a Salisbury solicitor when Norah Richardson mentioned it in her essay, 'Wiltshire Newspapers—Past and Present. Part III. South Wilts', *Wilts. Arch. Mag.*, 43 (1925–7), 37–8. It has since come to the Wiltshire Record Office (761/1). I am grateful to K. H. Rogers for locating the instructions book.   [84] PRO E. 112/1959/147.

[85] The complicated story of the changes in *Journal* management between 1770 and 1776 is told in Ch. 2.

a plan similar to that followed by John Newbery when he moved to London.[86] He continued to manage the paper throughout and, according to his Answers in the Exchequer case, he bought back the whole copyright about 1775. Although the *Journal* seems to have experienced difficulties outside the unilateral control of Benjamin Collins, it was clearly a very profitable enterprise if it could be expected to clear about £800 a year. The solicitor's instructions book suggests that the paper was valued at £5,200 in 1775. Benjamin Charles Collins (1758–1808) was apprenticed to his father and evidently in partnership with John Johnson in 1775; the younger Collins was 17 years old then and was to prove as capable a businessman as his father. Benjamin Collins could begin to think more seriously about banking and a more retired life.

Around this time Benjamin Collins stopped calling himself 'bookseller, printer, and stationer', and began to style himself 'Gentleman and Banker of Salisbury'. He had his portrait painted: he is in his late 50s or early 60s, wearing a frock-coat of dark blue velvet with the exaggerated buttonholes of the period sewn in gold thread; his wig is slightly old-fashioned, but appropriate for a man of his age. He looks the part of the banker. But in the background are symbols of the origins of his prosperity, two upright folio volumes draped with two newspapers. The volumes are unidentified (they are perhaps bound up copies of newspapers), but one of the papers is the *Salisbury Journal*, and the other is the *London Chronicle*.[87]

Collins was to maintain an active proprietorial interest in newspapers to the end of his life, even after he had retired from most other book-trade activities. Besides helping to establish the *Salisbury Journal*, the *London Chronicle*, and the *Public Ledger* earlier in his career, he also engineered the purchase of a controlling share in another provincial paper, the *Hampshire Chronicle*, in 1778, a share he was to hold until 1783 (less than two years before his death). He still owned the copyright of the *Salisbury Journal* when he died.

His eldest son William III apparently did not fulfil the promise of his early training with William Strahan, one of the best in the London book trade. Rather it was Benjamin Charles, the younger son, who was

---

[86] Welsh, *Bookseller of the Last Century*, 21.

[87] The portrait, recently discovered, now hangs in the *Salisbury Journal* office, Salisbury. The Detector, as might be expected, has something to say of Collins's appearance: 'His looks were shrewd, sly, methodical and plodding.—Practice had fixed upon his passive face the hollow varnish of a servile smile, which covered a depth of design and a latitude of principle equal to any attempt' (*Detector*, no. 1 [1786?], 5).

entrusted with the printing and publishing business.[88] Benjamin Charles
had been officially apprenticed to his father on 31 October 1775 (possibly
only as a formality) when he was nearly 17 years old. This was just after
Benjamin Collins had renewed his proprietorship in the *Journal* and had
found it necessary to acquaint the public that 'the printing, bookselling,
and stationary business, which has for so many years been carried on by
himself, and brother before him, is now continued by his son, Benjamin
Charles Collins, and J. Johnson, only, in the same house and shop on the
New Canal' (*SJ*, 23, 30 October 1775). Benjamin Charles soon demonstrated his skills, when he was questioned by Joseph Hodson's and George
Sealy's solicitor, 10 September 1776. The solicitor, attempting to demonstrate that Benjamin Collins was legally responsible for a share of the
bad debts in Sealy and Alexander's business, called him a sleeping partner. 'Charles [i.e. Benjamin Charles] replied you may call him *sleep*[g] if
you please but if the others had been *as active* as him there wou[d] <not>
have been so many bad debts.' When Benjamin Charles realized that
he might have provided the opposing solicitor with the evidence he had
been looking for, he recovered himself: he 'paused a Minute as if to
recollect himself & then said I mean if Hodson & Johnson had been as
active *in their Business* as my Fa[r] was in *his* there w[d]. not have been so
many bad Debts'.[89] Benjamin Charles was clearly in control when he
wrote to John Nichols in the early 1780s to advise him on securing a
copyright, finding the best London publisher, making the greatest profit on new parish register books, and avoiding overpriced bookbinders.[90]
He was his father's son.

While his sons and partners carried on the day-to-day business, Benjamin
Collins concentrated on converting more of his capital into property, the
traditional foundation of the English gentry. His will records estates in
Dorset, Somerset, Middlesex, Surrey, Huntingdonshire, and Wiltshire, as
well as property on the West Indian island of Montserrat. This last might
indicate that Collins was concerned in the sugar trade, since Montserrat
was a sugar producer. He might have inherited a little property when his
brother Francis, a prosperous Salisbury wine merchant, died in 1782,[91]

---

[88] The Detector alludes to 'a *dreadful* rupture' in the Collins family that Benjamin
narrowly avoided. Perhaps William Collins III may have been involved. He inherited a house
at Milford, plus the family banking business, which his father valued at only £2,000. On the
other hand, the printing and publishing business inherited by Benjamin Charles Collins was
valued at £6,500 (Benjamin Collins's will, PRO PROB. 11/1127/120).

[89] Solicitor's Instructions Book, WRO 761/1.

[90] Benjamin Charles Collins to John Nichols, 20 July 1781 and 23 Aug. 1783, Bodl., MS
Eng. lett. C.355, fos. 71–3.   [91] Francis Collins's will, PRO PROB. 11/1091/274–5.

but most of it seems to have been purchased. Indentures for a number
of these transactions are scattered in different record offices.[92] A printed
list of some of Collins's Salisbury freehold, copyhold, and leasehold hold-
ings to be sold at auction by his executors in 1789, four years after his
death, provides details of property with an annual value of nearly £400.[93]
Collins was able to settle £1,353 6s. 6d. on his daughter Jane when she
married George Leonard Staunton (later Sir George) in 1770; he lent
Staunton £4,000 at the same time—'on a mortgage of his Estate at Gren-
ada at lawful interest'—and later he acted as business agent for his son-
in-law.[94] Two of his other daughters received similar dowries. He insured
the silver plate alone, in his house on the New Canal, for £2,000.[95] He
began buying and selling East India Company Stock, starting with a purchase of £700 in 1769 and turning over £3,000 between 1774 and 1783.[96]
He was Chairman of the Salisbury Infirmary in 1775 (*SJ*, 22 May 1775)
and he was officially appointed 'to receive the deficient GOLD COIN of

[92] In the Wiltshire Record Office there are the following documents: lease of 8 acres at
Shepton Montague to Richard Hoare, 12 Nov. 1779, WRO 383/646; lease and release by
Samuel and Susannah Eyre of 6 Salisbury properties, 7 Nov. 1780, WRO 1075/87; and
leases and releases of property in Wilton, 1767, WRO 130/39. The Hampshire Record
Office holds documents relating to the sale of property in Eling near Southampton to
Benjamin Collins and George Pinckney (HRO 23M58/700–1). The Isle of Wight Record
Office has a lease for 99 years determinable on the life of Collins's eldest daughter Elizabeth
for land in the parish of Brading (HG/2/151).

[93] *Particulars and Conditions of Sale, of Several Freehold, Copyhold, and Leasehold Messuages,
Lands, Tenements, and Hereditaments, situate in New Sarum, Laverstock, Ditchampton, and
Milford, Wilts, to be Sold by Auction, in Lots, by Mr. Richard Smith, at the White Hart Inn,
in the City of New Sarum, on Monday the 7th Day of September, 1789, by the Direction of
the Devisees in Trust and Executors of Benjamin Collins ... Deceased* (Salisbury: Collins
[1789]). Sold at the same time were 'Two Tickets of 40l. each, payable to the Bearer, with
Interest at 4 per Cent. and charged on Tolls and Duties [on the Eling Turnpike] ...' (The
Particulars, as well as a number of manuscript indentures relating to the Bell Inn, Salisbury,
owned by Collins from the 1770s, are the property of June Coates, Old Bell Inn, Ann St.,
Salisbury.)

[94] A note dated 21 July 1771 in Collins's hand of particulars of the marriage settlement
is in the Staunton papers, Beinecke Library, Yale University. Three letters from Benjamin
Collins to George Leonard Staunton in 1779 and 1781 indicate that Collins handled business matters for his son-in-law, particularly when Staunton was abroad (Benjamin Collins
to George Leonard Staunton, 7 Dec. 1779, 2 Jan. and 15 Feb. 1781, Staunton Papers, Duke
University). Staunton in turn assisted Collins. With reference to Edmund and Richard
Burke, George Leonard wrote to his wife Jane that 'Your father will thus have through me
a friend at the treasury' (George Thomas Staunton, *Memoir of the Life & Family of the Late
Sir George Leonard Staunton, Bart.* (Havant: Henry Skelton for private circulation, 1823),
268).

[95] Sun Policy No. 396091, dated 12 Mar. 1778, Guildhall Library, London, MS 11936/
264. Another Sun Policy, No. 384499 dated 26 May 1777, insured the house for £600 (MS
11936/256).

[96] Stock Ledgers, India Office Library, London, L/AG/14/5/18 and 20.

the realm' during this time (*SJ*, 29 April 1776). Benjamin Collins was evidently a prosperous and acceptable businessman.

But he does not seem to have been a particularly generous man. For example when his youngest daughter Charlotte eloped with a journeyman named Bacon before she was of age, her family disapproved, and the Detector describes how 'Mrs. Bacon, like a prudent woman, threw herself at the feet of her father, in hopes of effectually removing every obstacle to their happiness'. Her father was unmoved—the Detector says that Collins 'consoled himself with the thoughts of benefiting from his child's breach of duty, by annually hoarding the expence of her maintenance' —and a family conference turned her out with a charitable 20 guineas.[97] There must be some hyperbole in the Detector's account, but his story is supported by Collins's will, in which Charlotte's one-eighth portion of the estate is to remain in her mother's hands during Charlotte's lifetime, with Mary Collins to exercise complete freedom in giving or withholding all or part of that share. This is confirmed by a codicil to the will, written after Charlotte had become 21. To be fair to Collins, the same codicil instructs William to pay Charlotte an annuity of £25, and Benjamin Collins's reaction to a marriage he viewed as unfortunate cannot have been untypical of other eighteenth-century fathers.[98]

When James Linden, the printer who had set up the *Hampshire Chronicle* in 1772 in competition with the *Salisbury Journal* and had later become bankrupt, set up yet another rival paper in the late 1770s, he seemed to be facing a second bankruptcy. The new partners in the *Chronicle*, directed by Benjamin Collins, decided not to bring a lawsuit against Linden because of his 'very indigent and necessitous Circumstances'.[99] Collins's motives were not philanthropical; rather they derived from an understanding that Linden's financial condition would bring about his collapse, so saving the partners the expense of a court case. John Wilkes, in his Bills, reports that Collins at least once 'fell into passionate and Abusive Expressions' during discussions about the management of the *Chronicle*, something that Collins himself admitted in his Answers.[100]

There is no evidence that Collins was especially civic-minded either. The *Salisbury Journal* of course performed a service for the city and region,

---

[97] *Detector*, no. 2 [1786?], 7–8.

[98] Mary Collins was more liberal in her will: Charlotte, a widow by 1808, was to have the dividends and interest from three-quarters of her mother's bank stock (the other quarter, plus a pianoforte, going to Charlotte Mary Bacon, Charlotte's daughter), £100 immediately on Mary Collins's decease, most of her plate, and all of her bed and table linens and china (PRO PROB. 11/1477/168).   [99] Wilkes's Bills, PRO E. 112/1959/147.

[100] Ibid.

but that was probably not the primary reason Collins retained his interest in the paper. He held public office only once, when he was alderman for 1753 (*SJ*, 2 October 1752), but he declined the honour the following year and paid his fine.[101] He was not active in church affairs. He did in fact subscribe to the Salisbury Infirmary, was a 10-guineas benefactor, and was Chairman for a time, but that, the Detector says, 'secured him their printing, stationary, and advertisements—this of course introduced him to all the nostrums and quack medicines of his day'.[102] His brother Francis remembered the Infirmary in his will; Benjamin did not.

Benjamin Collins died in February 1785 and was buried according to his wishes in St Edmund's churchyard, 23 February 1785.[103] The *Reading Mercury* ran the briefest notice, 21 February: 'On Wednesday died, at Salisbury, Benjamin Collins, Esq; banker'. The *Sherborne Mercury* was equally laconic; likewise the *Salisbury Journal*: 'Wednesday evening died, at his house on the Canal, in the 68th year of his age, Benjamin Collins, Esq. of this city.' The paper's imprint changes on that date, too, from 'Printed by J. Johnson' to 'Printed by and for Benjamin Charles Collins', reminiscent of the abrupt transition from William to Benjamin Collins in 1740.[104]

When Benjamin Collins died, he was worth between £85,000 and £100,000.[105] He was a man who began a provincial bookselling career with capital of perhaps £100 left him by a father who made soap and candles for a living. Within ten years he directed a flourishing book business, buying and selling copies, printing, binding, and publishing books, and inventing and selling the medicines that were a part of the stock of most provincial bookshops. An important component of his early success

---

[101] Collins was certainly not the only man to do this. His grandson, George Thomas Staunton, son of Sir George Leonard and Jane Staunton, wrote that Collins was invited to stand for Parliament, but, 'to the regret of his friends, his modesty, and an attachment to a country life, induced him to decline'. I have been unable to verify Staunton's claim (*Memoir of Sir George Leonard Staunton*, 17).

[102] *Detector* no. 2 [1786?], 8–9. The Detector is correct in saying that Collins printed material for the Infirmary. [103] St Edmund's Parish Register, WRO 1901/4.

[104] This is not to suggest that there was anything at all unusual in these brief notices of a death. Few 18th-cent. personalities received more than a line or two of notice at their passing.

[105] Collins's grandson, Sir Benjamin Collins Brodie (1783–1862), Queen Victoria's surgeon, wrote that his mother Sarah Collins Brodie had inherited 'a fortune of £10,000 as her share of her father's fortune' (*Autobiography of the Late Sir Benjamin C. Brodie, Bart.* (London: Longman, Green, Longman, Roberts & Green, 1865), 6). Sarah's inheritance was a one-eighth portion of Benjamin Collins's estate, and probably did not include her dowry of £1,200. Also not included in the eight shares was an annuity for Benjamin Collins's brother Joseph and various sums to other relatives.

was a relationship with the London book trade that could be called a privileged one—a relationship founded on Collins's good business sense and ingenuity, the *Salisbury Journal*'s established network in the provinces, and Collins's ability to finance books. Diversification in his middle years brought more wealth from moneylending, banking, and real estate, as well as from the buying and selling of more productive copyrights. Collins could afford to retire in his 60s, at last a banker and a landed gentleman.[106]

[106] An earlier version of this chapter was published as 'Benjamin Collins, The *Salisbury Journal*, and the Provincial Booktrade', in the *Library*, 6th ser., 11 (1989), 116–38.

2

The Commercial Structure of a Provincial Newspaper: Management and Distribution

THE life of a periodical depends on effective distribution. In the distribution of any successful mid-eighteenth-century provincial newspaper there were several levels of administration: at the top were the owners, proprietors, or partners, such as Benjamin Collins, who might themselves (especially earlier in the century) print, manage, and sell the paper locally; at a second level were the managers who were employed in editing, bookkeeping, printing, and so on; then came the newsagents in the towns and villages within the paper's circulation area; then distributors, who were appointed to carry bundles of newspapers to those agents and perhaps to deliver papers along the route; and finally there were the postmen, newsmen, carriers, and hawkers whose job it was to put the papers in the hands of the readers.[1] Personnel on all these levels contributed to a complex administrative network that radiated from the hub of the newspaper printing office, Salisbury for the *Salisbury Journal* for example, but a Salisbury–Winchester nexus for the *Hampshire Chronicle*. Underlying that was an associated system of smaller news-agency centres with radii extending to most of the towns, villages, and major houses in the area. The commercial health of the newspaper depended on a well-run, comprehensive distribution system, for it was by this means that readership was sustained and encouraged, advertising revenue was generated, and many of the books, medicines, and other goods marketed by the proprietors were conveyed to their customers.

The very earliest provincial newspapers, set up after the lapse of the Printing Act, were most often owned and operated by single printers who sometimes had trained in London and then returned home to set up in business. William Bonny, Francis Burges (ST2:0908), and Samuel Farley

---

[1] See G. A. Cranfield, *The Development of the Provincial Newspaper 1700–1760* (Oxford: Clarendon Press, 1962), 190–206, and R. M. Wiles, *Freshest Advices: Early Provincial Newspapers in England* (Columbus: Ohio State University Press, 1965), 95–146.

(ST2:0913), who established England's earliest provincial newspapers, are but three examples.[2] Similarly the *Sherborne Mercury* was established 22 February 1737 by two printers, William Bettinson, who claimed to come from London, and G. Price. They were later to be joined by the young John Newbery.[3] By the middle of the century many provincial papers, like their London counterparts, were owned and managed by consortia of booksellers and printers.[4] This had a good deal to do with the risks involved in establishing a newspaper—personnel, equipment, and paper, which had to be pre-stamped in London after 1712, had all to be deployed for weekly production; it was only when subscribers and advertisements reached certain stable levels that the reasonable, steady income that made newspaper work so attractive was ensured. The successful model of the London bookselling conger, in which booksellers had joined together since the late seventeenth century to share the risks and profits in major expensive books, or the more esoteric ones, was another imitable factor.[5]

That said, it is sometimes difficult to determine the precise make-up of the partnership in a given newspaper, for it can be obscured in an imprint that lists the publisher, printer, or agents but not the owner-partners behind them. That this was a quite deliberate practice on the part of the proprietors is suggested by Thomas Brewman, sometime publisher of the *Public Ledger*, one of Benjamin Collins's London papers: 'it is and hath been some times customary amongst printers to make use of the Names of Persons as Publishers who have no concern therein . . .'[6] There are many reasons newspaper owners might have for camouflaging the nature

---

[2] Burges and Farley were both apprenticed to Freeman Collins and freed in the same year, 1699.

[3] Charles Welsh, *A Bookseller of the Last Century: Being Some Account of the Life of John Newbery, and of the Books He Published, with a Notice of the Later Newberys* (London: Griffith, Farran, Okeden & Welsh; New York: E. P. Dutton, 1885), 160–1, 336; S. Roscoe, *John Newbery and His Successors 1740–1814: A Bibliography* (Wormley, Herts.: Five Owls Press, 1973), 11, 16.

[4] Michael Harris, 'The Booksellers and Group Ownership' in his *London Newspapers in the Age of Walpole: A Study of the Origins of the Modern English Press* (London: Associated University Presses, 1987), 65–81. Harris finds that 'by 1730 a large proportion of the principal London newspapers was in the hands of the booksellers . . .' while 'the cut-price papers, like the provincial weeklies, remained consistently in the hands of the printers' (p. 66). In fact the provincials did not invariably remain with the printers.

[5] For discussion of London congers, see 'The Trade in London', in Norma Hodgson and Cyprian Blagden, *The Notebook of Thomas Bennet and Henry Clements (1686–1719), with Some Aspects of Book Trade Practice*, Oxford Bibliographical Society Publications, NS 6 (Oxford: Oxford University Press, 1956), 67–100; Terry Belanger, 'Booksellers' Sales of Copyright: Aspects of the London Book Trade, 1718–1768', Ph.D. diss. (Columbia University, 1970), and his 'Booksellers' Trade Sales, 1718–1768', *Library*, 5th ser., 30 (1975), 281–302.

[6] Thomas Brewman's Answers, *Collins v. Faden*, PRO CH. 12/1254/11.

of their relationship with their property. Other business activities might conflict. By the 1770s Collins was an established bookseller, banker, and dealer in far-flung real estate, all activities that could have derived from and been promoted by his newspapers. Clearly it would not have been politic for Collins and Company to publicize its true interests during the takeover or destruction of a competing paper such as the *Hampshire Chronicle*. And in the age of the 'anonymous' pamphlet, such knowledge would have been common anyway among those who needed to know.

Disguising ownership was an attempt to detour certain legal problems as well as a defensive tactic that could prove useful in either town and country. Usually it is only when account books or other documents happen to survive that a paper's full commercial structure, with all its financial backers (silent and confessed), is evident. Account and minute books for several London papers exist to support a theory of widespread group ownership in the capital;[7] indeed group ownership on a rather large scale has been documented for Collins's *Public Ledger*, where twenty-four shares were divided among more than a dozen shareholders.[8] Very few working records have been recovered for eighteenth-century provincial newspapers, but it is fortunate that among them are those for the *Hampshire Chronicle*.[9]

By mid-century, the fact of group ownership—if not the precise details —becomes evident for many provincial newspapers from their imprints alone. R. M. Wiles was able to note in his *Freshest Advices* almost forty provincial newspaper partnerships before 1760.[10] Not all these were un-diluted *owner*-partnerships, but Wiles's list provides some idea of the prevalence of group management outside the capital. The account books for the *Hampshire Chronicle* reveal that James Linden, who founded the paper in 1772 and whose name is in the imprint with J. Webber and J. Wise,[11] was also for a time in commercial partnership with John Wheble, whose name is not in the imprint. And the 'T. Baker & Co.' that took over when Linden filed for bankruptcy in 1778 included—besides Thomas Baker of Southampton, who later dropped out of the venture—Benjamin

[7] There are substantial records for at least three London newspapers—the *Grub Street Journal* (for 1730 to 1738), the *General Evening Post* (for 1754 to 1786), and the *St James's Chronicle* (for 1754 to 1815). See Michael Harris, 'The Management of the London Newspaper Press during the Eighteenth Century', *Publishing History*, 4 (1978), 99–100, and his *London Newspapers*. [8] PRO CH. 12/104/32 and CH. 12/1254/11.
[9] PRO E. 140/90–1, E. 112/1959/147; for other accounts of provincial newspapers see Hannah Jane Barker, 'Press, Politics and Reform: 1779–1785', D.Phil. thesis (Oxford University, 1994), 133–64, and her essay 'Catering for Provincial Tastes: Newspapers, Readership and Profit in Late Eighteenth-Century England', *Historical Research*, 69/168 (1996), 42–61. [10] Listed in the index under 'Partnerships', p. 549.
[11] *The Hampshire Chronicle 1772–1972: A Bicentenary Publication* (Winchester [1972?]).

Collins, Benjamin Charles Collins, and John Johnson, all of Salisbury; John Wilkes of Winchester; and John Breadhower of Portsmouth. Benjamin Collins and Company held the controlling interest. While Benjamin Collins himself owned outright only a one-sixteenth share, his son Benjamin Charles and John Johnson jointly owned a four-sixteenths share at first, then bought another four-sixteenths held in trust for them by Baker, so that through them Benjamin Collins controlled more than half the copyright: Benjamin Charles was under age and apprenticed to his father at the time, and Johnson was employed by the elder Collins to manage his printing office in Salisbury. Wilkes was a minor co-proprietor as well as manager and printer of the paper in Winchester, and the bookseller John Breadhower had been invited to join the venture because Benjamin Collins thought that 'many of such Papers might be distributed and sold at Portsmouth . . . in Case they had a Partner residing there and interested in the success of the said Undertaking.'[12] Yet the imprint smoothed over these complications and simply suggested that T. Baker and Co. were in charge. The *Hampshire Chronicle* under its new ownership is probably typical in its administrative structure of moderately successful country newspapers—like the *Salisbury Journal* it is still in operation today—and its records demonstrate that provincial distribution networks in the mid-century sometimes began with a group of strategically placed owners who ran their investment in a series of regular committee meetings.

The pattern reverts to individual ownership and management for the *Salisbury Journal* for most of its first fifty years. It was probably begun, both in 1729 and in 1736, in partnership—the co-proprietors were almost certainly the brothers William and Benjamin Collins, perhaps also with Charles Hooten the *Journal*'s printer in 1729. Edward Easton, who worked closely with the Collinses early on, and William Bettinson, who actually printed the *Journal* for a time, are other possibilities. But when William Collins died or left off business in 1740, Benjamin became sole proprietor. Although the paper's imprint says that it is 'Printed by *B. COLLINS* and COMP. at the PRINTING-OFFICE on the DITCH' (*SJ*, 12 August 1740), there is no evidence to indicate that the 'COMP.' was anything other than the assortment of journeymen or apprentices and others who had helped in production since before William Collins's departure. Benjamin Collins, with and without Company, remains the primary name in the imprint from August 1740 until 1 January 1770, and indeed he was later to claim in print and in court that the paper had been solely his from 1740.

---

[12] John Wilkes's Bills of Complaint (PRO E. 112/1959/147).

When the Salisbury printer Joseph Hodson tried to recover bad debts from Benjamin Collins in the 1770s, he employed a local solicitor, whose 'Instructions Book' survives. In it a change in the top level of the *Journal*'s administration is recorded.[13] Evidently Benjamin Collins had retained half the copyright in the *Salisbury Journal*, but had sold the other half to John Alexander and George Sealy in one-quarter shares, effective from 1 January 1770. Both had solid Salisbury connections: George Sealy had been apprenticed to Collins in 1755; John Alexander (ST3:7947) was a letterpress and copperplate printer who had been in business in Salisbury from at least 1763, after serving a London apprenticeship with William Strahan.[14] Alexander began business in Salisbury about the time William Collins III was starting his apprenticeship with Strahan. By 1770 Benjamin Collins was in his mid-50s and involved in banking and real estate, so he may well have found it profitable to sell shares in the *Journal* and comfortable to turn over part of its management to others. After John Alexander's death in mid-1772 however, Collins saw the opportunity to buy back his one-quarter share. Then when Joseph Hodson and John Johnson entered the partnership in 1773 they jointly purchased Alexander's former share from Collins, as well as George Sealy's one-quarter share. Sealy was to be paid £1,300 for his. Collins turned over his half share about the same time, but continued to manage the paper in return for an annuity of £400, which was reckoned to be about half the annual clear profits. These figures incidentally suggest that the part a newspaper played in a provincial business could be a very valuable one.

Some of these administrative adjustments are confirmed in *Journal* imprints for 1770–5 (see Table 2). A succession of names are recorded in the imprint from 1770 to 1775, evidence of further changes in owners and managers: Alexander was dropped in mid-1772; a new printer, Joseph Hodson, was added in October of the same year; in December 1772 John Wilkes of Winchester joined Sealy and Hodson; then it was J. Hodson and Co. with Wilkes in mid-1773; then Hodson and John Johnson in

---

[13] WRO 761/1.

[14] George Sealy's apprenticeship is recorded in the Inland Revenue records, PRO IR. 1/20/133 (see Ian Maxted, *The British Book Trades, 1710–1777: An Index of Masters and Apprentices Recorded in the Inland Revenue Registers in the Public Record Office, Kew* (Exeter: Ian Maxted, 1983), no. 0365e). A John Alexander, son of the late John Alexander of Bengal, was apprenticed to William Strahan, 7 Feb. 1749, with payment made by Samuel Bennet (D. F. McKenzie, *Stationers' Company Apprentices 1701–1800* (Oxford: Oxford Bibliographical Society, 1978), 339). His son John (ST3:7999) was apprenticed after his decease to William Strahan II (ST3:7993) in 1778 (ibid. 341). John Alexander advertised his services as printer in the *Salisbury Journal*, 31 Oct. 1763, noting that 'Orders from any Part of the Country will be duly attended to.'

TABLE 2. *Transitions in* Salisbury Journal *management and ownership,*
1764–85

Date	Imprint	Proprietors
1764–70	Printed by B. Collins	Collins
1 Jan. 70	Printed by J. Alexander, sold by G. Sealy	Alexander (1/4), Sealy (1/4), Collins (1/2)
1 June 72	Printed and sold by G. Sealy	Sealy (1/4), Collins (3/4)
26 Oct. 72	Printed by J. Hodson, sold by G. Sealy	Sealy (1/4), Collins (3/4)
7 Dec. 72	Printed and sold by Sealy and Hodson; and J. Wilkes	Sealy (1/4), Collins (3/4)
7 June 73	Printed and sold by J. Hodson and Co.; and J. Wilkes	Hodson & Co. (i.e. Hodson, Johnson, Easton?)
6 Sept. 73	Printed and sold by Hodson and Johnson; and J. Wilkes	Hodson & Co.
3 July 75	Printed by J. Johnson	Collins?
21 Feb. 85	Printed by and for Benjamin Charles Collins	B. C. Collins

Salisbury with Wilkes in September 1773; in 1774 Wilkes was removed
from his prominent position in the imprint and placed in the list of
Journal agents at the foot of page 4; Hodson advertised his new reading
room in mid-June 1775, but two weeks later he was out of business and
the Hodson–Johnson partnership was officially dissolved, leaving only
John Johnson in the imprint.[15] Typically these changes of imprint do not
tell the whole story, but they are an indication of adjustments at the
highest level of the paper's commercial structure. Some of these changes
of management may have been in response to serious competition from
the *Hampshire Chronicle* after 1772. At any rate *Salisbury Journal* readers
must have been confused, and in the end Benjamin Collins felt it necessary to announce that 'the PRINTING, BOOKSELLING, and STATIONARY
Business, which has for so many years been carried on by himself, and

[15] The notice of the end of the partnership appeared in the *Journal*, 3 July 1775. Two
weeks before, Hodson had advertised that his 'NEW READING ROOM, near the POULTRY
CROSS, is this day opened . . .' (*SJ*, 19 June 1775), but after leaving off business in Salisbury,
Hodson evidently joined James Linden in Southampton—the two names appear in the
imprint of the *Hampshire Chronicle* (published from Southampton 1772–8) in 1776.

Brother before him, is now continued by his Son, BENJ. CHARLES COLLINS, and J. JOHNSON, only, in the same House and Shop on the NEW CANAL, as usual' (23 October 1775). Despite this announcement, only John Johnson's name appeared in the imprint until 1783. The usual proprietorial diffidence plus the fact that Benjamin Charles was just 17 years old in 1775 and had only recently been apprenticed to his father account for this discrepancy.

Collins's printed notice and the 'Instructions Book' are clues to the real ownership and management of the *Salisbury Journal*, which of course are further clarified in Collins's Answers to John Wilkes's Bills of Complaint in a Court of Exchequer case. Here Collins stated that in 1775 he had purchased

of Mr Edward Easton Joseph Hodgson [*sic*] and John Johnson their stock and their Trade of printers and the good will thereof and the copy right of a certain Newspaper called the Salisbury and Winchester Journal then printed and published in Salisbury and thereupon he . . . did employ . . . John Johnson to conduct the Printing Office and he did employ [Benjamin Charles Collins] to conduct the Business of the Shop then kept by him in Salisbury . . .[16]

In December 1772 the *Salisbury Journal*'s title had been altered to the *Salisbury and Winchester Journal*, just when the *Hampshire Chronicle* had become a threat, and John Wilkes in Winchester had become involved. There is no evidence of any other newspaper bearing the same title, so Collins must have been buying back his whole interest in the newspaper in 1775.

Collins further stated in his Answers that in 1778

the said Trade of a Printer Bookseller and Stationer so carried on in the name of [Benjamin Charles Collins and John Johnson] . . . was the proper Trade of him [Benjamin Collins] . . . and that he hath not at any time whatsoever assigned or conveyed or covenanted to convey to [Benjamin Charles Collins and John Johnson] . . . any part or share of and in the said Trade but that the same was . . . at his own disposal . . .[17]

Strictly speaking, Benjamin Collins may not have covenanted to convey anything at all to his son and John Johnson, but he had in fact written his will by this time and in that document he leaves to his son 'the several Trades or Businesses of a Printer Bookseller Bookbinder Stationer and Vender of Medicines . . . now carried on by and in the Name of my son . . . and John Johnson for my Use and Benefit'. Collins goes on to describe

[16] Benjamin Collins's answers are dated from the Antelope Inn, Salisbury, 27 Nov. 1783 (PRO E. 112/1959/147). [17] Ibid.

another bequest, namely 'my Copyright or Right of Printing Publishing and vending the Salisbury Journal'.[18]

A final clue in this single complicated example comes from Collins's embittered opponent, the pseudonymous Detector. When the Detector wrote about Collins in 1786–7, a year or so after his death, he suggested that Collins had provided all the newspaper's financial backing.[19] Indisputably the sole proprietorship of the *Salisbury Journal* was back in its founder's hands at least from March 1778 when the will was written, until June 1784 when a codicil confirmed the legacy. There is no reason to doubt that Benjamin Collins continued to own the copyright until his death seven months later in February 1785.

It can be established, then, that Benjamin Collins had financial control of the *Salisbury Journal* from 1740, when his elder brother disappeared from the scene, until 1785, with a hiatus of perhaps five years (1770–5) when some or all of his shares were sold and then repurchased. (There is a good parallel example in Ralph Griffiths and his *Monthly Review*: Griffiths sold shares in the *Monthly Review*, including a quarter share to Benjamin Collins, in 1761 to avoid bankruptcy and then in 1789 he bought back Collins's share from his estate.[20]) For much of this time decisions on the top-level administration of the paper must have belonged solely to Benjamin Collins, although some of those decisions will have been founded in management practice established when he was in partnership with his brother William or in consultation with family and employees. So too, Collins would have had the final word, whenever he wished, on the hiring of agents to promote distribution, the design of routes for his newsmen, the training of distributors, the collection of news, the supervision of the printing-office staff, the management of office accounts, the layout of the newspaper, and so on. In the *Salisbury Journal* is the example of a country newspaper more or less under the control of one man. Yet before 1740, when William Collins was still in evidence, and after 1775, when Collins took his second son and John Johnson into non-shareholding partnership, the *Journal* followed what was becoming a common style of provincial joint-management.

---

[18] Since Collins was careful to designate part shares in the copyrights of a number of books that Benjamin Charles will inherit, it is clear that he intended his son to take over his sole ownership of the newspaper (Benjamin Collins's will, 25 Mar. 1778, PRO PROB. 11/1127/120).

[19] 'It is an erroneous opinion, that the paper in circulation leaves a banker [Collins] with a large surplus of running cash' (*The Detector*, no. 1 [1787?], p. 9).

[20] Receipts from Benjamin Charles Collins to Ralph Griffiths, Bodl. MS Add. C.89, fos. 119*, 119**.

Meetings of the proprietors formed the basis for most administrative decisions on the co-owned papers. This form of management has been well documented for some London newspapers in the minutes of meetings of the proprietors of the *St James's Chronicle*, the *General Evening Post*, and the *Grub Street Journal*.[21] Michael Harris, in his examination of these records found two levels of managerial meetings for the *Grub Street Journal* in the 1730s: general meetings to establish overall policies and to negotiate critical issues like the hiring of a new printer, and meetings at which a smaller committee decided routine questions.[22]

In the provinces, where co-proprietors might live and conduct business in several different towns and so have little opportunity to meet casually, regular meetings were even more important. The records of the *Hampshire Chronicle* document the mechanics of such group-management for one Wessex newspaper, and they are of course relevant to the running of another, for they record something of Benjamin Collins's method of newspaper management both as co-owner (in his *Chronicle* interests) and as sole owner (in the frequent reference to the model of the *Salisbury Journal*). Legally he held only a one-sixteenth share in the new enterprise, but it is clear from the minutes of one partners' meeting and the Exchequer Bills and Answers—indeed from the fact that Collins is the first to be named in Wilkes's lawsuit—that he dominated the partnership.

The records of the *Hampshire Chronicle* that illustrate the lawsuit are among the few that document the higher administrative operations of an eighteenth-century provincial newspaper. Benjamin Collins's takeover of the bankrupt *Hampshire Chronicle* in 1778 was engineered in this way: Collins, together with his son and John Johnson, agreed to approach James Linden, a schoolmaster-turned-printer/bookseller, with a bid to purchase the copyright of his newspaper. This was in response to Linden's advertisement offering to sell the paper in May. Clearly one element of Collins's plan was to bring in strategically based partners: John Wilkes was invited to join the enterprise to facilitate moving the *Chronicle* from Southampton to Winchester and to act as local manager.[23] (The stated

---

[21] Richmond P. Bond and Marjorie N. Bond, 'The Minute Books of the *St. James's Chronicle*', *Studies in Bibliography*, 28 (1975), 17–40. The ledgers for the *General Evening Post* are in the W. S. Lewis Collection, Yale. Michael Harris has an enlightening discussion both of these account books and of those for the *Grub Street Journal* in his chapter on group ownership in *London Newspapers*, 65–81.

[22] See 'The Minute Books of the Partners in the *Grub Street Journal*', reproduced in *Publishing History*, 4 (1978), and Harris, *London Newspapers*, 73–7.

[23] John Wilkes (d. 1810) apparently began his career as a bookseller in Winchester in 1762 (Plomer, *A Dictionary of Printers and Booksellers 1726–1775* (London: The Bibliographical

purpose of the move was that Winchester's more central location in the county would allow the new owners to distribute the paper 'much earlier than was ever usual',[24] but it also had something to do with the interaction of the two rival papers.) John Breadhower was supposed to promote the paper in Portsmouth.[25] Thomas Baker, with a Bill of Indemnity, first acted on the partners' behalf to negotiate the purchase of the copyright, and managed to reduce the asking price of the transaction. Later he held four shares in trust for Collins and Company, encouraged Southampton readership, and probably kept watch on James Linden's activities, which for a time included printing another rival *Hampshire Chronicle*.[26] After the *Chronicle* had changed hands for 200 guineas in May,[27] Articles of Agreement dated 3 June 1778 were drawn up. A number of the articles dealt specifically with distribution; one required the new proprietors to organize half-yearly meetings in rotation.

Minutes survive for the first one, 23 November 1778 in Salisbury, as well as general descriptions of subsequent meetings in the Bills and Answers, and from these can be seen the sorts of decisions reserved for the proprietor-partners of a provincial newspaper. Profit and loss were

---

Society, 1932), 264; and F. A. Edwards, 'Early Hampshire Printers', *Papers and Proceedings of the Hampshire Field Club*, 2 (1891), 114). Wilkes first appeared in the imprint of the *Salisbury Journal*, 7 Dec. 1772 as an agent, and was probably related to the Richard Wilkes who had been apprenticed to Benjamin Collins in 1766 and who would have been free of his apprenticeship about this time (PRO IR. 1/56/43; see Maxted, *British Book Trades: Masters and Apprentices*, no. 0365g). A John Wilkes was later found in London, in Ave Maria Lane. He became free of the Stationers' Company by redemption in 1792, and took on two apprentices, his son John in 1793 and John White of Winchester in 1794 (McKenzie, *Apprentices 1701–1800*, 377).

[24] *HC*, 1 June 1778.

[25] John Breadhower is listed in neither Plomer nor McKenzie. There was a bookseller/ *Salisbury Journal* agent named Breadhower in Gosport in 1773 (*SJ*, 1 Feb. 1773). From at least 1777, when he advertised for an apprentice bookseller, John Breadhower was in Portsmouth (*SJ*, 14 Apr. 1777). He makes another appearance as *Salisbury Journal* agent from 28 Apr. 1783, soon after the *Hampshire Chronicle* partnership was dissolved.

[26] This Thomas Baker may be the same Thomas Baker, bookseller of Southampton, who became free of the Stationers' Company by redemption, 9 June 1789, and went on to bind three sons, Thomas (1791), Edward (1792), and Alfred (1793) to himself as apprentice booksellers (McKenzie, *Apprentices 1701–1800*, 15). Baker was in business in Southampton from at least 1767, when he began advertising his Circulating Library (which had already met with 'great Encouragement') in the *Salisbury Journal* (10 Aug. 1767); he was still listed as a *Journal* agent in 1785. As bookseller, newspaper agent, and circulating library proprietor, Baker would have been in direct competition with James Linden. Plomer finds Baker in business from 1767–76 (*Dictionary 1726–1775*, 12).

[27] Baker's original bid on behalf of the partners was for £275, but because Linden's assignees delayed the transaction, Linden could be forced to sell at the lower price (PRO E. 112/1959/147).

naturally of overriding concern, probably most sharply defined at this first meeting, when the account books were examined. Benjamin Collins, by now a banker with over forty years' newspaper experience, stated years later that he had had reservations about the accounts because Wilkes 'had not therein specified the particulars of his Receipts Charges and Disbursements and because he did not produce any Vouchers to verify the said Accounts'.[28] Yet the books passed inspection because the proprietors, every one of them, were impressed with what seemed to be a profit of £100. (The profit, it transpired, was merely a clerk's error.) Other points on the agenda, while basically financial, had more to do with the distribution and local management of the paper.

Whether the owners of a paper lived at a distance from each other, or all in the same town, experience suggested that one person should take charge of the routine work. Many consortia appointed managers, often from within their own number. This is a practice documented for every one of Benjamin Collins's papers: his own son and John Johnson managed the *Salisbury Journal*, John Wilkes the *Hampshire Chronicle*, and William Faden and Charles Spens started off his two London papers, the *Public Ledger* and the *London Chronicle* respectively. The most detailed account of a country manager's job is to be found in the *Chronicle* records for John Wilkes.

A Winchester bookseller, Wilkes had long been known to Benjamin Collins. Probably he was related to the Richard Wilkes who was bound to Collins in 1766. He had advertised a circulating library in 1771, and was a *Salisbury Journal* agent by 1772. He actually became a one-quarter-share partner in the repossessed *Hampshire Chronicle*, but it is clear that he was invited to join the enterprise because it was Collins's intention to transfer the newspaper from Southampton to Winchester, and he needed a man who knew the local trade. Wilkes soon learned to print the newspaper; his other duties were clearly priced and defined:

we shall not allow more than [£5 10s.] weekly for the printing and publication of the *Hampshire Chronicle*, Express Editor, keeping the Accounts, and all other Charges . . . We expect you to account for the Sale and Distribution of the said Paper at the full Retail price of . . . [3d.] each out of which . . . [9d.] upon each dozen sold will be allowed you for the Distribution; this . . . [9d.] per dozen to include every deduction whatever . . . And we also expect you to account for all the Advertisements that have been or shall be inserted . . .[29]

Wilkes was expected to report to the other partners at regular meetings, mark up an office copy of the paper, and make this and all accounts

[28] Ibid.   [29] Ibid.

available to the others. For much of his working life Benjamin Collins assigned a similar role to himself and his son, and John Johnson after that, but his account books did not survive to tell the full story.

The various agents recruited by managers and partners to see to distribution represent another level in the administration of eighteenth-century provincial newspapers. They were usually established business people, frequently booksellers or printers themselves, sometimes even co-operative newspaper proprietors, who agreed to organize local distribution and advertisement collections at a distance from the main office. The appointment of J. Smith, the first item in the Salisbury news section for 11 July 1774, briefly describes the job:

Advertisements for this paper will in future be taken in by J. SMITH, bookseller and stationer, in Marlborough, who is appointed an agent for the distribution of it in that town, and other places in those parts of Wiltshire where the Marlborough Journal was usually circulated, the publication of which is now discontinued.—All books, medicines, &c. advertised herein may be had of the said J. Smith; and all advertisements and articles of intelligence left with him, will be forwarded to the Printers with the utmost expedition.

The demise of a minor competitor, the brief-lived *Marlborough Journal*, is noted only in passing.

It is generally understood that agents worked for a commission, not just on each paper sold, but on advertisements and on any other goods that passed through their hands on the way from the newspaper printing office to the consumer. The formulaic 'Advertisements are taken in by . . .' in provincial newspaper imprints underlines this point. Obviously agents could take advantage of the newspaper route to promote their own concerns, books in particular. But there might be more to a newspaper agent's life than this, as becomes clear from the discussion of one agent at the November meeting of the *Hampshire Chronicle*'s proprietors. Thomas Baker, the bookseller who had acted for the partners in the original transaction, was retained as Southampton agent for the *Chronicle*. The partners agreed that Baker should be allowed the usual commission of 6*d.* per dozen for distributing the paper round that town, but decided that his proposed 'Charge of Five Shillings per Week for Agency, is unreasonable'. The source of the proprietors' alarm was the size of Baker's demand; there is no suggestion that the owners were surprised by the proposal itself. Clearly Baker thought that his claims to a regular agent's fee-income had a basis: a charge for agency could not have been unusual by this time, and a good, reliable agent must have been worth the additional expense of a small salary.

Another occasional source of agents' revenue was in the provision of local news to the editors. Most of any provincial newspaper's content was derived as a matter of course from the London and Continental printed papers to which the proprietor subscribed, and from the more expensive manuscript newsletters that were still in circulation in the eighteenth century. The *Chronicle*'s account books, however, provide evidence of the systematic provision of local material. Thomas Baker sent regular reports to both the *Salisbury Journal* and the *Hampshire Chronicle* and was paid for doing so—the November minutes record the decision that 'the same Allowance shall be made him for furnishing Intelligence, as is allowed to him at Salisbury'.[30] Such an income might be multiplied by as many newspapers as an enterprising journalist-agent could handle. A deliberate arrangement to collect country news from agents who were already in constant communication with the newspaper office made good sense: the proprietors were able to supplement their collection of London-derived news with the freshest local advice (which sometimes completed the circle by appearing in the London papers), while newsagents were able to supplement their incomes. Baker is the first provincial reporter-agent that can be documented in this way, but his role cannot have been without precedent. Newspapers in all parts of England interested in selling local or regional intelligence might well have looked to the services of literate, observant, and well-placed colleagues. Entries in the account books demonstrate that Baker was not the *Chronicle*'s sole agent-reporter.

Thomas Baker represents the upper rank of agent. He had been entrusted to arrange legal matters for Collins and Company; he felt entitled to a salary for agency services; he supplied Southampton news to at least two newspapers, the *Salisbury Journal* and the *Hampshire Chronicle*; and, in his own right, he had an established bookshop and circulating library. Aside from his journalism and his extra-commission revenue, most of Baker's newsagent activities must have been along the routine lines already described in other studies.[31] Newsagents were recruited by the newspaper's proprietors or their direct representative in the first place and were accountable to them or to a designated local manager. For example John Wilkes was responsible for keeping the *Chronicle*'s books and for collecting subscriptions and advertisement revenue from the outlying

[30] PRO E. 140/90.
[31] Notably by Wiles in *Freshest Advices* and Cranfield in his *Development of the Provincial Newspaper*. John Feather discusses newspaper distribution and its role in the expansion of the book trade in *The Provincial Book Trade in Eighteenth-Century England* (Cambridge, 1985), 17–20, 23–5.

agents every quarter. These agents were expected to take charge of finding reliable local carriers, newsmen, and hawkers (the equivalent of the
modern papergirls and paperboys) to deliver the papers weekly into the
hands of subscribers and casual purchasers. The newsagents, who were
intimately acquainted with the local newspaper and book routes, often
commissioned and trained the newsmen who walked them. The homely
details are documented on the debit side of the *Chronicle* cash books, where
there are, for example, charges for horse-hire and other expenses 'in
Journie with fresh Newsmen to shew them the Road'[32] and 'Jaques [the
Chichester agent[33]] paid Horsehire & Exp^s: instruct^s: Newsmen', among
a number of entries for training the newsmen.[34] Related expenditures are
for leather newsbags for the carriers, and paper and cord to wrap round the
bundles of newspapers, all items that would have been handled by the agent.

Customers with advertisements were frequently advised to send them
either directly to the printing office (always post paid), or through the
agents listed after the imprint. Advertising was a big money-earner, particularly for the Government, which could take in the high stamp duty,
and for the newspaper proprietors, but it could also make up a significant part of a newsagent's income. Almost half the basic fee for a short
advertisement went to the tax collector of course,[35] and only after an
agent's fee had been subtracted could the rest be regarded as profit for
the owners. Nevertheless eighteenth-century newspaper proprietors looked
to subscription revenue to cover production and distribution costs, and
regarded advertising as the real source of profits. One editor made this
explicit, when he wrote that 'The Profits of a newspaper arise *only* from
Advertisements'.[36] Newsagents received a fixed amount for each advertisement every time it appeared in the paper; a practice that is documented
for the *Hampshire Chronicle* in 1778, where there is a record that John
Breadhower be paid 'Three-pence for every Advertisement he sends to
the Paper, each Time it is inserted'.[37] Other papers similarly paid set fees.

---

[32] Ledger B, half-yearly entry dated 16 Sept. 1782, p. 124 (PRO E. 140/91).

[33] A Mr Jaques in Chichester was one of those offering subscriptions in John Ross's
Instructor's Assistant in 1764 (*SJ*, 16 July 1764). He is listed in neither Plomer nor McKenzie.

[34] Partners' cash book, entry dated 15 June 1778, p. 2 (PRO E. 140/90).

[35] The duty was 1s. per advertisement from 1712 (10 Anne, c. 18) until 1757 (30 Geo. II,
c. 19), when it was doubled; in 1780 (20 Geo. III, c. 28) it was raised again, to 2s. 6d.
Thereafter the duty fluctuated until 1853 (16 & 17 Victoria, c. 63), when it was abolished.
The tax was not related to the length of the ad.

[36] *Reading Mercury*, 10 July 1797, quoted in K. G. Burton, *The Early Newspaper Press
in Berkshire (1723–1855)* (Reading: published by the author, 1954), 45. Occasionally early
proprietors campaigned against the competition or tried to establish a new paper with 'free'
or 'duty-only' advertising (Wiles, *Freshest Advices*, 158–60).   [37] PRO E. 140/90.

For example the *Oxford Gazette and Reading Mercury* paid newsmen 2*d*. per advertisement in the 1750s.[38] The agent's allowance, like the tax, was evidently unaffected by the length of the notice—the advertisements recruited by Breadhower varied in length, but he was invariably credited 3*d*. each in his *Chronicle* accounts for example—although proprietors commonly set sliding rates for their customers according to length of advertisement. Soliciting and handling advertisements remained an integral part of a newsagent's job, one that brought greater profits for the proprietors and increased income for the agent. This also meant that, in an age of extended credit, debt collection and credit arrangements were commonly part of the job.

While the agent's advertising revenue, depending as it did on the variable needs of customers, might vary greatly from quarter to quarter, the commission for distributing the newspaper was a source of fairly steady income once circulation was established. Those who can be identified as agents in the *Hampshire Chronicle* accounts each received about the same number of papers (usually reckoned by the dozen) for redistribution from week to week, though the actual number allocated varied considerably from agent to agent: from as few as four papers for Elizabeth Martin in Waltham, who was probably acting as an informal agent delivering papers to a few neighbours, to about four dozen sent to Blake in Southampton, to ten dozen for Breadhower in Portsmouth. The thirteen dozen for Mr Underwood of Winchester were distributed by him to other agents on the network who then saw that the papers reached local customers. Underwood would have collected his newspapers directly from the printing office in the High Street each week. The biggest deliveries noted in the account books were usually to distributors, who were paid for each journey.[39] Their names were not listed with the newsagents' in the imprints of the *Hampshire Chronicle* since they did not provide the same sort of fixed contact for customers. This relationship between distributor and agent was repeated for the *Salisbury Journal* and indeed for other provincial newspapers of the time.

Both Thomas Baker and John Breadhower were explicitly allowed 6*d*. per dozen (or $\frac{1}{2}d$. each) for distribution,[40] which was the going rate mid-century.[41] Wiles records exactly the same amount paid to newsmen for *Adams's Weekly Courant*, 5 July 1757, and 'to the Person who sells' *Aris's Birmingham Gazette*, 4 July 1743. In the case of the *Hampshire Chronicle*,

---

[38] Cranfield, *Development of the Provincial Newspaper*, 234; and Wiles, *Freshest Advices*, 163. [39] Ledger B, PRO E. 140/91.
[40] PRO E. 140/90. [41] *Freshest Advices*, 100, 101.

the halfpenny was paid from John Wilkes's office in Winchester. As editor-printer-manager of the *Hampshire Chronicle* Wilkes was instructed 'to account for the Sale and Distribution of the said Paper at the full Retail price . . . out of which 9*d* . . . upon each dozen sold will be allowed . . . for the Distribution'—including charges for getting the papers to the newsagents.[42] This in turn suggests that the newsboys who finally delivered the goods to the customers received *their* commissions out of the agents' halfpenny-per-copy. Most, if not all agents had other business, and presumably could save on these expenses by sending apprentices or their own children on a weekly paper route. Given stable circulation figures, fees for distribution represented a steady income for the agent, albeit a small one in most cases. It is clear from the accounts that agents were not responsible for unusual delivery expenses, the Winchester printing office for example picking up the bill for transport by water (commonly called waterage) to the Isle of Wight.

The benefits of an agency, however, cannot be measured solely in terms of possible agency fees or commissions for receiving advertisements and distributing the paper. Many newsagents were primarily booksellers by trade or dealt in books and pamphlets as an adjunct to another business; many were schoolmasters, whose connection with the book trade is an obvious one, or apothecaries, with a historical connection; shopkeeper-agents had an interest in selling many other movable goods. The contact with the paper's proprietors, who would have had direct commercial links with London and were able to supply books, pamphlets, stationery, medicines, and perhaps other products at wholesale prices, was one that agents could exploit. So was the routine contact with a group of literate customers. Agents could advertise their own businesses at reduced, duty-only rates in the newspapers they distributed (at any rate, their names were listed at no charge), and they could take advantage of the newspaper's established distribution network to send other goods on their way.[43] Considered as a whole—including business contacts, fees,

---

[42] Bills and Answers, PRO E. 112/1959/147, p. 6.

[43] Certainly some London newspapers carried co-proprietors' advertisements for the cost of the duty only (Harris, *London Newspapers*, 59–60). This was probably also true for the provinces, although the evidence is not so clear-cut. At the very least provincial bookseller-agents would have been able to subtract the halfpenny commission from the price of the advertisement. Indirect evidence of special consideration for book-trade and medical advertising is to be found in the marked-up Beinecke Library copy of the *Salisbury Journal* from 1780, when most private advertisements are numbered in manuscript (a practice that was gradually introduced and was probably related to accounting), while book-trade and medical advertisements are not.

commissions, and advantageous advertising rates—the average provincial newspaper agency was probably not a bad proposition.

Much of the detailed information from the *Hampshire Chronicle* records may be readily translated to the *Salisbury Journal*, for the two newspapers shared proprietors, territory, and sometimes agents. The *Journal* agent's job was much the same as the *Chronicle* agent's. The names are known of over 170 people in sixty-nine towns who acted as agents for the *Salisbury Journal* at one time or another during its first fifty years. Doubtless there were more than 170 agents during this time, for the names are compiled from the lists that appeared sporadically in the newspaper as part of its colophon, and there were some years when no agents or only single agents were listed.[44] Obviously newsagents were still operating meanwhile and the *Journal* continued wide distribution, but there is no documented explanation for the omissions. The publication of agents' names may have coincided with increased competition, with campaigns to build up circulation, with the addition and subtraction of agents, or as a result of political or economic changes, like the list that appeared in 1757 just after the stamp duty was doubled. The lists varied in composition, from one agent to sixty; some agents were connected with the *Journal* for decades, others for weeks.

Many of the men and women who saw that the newspapers reached Wessex subscribers in the eighteenth century were closely allied to the book trade. Ninety-seven—more than half—of the 172 named *Salisbury Journal* agents were either described in the lists as booksellers, printers, stationers, or bookbinders, or found elsewhere in the paper selling books and pamphlets. At least seventeen were women; at least six were schoolteachers; three were apothecaries; there was a whipmaker, a goldsmith, a shopkeeper, a merchant, a postmaster, a tailor, and a cutler; for most of the rest, their one recorded activity is the distribution of copies of the *Journal* round certain towns.

This can be compared with the composition of *Hampshire Chronicle*

[44] No agents were listed during the following times: 6 Feb. 1738–19 Feb. 1739; 26 May–17 Nov. 1746; 13 June 1748–10 Sept. 1750, when a single agent, William Horton in Portsmouth, is noted; from this time until 18 Dec. 1752 only one agent at a time was named, including Horton, James Whiting in Romsey, and Thomas Burrough in Devizes; no agents are named until 7 Apr. 1755, when, again, a single bookseller is listed (Simon Knight at Newport, Isle of Wight); a list of twenty-three agents was added 2 June 1755 and dropped Sept.–Dec. 1756; a list of agents was added to a notice of the new stamp act (24 Oct. 1757), but otherwise there is no list 4 July 1757–8 Jan. 1770; 1 June–9 Nov. 1772; 21 Apr. 1777–28 Apr. 1783, when a list of forty-one agents is added; this long list is retained with various changes until 21 Feb. 1785, just after Benjamin Collins's death.

agencies from the late 1770s to the late 1780s, where the names of seventy-
five *Chronicle* agents can be compiled from the imprints of the paper's
first ten years. Twenty-seven of the seventy-five were described as printers,
booksellers, or stationers; that is, about one-third had commercial connections with books. Only one of the listed agents can be unambiguously
identified as a woman, Mrs Beeston a stationer at Lymington; one was a
schoolteacher; there were several *Chronicle* agents whose addresses were
local post offices; and the miscellaneous agents included a silversmith, a
baker, a hairdresser, a 'dealer in rum', a tailor, and a tallow chandler. The
main difference between *Journal* agencies and *Chronicle* agencies is in the
larger proportion of book-trade people among the agents for the longer-
established Salisbury paper. There was also a much greater percentage of
women making up the corps of *Journal* agents.

Seven or eight of the seventeen *Salisbury Journal* newsagents who can
be identified as women[45] were evidently successors to some male relative.
Ann Hillary in Salisbury took over the *Journal* agency as well as a book
and stationery shop immediately after her husband Joseph died in July
1774. She had one advertisement announcing the transition and calling
in debts owed to her husband (*SJ*, 25 July 1774); her name remained in
the *Journal* imprint for exactly one year until it was removed, and never
replaced, on 24 July 1775. Similarly Peggy and Bridget Elliot of Blandford,
sisters of Joseph Elliot, took over his bookselling and bookbinding business,
including the news agency, when he died early in 1757. Their first advertisement alerted clients to the fact that the sisters would welcome needlework too. For several years the Salisbury newspaper carried advertisements
for books sold by 'P. Elliot', presumably Peggy, until booksellers Samuel
Simmonds, J. Dempster, and William Sollers in sequence took over the
Blandford trade. In 1783 a Miss Wise, described as a druggist, became
the *Journal*'s agent at Newport, Isle of Wight, only after J. Wise, bookseller, was dropped from the imprint; the same is true for Mrs Tory in
Wimborne, who apparently succeeded William Tory in 1783; and for
Mrs Whiting, who followed the long-established James Whiting in Romsey
sometime after 1770. Whiting himself had taken over the agency from
a Mrs Rawlins, although his connection with her is unclear. It is impossible to say from the evidence whether these women became newsagents
and booksellers in the short term because of necessity and their commit-
ments to men in the book and newspaper trade, or whether a long-term

---

[45] Some of the agents identified only by surnames and first initials may also have been
women.

professional role was finally acknowledged only when no man's name was available.[46] Other women clearly were agents and booksellers in their own right. Few of these female agents are recorded in Plomer, although recent scholarship is beginning to discover a strong contingent of women in the book trade, many of whom either were in business for themselves from the start or carried on very capably after the demise of some male relative.

Agencies in three different centres, namely the Maynards of Devizes, Whiting in Romsey, and the Burdons in Winchester, suggest something of the business of eighteenth-century newsagents. Mrs Mary Maynard, Mrs Ann Maynard (who might have been one and the same), and a Miss Maynard carried on the tradition, established in the early years of the *Salisbury Journal*, of a close relationship between the Collins business and the book trade in Devizes.[47] Devizes is about 25 miles from Salisbury, with good communications along a centuries-old ridge road that was partly turnpiked early in the century; in fact the roads round Devizes were covered by the first Turnpike Act to affect Wiltshire.[48] In the eighteenth century the population of Devizes rose to about half that of Salisbury, placing it among the faster-growing and more populous Wiltshire towns, just behind Bradford and Marlborough, and along with Warminster and Trowbridge.[49] The Collinses had clearly found it useful to set up an agency there some time before June 1739, when the bookseller Thomas

---

[46] See e.g. C. J. Mitchell, 'Women in the Eighteenth-Century Book Trade', in O M Brack, Jr. (ed.), *Writers, Books, and Trade: An Eighteenth-Century Miscellany for William B. Todd* (New York: AMS Press, 1994), 25–75; Maureen Bell, 'Hannah Allen and the Development of a Puritan Publishing Business', *Publishing History*, 26 (1989), 5–66, and 'Mary Westwood, Quaker Publisher', *Publishing History*, 23 (1988), 5–66; and D. F. McKenzie's reassessment of Mary Simmons's 17th-cent. career in his unpublished Lyell Lectures (1988). Mid-18th-cent. women do not seem to have played a comparably prominent role in the provincial newspaper trade, however.

[47] Plomer has only 'Mrs. (   ) Maynard' (*Dictionary 1726–1775*, 166); there are no obvious connections in McKenzie, although Charles, son of John Maynard, who was made free of the Stationers' Company by patrimony in 1732, is a possibility (ST3:5323). The only contemporary noticed in the *Salisbury Journal* who might have been connected to these bookselling Maynards was a Michael Maynard of Newport, Isle of Wight, an insolvent debtor hoping to take advantage of the latest Relief Act (*SJ*, 22 May 1769).

[48] 6 Anne, c. 26 (*VCH Wiltshire*, iv. 257, 266); see also John Chandler, *Endless Street: A History of Salisbury and Its People* (Salisbury: Hobnob Press, 1987), fig. 21, 'Turnpikes and Railways in the Salisbury Area'. William Albert thinks that the 'lack of water transport and the consequent need to send goods by land carriage to London, may have led to the early turnpiking of roads near the cloth markets of Devizes, Chippenham and Calne' (*The Turnpike Road System in England 1663–1840* (Cambridge: Cambridge University Press, 1972), 38). See also Dorian Gerhold, *Road Transport before the Railways* (Cambridge University Press, 1993) and Eric Pawson, *Transport and Economy: The Turnpike Roads of Eighteenth-Century Britain* (London: Academic Press, 1979).

[49] Chandler, *Endless Street*, 46–7.

Sherwood was first listed as newsagent. Sherwood was followed in 1746 by William Leach, who combined the trades of snuff-making and selling stationery, and then by Thomas Burrough, who was silversmith, gold-smith, and bookseller. With Thomas Burrough it becomes evident that the Collins Devizes concern had expanded by the mid-1740s beyond a simple news agency into a local book-trade consortium, headed by Collins in Salisbury and including the agents in Devizes and Newport on the Isle of Wight. Advertisement after advertisement in the *Salisbury Journal* records books sold by Benjamin Collins in Salisbury, Thomas Burrough in Devizes, and Richard Baldwin in Newport, still apprenticed to Collins at this time. Most of the books and pamphlets they retailed were pub-lished from London, but there were occasional Salisbury imprints too. Other advertisements suggest that these agents relied on Collins's office for their job-printing needs, while Collins depended on Baldwin (and his successors in Newport) and Burrough to maintain local sales levels and perhaps to supply news occasionally.[50] The primary component of the relationship was of course the news agency for the *Salisbury Journal*.

So it is all the more interesting that at least the bookselling part of this important Devizes agency—and almost certainly the local distribu-tion of the *Salisbury Journal* as well[51]—was taken over by Mary Maynard in 1762, even though advertisements show that Burrough was still actively engaged in the Devizes book trade.[52] By this date the Salisbury–Devizes–Newport consortium had been replaced in the book advertisements by a larger, more fluid group of country booksellers, but Maynard's posi-tion, usually at the head of the list after Benjamin Collins, is evidence of her own seniority as well as of the enduring prominence of Devizes in the Wiltshire book trade.[53] Mary Maynard's business relationship with

---

[50] 'ALL Sorts of Blanks, Highway, Land-Tax, Assessors and Window-Tax Warrants, Common-Warrants, Orders of Removal Certificates, Summons, Kings-Bench and Common-Pleas Writs, all Sold at the Printing-Office in *Salisbury*; by *T. Burrough* in *Devizes*; *R. Baldwin*, at *Newport* . . . as cheap as in LONDON: And any particular Sorts printed at a few Days Notice, sent to either of the above Places' (*SJ*, 20 Nov. 1744). It is telling that while Baldwin and Burrough engaged in many other book-trade related activities (book-binding, stationery selling, bookselling, pamphlet selling, and so on), neither actually advert-ised as printer. Printing jobs seem to have been sent on to Salisbury, which could account for the 'few Days Notice' required.

[51] The transition took place at a time when agents were not listed in the *Journal*.

[52] e.g. in 1761 and 1762 Thomas Burrough was advertising library sales (*SJ*, 24 Aug. 1761, 14 June 1762). The next full-length list of agents did not appear in the *Journal* until 1770, but by then Ann Maynard, possibly in succession to Mary Maynard, had replaced Burrough as Devizes newsagent—this change may have taken place much earlier.

[53] While newsagents may have been listed in geographical order, provincial publishers in their book imprints loosely followed the London practice of listing the booksellers in order of seniority.

Benjamin Collins and his newspaper may be defined in terms of the *Salisbury Journal*: she was regularly listed there as the Devizes retailer for books and other goods from 1762 until at least 1767; and at one point she, like Benjamin Collins, was advertising tickets, shares, and chances in the Lottery (*SJ*, 10 November 1766). The books she helped to sell are a mixed lot—Knapp's *New Church Melody*, Brookes's *Natural History*, *Mother Goose*, *The Vicar of Wakefield*, Dodwell's *Sick Man's Companion*, and so on—not so much an indication of what Maynard herself decided to sell as an advertisement for what might be available in Devizes from London via Salisbury. In 1767 the *Family Guide to Health* was advertised as printed for J. Fletcher and Benjamin Collins and sold by 'Mrs. Ann Maynard' among others (*SJ*, 16 March 1767). Since both Mary and Ann Maynard are usually described as 'Mrs. Maynard', it is not known precisely when the name change had taken place, or even if there were actually two different persons.[54] When a new list of agents appeared in the first number of the *Salisbury Journal* for 1770, Mrs Ann Maynard was there in Thomas Burrough's place, confirming a position she had filled probably since 1762 when she became part of the regional bookselling scene. She in turn was replaced by a Miss Maynard in 1783 who remained the Devizes newsagent even after Benjamin Collins died. The Maynard business of books, newspapers, and related goods and services, owned and managed by women, was evidently a successful one, and certainly it was one on which Collins relied for twenty years and more.

Schoolmaster-newsagents are represented here by James Whiting of Romsey near Southampton.[55] Romsey is about 16 miles to the southeast of Salisbury on the important Portsmouth-to-Salisbury artery, in an area where Benjamin Collins was attempting to consolidate and extend the *Journal*'s readership from the 1750s against some competition from the *Reading Mercury*.[56] That Collins met with success was due in part to agents such as Whiting. He first advertised his joint occupations in the

---

[54] Mary may have chosen to use a second name after 1767. If so, she was not the only 18th-cent. bookseller to restyle her name: Richard Baldwin junior dropped the epithet once his career was well under way; Benjamin Charles Collins was known to his colleagues and friends as Charles; John Sadler Gale in Chippenham seems to have called himself J. Gale and S. Gale at different times; R. P. Durnford, a schoolmaster in Marlborough, began his bookselling career as R. Pye-Durnford.

[55] This James Whiting is not in McKenzie's *Apprentices*. Plomer finds a J. Whiting at work in Rumsey in 1768 (*Dictionary 1726–1775*, 261).

[56] The greatest concentration of *Salisbury Journal* agents was mostly to the south, southeast, and north-west. The *Reading Mercury* had agents in a number of towns to the northeast, east, and south-east of Salisbury, including Southampton, Portsmouth, and Winchester in the 1740s, and Southampton, Portsmouth, Windsor, Guildford, and Salisbury itself in the 1760s. See Burton, *Early Newspaper Press in Berkshire*, 85. See also the maps in Ch. 3.

Journal in 1751: 'All Sorts of Books are Sold and Bound; and Advertisements for this Paper are taken in by James Whiting, School-Master in Rumsey' (25 November 1751). He continued the book and teaching trades, selling a variety of books, and at the same time advertising that he boarded young men and taught them 'WRITING, ARITHMETICK, and MERCHANTS ACCOMPTS, After the true ITALIAN Method . . . with proper Assistants . . . on reasonable Terms' (*SJ*, 27 March 1758). His news agency was more complicated. Although Whiting had an advertising account with the *Journal* by 1751, he was not mentioned as an agent until 24 October 1757,[57] when subscribers, encouraged to abandon the expensive London papers for the more reasonably priced *Salisbury Journal*, were directed to Whiting and twenty-nine of his provincial colleagues. Eight months later the following notice appeared: 'This Journal which used to be distributed in Romsey and Places adjacent by Mrs. Rawlins, will for the future (our Customers are desired to take Notice,) be circulated by Mr. James Whiting in Romsey aforesaid' (12 June 1758). This marked the expansion of Whiting's news agency to include wider distribution; the notice also suggests the hidden infrastructure of a provincial distribution network. Mrs Rawlins must have been delivering the *Journal* 'in Romsey and Places adjacent' when James Whiting of Romsey appeared in the list of agents earlier, yet this is the only recorded notice of her in that role.

Similarly William Whitmarsh, whose name figures in no list of *Salisbury Journal* agents, felt it necessary to rebut

a false and malicious Report . . . lately raised, that WILLIAM WHITMARSH, junr. Taylor, of Winterbourn-Gunner, and Distributer of this Journal, is going to leave off distributing the same: This is to assure all his Customers, that he has not the least Intent of leaving it off, but is as willing as ever to serve his Customers with all Sorts of Magazines, Weekly Numbers, Books, Almanacks, &c. on the shortest Notice.

N.B. He continues on the Business of a Taylor, as usual . . .

(*SJ*, 13 December 1762)

The wording of this advertisement suggests a local news agency, rather than a carrier/distributor over long distances. And we know that James Dally distributed the *Journal* from Castle Street, Salisbury, to Stockbridge, Winchester, and Portsmouth only because he advertised for a young man to assist him (1 January 1759), but then he was probably a distributor, rather than a newsagent. At any rate Whiting continued selling books and newspapers at least until 1775, leaving schoolteaching to assistants or even

---

[57] The duty on newspapers and advertisements had been doubled from 11 July 1757.

abandoning it in favour of the book trade, when he found it more profit-able. He probably died before 1781 when a Mrs Whiting was listed in an advertisement as the retail outlet in Romsey for Dr Norris's Drops. Like a number of other eighteenth-century educators, James Whiting moved from the business of creating and shaping the provincial reading market to supplying that new market with reading material. He was joined by at least five other *Salisbury Journal* newsagent-schoolmasters—a Mr Johnson (in Alton), James Linden (Southampton), Jonathan Moore (Newport, Isle of Wight), a Mr Ross (Whitchurch), and Samuel Simmonds (Blandford).

One last example—of a more typical provincial bookseller and news agency—is the business of Thomas Burdon and John Burdon, booksellers in College Street, Winchester, agents first for the *Salisbury Journal* and then for the *Hampshire Chronicle*.[58] Thomas Burdon, who was the first of the family to make an appearance, was established in Winchester by the time the second edition of V. J. Peyton's *True Principles of the French Language*, printed for Davey and Law in London, was advertised in the *Salisbury Journal* late 1757. T. Burdon was one of the country booksellers mentioned, and he was joined by Benjamin Collins, James Fletcher in Oxford, Thomas Burrough in Devizes, and Samuel Gould in Dorchester. It seems likely that Thomas Burdon took over the business and shop of Richard Holloway, bankrupt about the same time, who had given notice in the *Journal* for 19 December 1757 that he had turned over his estate and effects to Davey and Law, the London booksellers who were his principal creditors. Thomas Burdon figured in a number of book advert-isements over the next thirteen years. John Burdon, who was probably his brother, joined him around 1759 when subscriptions to Doddridge's *Family Expositor* could be had from 'Messrs. Burdon' (*SJ*, 26 November 1759). By 1759, too, the Burdons were beginning to take an interest in the sale of provincial libraries, a direction the business was to follow under John Burdon from 1764: there are a number of his catalogues in the *Journal* advertising 'valuable and well-chosen Libraries' usually in 'very good Condition' and always 'sold remarkably cheap'. The two were closely connected with Winchester College, supplying the school with stationery, pens, ink, and books, as well as binding and repair services. There are receipts to document this aspect of the College trade; and it is likely that the boys were instructed to make most of their individual book purchases

[58] Plomer finds evidence of T. Burdon in St Michael's, Winchester, from 1760 to 1765. He married the widow Jane Widmore, 16 Apr. 1765, at St Michael's church. Plomer's dates for John Burdon's activities, including library sales, are 1773 to 1802, when he died (*Dictionary 1726–1775*, 39–40). Neither Burdon is in McKenzie.

at the Burdons' shop.[59] The *Salisbury Journal* agency is discovered first, not in the paper's imprint, but in an advertisement:

The Salisbury Journal, which used to be distributed in this City and Neighbour-hood by John Elkins, will for the future, be delivered by Stephen Tucker, from *Mr. Burdon's, Bookseller, in College-Street*; to whom, should any Omission happen by this Change of Hands, our Customers are desired to apply, and they will be punctually serv'd.   (*SJ*, 19 June 1758)

Once again details of a newspaper's distribution network are revealed only coincidentally: William Greenville—not Thomas Burdon—was the Winchester agent in the October 1757 list and it was not until 1776 that Burdon's name appears in the imprint, at that time replacing Mr Tombs the whipmaker. Yet here is Burdon in mid-1758, clearly a newsagent, taking responsibility (perhaps in conjunction with Greenville and later Tombs) for the proper distribution of the *Salisbury Journal* around Winchester. Like so many *Journal* agents, the Burdons combined newspaper management with an established bookselling business; and it was probably through book-trade contacts with Benjamin Collins that they entered into the agency in the first place.

London-based agents for the *Salisbury Journal* and *Hampshire Chronicle*, like their country colleagues, organized local distribution and acted as conduits for advertising revenue. But unlike the country agents, who were part of smaller newspaper-based distribution networks, the Londoners formed the centre of the greater national network that shipped information and wholesale goods through major provincial proprietors such as Benjamin Collins. The variety of London-provincial bonds that might be made are recorded in Collins's relationship with his London newsagents: for example he bought shares in copyrights from John Newbery and collaborated with him on children's books; he placed Richard Baldwin, while still his apprentice, in the important agency on the Isle of Wight, and maintained the connection when Baldwin moved to London; he held a number of shares with Stanley Crowder and other London booksellers. Collins invited the London book trade to share in his own London newspaper ventures and he colluded with the London booksellers when they were attempting to force the copyright issue. His London newsagents no doubt played a complementary part to Collins's regular bank, Baron Dimsdale and Company, in his London credit arrangements, at the very

---

[59] I am grateful to Claire Bolton, Oxford, for supplying me with information on the Winchester College side of the business.

least accepting payment from London customers who placed advertisements in the *Journal*.[60]

The London book and newspaper trade remained an integral part of the economic structure of eighteenth-century provincial newspapers as a source of news, credit, advertising revenue, books, medicines, and other products, all united in the person of the London agent. From the very beginning London booksellers had figured in *Salisbury Journal* advertisements. Almost from the beginning, which is to say from February 1739, London booksellers were included in the *Journal* imprint. The first was Thomas Astley, with whom the Collinses had numerous connections— they shared a Berkshire background of course, which could well have been the personal foundation of their commercial association; their names were linked in book imprints from as early as 1730, when Astley was one of the London retailers for a Salisbury-printed tract on Stonehenge; and Richard Baldwin junior, Benjamin Collins's first apprentice and another Berkshireman, went from his apprenticeship straight into partnership with Thomas Astley in 1746.[61] The unfortunate Astley was arrested for publishing details of Lord Lovat's trial in his *London Magazine* (along with Edward Cave of the *Gentleman's*); about a year later he suffered great losses in the devastating fire of 1748. Astley's successors to the London agency for the *Salisbury Journal* were the booksellers John Rivington (ST3:6844) after 1746, John Newbery from 1746 to 1755, Richard Baldwin junior (ST3:0376) from 1755 to 1770, and, from 1770, John Wilkie (ST3:1770), Stanley Crowder (ST3:4021), Thomas Carnan and Francis Newbery (ST3:2799), and Francis Blyth (ST3:7179). All were prominent in the London book trade, and most were Citizens and Stationers.

After September 1775 London booksellers no longer appeared in the imprint of the *Salisbury Journal*; rather their names were replaced by those of several London coffee-houses, the London, Chapter, Guildhall, and Peele's. This was not a new arrangement in 1775, as Collins's letter to John Nourse (ST3:5938) shows: in 1766 Collins could write that the *Salisbury Journal* was available every week 'at the Chapter Coffee House Pauls Church Yard, or at Mr Newbery's'.[62] The relationship between

[60] These bookseller/newsagents were by no means Collins's only London agents: William Strahan, who had no obvious interest in the *Salisbury Journal*, was the most important (see Ch. 1).

[61] See C. Y. Ferdinand, 'Richard Baldwin Junior, Bookseller', *Studies in Bibliography*, 42 (1989), 254–64, for discussion of both Baldwin and Astley.

[62] Benjamin Collins to John Nourse, 2 Jan. 1766, *Salisbury Journal* office, Salisbury. 1766 was a year in which the imprint carried no list of agents.

coffee-houses and newspapers was a longstanding one that went back to the seventeenth century when the coffee men realized that customers occupied in reading and discussing the news might spend more freely on refreshment. This was something that caught the attention of César de Saussure, one eighteenth-century visitor to England whose comments are famous:

Ce qui attire beaucoup de monde dans les cafés, ce sont les gazettes & autres papiers publics. Les Anglois sont grands nouvellistes. La plupart des artisans commencent la journée par aller au café, pour y lire les nouvelles. J'ai souvent vu des décroteurs & autres gens de cette étoffe s'associer pour acheter tous les jours la gazette d'un liard & la lire ensemble.[63]

In the late 1720s there was a brief commercial battle between the coffee-house proprietors and the newspaper proprietors that in the end only emphasized their interdependence. The coffee men objected to the expense of taking in so many newspapers and threatened to start one of their own, while the newspapermen countered that the customers who spent time reading the papers usually spent cash on overpriced drinks. There was a flurry of pamphlets around the topic.[64] By the middle of the eighteenth century it was common for coffee-houses all over the country to keep files of the London and provincial papers for the convenience of patrons who wanted to read them, subscribe to them, or place advertisements in them. There are several advertisements for provincial coffee-houses in the *Salisbury Journal* that specifically mention that newspapers will be available. The *Reading Mercury* could be consulted in two London coffee-houses —Sam's and the Horseshoe Inn—in 1743; by 1788 it was available at Peele's, the Chapter, and St Paul's.[65] Peele's in particular was noted for its files of newspapers and the Chapter was 'frequented by the booksellers, writers, and "men of letters"'. Thomas Gurney, its proprietor, wrote in 1798 that 'all the newspapers that are published in England, Ireland and Scotland are taken and the files may be regularly seen from June 1773 to the present time'.[66] The coffee-house historian Lillywhite describes three

---

[63] César de Saussure, *Lettre et Voyages de Mons' César de Saussure en Allemagne, en Hollande et en Angleterre, 1725–1729* (Lausanne: George Bridel; Paris: Fischbacher; Amsterdam: Feikema, Caarelsen, 1903), 167.

[64] One example that outlines both arguments, but favours the newspaper side, is *The Case between the Proprietors of News-Papers, and the Subscribing Coffee-Men, Fairly Stated* (London: printed for E. Smith, A. Dodd, and N. Blandford, 1729).

[65] Burton, *Early Newspaper Press in Berkshire*, 85. For the London coffee-houses, see Bryant Lillywhite, *London Coffee Houses: A Reference Book of Coffee Houses of the Seventeenth, Eighteenth, and Nineteenth Centuries* (London: George Allen & Unwin, 1963).

[66] Cited in Lillywhite, *London Coffee Houses*, 442.

of Collins's four London coffee-houses—the Guildhall, Peele's, and the London—as venues for Masonic meetings about this time. It is not clear exactly how much of the London newsagent's role was taken over by the coffee men, or if the coffee-house agents actually helped organize the distribution of provincial papers.

In London the last quarter of the eighteenth century saw the emergence of such agents as J. Hamilton and William Tayler who arranged advertising and postal distribution on a national scale. Hamilton advertised his 'first attempt to reduce the exorbitant expence of news-papers sent into the country' in the *Salisbury Journal*, 26 November 1770. As his notice suggests, he was concerned to get the London papers to provincial customers. Tayler's business was wider-ranging, handling subscriptions both ways (provinces-to-London and vice versa), but specializing in advertisements in the country papers. Calling himself 'agent to the country printers', he offered a list of fifty-one newspapers in 1778 in which he could readily place any customer's advertisement.[67] In the provinces, however, local newsagents continued much as before, collecting advertisements and organizing weekly distribution.

Like other provincial papers, the *Salisbury Journal* and the *Hampshire Chronicle* actually came into the hands of their subscribers by several means: postmen, carriers, distributors, newsmen, and hawkers. It is possible that the *Journal* was sometimes conveyed by water, perhaps along the River Avon, but there is slim evidence for this: however, one notice in the *Journal* of 6 July 1761 grouped together 'all Carriers, Coachmen, Watermen, Wherrymen, Dispersers of Country-Newspapers' who were liable to fines for carrying letters. The descriptions and the jobs themselves were not always clearly defined in the eighteenth century, and sometimes they were interchangeable. If accounts were kept of the people who actually delivered the provincial papers to subscribers—those who made up the numerous lowest ranks in the distribution system—they would have been kept by those local agents who hired, trained, and paid them. To date none of these records has been discovered. However, the public details printed in the local papers, as well as the surviving account books can provide a fairly detailed picture of how regional periodicals reached their customers.

Briefly defined, the *postmen* or *postboys* were employed by the Post Office to deliver mail through a network of post roads that became increasingly

---

[67] Michael Turner, 'William Tayler', unpublished paper; William Tayler, 'A Complete List of all the Country News-Papers throughout England' [1778], broadside advertisement.

extensive under Ralph Allen's management of the Bye Letter Office in the mid-century, but nevertheless remained a slow and expensive means of conveyance until the introduction of mail coaches in 1784.[68] A *carrier* was an individual, self-employed, who undertook to convey parcels and goods from place to place along established routes and at advertised times. The *newsmen* and *hawkers* were employed by the newspaper proprietors, either directly or through their agents, and were often restricted to delivering for a single newspaper concern: the distinction that might be drawn between the two is that newsmen delivered primarily to regular subscribers, while hawkers sold their papers on a more casual basis, sometimes crying them about town. A *distributor* might mean anyone—from agents to newsmen—who carried newspapers, but the term most often referred specifically to those who conveyed large bundles of newspapers to different agents for local delivery. In any event it was the constant concern of the proprietors and their agents that the news reach their customers quickly and expeditiously by one of these means.[69]

The post is a delivery system that is seldom mentioned in the Wessex papers; it does seem to have been infrequently used for provincial newspapers, limited no doubt by its expense, slowness, and occasional unreliability.[70] It was a different story in the capital of course, where a number of London-based officials with franking privileges undertook to send some of the London serials to the country—Edward Cave and his *Gentleman's Magazine* is a well-documented case.[71] Obviously the Post Office was sometimes employed for local delivery outside London too and certainly its use was encouraged for the transmission of advertisements—'post-paid'

---

[68] See Kenneth Ellis, *The Post Office in the Eighteenth Century: A Study in Administrative History* (London: Oxford University Press, 1958); Howard Robinson has an account of the Post Office in the mid-18th cent. in his *The British Post Office: A History* (Princeton, NJ: Princeton University Press, 1948), 99–112; see also Jeremy Greenwood's unpaginated, unfootnoted *Newspapers and the Post Office (1635–1834)* (Postal History Society Publications, 1971).

[69] There is no question that 18th-cent. proprietors were keenly interested in timeliness: the *Journal* planned a move from Saturday to Tuesday publication '*so that the freshest Intelligence by Monday's Post will by that means be inserted, and the same sooner and better Conveyed to our Readers*' (*SJ*, 19 Sept. 1737) for example, and there are occasional printed apologies for unavoidable delays in delivery.

[70] The Act of 1711 called for the following rates: 'In England and Wales a single letter was carried eighty miles for 3d . . . and beyond eighty miles for 4d. . . . Double letters, that is, letters of two sheets of paper, were levied "double postage". "Packets of writs, deeds, and other things" were charged at four times the single rate for each ounce' (Robinson, *British Post Office*, 96–7).

[71] A. D. Barker, 'Edward Cave, Samuel Johnson and the *Gentleman's Magazine*', D.Phil. thesis (Oxford University, 1981).

always—directly to the Printing Office, by which means the proprietor could avoid paying commission to an intermediary. At least two *Salisbury Journal* agents were themselves postmasters. The local use of the postal service and its contingent difficulties are demonstrated in one advertisement:

Several Gentlemen and others in *Shaftesbury* and the neighbourhood, having complained of their being lately disappointed of receiving the *Salisbury Journal* in the regular order they used to have it, are desired to take notice, that it was owing to the Post Office, from whence it used to be circulated, by Mr. Atchison, being moved to Mr. Pinhorn's, at the George; by whom it is now distributed early every Monday morning, and will be punctually sent to all Gentlemen and others that please to send their orders for it to the said Mr. Pinhorn, in *Shaftesbury*; *Mr. Gould*, at *Dorchester*; *Mr. Clench*, [Postmaster] at *Blandford*; or the Postmen, or News-Carriers . . .   (*SJ*, 1 February 1768)

There were other difficulties that arose from the vulnerability of the postboys. The *Journal* reported an attempted robbery, 11 December 1752, and the death of another postboy, squashed when his horse fell on him after it was shot by a highwayman (*SJ*, 17 December 1753). Severe winter weather usually brought the report of at least one postal carrier's death by freezing. During the fierce winter of 1766 one rather more fortunate young man retired to a warm public house, where he drank himself into oblivion. His luck failed him when he later forgot where he had left his postbag, claimed it had been stolen, and was detained in the Devizes bridewell for a time (*SJ*, 31 March 1766).

Common carriers, on the other hand, often appeared in the pages of local newspapers both in advertisements for their own regular delivery services and in notices about the distribution of the newspaper.[72] They received goods for delivery at designated points, very often inns, which involved financial collaboration with local innkeepers, and they travelled along published routes at set times of the week. The routes varied in distance, depending on population/customer density and the carrier's transportation—but the carrier's business inevitably involved a good deal of travel in all weathers and could not have been an easy life. John Sandell offered a typical service from Shaftesbury in which he set out

every *Monday*, *Wednesday*, *Thursday*, and *Saturday* (being the usual Days, from Shaston [i.e. Shaftesbury] to Compton, Funtmill, Sutton, Iwerne-Minster, Iwerne

---

[72] Pawson has a useful section on the 'Carrying Networks' in his *Transport and Economy*, 35–57; see also David Hey, *Packmen, Carriers and Packhorse Roads: Trade and Communications in North Derbyshire and South Yorkshire* (Leicester: Leicester University Press, 1980), especially the chapter on carriers, pp. 205–24.

Courtney, alias Shroton, Steepleton, Handford, Stowerpain, and Blandford, and from thence back to Shaston, Gillingham, Cucklington, Wincaunton, East, West, and Stower-Provost, as also Henstridge, and other places thereto Adjoining; and also to Motcombe, Mere, Sturton, Simbley, Knoyle, Hindon, and places adjacent. And likewise to Ludwell, Charlton, both Dunheads, both Hatches, Tisbury, and Chilmark, and all Places within Ten Miles round Shaston and Blandford, when and where all Persons may depend on having Things carried with Care and Industry . . .

N. B. The said Carrier has for many Years past, been used to these places in the Capacity of a Post-Man, and has thro' the whole Stage behaved with Honesty and Integrity . . .

He also carries the SALISBURY JOURNAL, and delivers it punctually once a Week, to such as are Quarterly Customers.   (*SJ*, 2 January 1749)

The Shaftesbury–Blandford segment alone meant a return journey of more than 25 miles and, all told, Sandell must have travelled at least 100 miles a week. As Ralph Allen extended his network of postal crossroads and by-roads, he made illegal the carriage of letters by anyone but formally employed postmen, so that such independent carriers as Sandell, whose advertisement appeared soon after a restrictive postal act had come into force, were compelled to concentrate more on the delivery of legal parcels, including newspapers. There were also individual private carriers who might undertake delivery of goods on a more casual basis; newspaper proprietors might have employed them on an *ad hoc* basis.

The common carriers often owned waggons and horses—'poor old Wall the Cranbourne Carrier' for example died after a fall from his (*SJ*, 20 May 1754) and was succeeded by John Beale of Cranbourne, who promised to deliver the *Journal* '*every* Monday *Morning*', and with it if desired, Dr James's fever powders (*SJ*, 22 July 1754). The age level for these commercial carriers was probably somewhat higher than that for postboys or newsboys. Wall, the Cranbourne man, was described as 'old', and other carriers were sometimes succeeded by widows and sons. For example Edward Pearcy, the London–Salisbury carrier, was succeeded by his wife and grown son (*SJ*, 20 April 1742); the widow of Samuel Birt, the Ringwood carrier, called in his debts (*SJ*, 14 October 1754); and John Sandell had been in business 'for many Years past' when he placed his advertisement in the *Journal*. The fact that carriers placed advertisements and newsboys did not is another indication of general differences in age and professional status.

It is not always clear just who paid the carriage on carrier-delivered newspapers. Wiles thought that subscribers 'would, of course, pay the charges',[73] yet an additional charge for this service does not figure—at least not explicitly—in advertisements for the *Salisbury Journal* itself. John Sandell's advertisement above suggests that quarterly subscribers might receive the *Journal* carriage-free. In fact competition from London in the first half of the century encouraged provincial proprietors to offer free delivery of their newspapers and other commercial goods to regular customers, whether by paid carrier or along the newspaper's own net-work: the *London Magazine* could be had carriage-free '*of the hawkers of this Paper*' (*SJ*, 18 April 1738) and 'Gentlemen in the Country' could 'be supplied with all Sorts of Books, Pamphlets, Plays, &c. free of Carriage, at the same Price as in London' (*SJ*, 4 September 1739). The availability of this service to provincial readers indicates that carriers were commis-sioned by the proprietors and their agents rather than by the subscribers, and were willing to work for the usual halfpenny a paper, commissions on advertisements, and customer contacts. Such an arrangement, in which the proprietors organized payment for carriage, would certainly have operated for the carriers and other distributors who delivered bundles of newspa-pers from the printing office to outlying agents. There is ample evidence for this practice in the account books. However, free delivery and other con-cessions were under pressure by the 1760s when new taxes cut into profit margins. After that provincial proprietors could at least promise that books were 'supplied on better Terms, (Carriage considered) than in London'.

For the distributors, hired specifically to take the newspapers to agents for local delivery and also to make themselves available to deliver other items along the way, payment was in terms of a fixed sum for each journey, rather than a commission on each paper carried. The *Hampshire Chron-icle* account books clearly show that the amount of payment depended on the length of the trip. For example, R. and W. Fry made weekly deli-veries along the routes to Poole (about 42 miles) and into Sussex (about 38 miles) for 1 guinea a trip, while T. Richardson in Petersfield and E. Whitenham in Droxford, whose journeys were shorter, each received 10s. a week.[74] Benjamin Collins, marketing his books by catalogue this time, pointed out that 'Orders from Gentlemen, &c. at a Distance, will be punctually observed, and small Parcels sent by the Distributers of the Salisbury Journal: By whom all Persons may be supplied with the Monthly Review, Magazines, and all periodical Publications; also new Books and Pamphlets, &c. as soon as possible after published' (*SJ*, 1 June 1767).

While the carriers and distributors were usually adult men who were

---

[73] Wiles, *Freshest Advices*, 128.   [74] Ledger B, PRO E. 140/91.

self-employed, owned a horse and perhaps a waggon, delivered goods of all kinds, themselves determined the geographical area to be covered, and probably contracted their services to the book and newspaper trade, the newsmen, newsboys, and hawkers were more often young, were employed directly by the newspaper they carried, usually walked, and followed a route tailored to the specific needs of the newspaper and its customers. There is very little to document this transient group. Part of their job was, of course, to deliver goods from the printing office or news agency to the customer. One crudely ironical letter published in the *Journal* was constructed around a request that two sets of Thomas Chubbs's posthumous works be sent by the newsman to a reading club that was 'very fond of Books which are wrote against Christianity'; payment was to be returned by the same means (*SJ*, 16 January 1749). Customers continued to take advantage of this dependable weekly service: newsmen carried items not directly related to the newspaper, as a not very timely notice in the news section of the *Journal* for 5 June 1775 shows:

Lost, or left somewhere, supposed to be sent by the newsman, on Sunday the 26th of March last, a small parcel tied up in a sheet of brown paper, and sealed, directed to Mrs. Jefferies, at Malmsbury, containing six pieces of Salisbury Lace, and twelve dozen of Lace Crowns and Seams, for childrens caps.

Other parcels and communications from the proprietors and agents to their customers found their way into the newsbags too, and their delivery must have been a means of supplementing newsmen's income.

Agents directly connected with the newspaper, if not one of the proprietors themselves, hired and trained the newsmen. The *Hampshire Chronicle* ledgers record expenses for showing 'fresh Newsmen' the road or 'instruct:ᵍ Newsmen'. The number of such entries indicates a fairly high turnover for what must have been a rigorous job.[75] Another recurring expense for the *Chronicle* proprietors was for leather newsbags[76]—at 5s. each the bags must have had room enough for the papers plus all the magazines, whole books, number books, pamphlets, and medicines the newspaper advertisements urged on their readers with the occasional promise of free carriage. Dependability and honesty were the usual requirements, but youth and strength were clearly assets for a job that demanded long hours of walking with a heavy load. James Dally, the Salisbury-based distributor who saw that the *Journal* reached Stockbridge, Winchester, and Portsmouth, specifically advertised for 'A Young Man about 17, 18, or 20 Years of Age' to carry the paper to quarterly subscribers (*SJ*, 1 January

[75] Ledger B, PRO E. 140/91.
[76] Cash Account Book for 18 May 1778–24 Mar. 1783, PRO E. 140/90.

1759). Newsmen were sometimes nicknamed Trampwell and one even 'walked 60 miles in 12 hours and 40 minutes' to win a wager of 10 guineas (*SJ*, 19 January 1767). Possibly the luckiest newsman was a Mr Penny who won a £10,000 prize, immediately farmed his walk, and went on to sell 'spirituous liquors and made-wines' (*SJ*, 13 June 1763). And newsmen were regularly restricted to delivering for only one concern, as recorded in articles of agreement among the new proprietors of the *Hampshire Chronicle* in 1778:

The newsmen employed or that have been employed in the Distribution of the Salisbury Journal shall not be Employed to distribute the Hampshire Chronicle nor shall the Newsman [*sic*] employed or <that> have been employed in the distribution of the Hampshire Chronicle be employed or distribute the Salisbury Journal without the Consent of the Proprietors . . .[77]

Hawkers, more strictly defined,[78] were certainly a part of the weekly life of most provincial towns throughout this period, although they are rarely mentioned—they were so much an ordinary part of the scene. Not a single *Salisbury Journal* hawker is mentioned by name in that newspaper, but a little can still be said about the hawker's role in the distribution network and how that differed from the newsboy's. First of all the hawkers relied on casual sales, while the newsboys delivered papers to a set of subscribers. This meant that the hawkers of newspapers were effectively restricted to the more populous towns and perhaps a few nearby villages and inns; it would not have been worth anyone's while to tramp the countryside with the sole purpose of finding occasional readers, although there was nothing to stop anyone who hawked other goods to the country market from adding a newspaper to his repertoire. Then the hawkers were more vocal, relying on voice and perhaps acting ability to sell the paper. The newsboys occasionally cried the papers too, but along designated routes and for customers who were expecting regular delivery. Richard Cruttwell for example was looking for 'Some industrious Men, of good character, who have clear and audible Voices . . . to distribute this Paper in different Country Circuits'.[79] Finally the hawkers usually received their bundles of papers only after the newsboys had begun their

---

[77] Wilkes *v.* Collins *et al.*, Bills and Answers, PRO E. 112/1959/147. Burton notes the same pattern in the Berkshire press: newsmen 'were employed directly by the newspaper concerned and, unlike the agents, distributed for only one newspaper' (*Early Newspaper Press in Berkshire*, 62).

[78] The term was sometimes more loosely used to describe anyone who delivered a paper, as e.g. in the notice '*WHEREAS Gentlemen have been discouraged from subscribing to the* SALISBURY JOURNAL *by the Disappointments of the Hawkers*' (*SJ*, 23 Jan. 1737/8).

[79] *Bath and Bristol Chronicle*, 25 Apr. 1771, cited in Roy M. Wiles, 'The Relish for Reading in Provincial England Two Centuries Ago', in Paul J. Korshin (ed.), *The Widening*

weekly rounds. The subscribers' greater financial commitment helped secure them priority delivery: John Jefferson Looney records a *York Mercury* notice urging subscribers to submit their names for regular delivery 'every Monday morning, before they are cry'd about the City by the hawkers, they omitting many families which should have them left at their houses' (*York Mercury*, 18 April 1720).[80] This last step in the distribution of eighteenth-century newspapers has twentieth-century parallels in the early delivery of the daily papers to regular customers (some of whom still pay in the same quarterly instalments), and the people who sell the same newspapers on street corners a little later in the day.

The business of getting the newspaper to the country customer in the eighteenth century was based on effective organizational techniques incorporating London models, but adapted to provincial needs. The administration of eighteenth-century country newspapers was structured around the requirements of distribution: provincial proprietors, like their colleagues in the capital, sometimes spread the risks in group ownership and management, although there were more country than London newspapers under the control of a single owner in the early part of the century. A close relationship between the London and the provincial book and newspaper tradesmen at this level was a component in any successful country newspaper. Commercial conditions outside London—in particular a much more widely scattered consumer population—required a highly organized regional network of reliable agents run along the lines of the large distribution network radiating from London. Provincial newsagents in turn were responsible for their own local networks of postmen, carriers, and newsmen. In many respects the provincial newspaper distribution network exemplified a division of labour with the purpose of supplying the reader with an efficient, regular delivery of goods.

The division between distribution and circulation is largely arbitrary, for the two are so closely connected. But if the multilayered distribution network was the means, then the end was circulation. The area into which a newspaper penetrated, the economic considerations that defined and redefined that area, and the readers who finally read the paper are the components.

Circle: Essays on the Circulation of Literature in Eighteenth-Century Europe (Philadelphia: University of Pennsylvania Press, 1976), 89.

[80] Cited in John Jefferson Looney, 'Advertising and Society in England 1720–1820: A Statistical Analysis of Yorkshire Newspaper Advertisements', Ph.D. diss. (Princeton University, 1983), 40 n. 43. In 1737 William Collins threatened that 'there will be no more printed, than will Supply the Subscribers' (*SJ*, 25 June 1737).

3

From Newsagent to Reader: Defining Readership

WHEN Samuel Farley attempted to establish a newspaper in Salisbury in 1715 he hoped (as we have noted) to find 200 subscribers within a radius of the market towns 'forty Miles distant from this City'.[1] Within this 40-mile radius were Marlborough, Devizes, Warminster, Shaftesbury, Yeovil, Poole, Southampton, Winchester, Andover, and Newbury, not one of which had a newspaper in 1715; yet Samuel Farley's venture failed. The costs of his proposed thrice-weekly distribution to a thinly scattered subscribing population, evidently amounting to under 200, were too great a deterrent. The *Salisbury Journal* that began in 1729 failed too, and for many of the same reasons—few subscribers, large territory, insubstantial income, large outgoings.[2] However, the *Salisbury Journal* was successfully re-established in 1736.

What made the difference after 1736? What were then the *Journal's* 'spheres of influence', the towns and villages where its readers lived, the area of effective circulation, advertising, and sales? Graham Cranfield makes a good case for plotting a newspaper's geographical area of readership by its named agents, suggesting that 'most of the advertisements came either from the immediate neighbourhood of the printing-office, or from places near the various agents'.[3] Advertisements would have been placed in the expectation that they would be read and acted upon by at least a few local readers; and the agents who handled them would have had a natural interest in promoting newspaper subscriptions and advertising within their own spheres of influence, for commissions made up a

---

[1] Farley extended his catchment area to include Exeter, where he had business and family connections.

[2] There is no known record of this *Journal's* circulation area though, for the one extant issue, the last one (no. 58, 6 July 1730), does not include a list of agents. Nor do the few advertisements give much of an idea of the paper's geographical scope.

[3] G. A. Cranfield, *The Development of the Provincial Newspaper 1700–1760* (Oxford: Clarendon Press, 1962), 203. Roy Wiles cautions against relying solely on advertisements to describe circulation area—an advertisement from a far distant town did not necessarily mean that a newspaper was regularly read there (*Freshest Advices: Early Provincial Newspapers in England* (Columbus: Ohio State University Press, 1965), 113–14).

portion of their income. In the case of the *Salisbury Journal* the very close correlation between advertisements for educational establishments and the locations of news agencies makes Cranfield's point: with few exceptions the towns that advertised schools actually had a *Journal* newsagent resident or nearby.[4]

Advertisements and lists of agents are the most obvious, indeed sometimes the only form of evidence for distribution, circulation, and readership. But there are problems with such evidence. Behind the imprints and lists of newsagents lies a whole commercial infrastructure that remained hidden except for occasional accidental glimpses: for example someone might be described as a newsagent in an advertisement on one page, but fails to make the list of agents on page 4; sometimes correspondence or account books provide the chance clues.[5] The postal system, which was a means of conveying provincial papers to readers well beyond any local distribution network, similarly was seldom mentioned as such. In addition years could go by when no newsagent was listed, or only one agent might be named at a time. Nevertheless a careful compilation and analysis of lists of newsagents can recover significant patterns of newspaper readership and influence in the provinces during the mid-eighteenth century. For the *Salisbury Journal* the early years saw agencies that were few in number but extensive in geographical terms; later, in the face of growing competition and in order to make distribution more efficient, agencies were concentrated into smaller areas. The facts of readership and circulation are closely tied to the facts of distribution, for distribution is the means to readership and circulation. Newsagents were the intermediary between reader and newspaper proprietor; and of course most of them could be described as newspaper readers themselves. An examination of nine major

---

[4] The educational advertisements in the *Salisbury Journal* were recorded in every detail for this study, making them particularly suitable for comparison. An exception to this rule of advertising, for example, was a Mr Taylor who advertised his school at Bowes near Richmond in Yorkshire ('every Branch requisite for the University, Army, Navy, or commercial Business' taught)—details were to be had from Richard Carr, Portsmouth; Henry Brough, Gosport; James Taylor at Sir Thomas Ridge's, Portsmouth; and Benjamin Collins (*SJ*, 11 Oct. 1762). It seems, though, that James Taylor, then residing in Portsmouth, was hoping to take local students with him to Yorkshire when he took over his late father's school, and this advertisement was aimed at them.

[5] U. Janssens-Knorsch tracked the distribution of the London-printed *Journal Britannique* through its published lists of agents. Ten years after his original research, when he was reading through unpublished correspondence, he learned of another agent who saw to it that copies of the *Journal* came into the hands of Frederick the Great in Berlin ('The Mutual Admiration Society—or Who Reads Whom in 18th-Century Journalism', in Hans Bots (ed.), *La Diffusion et la lecture des journaux de langue française sous l'Ancien Régime* (Amsterdam: APA–Holland University Press, 1989), 21–9).

lists of *Salisbury Journal* agents from 1739 to 1785 and comparison with those of other regional newspapers form the basis of this discussion, in which newsagents are considered for the part they played in defining numbers of readers and describing the area in which they lived.

The first *Salisbury Journal* agent to be named was one J. Everard in Andover. All that we know of him was that he was a silk dyer by trade who sold copies of the *Journal* and took in advertisements for at least a few months from 21 November 1737 until 6 February 1738. It is not clear why only Everard is mentioned, for there must have been others selling the paper by the end of 1737. Nor is it clear why he is named at all, unless, as is quite likely, the notice doubled as an advertisement for his other business concerns. The *Sherborne Mercury*, which was established about the same time as the *Journal* and, based as it was only about 35 miles from Salisbury, shared some of the same circulation area, listed two agents with its initial number of 22 February 1737, Mr Gould in Dorchester, and Mr Stoodly in Weymouth.[6] By November 1737 when Everard is first mentioned in the *Journal*, the *Mercury* could list newsagents in Dorchester, Taunton, Weymouth, Froome, Beaminster, Bridgwater, Axminster, Honiton, and Yeovil, defining a roughly circular area to the south and west of Salisbury.[7] Several of the *Mercury* agents—namely Gould, Chauklin of Taunton, and Geare on the Isle of Wight—were later incorporated into the ranks of *Salisbury Journal* agents. It is reasonable to assume that *Salisbury Journal* agents other than Mr Everard were in business in 1736 too, and that their names were published by word of mouth, handbills, or through the post.

The first real list of *Salisbury Journal* agencies appeared in the newspaper about a year after Everard. On 27 February 1739 agents were named in seven towns, including London, describing an area rather greater than that proposed by Samuel Farley a quarter century earlier (see Map 1).[8] One might expect to find agents listed in order of seniority, as in book

---

[6] J. Gould advertised books in the *Salisbury Journal*, 1736–45, but was not a listed agent. Samuel Gould of Dorchester was a *Journal* newsagent from Nov. 1746; according to an advertisement his territory included 'Dorchester *and* Weymouth, *and the Neighbourhood thereof*' (*SJ*, 17 Jan. 1757).

[7] The *Sherborne Mercury* agents listed 8 Nov. 1737 included Gould in Dorchester, Mrs Chauklin in Taunton, Stoodly in Weymouth, Edward Wiltshire in Froome, George Evely, a cutler in Beaminster, Benjamin Beal in Bridgwater, William Willmington in Axminster, William Beere, a currier in Honiton, and Thomas Geare in Yeovil.

[8] The agents, besides Collins, included 'T. ASTLEY, Bookseller in St. *Paul*'s Churchyard, *London*; N. POOL in *Farringdon, Berks*; Mr. HARRIS, jun. Bookseller in *Gloucester*; R. WARN, Bookseller in *Chippenham, Wilts*; W. BETTINSON, Printer in *Sherborne, Dorset*; Mrs. CAULKLIN, Bookseller in *Taunton, Somerset*; Mr. WELCH in *Limington, Hants . . .*'

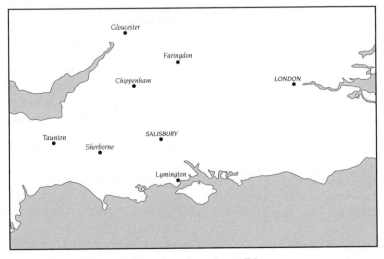

Map 1   *Salisbury Journal* agencies, 27 February 1739

imprints; instead the agents are listed in geographical order, starting with Salisbury and then working counter-clockwise from London. Their average distance from the printing office in Salisbury was 47 miles (not counting London).

Effective circulation and sales depended a good deal on contacts, both commercial and personal, and William and Benjamin Collins's own connections give shape to the area where they sent their *Journal* and collected advertisements. Faringdon, about 60 miles north of Salisbury, might seem an unusual choice for a news agency unless it is recalled that William and Benjamin Collins were both born there and still had friends and relatives there. Richard Baldwin, who was to become Benjamin Collins's first apprentice printer in 1740, had family in Faringdon too, including his uncle Robert, the local apothecary, and two cousins who were to become prominent with him in the London book trade.[9] Although the agent named there, N. Poole, remains otherwise unidentified, it is most likely that the *Salisbury Journal* initially found its way to Faringdon because of family or other personal links.

By 1739 competition from other country newspapers had to be reckoned with. The *Journal*'s catchment area then overlapped with those of a number of older papers: the *Gloucester Journal* (est. 1722), the *Reading*

---

[9] Henry Baldwin (1734–1813) and Robert Baldwin (1737–1810).

Mercury (est. 1723), the *Reading Journal* (est. 1736), and the *Sherborne Mercury* (est. 1737).[10] The Gloucester agency for the *Salisbury Journal* in the person of the bookseller Gabriel Harris junior, who extended the area of circulation to the north and west, was introduced as a result of competition with Robert Raikes's *Gloucester Journal*. For the nine months preceding this first list the two *Journals* were openly competing for subscribers: The *Salisbury Journal* had accused the *Gloucester* of dressing up Saturday's post as Monday's (22 May 1738), of pre-empting real news for Raikes's innovative but unsuccessful 'Country Common-Sense' (3 July 1738), and of publishing fictitious news of the Salisbury Assizes (31 July 1738). The Collins brothers went so far as to suggest that their paper could deliver fresher news to Gloucester readers than their own local could provide. That Raikes and the Collinses took identifiable stands on the Melksham riots of 1738 (Raikes in sympathy with the weavers as one would expect, the Collinses with the clothiers) provided a clear-cut editorial issue by which each side hoped to poach subscribers from the other's territory.[11] In a common pattern, however, competition eventually gave way to collaboration, and by 1755 Robert Raikes was himself a *Salisbury Journal* agent in a reciprocal arrangement with Benjamin Collins.

The *Sherborne Mercury* competed with the *Journal* for the same regional market. Despite that, Collins and William Bettinson, printer-proprietor of the new Sherborne paper, provide an early example of the combination of two proprietors to promote their own separate local newspapers; indeed Bettinson was one of the very first agents listed in the *Journal*. This can be explained by a commercial relationship that was much closer and more complicated than the imprint reveals. Until this first list of agents in early 1739, the *Salisbury Journal* always records that the paper was 'Printed for *William Collins* Book-seller in *Silver-street*'. 'Printed for' carries the usual suggestion that someone else actually printed the newspaper for its owner, in this case William Collins. Coinciding with the addition of the 1739 agency's list is a change in imprint that marks an important development: the paper is now 'Printed by WILLIAM COLLINS and Comp. at the PRINTING-OFFICE on the Ditch in SALISBURY; where Printing in general is perform'd in as handsome a Manner, and as cheap

---

[10] See Wiles's useful Chronological Chart in *Freshest Advices*, Appendix B.

[11] It is relatively unusual to encounter a sustained editorial position in an 18th-cent. provincial newspaper. Most claimed to be 'impartial', probably in the hopes of attracting as many readers as possible. That the *Salisbury Journal* version of the Melksham riots was adopted by Thomas Astley's *London Magazine*, while Edward Cave's *Gentleman's Magazine* reprinted opposing essays from the *Gloucester Journal* is also testimony of the close connections between the provincial newspapers and their London agents.

as in any Part of the Kingdom' (*SJ*, 27 February 1737). William Collins and Company had acquired a printing press and learned how to print.

The apparent absence of any printer to replace Charles Hooten in Salisbury before this, typographical peculiarities in some of the early numbers of the *Journal*, the relatively unusual fact of Bettinson's reciprocal news agency, and then a typographical comparison of early numbers of both newspapers all suggest that William Bettinson was printer of both the *Salisbury Journal* and the *Sherborne Mercury* from at least October 1737 until the Collinses acquired their own printing-house accommodation in 1739.[12] The connection with Sherborne and Bettinson continued in mutual news agencies for several years after the *Salisbury Journal* became self-sufficient.

The London news agency, vital for the survival of any early provincial paper, was provided at this time by Thomas Astley, whose close relationship with the Collinses has already been discussed. While there were no doubt *Journal* subscribers and readers who lived in the capital, the phrasing of the imprint—'Advertisements for this Paper are taken in by . . .'— gives the impression that the purpose of the London agents was primarily to handle advertising accounts, and to provide the relevant back files for customers to consult. This emphasis on advertising was indicative of things to come, since London bookseller-newsagents for many of the provincial newspapers were later replaced in the imprints by coffee-houses offering similar services, especially the provision of newspaper files for potential advertisers. By the end of the eighteenth century there was a further development in the system in the establishment of London agents such as William Tayler, who organized advertisements for the whole range of provincial newspapers from a central London office. A similar phenomenon can be observed in large towns that were outside a country paper's local catchment, where personal agencies were replaced or supplemented by a list of coffee-houses. The *Salisbury Journal* for example replaced booksellers in Bath, Bristol, and Exeter with coffee-house agencies, but at a slightly later date than their London colleagues. Further confirmation is found in a printed receipt dated 1781 in the Salisbury and South Wiltshire Museum, which notes that the *Journal* is 'forwarded by Post to the several Coffee-Houses in the Cities of London, Bath, Bristol, Exeter, &c.'.

Of the other agents in the *Journal*'s 1739 list—R. Warne in Chippenham,

---

[12] Bettinson did not print the new *Salisbury Journal* from the very start, but its printer for the first nine or ten months is unknown. The switch to Bettinson saw a marked improvement in typography and regularity of publication.

Sarah Chauklin in Taunton, and Mr Welch in Lymington—less is known. Their initial contact with the Collinses would have been through the growing provincial book trade: all three had already figured in *Journal* book advertisements. While there is still a great deal to be learned about the biographical side of these provincial book-trade networks (particularly in the area of family-related connections), the list appended to the 1739 imprint clearly shows that William and Benjamin Collins had by then set up a small network of agents, solidly grounded in personal and business contacts, that ensured them a reasonable chance of consolidating readership and advertising sales.

The next important list is that following the imprint of 15 December 1741, which reflects both additions to the network of agencies as well as some contraction in the geographical area:

ADVERTISEMENTS are taken in by T. ASTLEY, Bookseller, in St. *Paul's* Church-yard, *London*; N. POOL, in *Farringdon, Berks*; Mr. HARRIS, jun. Bookseller, in *Gloucester*; R. WARN, Bookseller, in *Chippenham, Wilts*; W. BETTINSON, Printer, in *Sherborn, Dorset*; T. GEARE, Bookseller, and Distributer of this Paper in the *Isle of Wight*; Mr. WELCH in *Limington, Hants*; W. FREDERICK Bookseller at *Bath*, THO. SHERWOOD in Devizes . . .

The average agency distance from Salisbury was about 39 miles at this time. Within 40 miles north-west of Salisbury there were now three agencies—in Bath, Chippenham, and Devizes—rather than just the one in Chippenham. This was to become an area in which *Journal* agents, and so presumably *Journal* readers, were to be most concentrated; in the meantime, more agents in this region provided useful support in the competition with the *Gloucester Journal*. Bath, a popular resort full of readers with the time and money for newspapers, would have been an attractive news agency and William Frederick, a well-known bookseller there, was incorporated into the *Salisbury Journal* network by April 1739. But unlike most of the others, Frederick was first introduced to *Journal* readers as a newsagent rather than as a bookseller in the advertising section, so this could have been a case where the Collinses actively solicited the help of a reputable bookseller in order to attract subscribers in his town. Devizes, which proved to be an important link in the *Journal*'s early distribution network, might represent a similar case, in that the news agency there may have been based on aggressive commercial tactics rather than on the development of existing book-trade contacts. Thomas Sherwood was the Devizes agent from at least mid-1739 until 1744, but he was never described in the lists as a bookseller. By contrast the transfer of Sarah

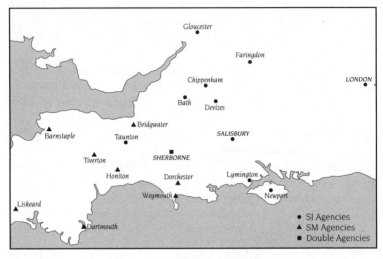

Map 2 *Salisbury Journal* and *Sherborne Mercury* agencies, 15 December 1741

Chauklin's distant Taunton news agency to Bettinson's *Sherborne Mercury* reduced the *Journal*'s average distribution area in this 1741 list and may therefore have been part of the same plan to consolidate readership, or even a gesture of co-operation. In the absence of direct evidence, one can, of course, only speculate on a newspaper proprietor's motives for adding one agent and shedding another.

Further evidence of the co-operative business arrangements between the Collins brothers and William Bettinson may be found in a comparison of the catchment areas for their two newspapers in December 1741 (see Map 2). The *Sherborne Mercury* listed nine agents in its 15 December 1741 number: 'Mr. *Gould* at *Dorchester*, Mrs. *Chauklin* at *Taunton*, Mr. *Shute* at *Tiverton*, Mr. *Gaydon, jun.* at *Barnstaple*, and Mrs. *Hayman* at *Dartmouth*, Booksellers; Mr. *Beere* at *Honiton*, Mr. *Rogers*, Tobacconist, at *Liskeard* in *Cornwall*, Mr. *Stoodly* at *Weymouth*, Mr. *B. Beale* at *Bridgwater* . . .'[13] The *Sherborne Mercury* and the *Salisbury Journal* each now had a clearly defined, distinct region of circulation, although each continued to offer a subscription service for the other. Such an arrangement could only have been the result of co-ordinated effort.

[13] Samuel Gould did not become a *Salisbury Journal* agent until 1746, although he appears in book advertisements in the *Journal* from 1743; Sarah Chauklin's name appeared in *Journal* lists only from Feb. 1739 to Apr. 1740, although she advertised books until 1762 and did not die until 1772.

By 23 March 1742 Collins had improved on the list of three months earlier, notably in the addition of John Newbery in Reading.[14] This was the beginning of a close professional and personal association with Newbery, who was still a partner in the *Reading Mercury* and based in Berkshire, that developed into a complex one that became concerned with buying and selling copyrights, sharing ideas for children's books and serial publications, and the sale of medicines. Benjamin Collins even followed his associate's example in arranging to retain a moiety of the profits from his printing business in 1770 when he was thinking of retiring.[15] The reciprocal nature of their relationship is demonstrated in Map 3, where it is clear that the younger *Journal* was allowed some room to grow. Newbery's move to London in late 1743 or early 1744 left his partner C. Micklewright in charge of Newbery's Reading operations, including the *Salisbury Journal* agency.[16] The new Oxford agent in 1742, bookseller James Fletcher, was born in Salisbury in 1710. Although he was working in Oxford by 1730 and had an office in London—at the Oxford Theatre in St Paul's—his birthplace may have been the factor that drew him into the *Journal*'s network.[17]

By early 1746 Benjamin Collins had agents in twelve provincial towns averaging 43 miles from Salisbury (47, counting the London agency): Reading, Oxford, Gloucester, Bristol, Bath, Devizes, Shaftesbury, Exeter, Poole, Lymington, Newport, and Portsmouth.[18] The *Sherborne Mercury*'s

---

[14] Agents for 23 Mar. 1742 include T. Astley in London, Newbery, J. Fletcher in Oxford, W. Frederick in Bath, J. Collet in Bristol, G. Harris jun. in Gloucester, T. Sherwood in Devizes, R. Welch in Lymington, R. Woolridge in Shaftesbury, and T. Geare in Newport. Because this list comes only three months after the last one discussed, it is considered primarily for the introduction of John Newbery and James Fletcher.

[15] Solicitor's Instructions Book, WRO 761/1.

[16] See Sidney Roscoe, *John Newbery and His Successors 1740–1814* (Wormley, Herts.: Five Owls Press, 1973), 5 n. and 34. Charles Welsh, in his *A Bookseller of the Last Century: Being Some Account of the Life of John Newbery* (London: Griffith, Farran, Okeden & Welsh; New York: E. P. Dutton, 1885), quotes from Francis Newbery's autobiography about Newbery's move to London: 'he became unable to attend to the business at Reading, and therefore gave it up, reserving to himself an annuity from its profits' (p. 21). C. Micklewright was possibly the Charles Micklewright who had been apprenticed to John Matthews in 1713 (ST3:5301).

[17] H. R. Plomer, *Dictionary of Printers and Booksellers Who Were at Work in England, Scotland, and Ireland from 1726 to 1775* (London: The Bibliographical Society, 1932), 94.

[18] 'ADVERTISEMENTS for this PAPER are also taken in by *J. Rivington* and *J. Newbery*, Booksellers, in St. *Paul's* Church-Yard, LONDON; *C. Micklewright*, Printer in *Reading*, BERKS. *J. Fletcher*, Bookseller in *Oxford*. *W. Frederick*, Bookseller in *Bath*. *R. Hayward*, Apothecary in *Bristol*. *G. Harris*, Bookseller in *Gloucester*. *J. Mackmyn*, Bookseller in *Exeter*, DEVON. *R. Woolridge*, in *Shaston*, DORSET. *R. Welch*, in *Lymington*, HANTS. *R. Baldwin*, Bookseller at *Newport, Isle of Wight*. *W. Owen*, Printer in *Portsmouth*. *T. Burrough*, in *Devizes*. *J. Brassett*, in *Pool*. And by the several Distributers of this PAPER in the Counties of *Wilts, Dorset, Hants, Somerset, Gloucester, Oxford* and *Berks* . . .'

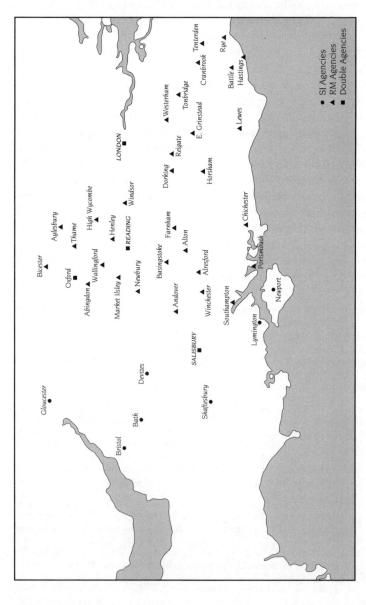

Map 3. *Salisbury Journal* and *Reading Mercury* agencies, 1743

Note: *Reading Mercury* agencies are based on Cranfield, *Development of the Provincial Newspaper Press*, Fig. 5.

imprint of the same date shows that two of its nine agents are new, but otherwise there are no changes in number of agents or in area covered. The addition of Reading, Oxford, Bristol (all over 50 miles away), and especially Exeter (85 miles away) accounts for this expansion of *Journal* territory. There was also a hiatus in two nearby agencies, when R. Warne the Chippenham agent was temporarily dropped from the list (but evidently reinstated in 1755) and William Bettinson died, not to be replaced until 1755 when Robert Goadby became the Sherborne agent. Among the newcomers—'new' that is in terms of *Journal* agents—were John Rivington and John Newbery, booksellers in St Paul's Churchyard, London, who together replaced Thomas Astley. The close personal and professional connections between Benjamin Collins and Richard Baldwin have been documented: the Isle of Wight agency, where he now replaced Thomas Geare, represented for the 18-year-old Richard Baldwin an intermediate step between the early years of his apprenticeship with Collins in Salisbury and a successful London book-trade career that was to begin with freedom of the Stationers' Company and partnership in the *London Magazine* with Thomas Astley.

The new agencies of the apothecary R. Hayward (replacing the bookseller R. Winpenny) in Bristol, the bookseller Joseph Braffett in Poole,[19] and the printer William Owen in Portsmouth, besides making the *Journal* more readily available there, also encouraged the flow of important trading, shipping, military, and colonial news from those ports to Salisbury. The Bristol agency, even as an adjunct business in Hayward's apothecary shop, must have been worth retaining, for in 1746 Bristol was the largest outport in Britain and had the second largest population in the provinces. Another new name, Robert Woolridge, continued the agency he had established in 1742 in Shaftesbury (which was also the home of Benjamin Collins's first wife Edith Good). Woolridge, sometimes in partnership with M. London, advertised books in the *Salisbury Journal* from 1739 into the 1770s. Frederick in Bath, Harris in Gloucester, and Welch in Lymington continued as *Journal* representatives, while Thomas Burrough, silversmith and bookseller, succeeded Thomas Sherwood in Devizes.

J. Mackmyn's Exeter agency is not very easy to explain in economic terms, for Exeter is much farther from Salisbury than most of its other agencies; in addition Exeter was evidently experiencing difficulties in its mid-century transition from textile town to 'commercial and banking

---

[19] Occasionally spelled 'Brassett' in the 1740s (and he is so listed in Plomer), but by the 1750s the spelling had settled to Braffett. He was still in business, with 'Mr Rule', in 1785.

centre'. There was a related loss of population until the 1770s.[20] There had been of course an earlier connection between Exeter and Salisbury in the textile trade, and the newspaper Farleys had worked in both towns at the beginning of the eighteenth century, but by the 1740s there were no obvious reasons for Collins to locate an agent there: few booksellers—or any other Exeter residents—advertised in the *Journal*. Mackmyn's short-lived relationship with the *Journal* seems to prove the point of commercial difficulty; Collins did not try to re-establish an Exeter readership until 1770.

From 1746 until 1755 there was no real list of agents added to the *Journal*'s imprint. Midway between, in an effort to capture and consolidate more of the port-towns reading market, Collins began to publish a local edition of the *Salisbury Journal* from Portsmouth and Gosport, 'The *Portsmouth* and *Gosport* Gazette, And SALISBURY JOURNAL'. The change was first noted in the main *Salisbury Journal* as from 16 April 1750, and nine later numbers from February 1752 to November 1752 are extant, so the arrangement survived for at least two and a half years.[21] The effect was described to the Portsmouth and Gosport readers:

> *As this (now united) is one of the most extensive* Country Papers *in the Kingdom, being circulated Weekly in great Numbers, throughout the Counties of* Hants, Wilts, *and* Dorset, *with Parts of* Berks, Gloucester, *and* Somerset, *and the Isles of* Wight, Purbeck, Jersey, *and* Guernsey, *the Advantages of Advertising therein, beyond what it was before, when confin'd to only* Portsmouth, Gosport, *and the* Common, *is to* [sic] *obvious to require any Thing to be said in Favour thereof.* (*SJ*, 16 April 1750)

But after assessing the benefits and costs of serving such an extensive readership, Collins, influenced by distribution costs, competition from other provincial newspapers, and probably a rise in readership closer to home, came to see merit in a more compact network. Two lists of agents about two and a half years apart serve to demonstrate: the first is from mid-1755 when the *Journal* was calling itself 'one of the most extensive Country Papers in the Kingdom' (see Map 4).[22] The number of agencies

---

[20] P. J. Corfield, *The Impact of English Towns 1700–1800* (Oxford: Oxford University Press, 1982), 26, 109.

[21] The Beinecke Library, Yale University, has what appears to be the first local issue, for 16 Apr. 1750, in its run of the *Salisbury Journal*. Wiles records the nine other nos. (24 Feb.–13 Nov. 1752) in the Bodleian Library, Oxford (*Freshest Advices*, 482).

[22] 'ADVERTISEMENTS for this JOURNAL . . . are taken in by R. BALDWIN, in Paternoster-Row, and J. NEWBERY, in St. Paul's Church Yard, London; C. MICKLEWRIGHT, in Reading; S. [i.e. N.?] POOLE, in Farringdon, Berks; J. FLETCHER, Bookseller, in Oxford; J. LEAKE and W. FREDERICK, at Bath; T. CADELL, at Bristol; T. BURROUGH, Bookseller, at Devizes; R. WARNE, at Cheppenham; W. CROUCH, at Marlborough; R. RAIKES, at Gloucester;

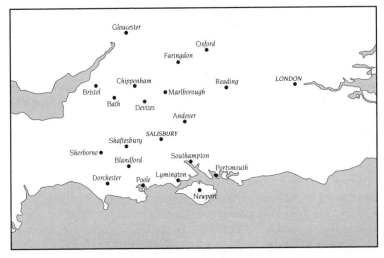

Map 4   *Salisbury Journal* agencies, 2 June 1755

had increased from thirteen in 1746 to twenty, while the average distance from Salisbury had decreased from 43 to 37 miles (or from 47 to 39 miles, if London figures). The addition of agencies in Blandford, Dorchester, Marlborough, and Southampton, and the reintroduction of those in Andover, Chippenham, and Sherborne seem to indicate greater circulation levels in the area closer to Salisbury, or at least some effort towards that end, for all these towns are within 40 miles of Salisbury. On the other hand Faringdon was in the picture again, along with Gloucester, Oxford, and London, all of them 60 miles or more from Salisbury, but all representing substantial markets that warranted the costs of covering them.

William Frederick in Bath, Thomas Burrough in Devizes, 'S. Poole'[23] in Faringdon, John Newbery in London, Richard Baldwin (now able to replace John Rivington in the London news agency), James Fletcher in Oxford, Joseph Braffett in Poole, and C. Micklewright in Reading would have been familiar names to *Salisbury Journal* customers in 1755. These

S. Poole, Bookseller, at Andover; R. Carr, at Portsmouth; J. Fyfield, at Southampton; Mr. V. Howe, in Lymington; S. Knight, at Newport, Isle of Wight; J. Braffett, at Poole; S. Gould, at Dorchester; R. Goadby, in Sherborne; J. Elliot, in Blandford; R. Woolridge and M. London, in Shaftesbury . . .' (*SJ*, 2 June 1755).

[23] Probably in error for N. Poole. The initial was changed to 'N.', 22 Sept.; the original mistake was probably due to the similarity of the Andover agent's name—S. Poole—in the same list.

same readers would have known of Robert Raikes, proprietor of the former rival *Gloucester Journal*, now a Gloucester agent for the *Salisbury Journal*. Thomas Cadell (ST3:3922) had returned to Bristol after serving an apprenticeship under Richard Hett (ST3:1771) in London,[24] and his strong professional connections with the London book trade might have made him a more useful agent than his predecessor, Hayward the apothecary. Most of these agents were independently successful booksellers based in relatively prosperous, populous towns. Their connections with the *Salisbury Journal* contributed to increased stability and readership in the mid-century.

Replacement agents saw that the *Journal* provided uninterrupted service to readers in other towns: V. Howe took over from Mr Welch in Lymington; Richard Carr followed Mr Owen in Portsmouth; and Simon Knight 'the Organist' succeeded Richard Baldwin and Jonathan Moore in Newport on the Isle of Wight. The Isle of Wight market for books and newspapers seems to have been a particularly difficult one, if the relatively high incidence of agency turnover and bankruptcies is any indication. Eight Newport agents are listed from 1741 to 1785, a comparatively high figure. Peter Milligan and Simon Knight both evidently experienced financial difficulties. The Newport agents were among the most diversified, advertising a wide variety of other goods and services—for example spectacles, a boarding school where boys are taught 'as much in one Year, as by ordinary Methods in Three', wall coverings, and musical instruments.

By adding new agencies in Blandford, Dorchester, Marlborough, and Southampton as well as reinstating the ones in Andover, Chippenham, and Sherborne, Collins was filling in the gaps in a distribution network that was now serving a more local area of readership. The agents for these towns (Joseph Elliot, Blandford; Samuel Gould, Dorchester; William Crouch, Marlborough; J. Fyfield, Southampton; Sarah Poole, Andover; R. Warne, Chippenham; and Robert Goadby, Sherborne) were primarily booksellers by trade, most of them representing a reputable, moderately successful middle rank of provincial bookseller, a status suggested by the steady numbers of book advertisements and apparent stability of business. Robert Goadby was exceptional: a learned man, formerly of Bath, The Hague, and Yeovil before finally settling in Sherborne in 1749, he alone of this group was a member of the Stationers' Company.[25] He took

---

[24] Thomas Cadell, son of James Cadell of Bristol, linen-draper, served his apprenticeship under Richard Hett, 7 May 1728–3 June 1735 (D. F. McKenzie, *Stationers' Company Apprentices 1701–1800* (Oxford: Oxford Bibliographical Society, 1978), 170).

[25] By translation from the Founders' Company (ibid. 142).

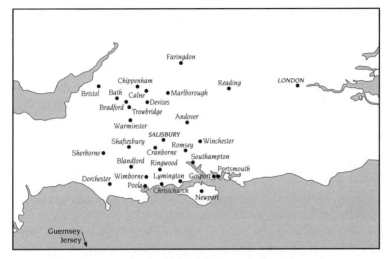

Map 5   *Salisbury Journal* agencies, 24 October 1757

over the *Sherborne Mercury* from the Bettinson family and thereafter his relationship with Collins and the *Salisbury Journal* was probably within much the same collaborative parameters as William Bettinson's had been, although Goadby's reputation was more broadly established. This process of filling in the local distribution networks is even more evident in the agents listed in October 1757 (see Map 5).[26]

The Government's latest Stamp Act, taxing all newspapers another $\frac{1}{2}d$. per copy and advertisements another 1s. per issue, had come into force only a few months before this.[27] It was not by chance that the Government's

---

[26] The agents are ranged in two columns: '[col. 1] T. Burrough, Bookseller, in *Devizes*, W. Frederick, Bookseller, in *Bath*, W. Crouch, in *Marlborough*, R. Warne, in *Chippenham*, J. Paradise, at *Caln*, J. Stuart, at *Bradford*, J. Wynn, at *Trowbridge*, P. Davies, at *Warminster*, R. Woolridge, at *Shaftesbury, Dorset*, R. Goadby, at *Sherborne*, S. Gould, at *Dorchester*, P. Elliot, at *Blandford*, J. Braffett, at *Poole*, Wm. Tory, Jun. at *Wimborne*, J. Beal, at *Cranborne*, [col. 2] John Compton, at *Ringwood, Hants*, J. Lockyer, at *Christchurch*, W. Sparrow, at *Lymington*, Wm. Woods, at *Southampton*, P. Milligan, Bookseller, at *New-Port, in the Isle of Wight*. P. Cailleteau, Merchant at Southampton, for the Islands of *Jersey* and *Guernsey*, J. Miller, at *Gosport*, R. Carr, Bookseller, at *Portsmouth*, W. Greenvile, at *Winchester*, T. Noyes, Bookseller, *Andover*, J. Whiting, at *Romsey*, C. Pocock, at *Reading, Berks*, N. Poole, at *Farringdon*, [new line:] Or the Distributers of the said Journal in the Counties of *Wilts, Dorset, Hants, Somerset*, and *Berks*. [new line:] ☞ or Advertisements for the said Journal are also taken in by the above-mentioned, and by *J. Newbery*, Bookseller, in St. *Paul's-Church Yard*, and *R. Baldwin*, in *Pater-noster-row, London*' (*SJ*, 24 Oct. 1757). The list was repeated, 7 Nov., with some alterations, two of which are worth noting: 'G. Compton' for 'John Compton', and 'T. Sparrow' for 'W. Sparrow'.   [27] 30 Geo. II, c. 19 (*SJ*, 5 July 1757).

measure and the consequent campaigns by the newspaper editors took place during the first phase of the Seven Years War, when public demand for news was high. Country proprietors were quick to capitalize on an expected drop in provincial subscriptions to the high-priced London papers, pointing out that a local one surely represented better value, for as a matter of course it contained news selected from most of the London papers, some of the Continental ones, a written newsletter or two, and local reports, as well as that other useful record of provincial life, the local advertisement. Benjamin Collins's strategy employed an open letter to his readers discussing the problem in ideological terms—the tax was described as an 'additional Clog on the Freedom of the Press'— before getting down to a discussion of its practical effects on the price of the *Salisbury Journal*. He concluded by comparing the cost of separate subscriptions to four popular London papers (the *London Evening Post*, the *General Evening Post*, the *Whitehall Evening Post*, and the *Evening Advertiser*—at £2 2s. 6d. each annually) to that of the demonstrably less expensive *Journal*, 'which not only contains the Marrow of them all, but the Gazette News, and other Intelligence three Days before any of 'em' (*SJ*, 4 July 1757). It was probably merely oversight that made Collins omit the fact that the *Evening Posts* were thrice-weeklies, geared to postal distribution to a provincial market,[28] while the *Journal* was issued only once a week. Collins complained that this tax-driven price rise would affect cost-effective quarterly subscriptions to the *Salisbury Journal*; he was eager to attract new subscribers as well as to retain former subscribers. No doubt a reading élite—the local gentry, politicians, and higher clergy who had professional interests in all the London news—continued to subscribe to their several London and local papers. But others might be persuaded to give up the Londons for the *Salisbury Journal*, and Collins wanted to leave them in no doubt where they should go to register their subscriptions.

To this end a new list of agents was published on 24 October 1757, not in the usual position at the foot of page 4, but on page 3, just after an engaging account of the 'The Woman of Kent' who refused to sleep with her husband until he had performed his patriotic duty to join the militia. After a period in which agencies had not been advertised in the *Journal*, Collins was motivated by the need to make a quick commercial recovery after the Stamp Act, and perhaps even to gain from it, if he could win

---

[28] The post left London for the provinces three evenings a week. The development of the London thrice-weeklies is discussed in Michael Harris, *London Newspapers in the Age of Walpole* (London: Associated University Presses, 1987), 33–5.

back old readers, lure enough new ones away from the London papers, and demonstrate plausible reasons for restricting credit and concessions. The discount on quarterly subscriptions was the first to go:

> while our Number sold was much larger, and our Expences and Hazards in carrying it on abundantly less, the Quarterly paper was always given in; but a Moment's Consideration must convince every one, that tho' this cou'd be done in a flourishing Trade, and under a *single Tax*, it cou'd by no Means be afforded in an impoverish'd one, overburthen'd and almost ruin'd under the grievous Load of a *double Tax*. (*SJ*, 17 October 1757)

Despite the outcry, most provincial newspapers in fact were able to weather the new tax.[29]

The 1757 notice, probably including every available agent, listed almost 50 per cent more than that of 1755, yet showed another decrease in geographical area covered. Even if the anomalous Jersey and Guernsey agencies (each over 100 miles distant, but in fact served by a single man, the Southampton-based merchant P. Cailleteau) are both included, there is a slight reduction, from an average 39 to 37 miles from Salisbury; excluding the Channel islands gives an average of 31 miles; and dropping London from the equation brings the average down to 29 miles. Readers within distribution range of thirty towns and villages now had ready access to the *Salisbury Journal* and all the products it advertised.

Map 5 shows that the area of densest coverage in 1757 extended to the north-west and directly south of Salisbury. While this pattern was roughly predicted in the earlier lists, it is confirmed in the new 1757 agencies: eight of the twelve new agents were so located, nine were within about 30 miles of Salisbury. At least six of them did not seem to have any overt connections with the book trade; they appeared in the *Journal* as agents only, and did not advertise books.[30] John Beale, an agent whose name appeared for the first time in the 1757 notice, had in fact delivered the paper from Cranborne since at least 22 July 1754 when customers were desired to note that '*At* CRANBORNE, *this* JOURNAL *is now delivered out by* JOHN BEALE, *every* Monday *Morning* . . .' Four of the others, Stuart in Bradford, Paradise in Calne, Davies in Warminster, and Tory in Wimborne, first advertised books in the *Journal* in 1757. Only two were established booksellers who could have carried with them additional

---

[29] See Wiles's Chronological Chart, *Freshest Advices*, facing p. 373.

[30] These were Lockyer in Christchurch, Beale in Cranborne, Miller in Gosport, Cailleteau in Southampton serving Jersey and Guernsey, Compton in Ringwood, and Wynn in Trowbridge.

subscribers and advertisers from a charted reading market: they were James Whiting the schoolmaster-bookseller of Romsey, and William Greenville of Winchester.

Dropping other agencies from the printed list gave further definition to *Salisbury Journal* territory in the later 1750s: Thomas Cadell in Bristol, who was later replaced, Robert Raikes in Gloucester, who died in 1757, and James Fletcher in Oxford were omitted from late 1757. While every list of *Journal* agents included a distant agent or two (responding to temporary demand or in the hopes of creating a more extended market) the trend at this time was towards servicing the needs of a reading population that was closer to hand.

For over twelve years, that is from late 1757 until 1770, the *Salisbury Journal* carried no rota of agents. Other country papers discontinued their listings of news agencies in the 1760s too, which suggests that by this time the process for subscribing and advertising with provincial newspapers was a well-established one, generally understood by the local reading public. The proprietors could afford to use the column space for other purposes. J. Jefferson Looney thinks that 'around 1760 networks of agents begin to disappear from the publishing information newspapers carried each week, either because space was becoming too valuable to permit allocation of several inches a week to giving the network or because the list had grown to impractical lengths'.[31] This mechanism could be disrupted by a major change in management or territory, however, and in that case a new list might serve to forestall confusion. Indeed the *Journal*'s printed list of agents reappeared in 1770, coinciding with a series of administrative changes after Benjamin Collins apparently sold at least two quarter-shares in the copyright.[32] The new imprint for 1 January 1770 notes that it is now 'Printed by J. ALEXANDER, and Sold by G. SEALY, at the Printing-Office, on the New Canal . . .' with the further notice a week later that

THE *Proprietors of this Journal beg leave to observe to the public, that, in return for their favours, they have now very considerably enlarged their plan; and extended the size of their paper almost beyond any other in the kingdom, which will not only enable them to be still more copious in their intelligence, but also more immediately obliging their correspondents, by obviating their frequent complaints of advertisements and letters, &c. being postponed or omitted, which has often been the case merely for want of room.*

[31] 'Advertising and Society in England 1720–1820: A Statistical Analysis of Yorkshire Newspaper Advertisements', Ph.D. diss. (Princeton University, 1983), 42.

[32] See Ch. 2, Table 2.

The great sale, and very large extent in the circulation of this Journal make it unnecessary to say any thing, in favour of advertising therein . . .
(*SJ*, 8 January 1770; slightly expanded 15 January 1770)

Appended was a new list of London and provincial agents, the country newsagents still twenty-eight in number after twelve years.[33]

The distribution and composition of agencies was somewhat different though (see Map 6): The bookseller Barnabas Thorn was an addition, the last *Journal* newsagent in Exeter to be listed, perhaps as part of an attempt to take advantage of Exeter's improving economic condition at this time. Likewise with Mrs Farley (that is the printer Hester Farley, daughter of Felix Farley) the *Salisbury Journal* renewed its connections with Bristol and the Farley family one more time. Other new agents included Joseph Pote (ST3:1180) the well-known Windsor and Eton bookseller, J. Wimpey of Newbury, bookseller, and Arthur Brown, a Honiton bookseller. The additions, all of them relatively distant from Salisbury, extended the average radius of circulation to 36 miles (38 miles with London). But these far-off newsagents coincide with a change in proprietorship, and therefore may reflect the commercial connections and business tactics of the *Journal*'s new part-owners, rather than of Benjamin Collins.

Otherwise the area where *Salisbury Journal* readers lived, as defined by news agencies, remained much the same: the concentration to the north-west remained precisely as it was in 1757, with agents in Chippenham, Calne, Bath, Bradford, Trowbridge, Devizes, and Warminster. Coverage of the area due south of Salisbury remained unchanged except that there was no longer a Lymington agent. The outline of the local area of readership, including the Isle of Wight and the ports of Southampton

---

[33] 'In London, by J. Wilkie, and J. [i.e. T] Carnan and Newbery, booksellers, in St. Paul's church-yard; R. Baldwin, and S. Crowder, in Pater-noster-row; and F. Blyth, at the Royal Exchange. [Then listed in one column:] In Reading, by Mrs. Smart, bookseller. Windsor, Mr. Pote, bookseller. Newbury, Mr. Wimpey. Marlborough, Mr. W. Crouch, bookseller. Devizes, Mrs. Maynard, ditto. Calne, Mr. T. Peters, ditto. Chippenham, Mr. Gale and Mr. Simpson, ditto. Bath, Mr. Frederick and Mr. Lake [i.e. Leake], ditto. Bristol, Mrs. Fatley [i.e. Farley], printer. Exeter, Mr. B. Thorn, bookseller. Honiton, Mr. Brown, bookseller. Sherborne, Mr. Goadby, printer. Weymouth, Mr. Crouch. Dorchester, Mr. Gould, bookseller. Blandford, Mr. Clench, post master. Wimborne, Mr. Wm. Tory, bookseller. Christchurch, Mr. G. Lockyer. Ringwood, Mr. James Collins. Southampton, Mr. James Linden, bookseller. Portsmouth, Mr. R. Carr, bookseller. Gosport, Mr. Wm. Dawkins, bookseller. Newport, Isle of Wight, Mr. Wise, bookseller. Romsey, Mr. James Whiting, bookseller; Andover, Mr. T. Baldwin, bookseller. Warminster, Mr. P. Davies, bookseller. Trowbridge, Mr. J. Marler, bookseller. Bradford, Mr. J. Stuart, bookseller. Poole, Mr. J. Braffett' (8 Jan. 1770). J. Beale in Cranborne, a *Journal* newsagent in 1757, was added to this new list, 15 Jan. 1770. The omission of his name, 1 Jan. 1770, may have been simply oversight.

and Portsmouth to the south-east, seems to have stabilized under Benjamin Collins's direction between the mid-1750s and 1770.

Of the twenty-three country towns and villages listed in both 1757 and 1770, ten had different agents in the new listing, a change in personnel only to be expected after twelve years. But thirteen—more than half— continued in their agencies. London had several additional agents: in 1757 *Journal* customers in London were directed to John Newbery and Richard Baldwin; in 1770 they could consult John Wilkie (ST3:4287?), and John Newbery's successors Thomas Carnan and Francis Newbery (ST3:2799) in St Paul's Churchyard; Richard Baldwin and Stanley Crowder (ST3:4021) in Paternoster Row; or Francis Blyth (ST3:7179) at the Royal Exchange. The distribution of newsagents in London's three major publishing-trade districts was clearly strategic in 1770, but London bookseller-newsagents were soon to be superseded by the coffee-houses (the London, Chapter, and Guildhall for the *Salisbury Journal* according to the imprint of 16 November 1772).

The most notable change in 1770 was a more overt emphasis on the book trade, when nearly all the agents were described either as booksellers or printers. Twenty-two of the twenty-eight provincial agencies are actually described as booksellers or printers. Of the remaining six, two can in fact be identified as booksellers by trade (Wimpey in Newbury and Braffett in Poole, whose descriptors were omitted); one, Mr Clench in Blandford, was a postmaster, and another, James Collins in Ringwood, was a shopkeeper; the trades of the remaining two are unknown. This can be compared with the 1757 list in which only five of the twenty-eight provincial agents are actually described as booksellers, and a total of nineteen in that list can be identified as booksellers from other evidence. This was symptomatic of the trend towards greater specialization of manufacture through the eighteenth century, but translated into newspaper-trade terms suggests that newsagents were preferably recruited from those who already dealt with paper products such as books, stationery, and printed forms and advertising and were thereby links in established trade networks. The cutlers, silversmiths, apothecaries, and others who had handled newspapers as a sideline earlier in the century were outdated. Potential subscribers and advertisers within the distribution radius of Salisbury could logically assume that their local bookseller was also an agent for the *Salisbury Journal*.

The bias towards the book trade was there from the beginning of course, for the businesses of newspapers and of books were naturally closely allied: newspapers, as Michael Harris has suggested, were the engines that drove the book trade. What was different in the 1770 list was that it drew the reader's attention to the connection, even through the typographical arrangement of the newsagents' names in a column to give prominence to their epithets. This emphasis is not uniformly evident within the last three lists to be discussed, but both the 1783 and 1785 lists are prefaced with the observation that 'To each Place is annexed the Name of some respectable Bookseller, or other Person . . .' The fact that so many towns and villages could now support a local bookseller, or even a printer, is further evidence of the growth of the reading population in eighteenth-century provincial England.

Benjamin Collins sold some of his shares in the *Salisbury Journal* in 1770 and bought them back five years later,[34] in the meantime employing his son Benjamin Charles to run the 'Business of the Shop then kept by him in Salisbury' and John Johnson to run his printing office. If Collins senior's intention was now to retire to the comparatively quiet life of a country banker, his timing was not good. Evidence suggests that the *Journal* was experiencing difficulties under its new managers, not the least of which would have been James Linden's rival newspaper, the *Hampshire Chronicle*, founded in July 1772. Exactly what the *Journal* proprietors had against the new paper may be seen in Map 6, which shows the distribution of *Chronicle* agents into *Salisbury Journal* territory. The *Journal* (17 August 1772) took the threat to its readership seriously:

THE SALISBURY JOURNAL presents his most respectful compliments to his Readers in general, throughout the county of Hants, and hopes, as he has been their faithful servant for upwards of thirty years past, and punctually supplied them with the earliest and most authentic intelligence during the whole time, that they will take no part in the very unnecessary opposition forming against him, in one part of their county, but continue to give him their usual kind reception, and he will make it his constant endeavour still more and more to merit their favours.

* ** The SALISBURY JOURNAL is, without exception, the most extensive Country Paper in the kingdom, being circulated weekly by upwards of twenty distributors, (besides the mails, carriers, and other conveyances) in the most regular manner, throughout the counties of *Wilts, Hants,* and *Dorset,* part of *Somersetshire, Gloucestershire, Berkshire,* and *Oxfordshire,* the isles of *Wight, Purbeck, Jersey,* and *Guernsey*; and to numbers of Gentlemen residing out of the reach of the distributors, it is constantly sent by the post; also to some of the most public Coffee-houses

---

[34] Bills and Answers dated 27 Nov. 1783 (PRO E. 112/1959/147). The transaction probably took place in late June or very early July: the imprint first reflecting the change in management appeared with the 3 July 1775 number.

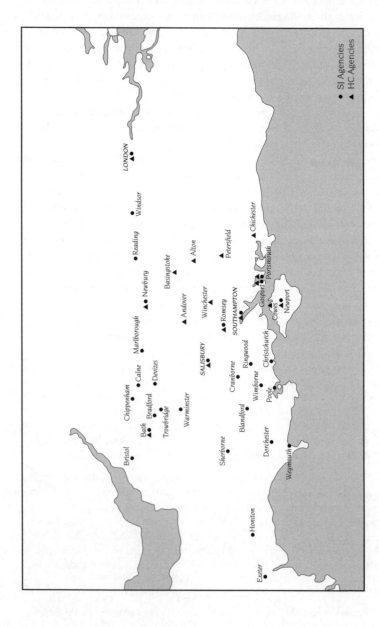

Map 6 *Salisbury Journal* agencies, 8 January 1770, and *Hampshire Chronicle* agencies, 24 August 1772

● SJ Agencies
▲ HC Agencies

LONDON

Windsor

● Reading

● Newbury

Basingstoke ▲

▲ Alton

▲ Petersfield

Chichester ▲

Portsmouth

Gosport

Cowes

Newport

● Marlborough

▲ Andover

Winchester ▲

Romsey ▲

SOUTHAMPTON

● Chippenham

● Calne

● Devizes

SALISBURY ▲

Cranborne

Ringwood

Christchurch

Wimborne

Poole

● Bradford

Bath ▲

Trowbridge

● Warminster

Blandford

Bristol ●

Sherborne ●

Dorchester ●

Weymouth ●

● Honiton

Exeter ●

in London; from whence it may reasonably be concluded there is not the least occasion for any other News-paper in this part of the kingdom, (so amply supplied already) on any pretence whatever, especially at a time of profound Peace, when there is so very little stirring, that even a single column of the SALISBURY JOURNAL would easily contain all the material news of the whole week. Indeed to the Merchant, the Tradesman, the Manufacturer, and, in short, every Man of Business, the great number and variety of Advertisements in an old established Journal, are not only matter of amusement, but of real use, which a *new paper*, printed in a corner of the county, hemm'd in on one side by the sea, without any resource of country, but what is already supplied, on the other, can never attain to, as the inutility of advertising therein is too obvious to need the least observation to be made thereon.

THE EDITOR.

This 'card' was left by an alarmed editor (almost certainly Benjamin Collins temporarily out of retirement), addressed to all his Hampshire readers, but more particularly to those who had thoughts of taking the new *Hampshire Chronicle*. It has quite a bit to say about newspaper strategy, circulation, distribution, and content, and is most convincing in its description of *Journal* readership. It is clear that Hampshire folk had been reading the Salisbury paper since its inception 'upwards of thirty years past', and that its very extensive distribution should have confirmed them in their choice of reading material. Hampshire readers were concerned that their newspaper reach them regularly, punctually, and of course with all the news. But the real emphasis here is on the effective advertising a long-established newspaper can provide: Collins's card suggests that any local subscriber will find advertisements a good read, but one category of reader 'the Merchant, the Tradesman, the Manufacturer, and, in short, every Man of Business' will find them indispensable. The 'Gentleman' is the other category specifically mentioned.

James Linden did manage to establish a newspaper that is still running today—many of Collins's readers were persuaded to change allegiance—but he himself was driven to bankruptcy within a few years, the *Hampshire Chronicle* was bought out by a consortium controlled by Collins, and Linden returned to schoolteaching. In the end Collins was able to keep all his readers, though eventually he had to oversee both titles, the *Salisbury Journal* and the *Hampshire Chronicle*, to do so. The struggle to retain its Hampshire readership is evident even in *Journal* imprints. There were five major changes in imprint during this time, and the number of country towns with agents fluctuated greatly, dropping to only sixteen in late 1772, rising to twenty-nine in March 1774, then dropping to twenty-three when Collins resumed control. The *Journal* gave itself a more comprehensive name in December 1772, the *Salisbury and Winchester Journal*. Constant transitions do not boost readership. In July 1775 a new imprint with a new list of agents sought to stabilize the situation.[35]

Twenty-three provincial towns were listed with a total of twenty-nine agents, including Joseph Hillary, the first agent in Salisbury outside the *Journal* printing office. This drop in numbers probably had more to do with the battle for readers in the early 1770s than with Benjamin Collins's return. Nevertheless the borders of local readership survived roughly intact: there was a continued concentration of agencies to the north-west, the south, and the south-east, reinforced by new agents in Tippet (now called Tidpit), a village about 10 miles more or less south of Salisbury, and West Cowes on the Isle of Wight (see Map 7). Even with the loss of named agencies in Calne, Christchurch, Sherborne, Trowbridge, and Weymouth, and the addition of agencies in Stockbridge and Whitchurch to the east, the geographical shape of the local reading market remained much the same, albeit secured through a different distribution of agents. The catchment area was further defined with the pruning of the more distant branches of the *Journal* distribution network (that is Honiton, Exeter, Windsor, Reading, and Bristol). Of course, by this time some of these towns may well have been served by coffee-houses rather than personal agents; indeed, a printed receipt from Collins and Johnson in 1780 notes that the *Journal* was posted to coffee-houses in London, Bath, Bristol, and Exeter.[36]

At any rate London was now the only town in the published list that was much more than 40 miles from Salisbury. The effect was greatly to

---

[35] The list itself is important primary evidence, and this and the last two lists of agents discussed will be cited in full. That for 3 July 1775 reads: 'at the *London, Chapter, Guildhall*, and *Peele*'s Coffee-Houses, in *London*;—also by [in 4 cols., col. 1:] Mr. BAKER, Bookseller, at Southampton. Mr. BALDWIN, at Andover, *Hants*. Mr. BEALE, at Cranbourn, *Dorsetshire*. Mr. BRAFFETT, at Poole, *Dorsetshire*. Mr. BREADHOWER, at Gosport. Mr. CARR, Bookseller, at Portsmouth, *Herts*. [col. 2:] Mr. COLE, at Stockbridge, *Hants*. Mr. COLLINS, Shopkeeper, at Ringwood, *Hants*. Mr. CROUCH, at Marlborough, *Wilts*. Mr. DAWKINS, at Gosport, *Hants*. Mr. DAVIES, at Warminster, *Wilts*. Mr. DEACON, at West-Cowes, Isle of Wight. [col. 3:] Mr. DEMPSTER, Mr. CLENCH, and Mr. SIMMONDS, at Blandford, *Dorset*. Mr. FREDERICK, and Mr. CRUTTWELL, Bath. Mr. GOULD, at Dorchester. Mrs. MAYNARD, at Devizes, *Wilts*. Mr. ROSS, School-master, at Whitchurch, *Hants*. [col. 4:] Mr. SMITH, in Marlborough, *Wilts*. Mr. SIMPSON, at Chippenham, *Wilts*. Mr. STUART, at Bradford, *Wilts*. Mr. TORY, in Wimborne, *Dorset*. Mr. WHITING, at Romsey, *Hants*. Mr. WOOLRIDGE, at Shaftesbury, *Dorset*. [across the bottom:] Mr. WARNE, at the Angel, Tippet; Mr. WISE, at Newport, *Isle of Wight*; and Mrs. HILLARY, *Sarum*.—Of whom may be had, all the BOOKS and MEDICINES advertised in this *Paper*.'

[36] Salisbury and S. Wiltshire Museum, Salisbury.

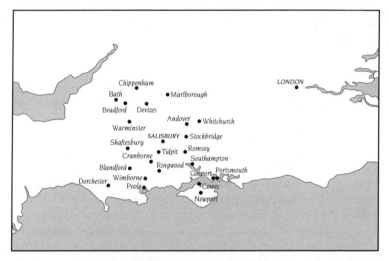

Map 7   *Salisbury Journal* agencies, 3 July 1775

reduce the total geographical area in which readers had access to the *Salisbury Journal* through intermediary personal agents: from an average of 36 miles distance from Salisbury to 25 miles (or 38 miles to 28 miles taking London into consideration). The list of 3 July 1775 marked a return to the wholly competent management of Benjamin Collins, now in partnership with his son Benjamin Charles and with John Johnson, a combination that was to last until Collins senior's death ten years later. One gauge of the effectiveness of this arrangement is the next available list of agents, the one that appeared in 1783.[37]

---

[37] 'This Paper is published every SUNDAY and MONDAY through the extensive Counties of WILTS, HANTS, DORSET, SOMERSET, and Part of BERKS; particularly in the following Cities and Towns, and also in all the intermediate Villages.—To each Place is annexed the Name of some respectable Bookseller, or other Person . . . [in 6 cols., col. 1:] Andover, Hants, Mr. Baldwin. Blandford, Dorset, Mr. Simmonds. Bradford, Wilts, Mr. Stuart. Bridport, Dorset, Mr. Ackerman. Castlecary, Somerset. Chippenham, Wilts, Mr. Angell. Christchurch, Hants, Mr. Lockyer. Corfe-Castle, Dorset, Mr. Ingram. Cowes, Isle of Wight, Mr. Deacon. [col. 2:] Cranborne, Dorset, Mr. Beale. Devizes, Wilts, Miss Maynard. Dorchester, Dorset, Mess. Gould and Thorne, and Mr. Lockett. Fareham, Hants. Fordingbridge, Hants, Mr. Slann. Frome, Somerset, Mr. Daniel. Gosport, Hants, Mr. Dawkins. Hindon, Wilts, Mr. Bennett. [col. 3:] Lavington, Wilts, Mr. Holmes. Lymington, Hants, Mrs. Beeston. Marlborough, Wilts, Mr. Harold. Melksham, Wilts. Mere, Wilts, Mrs. Pittman. Milborne Port, Dorset. Newport, Isle of Wight, Miss Wise's. Petersfield, Hants. Poole, Dorset, Mr. Braffett and Mr. Rule. [col. 4:] Portsmouth, Hants, Mr. Breadhower. Ringwood, Hants, Mr. Greaves. Romsey, Hants, Mrs. Whiting. Shaftesbury, Dorset, Mr. Adams, and Mr. England. Shepton Mallet, Somerset, Mr. Cary. Sherborne,

Within eight years of Collins's renewed proprietorship, the number of towns incorporated into the *Salisbury Journal*'s network of agencies more than doubled, from twenty-three in 1775 to fifty-three in 1783 (see Map 8). Twelve of the towns—Castlecary, Fareham, Melksham, Milborne Port, Petersfield, Swindon, Taunton, Waltham, Westbury, Whitchurch, Wickham, and Wilton—do not have a named agent, and they were probably listed as territorial markers staking a claim until proper newsagents could be engaged, or as assurance to local readers that the *Journal* was soon to be more readily accessible. Most of them were within the catchment area already described. Taunton, which was listed without an agent in 1783, was the only one of these towns any great distance from Salisbury, so the picture in Map 8 is one of great concentration of news agencies within a well-defined distribution area. The average distance was slightly greater than in 1775: 28 miles including only those towns with personal agents; 29 miles adding the small provincial towns without agents.

That still left 37 provincial towns and villages (not counting the coffeehouse agencies) with 'some respectable Bookseller, or other Person' who would forward readers' book orders, subscriptions, and advertisements to the printing office in Salisbury in the 1780s. Booksellers were in the majority, although agencies for a number of the smaller intermediate villages were filled with 'other Persons' who had no evident connection with the book trade. Not every Wessex village had a resident bookseller in the eighteenth century; but certainly any Wessex reader could expect to find a means to books and newspapers within easy reach. Readers placed farther afield found a different sort of agent: from at least the early 1780s subscribers and advertisers in populous cities such as Bath, Bristol, and Exeter, as well as London, could find most provincial newspapers in the coffee-houses, which had for years made a commercial point of providing an attractive selection of London and country papers. When these agencies are added to the network, the average distance from Salisbury of all the 1783 agents becomes nearly 32 miles.

One last list of agents completes this outline of regional newspaper

Dorset, Mess. Goadby and Co. Southampton, Hants, Mr. Baker. Stockbridge, Hants, Mr. Hulbert. [col. 5:] Sturminster, Dorset, Mr. Colburne. Swindon, Wilts. Taunton, Somerset. City of Winchester, Mr. Sadler. Waltham, Hants. Wareham, Dorset, Mr. Dampier. Warminster, Wilts, Mr. Davies. City of Wells, Somerset, Mr. Cass. Westbury, Wilts. [col. 6:] Weymouth, Dorset, Miss Thorne. Wilton, Wilts. Wimborne, Dorset, Mrs. Tory. Wincaunton, Somerset, Mr. Mogg. Wickham, Hants. Whitchurch, Hants. . . . [new para.:] This Paper is also forwarded by the Post to the Houses of many of the principal Nobility and Gentry in London and the Country; also to the several Coffee-houses in London, Bath, Bristol, Exeter, &c. . . .' (*SJ*, 28 Apr. 1783).

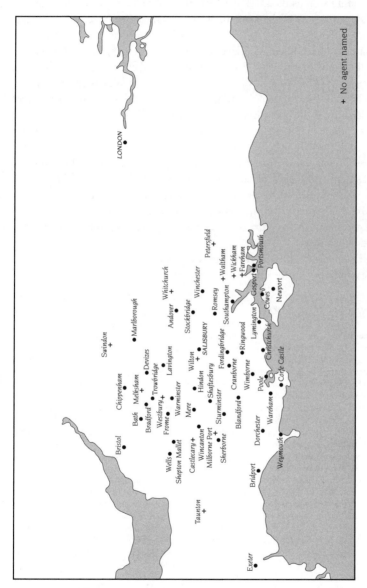

Map 8 *Salisbury Journal* agencies, 28 April 1783

LONDON

Bristol

Taunton +

Exeter

Bridport

Weymouth

Wells

Shepton Mallet

Castlecary +

Wincanton

Milborne Port +

Sherborne

Bath

Bradford

Westbury +

Frome

Warminster

Mere

Chippenham

Melksham +

Trowbridge

Devizes

Lavington

Hindon

Shaftesbury

Sturminster

Blandford

Dorchester

Wareham

Corfe Castle

Poole

Wimborne

Cranborne

Fordingbridge

Wilton

SALISBURY

Swindon +

Marlborough

Whitchurch

Andover +

Stockbridge

Winchester

Romsey

Southampton

Ringwood

Christchurch

Lymington

Cowes

Newport

Gosport •

Portsmouth

Petersfield +

Waltham +

Wickham +

Fareham +

+ No agent named

readership. It is the one published in January 1785, just a month before Benjamin Collins died.[38] The distribution of agencies is similar to that of 1783, with most of the same towns represented (see Map 9). The significant difference is that by 1785 many of the vacancies for *Journal* newsagents had been filled: Mr Gardiner handled the newspaper in Castlecary; Hallett in Milborne Port; Poole in Taunton; Baker in Waltham; Phipps in Westbury; Miss Wilce in Wickham; and Barnard in Wilton. A few towns— Melksham, Petersfield, Swindon, and Whitchurch—were dropped, so that Fareham was the only place without an agent. There were a few additions: Case junior in Amesbury; Peacocke in Basingstoke; and Dawkins junior in Guildford. In April 1783 Collins and Johnson had listed fifty-three cities, towns, and villages, forty-one with agents of one kind or another. Less than two years later, in January 1785, they listed fifty-two places, all but one supplied with agents. The overall impression is that the *Salisbury Journal* inherited by Benjamin Charles Collins in 1785 was a lively commercial concern, supported by a constantly growing number of readers and subscribers.

These eighteenth-century lists of agents were both descriptive and prescriptive—on the one hand they represent efforts to meet a perceived

[38] 'This paper is published every SUNDAY and MONDAY through the extensive Counties of WILTS, HANTS, DORSET, SOMERSET, and Part of BERKS; particularly in the following Cities and Towns, and also in all the intermediate Villages. . . . [in 6 cols., col. 1:] Amesbury, Wilts, Mr. Case, jun. Andover, Hants, Mr. Baldwin and Maud. Basingstoke, Hants, Mr. Peacocke. Blandford, Mr. Simmonds & Mr. Sollers. Bradford, Wilts, Mr. Stuart, Boookseller [*sic*]. Bridport, Dorset, Mr. Ackerman, Ditto. Castlecary, Somerset, Mr. Gardiner. Chippenham, Mr. Angell and Mr. Forty. Christchurch, Hants, Mr. Lockyer. [col. 2:] Corfe-Castle, Dorset, Mr. Ingram. Cowes, Isle of Wight, Mr. Deacon. Cranborne, Dorset, Mr. Beale. Devizes, Wilts, Miss Maynard, Bookseller. Dorchester, Dorset, Mess. Gould and Thorne, and Mr. Lockett, Booksellers. Fareham, Hants. Fordingbridge, Hants, Mr. Slann. Frome, Somerset, Mr. Daniel, Bookseller. [col. 3:] GOSPORT, Hants, Mr. Watts, jun. Guildford, Surry, Mr. Dawkins, jun. Hindon, Wilts, Mr. Bennett. Lavington, Wilts, Mr. Holmes. Lymington, Hants, Mr. R. Jones. Marlborough, Wilts, Mr. Harold. Mere, Wilts, Mrs. Pittman. Milborne Port, Somerset, Mr. Hallett. [col. 4:] NEWPORT, Isle of Wight, Miss Wise's, and Mr. Albin, Druggists. POOLE, Mr. Braffett and Mr. Rule. PORTSMOUTH, Mr. Breadhower. Portsmouth Common, Mr. Crist. Ringwood, Hants, Mrs. Freames. ROMSEY, Hants, Mrs. Whiting. Shaftesbury, Mr. Adams, and Mr. England. Shepton Mallet, Somerset, Mr. Cary. [col. 5:] Sherborne, Dorset, Mess. Goadby and Co. and Mr. Gander, Booksellers. SOUTHAMPTON, Hants, Mr. Baker. Stockbridge, Hants, Mr. Hulbert. Sturminster, Dorset, Mr. Colburne. Taunton, Somerset, Mr. Poole. City of WINCHESTER, Messrs. Robbins and Gilmour, Printers and Booksellers. Waltham, Hants, Mr. Baker. [col. 6:] Wareham, Dorset, Mr. Dampier. Warminster, Wilts, Mr. Davies. City of Wells, Somerset, Mr. Ca[ss]. Westbury, Wilts, Mr. Phipps. Weymouth, Dorset, Miss Thorne. Wilton, Wilts, Mr. Barnard. Wimborne, Dorset, Mrs. Tory. Wincaunton, Somerset, Mr. Mogg. Wickham, Hants, Miss Wilce. [new line:] With many other smaller Towns, which want of Room obliges us to omit. . . . also to the several Coffee-houses in London, Bath, Bristol, Exeter, &c. . . .' (*SJ*, 17 Jan. 1785).

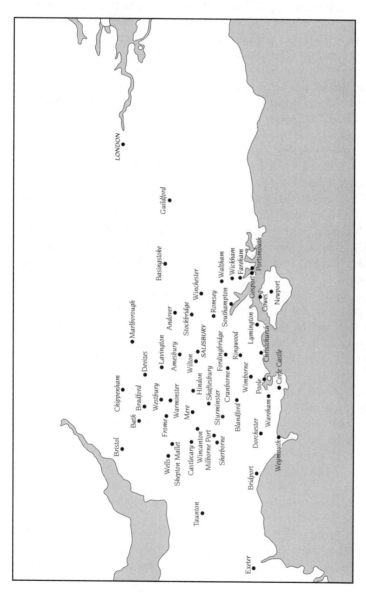

Map 9   *Salisbury Journal* agencies, 8 January 1785

local demand for reading matter, but on the other they attempt to increase that readership through the marketing efforts of more and more
local agents. Collins occasionally discussed the logistics of getting the
Salisbury Journal to new subscribers in out-of-the-way places, suggesting
in 1756 that the 'great Number of Gentlemen and others, who live some
at a great Distance, and others out of the Road of any Distributer or Post-
Boy' should appoint a neighbourhood location within the established
postal and newspaper circuits where 'one or more Papers' could be left
for collection. Enough readers put to such inconvenience might be sufficient cause to set up a new agency though: anyone who regularly received
the *Salisbury Journal* was not only a paying newspaper subscriber but was
also a likely customer for all the other reading material advertised in its
columns—books sold in parts, subscription books, books sewn, bound, or
in blue covers, magazines, almanacs, etc.—as well as stationery supplies,
medicines, or other goods.

A general pattern of reader distribution can be detected in all this:
early *Salisbury Journal* readers made a thinly scattered, widespread
population that stretched from Taunton to Gloucester, Faringdon, and
London in the 1730s, 1740s, and early 1750s. Competition with other
newspapers was relatively limited at this time and William and Benjamin
Collins were able to employ *Journal* newsagents wherever they had good
personal and business contacts.[39] Readership seems to have multiplied
and consolidated during the late 1750s and the 1760s coinciding with the
eventful Seven Years War, and was strong enough to override the temporary effects of the additional stamp duty imposed in mid-1757. Pressure from new subscribers for uninterrupted service to those intermediate
towns and villages must have assisted the process of filling in local agencies. During this time *Journal* territory assumed a geographical shape that
would be recognized by its present editor. The 1770s and 1780s found
roughly the same territory populated by more agents serving more readers.
Those readers who lived and travelled far away from Salisbury (that is
within the catchment area of another provincial newspaper) still had a
good chance of reading the *Salisbury Journal* in other local coffee-houses
and reading-rooms.

The trend towards a more concentrated reading population is evident
still. More than 200 years later the present *Salisbury Journal* reaches about
25,000 households within a territory that is defined to a certain extent by

---

[39] There were about thirty provincial newspapers in business in 1740 (see Wiles, *Freshest
Advices*, Appendix B).

competing newspapers and is considerably smaller than that enjoyed in the eighteenth century. No longer family-owned, the *Journal* is evidently the most successful in the Southern Newspapers Group. And until recent years when wholesalers have taken over, a similar system of distribution from printing office to local newsagents to readers was in operation—a system that Benjamin Collins would have had no trouble recognizing.[40]

Fairly accurate figures for the geographical area in which the *Salisbury Journal* was distributed and read can be constructed from lists of agents, but they cannot reveal much about the number of papers printed nor say precisely who read them. In fact very little is known about edition sizes for any provincial newspaper. Cranfield thought that 100 to 200 paying subscribers was viable early in the century, figures borne out by Samuel Farley's hope for 200 subscribers to his *Salisbury Post Man* in 1715.[41] K. G. Burton estimated that the *Reading Mercury* sold 'no more than 400 copies each week when it was first issued [in 1723], and by the end of the century the probable weekly issue was about 1000 copies'.[42] Evidence collected by Cranfield, most of it of course based on claims made by the newspapers themselves, suggests that edition size remained around 200 to 300 for most provincial papers until the 1730s; after this there was a steady increase. Concrete support for this is to be found in the ledgers of Christopher Etherington's *York Chronicle*, which R. Davies was able to consult in the mid-nineteenth century before they disappeared: The *York Chronicle* was printed in two editions of 3,000 in 1772 to be given away free during an intensive campaign for subscribers; the first edition that was actually *sold* numbered 1,650, and production then reached a high of 2,000 in 1773. Etherington had printed 15,000 copies each of his pro-spectus and an accompanying circular letter, which he sent out in 130 parcels to 'agents in all the principal towns within the counties of York, Lincoln, and Durham, and in several towns in each of the other north-ern and midland counties'. The more important towns, including Lon-don, received 1,000 copies, others 100 to 500.[43] The *Hampshire Chronicle* account books record that it was regularly published in editions of just over 1,000 in the late 1770s, lending further support to the idea of in-creasing circulation figures through the century. The *Hampshire Chronicle*

[40] *Salisbury Journal and Times Series: The Facts* [Salisbury, 1989].

[41] Cranfield, *Development of the Provincial Newspaper*, 169.

[42] K. G. Burton, *The Early Newspaper Press in Berkshire (1723–1855)* (Reading: pub-lished by the author, 1954), 5.

[43] Robert Davies, *A Memoir of the York Press, with Notices of Authors, Printers, and Stationers in the Sixteenth, Seventeenth, and Eighteenth Centuries* (Westminster: Nichols & Sons, 1868), 332–5.

was contemporary with the *Salisbury Journal*, the two papers had a shared management, and their catchment areas overlapped, but the *Chronicle* was a paper recently rescued from bankruptcy in 1778 that had to compete for subscribers with the long-established *Salisbury Journal*, *Reading Mercury*, and *Reading Journal*.[44] There are no solid production figures for the *Salisbury Journal*; the *Chronicle*'s can only suggest that at this time the more successful *Salisbury Journal* must have been produced in greater numbers.

Evidence for *Salisbury Journal* readership may be found in the newspaper itself, as well as in one surviving invoice. Early on William Collins made it clear that production, distribution, and circulation had to be closely linked, when he urged those interested in seeing the next number of the *Journal* to contact him within a few days—'otherwise there will be no more printed, than will Supply the Subscribers' (*SJ*, 25 June 1737). Only a small percentage of the edition would have been intended for casual purchase, with the bulk of sales planned for regular subscribers. References to numbers of subscribers are usually oblique and overly generous: in 1745 Benjamin Collins claimed that his was 'one of the most extensive *Country Papers* in the *Kingdom*, being distributed Weekly in great Numbers thro' the several *Counties* of WILTSHIRE, DORSETSHIRE, SOMERSETSHIRE, GLOUCESTERSHIRE, BERKSHIRE, HAMPSHIRE, and the ISLES OF WIGHT, PURBECK, JERSEY, and GUERNSEY' (*SJ*, 24 September 1745). 'Great' and 'extensive' are not very useful descriptors here, although it is helpful to know that distribution extended to Jersey and Guernsey twelve years before an agent was listed there. A correspondent, one Isaac Jones, wrote that 'your Paper is in high esteem and spreads over most of the Western Counties' (*SJ*, 17 December 1750); there were 'repeated Desires to be supplied with this Journal for a great Number of Gentlemen and others, who live some at a great Distance . . .' (*SJ*, 28 June 1756); Z.Z. of Southampton advertised for work, selecting the *Journal*, he said, because 'this Paper is so very extensive' (*SJ*, 27 August 1759); and A.B., another correspondent, reported the useful discovery that the Salisbury paper circulated in the Army, both among the regulars and the militia (*SJ*, 10 September 1759). A second A.B., this one purporting to be a Bristol commercial man, wrote at length about the advantages of subscribing to the *Journal*, which he saw 'in most places that I go to' on business trips through 'several counties' (*SJ*, 25 January 1762). A letter was printed demanding a strict account of

---

[44] In fact, both the *Salisbury* and *Reading Journals* at different times printed a local edition for Winchester, the town in which the *Chronicle* was based.

how money collected for victims of a fire in Wareham had been spent—
its author wrote to the *Journal* because 'I believe your Paper circulates
over Dorsetshire' (*SJ*, 22 August 1763). A cure for scald head (i.e. ring-
worm) was submitted by J. Cook, MD, who thought the medium of the
Salisbury Journal would best serve the public 'As your very useful and instructive Journal falls into a great number of hands' (*SJ*, 13 February 1764).
And a letter of complaint about the turnpikes began with the observation
that 'YOUR paper, I apprehend is read in every town and village in the
county of Wilts, it will therefore of course reach the eyes of the Surveyors
of the turnpike road leading from Weyhill to Devizes' (*SJ*, 18 September
1769). Quite likely Benjamin Collins would not have hesitated to manufacture a letter from A.B. or Z.Z. if he thought that might help circulation; but even if one or two of them can be discounted as self-advertisement,
these letters and notices provide general evidence for numbers, categories,
and locations of newspaper readers in eighteenth-century Wessex.

Few specific figures for subscribers are available. There was Farley's
hopeful projection of 200 subscribers in 1715. Another reference is very
suggestive. This is to 2,000 *London Magazine* titles printed by Charles
Ackers 'for Salisbury' April 1740; 2,000 titles were printed for Gloucester at the same time. Printed title-leaves were a common form of book
advertisement, designed to be posted outside booksellers' shops or, in
greater numbers, to be inserted as advertising into serial publications.[45]
The practice of using newspapers to carry loose, single-leaf advertisements is, of course, still common. It is likely that Ackers's *London Magazine* titles were delivered to the proprietors of the *Salisbury Journal* and
Gloucester Journal to take advantage of their established newspaper networks for cheap and effective co-distribution.[46] Certainly Ackers and
Collins had business dealings with each other and the *London Magazine*,
published by their close colleague Thomas Astley, was advertised in the
Salisbury Journal at this time. The connection has to be speculative, but
suggests nevertheless a plausible intermediate circulation figure of about
2,000 in the 1740s.

[45] D. F. McKenzie and J. C. Ross (eds.), *A Ledger of Charles Ackers, Printer of* The
London Magazine (Oxford: Oxford Bibliographical Society, 1968), 110. A rare title-leaf
advertisement for the *Gentleman's Magazine* with which the *London* was in fiercely direct
competition at this time, is bound up before the regular monthly title leaf in a 1739 volume
of the *Gentleman's* in the Bodleian Library, Oxford (Lister H. 107). The regular title-page
has the list of contents on the verso, while the advertisement has a puff for the magazine on
its verso.
[46] Ackers was to print *Journey to the World Underground* for Benjamin Collins and Thomas
Astley in 1742 (ibid. 160). The proprietor of the *Gloucester Journal* was Robert Raikes then.

In 1762 A.Z. wrote to Benjamin Collins complaining that the *Journal* was circulated in insufficient numbers: 'YOU must either print more Journals, or you must soon print less; for I am obliged to make my Paper serve myself and neighbours, purely because you don't supply them; for I take it for granted that is the case, because they can all very well afford to pay the trifling expence of it'; a larger edition would save his friends 'the trouble of continually sending (especially these cold winter nights) to borrow a Journal of your constant customer'. Collins's immediate printed response was a promise to increase edition size:

The obliging writer of the above letter having laid us under no restraint, we take the liberty to show it the Public, and beg the favour of all whom it may concern to take notice, that the first Monday after next Quarter-day, being the 29th instant, we shall print Five Hundred Papers extra, purposely to prevent any farther complaints of this sort. (*SJ*, 22 March 1762)

The proposed increase—itself two and a half times greater than the total number of subscribers Samuel Farley hoped for in 1715—is testimony to the growth of newspaper readership around Wiltshire over fifty years. Precisely how Collins ensured the distribution and sale of these extra 500 papers is unknown, but the size of the increase suggests a local market for editions on the order of 2,000–3,000 in the 1760s.

There was almost certainly a gradual rise in subscribers and casual purchasers from the inception of the *Journal* through the 1760s, although the trend was probably less marked under the new management of the early 1770s. Progress was resumed after 1775, and by 1780 the *Journal* partners could argue that the cost of advertising in their newspaper was justified by circulation figures of 'upwards of 4000'.[47] Allowance must be made for some exaggeration, but even so, the *Salisbury Journal* was probably one of the best-selling provincial newspapers in the mid-eighteenth century.

Two hundred subscribers to the *Salisbury Post Man* in 1715; 2,000 for the *Salisbury Journal* in the 1740s; perhaps 3,000 during the Seven Years War; and 'upwards of 4000' by 1780—these are figures for the readers who individually paid for the paper. It is impossible to deduce from these imprecise figures just how many people actually read, or indeed *heard*, the *Journal*. Obviously any newspaper circulated among many more than those who actually bought it; in addition a weekly such as the *Salisbury Journal* maintained a sort of currency for the seven days between issues,

[47] Printed receipt, Salisbury and S. Wiltshire Museum, Salisbury.

giving country readers plenty of time to share the printed news. Reading the newspaper aloud became a regular pastime in some families, as in the late eighteenth-century Berkshire family Charles Knight described, where his 'friend would make the stirring passing events of the week known to his household in reading aloud the "Reading Mercury", which was duly delivered at his door by an old newsman on a shambling pony'.[48] Anna Larpent, whose diaries record a diverse reading experience, also describes how her husband used to read the newspaper to her while she did household chores.[49] Similarly one paper might be passed around: A.Z. might complain of an obligation to share his paper with neighbours, but he was describing a common reading practice, one that newspaper proprietors did not always wish to encourage. Cranfield even records 'a Friendly Society of Neighbours' that purchased a joint subscription to the *Cambridge Journal* in 1746.[50] Coffee-houses and inns made a selling point of the newspapers and gazettes they provided either gratis or for a small fee, and many of their clients must have become accustomed to stopping in for a drink and the news. Thomas Benge Burr described coffee-houses and bookshops as 'places where the social virtues reign triumphant over prejudice and prepossession. . . . Here divines and philosophers, deists and christians, whigs and tories, scotch and english, debate without anger, dispute with politeness, and judge with candour . . .'[51] Benjamin Collins's brother Francis ran an engaging 'Coffee Room with a Collection of Maps, the Daily Advertiser, besides other papers; and . . . a good Fire' (*SJ*, 20 October 1755), and in Winchester John Childs notes that the *Salisbury Journal* would be available for reading at his coffee-house. Parson Woodforde, who was living in Somerset, wrote of paying to read the news on several occasions at various inns in the 1760s and 1770s.[52] Newspapers, both London and provincial, were often provided by local circulating libraries and reading rooms—in 1741 Edward Easton advertised that his

[48] Charles Knight, *Passages of a Working Life during Half a Century: With a Prelude of Early Reminiscences* (London: Bradbury & Evans, 1864–5), i. 22.

[49] John Brewer, 'Reconstructing the Reader: Prescriptions, Texts and Strategies in Anna Larpent's Reading', in James Raven, Helen Small, and Naomi Tadmor (eds.), *The Practice and Representation of Reading in England* (Cambridge: Cambridge University Press, 1996), 242. [50] Cranfield, *Development of the Provincial Newspaper*, 177.

[51] Thomas Benge Burr, *The History of Tunbridge-Wells* (London: printed; sold by M. Hingeston; J. Dodsley; T. Caslon; and E. Baker, Tunbridge-Wells, 1766), 126–7.

[52] *The Diary of a Country Parson: The Reverend James Woodforde, 1758–[1802]*, ed. John Beresford, 5 vols. (London: Humphrey Milford, Oxford University Press, 1924–31), i. 18, 21, 254. Thomas Turner, another contemporary, also wrote of making trips to read the news (*The Diary of Thomas Turner, 1754–1765*, ed. David Vaisey (Oxford: Oxford University Press, 1984)).

public library and reading-room in Salisbury had 'News-Papers to be seen every Monday' (*SJ*, 11 August 1741). He was one of many who advertised similar services. That reading newspapers was a constant (albeit sometimes solitary) pastime might be further demonstrated by the unfortunate minister of Weston Turville who was killed in September 1747 after his horse bolted—had he not been absorbed in reading the newspaper at the time, he might have kept his seat (*SJ*, 21 September 1747). Family reading, sharing among household members and neighbours, reading out loud, and coffee-house and reading-room circulation established a large multiple readership. It is safe to say that very few copies of any eighteenth-century provincial newspapers were enjoyed by only one reader.

Multiple newspaper readership may be well established, but it is difficult to arrive at some reliable figure by which the number of subscribers can be multiplied to estimate the total number of readers and auditors. In 1711 Joseph Addison thought that twenty readers per newspaper was 'a modest Computation'.[53] A more conservative multiplier of half that suggests 2,000 readers for Farley's 200 potential subscribers in 1715, 20,000 for the *Salisbury Journal* in the 1740s, 30,000 in the 1750s and 1760s, rising to as many as 40,000 by 1780. These sums can be set against the larger context of population figures for the counties in which the *Journal* circulated: Collins claimed that his newspaper circulated throughout the counties of Wiltshire, Hampshire, and Dorset, and parts of Berkshire, Gloucestershire, and Somerset, and for most of the *Journal*'s eighteenth-century history this claim is supported by news agencies and the geographical origins of its advertising. The 1801 census records a *de facto* population of 185,107 for Wiltshire, 219,170 for Hampshire, and 114,452 for Dorset, making a total of 518,729 for the area in which the *Journal* claimed most comprehensive circulation.[54] 'Parts' of Berkshire, Gloucestershire, and Somerset defies any precise definition, but total 1801 county populations were 110,752 for Berkshire, 250,723 for Gloucestershire, and 273,577 for Somerset.[55] Major towns in which the *Journal* was regularly distributed included Chippenham (3,366 in 1801), Devizes (3,547), Lymington (2,378), Marlborough (2,367), Poole (4,761), Portsmouth (7,839), Shaftesbury (2,433), and Sherborne (3,159), and, of course, Salisbury itself. Salisbury had 6,678 residents in 1695, 6,586 in 1753, and

[53] Addison, *Spectator*, 12 Mar. 1711.
[54] *VCH Wiltshire*, iv. 339; *Hampshire*, v. 437; and *Dorset*, ii. 266.
[55] *VCH Berkshire*, ii. 236; *Gloucester*, ii. 175; and *Somerset*, ii. 340.

7,668 in 1801.[56] After adjusting for a smaller population in the mid-eighteenth century, the only thing that can be suggested is that something like 5 per cent of the local population may have been *Journal* readers in the last quarter of the eighteenth century. But the usefulness of such calculations is obviously limited.

If the number of Wessex newspaper readers and the area in which they lived can be loosely defined, what then can be said about the readers themselves? In general the range of *Salisbury Journal* readership today is a wide one, from the highly literate to those who usually prefer to read the *Sun*; every socio-economic group is represented. The range was not so extensive in the mid-eighteenth century. The literate naturally formed a part of the *Journal*'s reading population then, and some of them would also have read what has been called the élite press, that is the Continental and official London newspapers.[57] But generally those who might have been *Sun* readers now were possibly not even functionally literate in the eighteenth century. Likewise the very wealthy, the prosperous business and farming classes, and the educated middle classes could be numbered among the *Journal*'s subscribers, while there were probably few from the labouring classes, who had less opportunity to learn to read and little leisure to practise that skill.

Broad conclusions about the Wessex reading population can be drawn from the social and economic history of the region.[58] The area was largely agricultural and pastoral, particularly in Dorset where the towns did not come into prominence until sea-bathing became fashionable in the mid-century. Hampshire produced wheat, barley, oats, peas, sheep, and pigs, and bees were reputedly 'much cherished' there, while much of rural Wiltshire was divided into 'sheep-and-corn country' or 'cheese-and-butter country'. Earlier in the century Defoe had noticed, with some amazement, the very large size of Wessex flocks.[59] The second half of the century brought improved farming techniques, the establishment of

[56] The 1695 and 1753 figures are reported in *SJ*, 2 July 1753. John Chandler discusses these and the 1801 census in *Endless Street*, 33–47, 285–6.

[57] John C. Merrill, *The Élite Press: Great Newspapers of the World* (New York: Pitman, 1968), 7; Jeremy D. Popkin, 'The Élite Press in the French Revolution: the *Gazette de Leyde* and the *Gazette universelle*', in Harvey Chisick (ed.), *The Press in the French Revolution* (Oxford: The Voltaire Foundation, 1991), 85–98.

[58] The following sketch is drawn primarily from the various Victoria County Histories. But see also Peter Borsay, *The English Urban Renaissance: Culture and Society in the Provincial Town, 1660–1770* (Oxford: Clarendon Press, 1989).

[59] Daniel Defoe, *A Tour thro' the Whole Island of Great Britain, divided into Circuits or Journies* (London, 1724), i, letter 3, p. 26.

larger cloth manufacturing centres, and a remarkable rise in wheat prices, which meant poverty and distress, as ever mainly for the labouring classes and small farmers: large farms absorbed the smaller ones, and there were fewer opportunities for the poor to supplement their income at home in cloth-related piece-work. Substantial farmers—who after all would have been more likely than farm labourers to subscribe to the local newspaper— were able to benefit under these economic conditions, however, turning their high profits to agricultural improvement. Evidence for the significance of this segment of the provincial reading population is to be found in a notice that

The Salisbury Journal of the 11th inst. containing some curious and useful instructions concerning cheap *fuel, hay-making, and fattening cattle*, &c. being all sold off, and many since called for; a new edition is this day published and sold at the Printing-Office; and may be had of the distributers of this Journal.

(*SJ*, 25 June 1764)

The only time a second edition of the *Journal* was produced during the mid-century was when there was heavy demand for agricultural advice.

   The regional cloth industry appears to have reached a zenith in the sixteenth and seventeenth centuries, and was evidently in general decline through the eighteenth. But specialist cloth manufacturing remained a considerable business in small urban centres such as Bradford-upon-Avon. Collins's reports of the Melksham weavers' riots, for example, favoured the clothiers who were, again, more likely than their employees to take out subscriptions to the *Journal*. Two cathedral cities, Salisbury and Winchester, with a sizeable clerical population, fell within the *Journal*'s catchment area. There were plausible claims of a *Journal* readership among military and naval men too, who made up a large element of the port towns served by the *Salisbury Journal*. And a growing middle class, with more leisure and more money, must also be counted among provincial newspaper readers.

   Defoe's notes on the inhabitants of Salisbury describe a good many newspaper readers:

The People of *Salisbury* are gay and rich, and have a flourishing Trade; and there is a great deal of good Manners and good Company among them; I mean, among the Citizens, besides what is found among the Gentlemen; for there are many good Families in *Salisbury*, besides the Citizens.

   The Society has a great Addition from *the Closs* [*sic*], that is to say, the Circle of Ground wall'd in adjacent to the Cathedral; in which the Families of the Prebendaries and Commons, and other of the Clergy belonging to the Cathedral have their Houses, as is usual in all Cities where there are Cathedral Churches. These are so considerable here, and the Place so large, that it is (*as it is call'd in general*) like another City.[60]

The climate these townspeople created probably encouraged the Collins brothers to set up a newspaper there in the first place.

A few of the individuals who read the *Salisbury Journal* in the eighteenth century are known by name. It is safe to say that nearly every one of the agents who handled the *Journal* read the paper at least occasionally. There are records of purchases in the Earl of Radnor's house accounts that suggest that he was among the local newspaper-reading élite, subscribing to provincial and London papers. The *Journal*'s one known war correspondent signed his account of the defeat at Agria: he was Samuel Beaven.[61] The pseudonymous Detector, who despised Benjamin Collins so much that he published at least three numbers of a periodical devoted to attacking him after his death, was clearly a *Journal* reader. Editors of other papers had to read the Wessex paper too. And many of those who advertised in the paper must have been regular readers—the advertisements in any provincial paper taken all together describe a sort of Every Reader. Some of those were actually signed: the bookseller Daniel Browne used the columns of the *Journal* to apologize to the Right Hon. Lord L——r for publishing a false account of a duel in which the peer had been involved ('as I cannot make any other Satisfaction, for the Injury I have done the unhappy Nobleman, I hope he will accept of this, nor should it have been printed had I seen it' (*SJ*, 9 March 1752)). They also describe a few non-readers in great physical detail, such as illiterate apprentices or soldiers who fled their service,[62] or Edward Uphill the runaway husband whose wife 'will be obliged to any Person that will inform him of this Advertisement, as he cannot read himself'.[63] Frequently the printed apologies for slanderous or aggressive behaviour bear only the mark of the defendant, a sign that even the illiterate readily understood the value of a widely distributed newspaper.

---

[60] Daniel Defoe, *A Tour thro' the Whole Island of Great Britain, divided into Circuits or Journies* (London, 1724), i, letter 3, p. 29.

[61] *SJ*, 29 Nov. 1759. Possibly related to the '*Mr. Beavan at Melksham*' who had lost a 'thin Parcel of Writing-Paper' in Salisbury in 1746 (*SJ*, 3 Nov. 1746).

[62] Almost invariably unattractive in appearance. The description of the apprentice John Barnes is typical: 'about 19 Years old, about five Feet four Inches high, pitted with the Small-Pox, talks lisping, and his Shins grown much out' (*SJ*, 30 Jan. 1764); or Thomas Scammell, a runaway husband who was described as having a 'dark complexion and hair, bald pated, flat nose, . . . and rather corpulent' (*SJ*, 1 Jan. 1781).

[63] Uphill was a sawyer who was fleeing a small debt (*SJ*, 17 May 1762).

All these elements—the network of newsagents, population records, socio-economic studies, estimated production figures, the paper's advertisements, speculations about numbers of readers—help to describe Wessex readership in the mid-eighteenth century. The picture is further enhanced by a study of the content of the newspaper and how it was organized, for the news an editor brought to his readers, his selections from the London papers and the editorial amendments and abridgements he made to them, his own rarely stated editorial positions, even the way the news was physically presented are ways in which the newspaper described its audience.

4

Production and Policy: The Shape of a Provincial Newspaper

EACH number of a provincial newspaper contained a measure of news and advertising, often with the addition of literary or political essays, letters to the editor, and verse. Editorial decisions ultimately determined the content of any newspaper, but behind those decisions lay a number of practical factors: what the market wanted; what the editor thought the market wanted; the news available from readers and other reporters; the supply of stamped paper; the timing of the post that brought the London and Continental newspapers; the availability of an express delivery service; and the requirements of advertising. Even more fundamental was the framework imposed by the technologies of the day: the size of hand-made paper, the limits of manual press production. All these governed the physical amount of news and advertising that could be printed, the way in which the contents were ordered, and even the very day on which a weekly paper might be published.

By the time William Bettinson, William and Benjamin Collins, John Newbery, Robert Raikes, and others first began publishing their papers in the 1720s and 1730s, the physical size of newspapers had effectively been determined by the two Government Stamp Acts of 1712 and 1725: both laws required a duty of $1d.$ per sheet or $\frac{1}{2}d.$ per half-sheet on each copy of the paper sold. After 1712 a number of proprietors had been able to exploit a loophole in the first Stamp Act, printing their newspapers on one and a half sheets, rather than the usual single sheet, and calling them pamphlets—pamphlets were taxed on the whole edition rather than on every copy—but the 1725 Act defined *newspaper* with more precision and thereby eliminated the loophole. After 1725 when the tax was not only unavoidable but closely pegged to sheets used, many newspaper proprietors found it economical to print on single half-sheets and pay the minimum tax of $\frac{1}{2}d.$ a copy. Since neither Act defined the size of a sheet, paper for newspaper work was made as large as possible within the contemporary hand-manufacturing limits,[1] the early *Salisbury Journal* was printed on a

---

[1] On paper size see e.g. Philip Gaskell, *A New Introduction to Bibliography* (Oxford: Oxford University Press, 1972), 66–8, and Table 3: 'Paper Sizes and Watermarks', 72–5.

large half-sheet, folded once to make four pages. This was a format shared by practically all the mid-eighteenth-century newspapers.

From its inception the *Journal* had to work within the limits of economical half-sheet production by using smaller type sizes or different layouts. If the proprietors wanted more news or advertising they had to create the space for it, so sometimes advertisements spilled over into the margins, or the type in a column of news silently slipped one size down. In 1764 the editor of the *Journal* thought that he ought to announce that

This JOURNAL, (which begins the New Year with an entire new and beautiful Elziver Letter) for more amply accommodating our Readers with the Occurrences of the Times, is considerably enlarged; and, though not divided into four Columns, according to the present Mode, (which, while it *seemingly increases*, in *reality diminishes*, the Contents) is now the fullest, as well as most early and extensive Country Paper in the Kingdom.   (*SJ*, 2 January 1764)

Collins was not only concerned to make room for 'the Occurrences of the Times' of course; the dearth of marketable news after the Seven Years War encouraged many editors to cultivate the advertising side of business, and growth there required more space.

Until 1770 the *Journal* was printed three columns to a page in type of varying sizes, ranging in the early years from the double pica and great primer in the title section, to the long primer indiscriminately used for both news and advertising. Brevier type was employed when a story had to be squeezed in at the last minute and was regularly used for advertisements later in the century. Four pages at three columns each allowed twelve columns in all for news and advertising of course. Despite Collins's stated objections to the four-column page, the new management moved to that format and a smaller type size in 1770 to extend '*the size of their paper almost beyond any other in the kingdom, which will not only enable them to be still more copious in their intelligence, but also more immediately obliging to their correspondents . . .*' (*SJ*, 8 January 1770). Another Stamp Act in 1776 brought further improvements within the four-column, four-page definition, and, under Benjamin Collins's renewed management, another '*new Elzevir letter cast on purpose*' (*SJ*, 8 July 1776). Collins might have hoped that his readers believed by this suggestion that he had actually gone to the trouble of purchasing new type custom-made for the paper they were reading, but in fact so-called Elzevier was readily available to any printer interested in a good, readable type fount. With four columns and small-size type eighteenth-century provincial editors had just about reached the limits of weekly newspaper production. The Fourdriniers had still to invent their machine for producing paper in a continuous roll,[2] and stamp duty (already high at $\frac{1}{2}d.$ a copy, doubled in 1757, and raised again in 1776) was an economic disincentive to expanding the paper in any other ways. However, the developing interest in news from America pushed beyond that to the provision of a number of 'extras' along with the regular newspaper. These were single half-sheets, printed on both sides in the style of the *Journal*, and bearing the same date as the paper. These seem to have been issued free and unstamped to subscribers.

Economics and technology also determined that the text for the weekly news was almost always in words rather than in pictures, for making and printing expensive woodcuts or engravings to accompany something so ephemeral simply could not be cost- or time-effective. Therefore few illustrations found their way into any eighteenth-century provincial newspaper and most of those that did were either the small woodcuts commonly found with advertisements for quack medicines, or the woodcut newsboys, town crests, and views that formed part of the masthead. Occasionally, though, Collins and his colleagues made room for larger woodcuts to illustrate the news: 'An Exact *PLAN* of the Island of *CAPE BRETON*' was published 20 August 1745. The outline of the 1,680-carat Brazilian diamond sent to the King of Portugal, along with a written description of the gem, appeared in the 12 January 1747 number of the *Journal*. Constructed from one long type rule (of the sort that separated the paper's columns) and possibly copied from the illustration that had appeared in the December 1746 number of the *Gentleman's Magazine*, the simple oval outline was effective and striking.[3] The fireworks to celebrate the Peace of Aix-la-Chapelle, 7 October 1748, were depicted in an elaborate woodcut (*SJ*, 30 January 1749); '*A* REPRESENTATION *of the* Triangular MONUMENTAL STONE *of* WILLIAM RUFUS' was included in the number for 7 January 1751; and 'A PLAN of the Battle fought in North America Sept. 7, 1755, between the English Army under General Johnson, and the French under General Count Dieskau', appeared in the 8 December 1755 number. Provincial editors—and indeed the London editors—were fairly easy about sharing and copying the pictures: it is possible to find copies of a number of these illustrations in more than one newspaper. The seven news illustrations that appeared in the *Reading Mercury* before 1855 included the plan of Cape Breton (September 1745); order of battle, Straghallan Moor (May 1746); Aix-la-Chapelle fireworks

---

[2] The Fourdrinier machine was not in operation until 1803 (see ibid. 216).
[3] The illustration in the *GM* certainly preceded that in the *Salisbury Journal*, but whether or not that was the precise source of the *Journal* picture is unclear.

(January 1749); plan of battle between Johnson and Dieskau (December 1755); courtroom plan (April 1756); and Lunardi's Aerostatic Machine (September 1784).[4] Pictures in advertisements were more common and more predictable, but the distinctive portrait accompanying a notice for Edward Wilson, a London painter, is worth mentioning (*SJ*, 29 August 1749).

Otherwise typography could be made to underline an editor's point. On more than one occasion in the *Salisbury Journal* vertically aligned type was used along with the horizonal, as when for example Collins wished to demonstrate the seating arrangements at the Duke of Newcastle's lavish entertainment for the Prince of Hesse (*SJ*, 16 June 1746). Turned type was even used to demonstrate ironic meaning with reference to the *brave* Admiral Byng (*SJ*, 16 August 1756). The funeral procession for Frederick the Prince of Wales was imaginatively illustrated solely with type and rules —the words describing the coffin's trappings and carriage were arranged in the shape of a coffin and enclosed within a box constructed of rules (*SJ*, 22 April 1752). Advertisements were occasionally set in the margins, again in vertical and horizontal alignment; sometimes a late news bulletin found its way into the bottom margin of the first page. Some sections of the *Journal* were defined by drop initials, or by type initials enclosed in woodcut or metal factotums (which became particularly decorative during the late 1740s), or by vertical and horizontal rules, or by type ornaments, or, for a short time, by real headlines. There were recognizable headlines in the *Journal* for 6 April and 14 December 1747 for example. Although the use of italic type in a headline might not appeal to twentieth-century readers, the style of phrase and the emotional appeal of this headline are quite modern: '*A Man, his Wife, and three Children burnt to Death*' (*SJ*, 14 December 1747).

Brief, individual editorial comments or notes were set off in italic type, and were usually signalled by three asterisks arranged in a triangle or by a fist with pointing index finger; editorial interjections were usually enclosed within square brackets, although longer editorial items received no special typographical treatment. With the exception of a period during the late 1740s and early 1750s when he was younger and followed a more innovative line, Collins's approach to newspaper format, layout, and typography was generally a conservative one. It had to be, for the eighteenth-century country market wanted a country newspaper that *looked* like a

    [4] K. G. Burton, *The Early Newspaper Press in Berkshire (1723–1855)* (Reading: published by the author, 1954), 26–8.

country newspaper. And of course they wanted one that was published on time.

Newspapers were valued by their shareholders for the steady work and income they provided. The initial investment in printing press and type might be large for a newcomer, and subscribers difficult to round up, but once all that was established, a newspaper could be a great asset. A country weekly left the press and workmen free much of the time to take on other work, which, since London retained the market for most book production, could include the printing of advertisements, handbills, forms, warrants, and occasional small local books of sermons or verse. The ability to take on jobbing work at short notice depended on an efficient production schedule for the newspaper. One way of maximizing the compositor's time was to leave standing as much type as practicable from week to week, so that time could be saved on distribution and recomposition. A skeleton forme consisting of at least the title section on page 1 and the imprint on page 4 might be reprinted each week for months and even years, and could safely be left in standing type. Minor adjustments— the weekly change in date and number, small additions or subtractions to a list of newsagents—could be made to the skeleton forme without much trouble, and it was not reset until significant changes in news agencies required a new list, or a new masthead was substituted for a worn or outdated one. Type for repeat advertisements, frequently those for the books and medicines the paper's proprietor was concerned to sell, could be left in place too, usually for as long as the advertisements were current.

Since pages 1 and 4, already partly composed, made up the outer forme of the usual four-page newspaper, it made sense to fill in the remainder of that forme first with the news and advertisements received earliest in the work week. Once the type was composed and proof-read, the outer forme could be printed, and once printed it seems that additional corrections generally were not made to those pages, even when errors of fact were subsequently discovered. The 5 February 1739 number of the *Salisbury Journal* in the Beinecke Library shows signs of having been proof-read through pages 2 and 3, which suggests that the outer forme of this number had already gone past this stage.[5] Press economics made this the only realistic course. Newspapers had to be printed on prestamped (that is tax-paid) paper through at least the first half of the century and wastage and returns had to be kept to an efficient minimum. In the case of the *Salisbury Journal*, page 4 most often contained long

---

[5] There are proof-reader's symbols for deletion, word spacing, and turned type.

reruns of advertisements for book-trade-related goods; page 1 had the
stalest news and the occasional essay. The inner forme (pages 2 and 3)
usually carried additional advertising, as well as the most recent intelligence, with a section of page 3 always reserved for strictly local news.
This was composed during the week and was printed as soon as the last
news was received. This practice—printing the side of the half-sheet that
contained pages 1 and 4 early in the week, then printing the other side
(pages 2 and 3)—was one shared by many newspapers and explains
certain peculiarities that twentieth-century readers might find disconcert-
ing. The editor of the *York Courant* of 9 December 1746 usefully makes
this point of production:

As the Number of Courants *now printed is so very great, that we are oblig'd to go to
Press with one Side of the Paper on* Saturday; *and it's frequent to order an Advertisement to be continued till forbid; our Correspondents are desir'd to send in their Orders
of Discontinuance before that Day at Noon, otherwise their Advertisements cannot be
taken out.*

The *Salisbury Journal* for example had printed an advertisement 'in the
second Column of the last Page of this Paper, relating to Mr. Duckett's
being at the several Places therein mentioned'. A correction was received
in the Monday post, too late to make any adjustments in the advertisement itself, but still in time to find a place in the inner forme (*SJ*, 17
July 1739). Or there was a notice on page 3 that 'the estates and goods
(advertised on the 1st page of this Journal) belonging to Mr. Hatton
Figes, deceased, which were to have been sold by auction . . . are now
disposed of' (*SJ*, 1 January 1770). *Journal* readers in 1762 who first met
the continuation of an account of the ghost of Cock Lane on page 2 were
probably not startled to find the beginning of the story on page 4 (*SJ*,
25 January 1762). Almost every eighteenth-century country newspaper
at one time or another was guilty of printing news of a death or marriage
on page 4, with a retraction on page 2 or 3.[6]

The printers of the *Salisbury Journal* seem to have followed this efficient course for most of the newspaper's eighteenth-century life. However, a more unusual production method was employed from the *Journal*'s
beginning in late 1736 until mid-1739, a period when it was probably
printed outside Salisbury—certainly from October 1737 until February
1739 it was printed by William Bettinson in Sherborne, about 35 miles
away. From 27 February 1739 the *Salisbury Journal* was printed in the

---

[6] Roy Wiles discusses production in *Freshest Advices: Early Provincial Newspapers in
England* (Columbus: Ohio State University Press, 1965), 71–88.

Collins's printing office on the New Canal, from where it was also published. But during the initial term of contract printing, and continuing until May 1739, the paper seems to have been set, and possibly printed, one page at a time, in sequence from page 1 to page 4, with the news divided into three sections corresponding to the three postal deliveries, the 'stale Stuff' on page 1, the most recent on page 4.[7] The clues to this order of typesetting lie in the typographically smooth continuation of stories from one page to the next and the fact that page 4, rather than page 3, had the latest news. A compositor's error even implies that at least one issue of the *Journal* may have been printed page by page: page 4 of the 3 April 1739 number instructs that '*In the first Word of the first Column of the Paper, for ROHN, read JOHN*'. This note on page 4 suggests that the '*R*', enclosed in the factotum regularly beginning on page 1, had been left over from the week before when it had introduced the first story. An acute type shortage demanding instant recovery of the type used for the first page must have required its distribution before page 4 was set, even though the two pages were on the same side of the half-sheet. Unfortunately too few copies survive to establish any variation during the print runs. In these very early days of the *Journal*, stories and advertisements seem to have been set as they were received, and edited from page 1 through page 4. This was not the usual method, and was probably also dictated by shortage of type: a printer with little type could not afford to leave much text-type standing, but would distribute and reset it as soon as a page or forme had been printed. This was William Bettinson's style of production, and William Collins, who probably learned newspaper presswork from Bettinson, continued setting the pages consecutively for a few months after he took over the printing in late February 1739. Collins may not have set the type himself, possibly luring one of Bettinson's workmen or another printer to Salisbury to work under his management. At any rate he, or a new workman, switched to the more efficient, more common printing by formes in May 1739.

It is possible to form an idea of the *Salisbury Journal*'s normal weekly production schedule in the New Canal printing office: printing, proof-reading, and correcting the outer forme took place early in the work week and could be evenly paced, co-ordinated with other jobbing work. Composition of the inner forme began mid-week, incorporating advertising

---

[7] Wiles notes that some newspapers printed all the news together, rather than separating it according to delivery day—effective, but probably the least efficient production technique, since it meant delaying composition until all the news had been received (ibid. 77–9).

copy, which had to be in the office two or three days in advance of publication. When the *Journal* was published on Tuesdays the editors gave
notice that 'Such Persons as may have Occasion to Advertise in this
Journal, are desir'd to send in their ADVERTIIEMENTS [*sic*] by *Saturday*
noon, lest they should happen to be postpon'd 'till the Week following'
(*SJ*, 24 September 1745). There was a similar notice in the 19 August
1754 number. News selected from the correspondence and newspapers of
the first two posts could also be set in type mid-week, but with the arrival
of the week's third and last post there must often have been a rush to get
the paper printed, corrected, and issued on time.

It is difficult to say what personnel and equipment were involved in
the production of the *Journal*—William Bettinson certainly had a hand
in printing the newspaper during its early days, probably with some
assistance from William and Benjamin Collins. Then the Collins brothers
themselves opened their own printing office. After William I disappeared
in 1740 Benjamin Collins employed at least one or two apprentices at a
time, who were later joined by his sons, William II (ST3:7965, apprenticed to William Strahan in London from 1763 to 1770[8]), and Benjamin
Charles (apprenticed to his father in 1775).[9] One printing press worked
by two men was probably sufficient to meet the needs of the *Salisbury
Journal* when edition sizes were relatively small—it has been suggested
that about 250 sheets an hour could be printed on one side on a hand
press worked at full speed.[10] But circulation figures of 'upwards of 4,000'
claimed by the proprietors in 1780[11] probably would have required a
larger staff and more than one press.

Eighteenth-century provincial newspaper proprietors aimed to co-
ordinate publication with the post and, if they could afford it, a private
express-delivery service, as well as with days of increased local commercial

---

[8] D. F. McKenzie, *Stationers' Company Apprentices 1701–1800* (Oxford: Oxford Bibliographical Society, 1978), 340.

[9] Ian Maxted lists nine apprentices, including Benjamin Charles, for Benjamin Collins
(no. 0365), from 1740 to 1775 in his *British Book Trades, 1710–1777* (Exeter: Ian Maxted,
1983).

[10] 'The token of 250 sheets printed on one side was conventionally called an hour's work,
but this figure was at best a mean' (Gaskell, *New Introduction to Bibliography*, 139). Among
others, Wiles discusses production rates in *Freshest Advices*, 73–4 and 91 n. 31, as does D.
Nichol Smith, 'The Newspaper', in A. S. Turberville (ed.), *Johnson's England: An Account
of the Life & Manners of His Age* (1933; repr. Oxford: Clarendon Press, 1952), ii. 333–4.
Nichol Smith draws on Timperley's *Printers' Manual* (1838) for evidence. D. F. McKenzie's
'Printers of the Mind: Some Notes on Bibliographical Theories and Printing-House Prac-
tices' should always be read before theorizing about work in the printing office (*Studies in
Bibliography*, 22 (1969), 1–77).

[11] Printed *Salisbury Journal* receipt, Salisbury and S. Wiltshire Museum, Salisbury.

activity. In its first few years the *Salisbury Journal* was published irregularly on Saturdays and Mondays to coincide with the Saturday/Tuesday markets Salisbury has held since the fourteenth century,[12] or with a day on which the post was delivered. The post was sent from London on Monday, Thursday, and Saturday, and arrived in Salisbury the following morning each week. When the Collins brothers began printing the newspaper for themselves in February 1739, they experimented with Tuesday publication for a time, which enabled them to capitalize on casual sales from those attending the Salisbury market that day. But the advantages of meeting postal deadlines were just as important, as William Collins explained when Tuesday was first proposed in 1737:

THE publishing this Paper as usual, on Saturday Evening, being attended with many Inconveniences, the same will be published, after the last day of this Month, on every Tuesday Morning, so that the freshest Intelligence by Monday's Post will by that means be inserted, and the same sooner and better Conveyed to our Readers.

(*SJ*, 19 September 1737)

In fact the change to Tuesdays did not take place until 27 February 1738/9, nearly a year and a half after this notice, and the proprietors finally settled on a Monday publication date from 10 March 1745/6. While a Monday newspaper still had some currency for the Tuesday market buyers, production was now better timed with the arrival of the express news early Sunday morning. Printing was completed on Sunday and distribution began immediately after that. Some local subscribers must have had their copies by late Sunday. Simon Knight, a newsagent at Newport on the Isle of Wight, was able to promise Monday-morning delivery to his customers (*SJ*, 7 April 1755), and subscribers in the neighbourhood of Shaftesbury were promised delivery *early* Monday morning (*SJ*, 1 February 1768). Such efficiency was not universally appealing. In 1783 the curate of Wylye, John Eyre, complained to the Bishop of 'The soul-hurting printing, publishing, and vending the Salisbury Journal on Sundays to the profanation of the Lord's day'.[13]

The oldest news might have been placed on page 1, but that did not mean that provincial editors were not interested in timeliness; on the contrary a claim to publish the freshest advices was a real selling-point, and

[12] John Chandler, *Endless Street: A History of Salisbury and Its People* (Salisbury: Hobnob Press, 1987), 95.

[13] Mary Ransome, *Wiltshire Returns to the Bishop's Visitation Queries 1783*, Wiltshire Record Society, 27 (Devizes: Wiltshire Record Society, 1972), 248. The Bishop of Salisbury in 1783 was Shute Barrington.

proprietors went to great lengths to ensure that their offices received the printed and written news from London with the greatest expedition. About 1745 Benjamin Collins began employing a weekly express service that he said would 'furnish our Readers with the most authentick Intelligence several Days before it can be seen in any of the London Evening Papers', quite likely in response to the rising demand for news during the 1745 Rebellion. He may have been able to join with the proprietors of the *Reading Mercury* who announced a similar service in September of the same year that would enable them '(by means of an extraordinary Correspondence and Messengers employ'd on purpose) to publish our paper considerably sooner than usual, without omitting any of the freshest intelligence, even that which is brought by Sunday's post' (*Reading Mercury*, 30 September 1745). Later when the *Mercury* advertised for 'a Man to fetch the Express from London to Reading', they asked for someone based near Slough, between London and Reading, which gives some idea of the logistics involved (23 March 1772).[14]

There is no question that the *Salisbury Journal* and *Hampshire Chronicle* shared the expense of a service from London as there are records of this arrangement in the *Chronicle*'s account books. The *Journal*'s express delivery is not actually mentioned in print until 1752:

> No mention could possibly be made in our last of the KING's Return, by Reason our Express came away two Hours before his MAJESTY's Arrival; and, as usual, with one of the first printed Gazettes, &c. which had not a Word of his being come to Town, or so much as landed, or expected that Night, nor any Thing more relating thereto than what we gave in our last.   (*SJ*, 27 November 1752)

Collins, who was usually reliable in these matters, claimed in 1765 that it had been in operation for twenty years (*SJ*, 18 March 1765). The rider evidently left the capital Saturday evening with all the London papers, written newsletters, and other reports (some of which he himself may have been responsible for), arriving almost without fail on Sunday morning. It is in this context—the express rider's failure to turn up one Sunday morning in 1765—that Collins apologized for the necessity of deferring the week's latest news until the following week's *Salisbury Journal* ('it being only the second misfortune of the kind we have met with in twenty years') and speculated that the delay must have been the result of an accident. It was. The rider had dropped his dispatches on the road between London and Bagshot and was unable to recover them in the dark, '*whereby his arrival here was retarded 'till eight o'clock in the evening*' (*SJ*, 15 March

---

[14] Quoted in Burton, *Early Newspaper Press in Berkshire*, 31, 32.

1765). Such incidents were indeed rare; the only other delayed rider mentioned in the *Journal* was one who waited in London eighteen hours to verify news of George II's death (*SJ*, 27 October 1760). Such a fast, reliable service was expensive—the *Hampshire Chronicle* account books record that the express service managed by Collins and shared between the *Chronicle* and the *Salisbury Journal* in the late 1770s was more than 13*s.* a week. The *Chronicle* partners paid Collins and Company 13*s.* 5*d.* a week 'for the Express', quite likely from London to Salisbury rather than directly to Winchester. From September 1781 to March 1782 the *Chronicle* partners also paid A. Morley of Basingstoke 5*s.* a week for carrying the express—Morley may have met the London–Salisbury rider to see that the news reached Winchester more quickly. There are other payments by Collins and Company for 'bring:ᵍ Express & Carr:ᵍ Southton papers.'[15] Collins made sure his customers understood the care and expense this entailed in his discussion of the price rise occasioned by the 1757 Stamp Act:

And here we beg Leave to mention a Circumstance that is almost peculiar to the SALISBURY JOURNAL, and therefore may plead something in its Favour, and tho' nothing new, is in all Probability intirely unknown to many of our Readers, (who have often wondered by what Means we get our Intelligence so early) viz. that we are at the Expence of a constant Weekly Express from London, to bring us the last Advices both from Abroad and at Home; by which we are enabled, not only to be before the Post, but to furnish our Readers with the most authentick Intelligence several Days before it can be seen in any of the London Evening papers . . . (*SJ*, 17 October 1757)

Another constant expense of running a country newspaper, of course, included quarterly subscriptions to the major London newspapers, particularly the London thrice-weeklies, which were issued around four or five o'clock the evenings of post days, clearly with the provincial market in mind.[16] The *Hampshire Chronicle* partners, for example, paid nearly £11.00 for the 'Gazettes & Papers' in 1782.[17] Continental papers sometimes supplemented the printed London contributions, and all these were regularly mined by country editors for news. Whole stories, or extracts from them, were selected and then transferred, sometimes in a carefully

---

[15] (PRO E. 140/91). The express service was organized from Salisbury however— Wilkes claimed that it was so and Collins readily agreed (Bills and Answers, PRO E. 112/1959/147).

[16] See Michael Harris, *London Newspapers in the Age of Walpole: A Study of the Origins of the Modern English Press* (London: Associated University Presses, 1987), 33–5.

[17] Account books, PRO E. 140/91.

refashioned state, but more often with little or no adjustment, to the columns of provincial newspapers.[18] Much of the other non-commercial content of eighteenth-century newspapers was drawn from specialized periodicals such as the monthly literary magazines, bills of mortality, and lists of grain prices. This was true of both the London and the provincial newspapers, so in fact it is often impossible to say whether a country paper tapped these other serials directly, or indirectly through its London subscriptions. Alongside the printed news there were the handwritten newsletters, which remained an important source of information well into the eighteenth century.

The country proprietors strove to present their digests of news as a useful and economical alternative—all the important news from London for the modest price of a local paper. The practice was seldom defined as plagiarism; rather this sort of borrowing was viewed as a normal part of the editing process. Even more than other periodicals the magazines capitalized on this practice, taking the name—*magazine*—from this characteristic. Indeed the editors who constructed their newspapers out of this variety of published and unpublished news and essays were frequently called *authors* or *writers*. Often, but not always, editors of provincial papers identified their news sources in print, and on occasion they listed the papers from which they drew their information. When a local edition of the *Salisbury Journal*, called the *Portsmouth and Gosport Gazette, and Salisbury Journal*, was first published, readers would have been interested to know that the newspaper

> *will contain the earliest Intelligence in general; and in particular* Thursday's, *and* Monday's London Gazettes; *with* Thursday's, Saturday's, *and* Monday's GEN- ERAL, WHITEHALL, LONDON, *and* St. JAMES's Evening-Posts, *and all the* Daily- Papers *and written Letter, with an Account of* Prize-Money, *when and where to be paid, Ship News and all other material Occurrences, either at Home or Abroad . . .*
>
> (*SJ*, 16 April 1750)

In an effort to make the new price of his newspaper more palatable after the doubled stamp duty of 1757, Collins compared the prices of the *London Evening Post*, the *General Evening Post*, the *Whitehall Evening Post*, and the *Evening Advertiser* unfavourably with that of the *Salisbury Journal*, adding that the *Journal* contained 'not only . . . the Marrow of them all, but the Gazette News, and other Intelligence three Days before any of

---

[18] Wiles discusses the art of rewriting the news in *Freshest Advices*, 208–10; Jeremy Black looks at the problems of editorial selection in ch. 2 of his *The English Press in the Eighteenth Century* (Philadelphia: University of Pennsylvania Press, 1987), 25–49.

'em' (*SJ*, 4 July 1757). By comparison the editors of the *Reading Mercury* implied that they subscribed to all sixteen periodicals listed after the title of their 23 July 1744 number when they noted that sources of articles would be identified only when they were 'peculiar to each Paper, and not in any of the rest'.[19] The tireless efforts of the editor in reading through all these papers were probably supposed to spring to mind, but alternatively it was possible to include items from just as many periodicals by extracting them from the London thrice-weeklies.

The editor himself bore the greatest responsibility for how his paper looked and was organized. He had to treat copy from other sources with appropriate caution. Benjamin Collins seems to have taken special care when considering unauthenticated Wiltshire stories in London newspapers: in one case the account of a murder in Devizes was duly included in the *Salisbury Journal* because it was news in the London papers, but he added a proviso that the story was likely a false one since Collins had not had '*private Intelligence of the Affair*' (*SJ*, 17 February 1752). Sending details of fictitious marriages to unsuspecting editors seems to have been a popular eighteenth-century recreation, and interesting unions were reported in one issue of the *Journal* only to be withdrawn with or without real apology in another. For example 'In our Journal of the 2d inst. we copied a paragraph from one of the London papers, of the marriage of Mr. Davies, of Lymington, to Miss Scrimpshaw, of Petty France, Westminster, which was without foundation' (*SJ*, 30 May 1768). Perhaps the humblest apology in the *Journal* was the editor's to the Earl of Hertford after an offensive paragraph had been '*inadvertently copied from one of the London papers*' (*SJ*, 9 April 1764). Collins was compelled to adopt a professionally sceptical view of London-derived news, as he took the opportunity to explain to his readers in the 23 January 1769 number of the *Journal*:

The formal narrative from Oxford, of a young Gentleman and Lady having destroyed themselves out of a passionate fondness for each other: the account of the Bishop of Bath and Wells being given over, and that the Dean was to be appointed to that see in his stead; and many other articles of the same stamp, which we frequently see published in some of the London papers, are mere invention, calculated only to deceive and amuse, therefore, as near as possible, are always omitted in this journal.

Further explanation followed a few months later:

On Thursday many people were greatly alarmed at two striking paragraphs, in the papers of that day, one, *of advice being received Monday evening, that Gibraltar*

---

[19] Quoted in Burton, *Early Newspaper Press in Berkshire*, 13.

was taken by the French and Spaniards; the other, *of the Count du Chatelet (the French Ambassador here) setting out suddenly the same night for Paris*; both of which prove to be very false, and the inserting them was quite absurd and ridiculous.— Upon this occasion it may not be amiss to observe, that THURSDAY's POST being generally barren of authentic intelligence, is commonly made up, in a great measure, of imaginary accounts, and chimerical advices, calculated to alarm the public, and answer private ends, which the public would do well to pay no regard to, till they see what the Salisbury Journal says of the Monday following.

(*SJ*, 23 April 1770)

Anna Maria Smart took a similar view in the *Reading Mercury*:

It is well known to all those whose curiosity hastens them to the earliest intelligence, that the same even is every week affirmed and denied: that the papers of the same day, contradict each other, and that the mind is confused by opposite relations, or tortured with the narrations of the same transactions, transmitted, or pretended to be transmitted from different places. Whoever has felt these inconveniences will naturally wish for a writer who shall once a week collect the evidence, decide upon its probability, reject those reports, which, being raised only to serve the day, are naturally refuted before the end of the week, and enable the reader to judge the true state of foreign and domestic affairs.

(*Reading Mercury*, 25 January 1762)

The suggestion was not simply that provincial newspapers could provide a more economical source of news than any individual London paper, but that they could also make some claim to be authenticators of the London news. Paradoxically Ben Jonson's critique of the newspaper press in the 1620s, its content '*ill-cook'd! and ill-dish'd*' in a '*weekly cheat to draw money*', are echoed here by Anna Maria Smart. But whereas Jonson's *The Staple of News* (1626) was an impassioned plea for the responsible, mediating role of the *poet* in reporting the age, hers is a defence of the *editor* as the locus of integrity, which presciently suggests its fuller realization a century later.

As for the news from some foreign sources, it was sometimes disclaimer enough merely to state that an item was extracted from the Paris *A la Main*—a story about an alleged attack by Hussars on a baggage and hospital convoy was followed by the square-bracketed comment that 'This seems to be a very lame Story, but, however, it is well enough for the Paris A-la-main' (*SJ*, 19 July 1743), and a report from the same source that Lisbon literally had sunk after the earthquake of 1756 incorporated another aside, likewise within square brackets, that 'This Account deserves no Credit. The Paris Gazette of the 10th Inst. mentioned the Shock of the 21st ult. . . . but said nothing of the City's being overflowed'

(*SJ*, 26 January 1756). In this same number the *Journal* was able, however, to publish a straightfaced account of a miracle diet drink invented by a Paris physician to cure the gout. Another report from France was described as a '*cook'd up Paragraph*' (*SJ*, 9 October 1738). The Dutch sources were viewed with similar suspicion ('As several Mistakes have been made by our Writers, and those chiefly occasion'd by copying the Dutch Gazettes,' *SJ*, 9 November 1747).

Further difficulties arose for the provincials when their printed sources, particularly the official newspaper the *London Gazette*, proved not always to be full of marketable news. The editors of the *Journal* made a point of including news from the *Gazette* each week—in times of war or political crisis the official newspaper often contained the fullest and most accurate accounts. In times of peace the *Gazette* sometimes left something to be desired, as Collins occasionally complained: 'ALL the News in this Day's Gazette is the King's Speech, a List of Acts passed, (both which are in the former Part of this Paper) and the Contents of a Memorial, signed by M. de Behr' (*SJ*, 30 March 1752).

It was the policy of the *Salisbury Journal* to favour news from its own reporters over that derived from the printed and even written periodicals. This policy was shared by other papers.

We have taken some Pains to acquire better Lights than these [the Gazettes and Journals], and in order to make *this Paper* as useful to our Readers as possible . . . we shall give them first, such Accounts as we receive from our particular Correspondents, and then collect such Articles from the public Papers, without Favour or Prejudice, as seem most agreeable to Truth, and are written with Spirit and Judgment . . . (*SJ*, 10 March 1746)

The *Salisbury Journal*, like the *Hampshire Chronicle*, must have paid for these particular reports sometimes, perhaps supplementing a regular agent's sales commission with fees, or a small salary, or free or discounted newspapers for the regular provision of news.[20] The agents, who had established weekly communications with the printing office in Salisbury, were in a good position to exploit such opportunities, particularly if they were based in one of those entrepôts for news, a port town for example. It is quite likely too that the proprietors sometimes retained other paid

[20] Minutes for a meeting of the *Hampshire Chronicle* proprietors, 23 Nov. 1778, indicate that Thomas Baker was to receive 'the same Allowance . . . for furnishing Intelligence, as is allowed to him at Salisbury [i.e. by the *Salisbury Journal*]' (PRO E. 140/90). An entry in the account books shows that William Dawkins in Gosport was paid 1*g*. for a similar service (PRO E. 140/91).

reporters. These previously unpublished contributions—in their timing, the way they were written, how they related to other copy, and how they were edited—gave further definition to the physical paper.

The *Journal* encouraged all its readers to contribute newsworthy items on an *ad hoc* basis, regularly advising that the printing office and news-agents accepted both advertising and news. The formulaic 'Advertise-ments, Articles of Intelligence, &c. are taken in by . . .' frequently appeared at the head of lists of newsagents. These efforts met with some success, for there are occasional references in the local news sections to anonym-ous correspondents, many of whom probably had no professional connec-tion with the paper. Someone from the Isle of Wight sent a report on a plague ship that had docked there (*SJ*, 27 September 1743); '*Our cor-respondent in Purbeck*' wrote with the sad news of thirteen drownings in the mud flats near the Isle of Purbeck (*SJ*, 19 March 1759); and another reporter in Blandford contributed an item on the lack of charity shown by the wealthier farmers towards the poor in the area (*SJ*, 3 November 1766). 'Our correspondent in London, on whose veracity we can depend' was able to report on an engagement between the combined forces of France and Spain with England: the victorious English, he said, 'fought like devils' (*SJ*, 4 November 1782). Samuel Beaven, one of the few *Journal* correspondents whose name is actually known, wrote from on board the ship *Revenge* with an eyewitness account of the defeat at Angria:

as I imagine a particular Narrative, from an Actor in it, will prove more satis-factory, than what the London papers collect; I therefore send you the following, which please to receive as the first Offering of an Indian Correspondent; who intends (with your leave) occasionally transmitting what further occurs, in this Part of the Eastern World, within the Scope of his Intelligence, and what he can safely assert to you as authentic.   (*SJ*, 29 November 1756)

Mary Jeffery of the Bell Inn, Romsey, wrote with a report on the pro-gress of repairs after a fire there, which the *Journal* published, but clearly her motive for doing so was to let customers know when the Bell would be open for business (*SJ*, 16 October 1758). Contributions often took the form of newsy paragraphs derived from personal letters received by readers and passed on to the paper, as part of a letter from Malaga to 'a gentleman in this city' (*SJ*, 10 July 1775), or an '*Extract of a letter from Lieutenant Stoddart, of the Carcase bomb-ketch, to his wife in this city*' (*SJ*, 7 October 1776). A letter from Cape Breton via Gosport came with a puff for the *Journal*, describing it as 'having the Character of being one of the most authentic and best connected published, and free from those numerous Conjectures, and Hearsay Paragraphs (without any Foundation) with which many of the News Papers are filled' (*SJ*, 18 August 1746).

Editors were always happy to print genuine—or at least plausible —first-hand accounts of disasters or items of general social or cultural value. These individual lines of communication were encouraged because they sometimes enabled the country papers to publish accounts before any of their rivals, or to claim the greater truth. Editors cared about both. The *Journal* for 28 April 1766 for example carried in the Salisbury news section a report from Spain prefaced by the notice that '*The following particulars of the riot at Madrid, which have not before appeared in print, were sent by a person of distinction, who was present when it happened, and may be depended on.*' One of the inherent problems of such reportage was accommodating an author's bias. A week after the *Journal* had printed an account of the death of William Toy, son of Salisbury's most famous dancing master, at the hand of a local surgeon, one Hughes, a completely different version of the story was published in which it became clear that Hughes himself had supplied the first version. He had attacked young Mr Toy with the butt of his riding whip, after discovering that Toy was romantically involved with his daughter (*SJ*, 15, 22 February 1747/8).

There is no evidence that any of these casual correspondents were paid in cash, although Collins assured his readers that

All authentic articles of intelligence worthy notice, sent to the Printers of this paper, will be thankfully received, and immediately inserted, especially such as may be of use to the public, particularly of house-breakers, horse-stealers, *and* highway-men, *numbers of whom have been aprehended, and brought to justice, by the facts being circumstantially published, and the persons suspected described in this extensive Journal.*

(*SJ*, 21 February 1774)

Many amateur reporters must have been wholly satisfied with their editor's gratitude; and in fact some actually paid to have their stories published. These were such authors as 'Tom Sugar Loaf' who was instructed to '*appear himself in defence of his own charge, (which the Printer has no concern in) and pay the usual fee or 'twill not be inserted*' (*SJ*, 3 June 1765). Payment could find a peripheral story a place in the regular news columns, or it could disguise a commercial advertisement as news. Certainly any 'news' submitted to the *Salisbury Journal* that bore the least hint of the commercial was held back until the full advertising fee had been paid. This was a practice more strictly enforced from the late 1750s, when it becomes difficult to escape the notion that editorial policy could be waived in favour of a cash payment: '*C. Christian's epigram*', the editor notes, '*is on a local affair, in which we have no business to interfere, unless it be paid for as an advertisement. Somniphilos, the same'* (*SJ*, 1 April 1765), or '*A* CARD *to* C——x, *being entirely of a private nature, cannot be inserted but on the footing of an Advertisement'* (*SJ*, 24 February 1777). If these editorial interventions are anything to go by, their frequent appearance suggests that Collins was finding new ways of exploiting the paper's revenue-earning potential.

When the editor of the *Salisbury Journal* retained a reporter's first-person narrative, or prefaced an account with 'our correspondent writes' or 'we hear' or 'the following is said to be a genuine account', or noted that a story had first appeared in another newspaper, or presented it as an advertisement, he was acknowledging both an external source of news and the necessity of drawing on such material. Such a practice served to put some distance between the editor and the possibly inaccurate account that might appear in his paper. It also underlines an editorial problem common to all newspapers: editors wanted to fill their columns with engaging copy, but could not always be certain of the precise origins of reports sent from a distance, especially when a contributor was not one of their regular journalists; they often had to trust the accuracy of any plausible newsworthy item. Verification was a difficulty, and became more so as readers and contributors multiplied. A few fictitious stories may have been sent in good faith, but it is clear that some local correspondents exploited the anonymity of the newspaper press to make spurious points. One contributor, who had falsely represented a case between an inn-keeper and the Dorchester Corporation in March 1754, was reprimanded, but it took the editor two months to get to the bottom of the story:

Tho' inserted on the strongest assurances of its being matter of Fact, [it] is, we find upon Enquiry, false in every Particular, totally impertinent, and Calculated only to make Mischief and cast a Reflection on a Worthy Body of Men without the least just Cause. Such Paragraphs our Correspondents wou'd do well to observe, that whatever Credit they may gain for a Time, can in the End, only bring Scandal on their Authors. (*SJ*, 6 May 1754)

Even Samuel Johnson was not above such practical jokes, although one point of the stories he manufactured about spectacular battles between the Turks and the Russians and then planted in the *Public Advertiser* was to demonstrate to Mrs Thrale's mother that it might be useful to entertain greater scepticism towards what she found in print. At the same time Johnson made another point against the *Public Advertiser* for its unwitting acceptance of the fiction. This was a paper of which he did not approve.[21] After a number of embarrassing retractions, Benjamin Collins and his colleagues learned to withhold the more suspicious anonymous stories altogether, or at least until they were verified or the author identified. When the non-appearance of a contribution called for an explanation, communication with anonymous or pseudonymous authors necessarily was through the printed pages of the newspaper: '*The article of a treaty of marriage on foot between——we must beg our anonimous correspondent to excuse, or authorise the insertion*' (*SJ*, 10 September 1764). A 'Freeholder' was instructed that his contribution was '*illiberal and anonymous, therefore not admissable, especially as the author of the address, to which this is a reply, has openly set his name to it*' (*SJ*, 18 October 1779). '*The paragraph in our last, mentioning the death of Mr. Godwin-Seward, surgeon, of Romsey, was sent to us for insertion, and we had no reason to doubt its veracity; we now hear that it was false, and with pleasure contradict it*' (*SJ*, 26 February 1776). Godwin-Seward may have had a brush with death that was honestly mis-understood as the real thing and he may really have intended to bestow the legacies mentioned in the previous week's story—or perhaps this was the revenge of an unhappy patient. This note suggests the ease with which almost any reporter could have a story printed in the newspaper press. The *Salisbury Journal* carried a more broadly directed admonition after a spurious article about a marriage between one Mr Moxham and a Mrs Jackson of 'genteel fortune' had slipped through the editorial net (*SJ*, 19 August 1776): '*We are ever ready to oblige our correspondents with the earliest insertion of such articles as may be worthy public notice; but must desire they will send us only such as are authentic, and signed by their real names, otherwise they cannot have a place*' (*SJ*, 26 August 1776). Despite these editorial tactics false news stories continued to find their way into the pages of the *Salisbury Journal* and other Wessex papers, to be followed by a retraction when the mistake was discovered. In 1782 the *Journal* pro-prietors had to admit that 'We were misinformed in regard to a duel near Downton, as inserted in our last, no such thing having happened' (*SJ*, 9 September 1782).

The choice of news copy from all these sources, printed and manu-script, professional and amateur, was in itself an important editorial pro-cess. The editor's selection and adjustment of his texts naturally influenced both the content and the form of the paper. Production schedules had to

---

[21] Betty Rizzo accounts for this and Johnson's other motives in '"Innocent Frauds": By Samuel Johnson', *Library*, 6th ser., 8 (1986), 249–64. The text of the seven news items is included.

fit in with these routines. (Advertisements are another issue—more fully discussed in Chapter 6—for it was the paying readers to a large extent who determined their own text.) The policy that governed the selection of news was seldom stated. While a nineteenth- or twentieth-century style editorial—that is, a clear statement of opinion that would be at home on a modern leader page—was rarely encountered in the eclectic eighteenth-century newspaper, an editorial policy in embryo can be detected in occasional brief editorial comments and in the much less frequent clear-cut editorials. Even if the provincial editor borrowed most of his material,[22] the fact that he *chose* to include subjectively written copy without contradictory comment suggests a number of possibilities: the editor of the country paper may himself have shared those biases; perhaps he thought his readers shared those views and therefore hoped to cater to that market; or he may have decided that his readers ought to become acquainted with those views. The rules governing inclusion might have had a philosophical basis, or more often an economic one (just what would sell the paper), and most probably a combination of both.

The editorial task was not an easy one. It was governed by what the editor thought his readers wanted to read and by what the editor himself wanted his readers to read. In this sense newspapers—eighteenth-century newspapers as well as twentieth-century ones—continue to be both descriptive and prescriptive. Good editing involved a clear assessment of readership as well as an ability to service that market. Probably the single most important influence on circulation and readership was editorial policy, encompassing the selection of news, the arrangement of news and advertising, and the overall tone of the newspaper, in a synthesis that had to appeal to locals. But other practical factors played an important part too. Subscribers who were confident they could always find the most current news on page 3 would have found it easier to renew their subscriptions; the farmer who purchased a copy of the *Salisbury Journal* every market day might have developed a greater willingness to become a quarterly subscriber; another might have considered giving up a subscription to a London paper in favour of the less expensive country paper. The content of the *Salisbury Journal* reveals more of the complicated relationship between editorial policy, production, and the newspaper reader in eighteenth-century Wessex.

---

[22] Editorial essays, like other articles, often appeared in more than one newspaper. For example the *Salisbury Journal* published an attack on the 1776 Stamp Act in an 'extra' dated 6 May 1776. The same essay had already appeared in the *Reading Mercury* (29 April 1776; quoted in Black, *English Press*, 59–60).

5

Editors and Text

ANY eighteenth-century provincial newspaper editor could have en-dorsed an editorial essay that appeared in the *London Evening Post* in 1754. A number of them went so far as to reprint it:

Those who declaim against the *Liberties* taken by *News Papers*, in representing Grievances, proposing Remedies, and censuring Persons, know not what they say, or what they mean: It is *this Liberty*, that not only *protects* all the *rest*, but without *this Liberty*, the constitutional *Lenity* of our *Government* would be *pre-judicial* to the *Subject*; the *News Papers* expose *Crimes*, detect *Impositions*, bring *Contrivances* to *Light* that would be too *high*, too *low*, or too *hard* for the LAWS, and *Impunity* would render *intolerable.*—Pinch but one of these DECLAIMERS, he flies to a NEWS PAPER, and makes his CASE known to the PUBLICK.—For none are *quicker* in their *Feelings*, than Those who are *callous* in their *Comprehensions*.

(*SJ*, 18 March 1754)

The author of the essay promotes the newspaper as a necessary adjunct to the law, seeking and correcting misdeamours that fall outside the bounds of formal legal procedures. This is the newspaper at its most active. Other statements that highlighted this useful prescriptive role for the newspaper inevitably appeared in conjunction with rises in stamp duty ('this exorbitant Tax, this additional Clog on the Palladium of our Lib-erties'). An alternative definition was published about a month later, in another essay taken from the London papers, appropriately described 'A REFLECTION':

THE papers of the day are not only a daily amusement, but a daily lesson in life; every paper is a sort of tragi-comedy that represents the different distresses and pursuits of mankind; each compiler is a picturesque historian that presents you with something to laugh at, and something to bewail; and their compilations, though a chaos of confused matter promiscuously jumbled together, are aptly expressive of the miseries and follies of mankind. (*SJ*, 25 April 1757)

Of course, eighteenth-century newspapers could be, and were, both *pre-scriptive* in the manner of the first essay, and *descriptive*, as recorded in the second. The two roles are hardly exclusive, and the pragmatic editor moved easily between the two, occasionally making a corrective point with one story, simply reporting another. In the provinces, where most of the copy was selected from the London and some of it from the Continental papers, the very act of selection itself was the means of editorial expression. So, for example, the editor of the *Salisbury Journal* chose his weekly news, endeavouring to be a 'picturesque historian' who recorded the events of the day, exercised good judgement, and was concerned with the public good; who promoted prudence and decency; who traditionally sought both to amuse and instruct his readers; who undertook to get the news out as quickly and accurately as possible; and who helped, in that public-spirited way, to apprehend criminals. The aim was to sell as many newspapers as possible. Benjamin Collins did not, as did some other editors, make a feature of his impartiality, although that was the unstated basis of his claims to truth and verification. This was the editorial spirit that was supposed to rule the selection of general news items and essays.

Editorial essays of the kind that would be at home on a modern leader page are rare in the eighteenth-century provincial weeklies. More common were brief editorial notes, which were often set off typographically from the main text in italic type or within square brackets, or were signalled by a pointing hand or a triangle of asterisks. Very occasionally a whole news item that demonstrated a clear bias was published. A country editor did not actually need to write many column inches himself, even when he wanted to express an opinion; he had only to choose his copy. When an essay appeared in a local paper, it can usually be traced to some earlier printed source. Editorial essays, like other articles from the London papers, were often picked up by more than one country newspaper. For example the *Salisbury Journal* published an attack on the 1776 Stamp Act in an 'extra' dated 6 May 1776; the same essay had already appeared in the *Reading Mercury*.[1]

Obviously economic considerations—that is, competition—sometimes lay behind a provincial editor's published position. When the *Salisbury Journal* was trying to establish itself in Wessex, and saw the *Gloucester Journal* as a rival, Collins placed his newspaper in one camp in the escalating disagreements between weavers and clothiers. No reader could have mistaken Collins's position then, and wealthier subscribers, the weavers among them, might have found his views worth supporting. Later, when the *Journal*'s catchment area was secure, Collins was able to cultivate an editorial position that minimized the possibilities of alienating any

---

[1] Quoted in Jeremy Black, *The English Press in the Eighteenth Century* (Philadephia: University of Pennsylvania Press, 1987), 59–60.

subscribers at the same time as he sought to appeal to the broadest range of local readers. Indeed, into the nineteenth century the *Journal* was still described as one of the many 'neutral' provincial newspapers by the *Newspaper Press Directory* of 1857, which went on to describe the Salisbury paper as one that 'advocates the agricultural interest, and the Protestant principles of the Church of England.—The news of the week is given under different heads, admirably arranged; and the literary articles are well written.'[2]

It was unusual for editorial opinion to be expressed outright in the *Salisbury Journal*, but when it was, it took the conventional form of a brief note as, for example, the suggestion that only the ignorant would protest against inoculation for the smallpox (*SJ*, 16 November 1767), or that nine out of ten shooting accidents were the result of 'carelessness or inattention' (*SJ*, 14 December 1767). By the 1780s a similar observation about guns was directly attributed to the correspondent who had sent in a notice about the death of a child (*SJ*, 8 January 1781). The murder of an infant by its unfortunate mother almost always elicited a recommendation for a foundling hospital, this one reprinted from the *London Evening Post* after one mother had been hanged for such a crime: 'Several late Instances of murdering Bastard Children shews what great Use and Benefit an Hospital for such Infants would be to the Publick; for probably if these Creatures could have their Children taken off their Hands and not expos'd, they would not have lain violent Hands upon them' (*SJ*, 12 March 1737). The editor commented on the 'inhuman Practice of Boxing' when a baker lost his sight in a match (*SJ*, 22 June 1751) and objected, in the local news section, to new laws against smuggling that included bounties for informants on innocent purchasers: '*Amazing Stupidity! to encourage such Miscreants, and thereby subject a Family to Ruin, for the saving a Quarter of a Pound of Tea*' (*SJ*, 18 September 1752). He also opposed the barbarous pastime of cock-throwing, hoping that the death of a 7-year-old from an ill-aimed stick 'will be a warning to others to avoid such very cruel and dangerous Diversion' (*SJ*, 17 March 1755). Again this was comment on a local report. Pickpockets were also censured, within square brackets: 'Such cowardly Rogues ought to be search'd after, and not only sent abroad to serve in the Wars, but put in the Front of the most desperate Engagement, whereby they may peradventure be useful in screening the Lives of honest brave Men' (*SJ*, 29 May 1744).

---

[2] Charles Mitchell, *The Newspaper Press Directory . . . Entirely Revised for the Year 1857* (London: C. Mitchell, [1857]), 60.

Early provincial newspaper editors relied on a broad constituency for subscription and advertising revenue, one that they could not afford to alienate.
So proprietors such as Benjamin Collins usually indulged in uncontro-
versial editorial suggestions, some of them reprints, some of them clearly
their own, that readers of good sense could not fault: when economic
considerations allowed, Collins showed himself to be a conservative proprietor who appeared to temper his editorial conduct with a good deal of
humanity.

Besides these explicit, but relatively innocuous editorial statements,
the *Journal* on one or two occasions indulged in an interpretation of
the news that was quite distinctive and far from impartial. The earliest
example is coverage of the Wiltshire weavers' riots in Melksham during
the winter of 1738/9, discussed in greater detail later in this chapter. In
this case the *Journal* shifted from apparent objectivity to unqualified
support of management and the status quo, an editorial thread that ran
through later stories of property damage and lawlessness. Indeed when
there were corn riots in Salisbury some twenty years later the editor's
recommendation was that '*whatever be our publick Grievances, nothing is
more certain than that they can never be alleviated, but must unavoidably
become worse, by all outrageous and unlawful Proceedings*' (*SJ*, 9 May 1757).
In the very same number a paragraph selected from a London paper, but
based on letters from clothiers in the west of the country, described the
distressing situation of the local poor. Collins evidently did not see any
contradiction. The prevailing economic conditions meant that, as a rule,
Wessex readers were urged actively to support English trade, particularly
the home or British colonial manufacture of cloth, much of which was
based on the Wessex wool trade. Stories of royalty and nobility dressed in
exemplary, and entirely fashionable, English clothing were numerous; there
were always overtones of disapproval when sightings of French cambrics
were reported. In wartime this patriotism became more expansive, so that
a simple report of a musical disappointment on the Isle of Wight—the
failure of a 'grand Foreign Concert of Music' to materialize—could become an object lesson (*SJ*, 14 June 1756).

The *Journal* was on the more popular Tory side when it came to
coverage of Walpole's administration. This was particularly evident in
the satirical verse it published. When Admiral John Byng refused to put
his fleet at risk to protect Minorca the *Journal* mounted the Tory stand
again, lampooning Byng in prose and verse, comparing him unfavourably
with Blakeney, and even publishing the rather feeble poetical efforts of
a 'Young Lady' against Byng ('*Blakeney* we praise, and *Byng* we blame',

SJ, 2 August 1756). *Journal* disapproval was unrelenting almost to the very end, when Byng's graceful acceptance of court martial and execution had to be acknowledged. Collins thereafter seized the opportunity to advertise several printed versions of the trial and the Admiral's last words.

There was nothing impartial about the editor's position on the so-called Jew Bill in 1753 either. The *Journal* joined most of the rest of the country in a hysterical attack on a bill to naturalize Jews, publishing complaints to Wiltshire representatives about their support for it (*SJ*, 13 August 1753) and printing stories of alleged Jewish atrocities (*SJ*, 3 September 1753). There were anti-Semitic riots in the capital, and the bill was repealed. The *Journal*'s editorial position on popular controversial issues could usually be deciphered, even when it was not so direct.

Other broad editorial principles may be discerned in the way the news was handled. Collins, for example, was not above publishing sensational descriptions of hangings and crimes, which is hardly surprising in an age when public executions in England were intended to deter, instruct, and entertain; death was not always as private as it is today; and the detection of crime and the publication of its consequences were viewed as obligations of the newspaper press. The consequences of crime were definitely in the public sector. Even so, a blurry editorial line was drawn between what was considered decent and suitable for a local newspaper and what was not. Coverage in the *Journal* of Elizabeth Brownrigg's mistreatment and subsequent murder of one of her female apprentices in 1767 began with an account of Mrs Brownrigg's repentance and gallows warning, evidently taken as sincere (*SJ*, 21 September 1767). Mrs Brownrigg hoped that others would learn from her fate to avoid cruelty, and suggested that overseers might 'look now and then after the poor young persons of both sexes to see that their masters and mistresses used them well', a sentiment that Paul Langford finds indicative of the changing attitudes towards children and child labour in the eighteenth century.[3] Readers were interested, and Brownrigg's last words were followed the next week with constable John Wingrave's report (*SJ*, 28 September 1767). Wingrave's version of this highly marketable story was a balanced one, offering a few unsavoury details of the apprentice Mary Clifford's death but focusing a good deal of attention on how the crime was discovered with the help of observant neighbours. Editorial care seems to

---

[3] *A Polite and Commercial People: England 1727–1783* (Oxford: Clarendon Press, 1989), 501–3.

have been taken to ensure, so far as possible, that the *Salisbury Journal* capitalized on public interest and curiosity, while at the same time it presented lessons against cruelty and thereby avoided accusations of sensationalism. Details of another brutal murder were suppressed specifically because they might 'make too great an impression' (*SJ*, 29 June 1767).

The editorial line drawn around reports of a more private nature, however, was more straightforward, at least in theory: Collins made it fairly clear that 'personal Correction for private Vices, is not the Business of a Journalist'. He went on to explain that one anecdote that purported to be satire was beyond journalistic consideration, 'for if *Dismal*, as our Correspondent asserts, be only a malign Pauper, long since spew'd out of all good Company, (except being once k—d from a N——n's) he is certainly below the Reach of Satyr, and too contemptible for publick Notice' (*SJ*, 19 June 1758), although it is worth noting that the editor's parenthetical comment might have been enough for local readers to identify *Dismal*. Scandalous stories about local personalities were specifically excluded from the *Journal*, just as they were from other provincial newspapers. Such items appealed to a very limited market, usually carried with them the fear of libel action, and were difficult to substantiate, so that it was simply not worth publishing undiluted gossip as news. Typically the editor advises that '*The Warminster Witling has some humour, but rather too much ill nature and personal reflection for a public news paper*' (*SJ*, 3 March 1766), or that 'The account of a late fray between a man and his wife at L—k, had better be kept to themselves than made public, especially as they seem to be both to blame, and are both sufferers; therefore we advise them to kiss and be friends, and do so no more' (*SJ*, 31 March 1766). Comments of this sort were almost always set in italic type, a style that gave both emphasis (in its difference from the roman type of the text) and intimacy (in the slope of the letter) to these brief editorials. Another story was rejected because the Subject was 'of too private a Nature either to interest or entertain the Publick' (*SJ*, 12 April 1756). Nevertheless, similar accounts did occasionally appear as paid advertisements. The reclassification of a controversial personal item from news or literature to *advertisement* seems effectively to have shifted responsibility from editor to paying customer.

A newspaper's editorial framework provides a context for an investigation of its contents. It has been observed that in general eighteenth-century newspapers do not readily lend themselves to detailed content analysis: their 'conspicuous variety' is one problem; it is not always easy or even possible to separate the borrowed news items from those originally submitted by reporters or written in-house; the division between news and advertising was often obscured by the practice of puffing; and it is sometimes difficult to discern whether or not a news story was a paid-for, and possibly biased, contribution.[4] Even if the contents of a given newspaper were precisely quantified, it would be unrealistic to attempt to see direct correlations between the presentation of the news and the opinions of the readership or even of the editors. The relationship is particularly untidy for a country newspaper such as the *Salisbury Journal*, which was widely distributed through a diverse catchment area that included large commercial ports, wool and dairy country, and cathedral towns.

Yet reconstructing the very rough physical outlines of what was in the newspaper can be a fruitful starting point for discussion. The very first number of the new *Salisbury Journal* for 27 November 1736 may be taken as representative of the young provincial papers of the time. Four printed London news sources are cited, the *London Evening Post* of 20 November on page 1, and the *General Evening-Post*, the *Daily Gazette*, and the *London Gazette* on the second page. Other news is drawn from '*several* LONDON PRINTS', and an unspecified '*written Letter* LONDON 23 *Nov.*', along with letters from Leghorn and Paris (one of them in fact postdating this issue of the *Journal* with '*Nov.* 28 [NS]', since England had not yet adopted the New Style Calendar). There were also local and London reports. The most recent news appears in the form of a postscript in the third, and last, column on page 4; the oldest is on page 1.

As for the news itself in the first number of the *Journal*, reports with St Petersburg, Lisbon, and Vienna datelines are followed by a section headed 'LONDON' carrying three columns of news ranging from an account of the Princess of Wales's birthday celebrations to a description of one Mrs Jenning's coffin ('six Foot and a half long, and two Foot nine inches over, cover'd with Velvet'). The same section contains two items in which the editorial position is unmistakable. A report on a fatal accident in which sloppily constructed scaffolding played a part concludes that 'Accidents of this Kind are very common, tho' so easily avoided; but generally speaking those only suffer thro' whose Negligence these Disasters happen, and who with a very little Care might prevent any

---

[4] Jeremy Black discusses the general problems of precision in content analysis in his *English Press*, 26–8. Virginia Berridge has a useful discussion of the historiography and wider issues of the subject (with particular reference to late nineteenth-century newspaper reporting) in 'Content Analysis and Historical Research on Newspapers', in Michael Harris and Alan Lee (eds.), *The Press in English Society from the Seventeenth to Nineteenth Centuries* (London: Associated University Presses, 1986), 201–18.

thing of that Nature.' The next complains that, in spite of a new Gin Act, 'the Skirts of the Town are pester'd with great Numbers of these walking Distillers'. Even though both comments probably derived from London, it is significant that they were adopted by Wiltshire editors. The local Salisbury news consists of a brief notice of the death of Thomas Lewis, a former Member of Parliament for Salisbury. A curious mixture of Continental news, sensational crime, and lists of preferments, deaths, promotions, bankrupts, and stock makes up the rest. The lone advertisement is for William Salmon's *Builder's Guide* printed for James Hodges in London, and sold by William Collins and three other provincial booksellers. In 1736 the colophon names only William Collins, but within five years it would list the numerous agents who helped administer the *Salisbury Journal*'s distribution network. A woodcut headpiece with a view of Salisbury, flanked by the city seal on the left and the intertwined initials *BC* and *WC*[5] on the right are the only decorations, aside from one factotum and a few type ornaments.

By sampling whole numbers of the *Salisbury Journal* from each decade after this, the individual pattern of its contents can be reconstructed, and that pattern filled out by a catalogue of representative stories, genres, and subjects, an investigation that can in turn enlarge on the details of editorial method. For this sample the first number for each month from the first year of each decade from 1740 to 1780, and the first and last numbers published under Collins's management in 1736 and 1785, have been selected for basic commercial (that is advertisements) and non-commercial (that is news—including local, national, and international from any source—literary and political essays, and verse) categories. The exercise gives a general idea of the relative weight of the news, literary, and advertising content of the paper through its first fifty years. Even so simple and selective a method then yields something more of eighteenth-century editorial method and its dual descriptive-prescriptive nature, and suggests how the provincial newspaper shaped the provincial reading market and how the market shaped the newspaper.

The provincial newspapers, and most of their metropolitan counterparts, were looking for a balance between the provision of intelligence, which attracted subscribers but earned little or no direct income, and the sale of advertisements, which usefully attracted both readers and direct income. The first number of the *Salisbury Journal* in 1736 had about 10.4 columns of news and 1.6 columns of advertisements, so it was heavily

[5] Evidently standing for Benjamin Collins and William Collins.

weighted towards news; 87 per cent was news, only 13 per cent paid advertising. Thereafter the real profit-makers, the advertisements, steadily gained ground, propelled both by the proprietors' desire to make money and the consumers' to give notice. In 1740 the *Journal* averaged about 70 per cent news, 26 per cent advertising, while the remaining 4 per cent was divided between essays and verse. The *Salisbury Journal* had a literary element almost from the very beginning. The first poetry appeared in the 18 December 1736 number, 'A Receipt to Make an Epigram' ('A pleasing subject first with care provide,'). News made up about 60 per cent of the content in 1750, and advertising 29 per cent. In 1760 the non-commercial content of the paper took up just over half the column space (47 per cent news, 5 per cent essays, 1 per cent verse), but by 1770 advertisements took up well over half the paper's column space (56 per cent). The trend did not stop even there: in 1780 advertisements took up on average nearly 60 per cent of the space available. The *Salisbury Journal* saw growing numbers of subscribers at the same time, so it is evident that readers tolerated a large measure of advertising with their news; indeed many of them positively encouraged the trend. One could argue too, that a high level of paid advertising is one measure of a newspaper's influence. It is certainly a gauge of its economic success.

From the many that might have been discussed two topics in particular within the period have been selected for more detailed analysis. They complement the rather more superficial enumeration of subjects, which is dictated by the eclectic nature of most of the newspaper's contents and by the brevity of each item. One, from the *Journal*'s early days of news-dominated columns, is the Melksham riots; the other is the coverage of events leading to the American Declaration of Independence in July 1776. The editorial development of the story of the Melksham weavers' uprisings during the winter of 1738/9 is a useful case, for it reveals something of how the editors both responded to and in some ways manipulated their readers when their newspaper was very young.

The rioting began on 27 November 1738 and the first *Salisbury Journal* report, concerned primarily with the committal of one of the rioters to the local gaol, appeared about a week later, on 4 December 1738. The account was cursory, describing the riot in a relatively objective manner as one in which 'some Hundreds' of workmen assembled to march on Melksham where they destroyed looms, cloth, records, and securities belonging to the clothier Mr Colthurst, and then broke into his wine cellar. It was reported that John Crabb, the gaoled weaver, had offered to turn evidence against the ringleaders. The *Journal* editors offered no opinion, and concluded the report with the promise of further 'Particulars . . . as they occur'.

The next issue, 11 December, brought '*a more particular Relation of the rising of the Weavers and Sheermen*' possibly derived from one of the London papers. While the damage to Colthurst's property is given in detail, the essay cannot fairly be described as biased—the weavers are said to have acted only after Colthurst had unilaterally lowered prices, and it was noted that they had rejected Colthurst's offer of better rates on the reasonable grounds that he had made false promises in the past. Next week there was a one-line notice on page 3 about garrisons stationed in 'the Clothing Part of Wiltshire' to prevent further trouble, a report that was derived from the London papers, and, on page 4, a list of those committed to the county gaol. With a total of nine alleged rioters now in local custody, the managers of the *Salisbury Journal* must have begun to take a proprietorial interest in a controversial regional event that was beginning to interest the whole nation.

Yet the Wessex editors' position was not clarified until Robert Raikes's provocative 'Essay on Riots' had been published in his *Gloucester Journal*, 19 December 1738.[6] The 'Essay on Riots' would have been particularly inflammatory in Wiltshire, for Raikes seemed concerned to localize the problems. The opposite views of the Collins and Raikes establishments had already been defined by the rivalry between the two newspapers, much in evidence over the previous spring and summer: the *Salisbury Journal* claimed that the *Gloucester Journal* sometimes dressed up Saturday's news as Monday's (*SJ*, 22 May 1738); Raikes's efforts to incorporate his own literary essays into the Gloucester paper were ridiculed— his 'Country Common Sense' was described as '*a flat heavy Composition*' (*SJ*, 3 July 1738); and Raikes was accused of marketing 'Quack Intelligence' (*SJ*, 31 July 1738). The *Salisbury Journal* essay, published in the 8 January 1739 number, was in part reactionary, designed to counter Raikes's suggestions that some of the blame for the trouble lay with the master clothiers of Wiltshire and even with the Government—Raikes's proposal to form an official commission of enquiry into a number of issues was answered with a list of opposing heads of enquiry. At the same time the

---

[6] Raikes (1689–1757) was the father of Robert Raikes, prominent in the Sunday School movement (Roland Austin, 'Robert Raikes, the Elder, and the "Gloucester Journal"', *Library*, 3rd ser., 6/21 (1915), 1–24; H. R. Plomer, *A Dictionary of the Printers and Booksellers Who Were at Work in England, Scotland, and Ireland from 1668 to 1725* (London: The Bibliographical Society, 1922), 246; and Frank Booth, *Robert Raikes of Gloucester* (Redhill, Surrey: National Christian Education Council, 1980), 30–44).

Salisbury Journal essay was sharply focused on the pro-clothier view, a position that might have been calculated to appeal to at least one important section of Wiltshire readers.[7]

Thereafter the *Journal* editors departed from the rhetoric of objectivity to describe the 'Insurrection of the Weavers' in terms of 'outrageous Fury' and 'the Horrour of the neighbouring Country'. To verify this version of the story they produced an account of the riots signed by a number of Melksham clothiers and others whose property had been damaged, a document that could hardly be described as unbiased. The death in custody of two of the rioters was dismissed with a short notice (*SJ*, 15 January 1739). When news became scarce during the interval between the imprisonment of the rioters and their trials, the *Salisbury Journal* brought out a treatise on the woollen manufacture (*SJ*, 29 January 1739), and printed a letter signed by thirty-five clothiers who denied the *Gloucester Journal*'s allegations of paying workers in truck (*SJ*, 5 February 1739). When the Wessex cloth workers had rioted ten years before, they met with a sympathetic response at public and Governmental levels. This time the weavers' case was not so well received, and the story ended with the hanging of several of the ringleaders, a story the *Salisbury Journal* was able to report with evident satisfaction that justice had been done. It is impossible to gauge what part the *Journal* played in bringing that particular justice to life. In all this the Salisbury paper seemed to be responding to its Gloucester competitor, rather than initiating any controversy.

The rivalry between the two provincial papers was effectively translated to London, when the two versions of the story were reproduced, one in the *Gentleman's Magazine*, the other in the *London*, which competed head on with each other for the monthly magazine market. The *London Magazine* had in fact initially promised its readers Raikes's 'Essay', but thought better of the idea and instead reprinted the *Salisbury Journal*'s view:

In our last, we promis'd a certain Essay on Riots; but as we are since assur'd, that there are many Misrepresentations and false Insinuations in that Essay, with regard to the Master Weavers, Clothiers, &c. in and about Melksham; which are answer'd in the

---

[7] The Melksham rioting was a popular but divisive issue, and a great deal was published on the subject, including another answer to Raikes's 'Essay', a pamphlet by 'Philalethes': *The Case as It Now Stands, between the Clothiers, Weavers, and Other Manufacturers, with regard to the Late Riot, in the County of Wilts* (London: Printed for the Author, and Sold by T. Cooper, 1739). Here the weavers are accorded barely human status—apprentice weavers are placed 'into a Capacity of obtaining a comfortable Subsistence, with scarce any human Abilities. It is a Trade so easy in itself, that formerly it was deemed the proper Employment of a Woman . . .' (p. 13).

SALISBURY JOURNAL *of the 8th of this Month; we desire to be excus'd inserting the said Essay . . .*[8]

The *London*'s subsequent coverage of the affairs relating to the uprising was also derived from the *Salisbury Journal*. The significant role of the book-trade networks is evident: the *London Magazine* was run by Thomas Astley, a long-time colleague of the Collins brothers, and was later managed by Benjamin Collins's first apprentice Richard Baldwin. On the other hand the *Gentleman's Magazine*, edited by Edward Cave who long had had connections with Robert Raikes,[9] picked up the *Gloucester Journal*'s pro-weavers version.

Placed in this context of business networks and commercial rivalry the story of the Melksham riots shows how complicated any analysis of the news can be. The proprietors of a new Wessex newspaper aiming to attract readers from the longer-established Gloucester paper might have calculated some advantage from declaring a position on a controversial local affair. Certainly the bias towards the management side was sharpened only after the appearance of Raikes's 'Essay' turned the riots into a national journalistic issue. When the *Gloucester Journal* became involved in promoting the weavers' cause, reporting in the *Salisbury Journal* slipped into propaganda in favour of the opposite side. Weavers in the *Salisbury Journal* became lawless, insensible property wreckers; clothiers represented reasonable men who were no longer (if they ever had been) guilty of exploiting their employees, whose word was proof against their accusers. This is underlined by the London connections, when the rival provincial versions were picked up by rival metropolitan periodicals. It was no coincidence that one of Raikes's close London associates printed his story, while one of Collins's London colleagues printed his.

Perhaps the proprietors sought new *Salisbury Journal* subscribers among those who sympathized with the clothiers and their version was a deliberate appeal to that part of the market. Few weavers could have been interested in buying a newspaper. A personal element cannot be ruled out either: Collins's own biography suggests that he would have had a natural sympathy for the establishment cause; equally Robert Raikes,

---

[8] *LM* (Jan. 1739), 9.

[9] In 1728 Raikes was summoned to the House of Commons to face charges of printing reports of their Proceedings, which had been supplied by Cave (Austin, 'Robert Raikes', 16; see also Plomer, *Dictionary 1668–1725*, 246; for Edward Cave see Plomer, *A Dictionary of the Printers and Booksellers Who Were at Work in England, Scotland and Ireland from 1726 to 1775* (London: The Bibliographical Society, 1932), 47–8; and A. D. Barker, 'Edward Cave, Samuel Johnson and the *Gentleman's Magazine*', D.Phil. thesis (Oxford University, 1981)).

whose son played a leading part in the early Sunday School movement, might have been expected to side with a group he believed was oppressed. The private convictions of the two editors might well have been behind some of the reports. Even so, such concerns did not interfere for long, and by 1742 Collins and Raikes were able to overcome their differences. Raikes advertised for subscribers to Thomas Allen's *Archaeologia universalis* in the Salisbury paper, and in 1755 was listed among the *Salisbury Journal* newsagents.

The Melksham riots developed into a story that any sensible newspaper editor should have been happy to publish. The issues—alleged exploitation of workers and unlawful practice on the part of their employers, plus the undisputed facts of riot and destruction of property—were clearly national ones, especially after the London press had picked up the story. Reconstructing a larger context for the original reports assists in their interpretation. But whether or not the printed rhetoric of the Melksham riots was effective—did it persuade anyone that hanging the weavers was a just punishment? did it win over new readers?—remains an unanswered question.

The news in the more mature *Salisbury Journal* was not usually so open to detailed contextual analysis; perhaps it was not so keenly felt later, when Collins was more secure in his editorial position. Most reports have to be taken on face value. Nearly all the international and national news was derivative, of course, with stories routinely extracted from a range of printed sources. Yet editorial efforts to sustain a level of objectivity can be detected in other news, even in the coverage of such a controversial issue as American independence in the 1770s. 'W.X.Y.' was probably right when he wrote in early 1776

I Believe there is not a person in this kingdom but is more or less interested in the present struggle between us and our American Colonists, and not many so totally divested of all concern for the event, as to take no side in it; but every one seems to have attached himself to one or the other. (*SJ*, 11 March 1776)

Reporting of events leading to the American Declaration of Independence in July 1776 was conducted along the lines of an inquiry, with evidence presented for both sides, and sources identified so that no reader need be confused about the politics underlying any report. The editorial principle in operation in this second example seems to be to present the facts available so that the reader can himself refashion the story. Implicit in this principle is the acknowledgement that readers of both persuasions were numbered among *Journal* subscribers. One week might see the colonial rebels described as bullies and bluffers (*SJ*, 16 January 1775), while the next sees the publication of Chatham's conciliatory Bill for Settling the Troubles in America (*SJ*, 23 January 1775). One discussion corrects earlier reports, balancing the argument by describing the acceptable form of enthusiasm practised by many American colonists:

we hear that the greatest unanimity prevails in the Colonies. It is not a faction or tumultuous mob, as has been said, that oppose the measures of government, but gentlemen of the first rank and fortune, people of all degrees and professions, unite in a solemn engagement to defend their liberties. They profess the utmost loyalty to the King. They acknowledge the supremacy of Parliament in all matters of trade and commerce, and they regret that they should be driven by a vindict-ive Ministry into a contention with the good people of England; but they deem the power of taxing the Colonies, and altering their chartered form of govern-ment . . . to be unconstitutional, and an attempt to rob them of their property, and reduce them to a state of slavery. . . . This enthusiastic spirit runs through the whole Continent, manifesting itself, not in rash expressions of passion and animosity, but in a cool, serious, and obstinate determination to persist unto the last. (*SJ*, 26 June 1775)

Both sides of the colonial trade question were considered: one manufacturer wrote to support an embargo on all imports from America (*SJ*, 2 Janu-ary 1775), while there are a number of opposing reports from English port towns describing the hardships brought on by the subsequent loss of trade. Editors tried to maintain equilibrium, but they were also con-cerned that the information they passed on to their readers was reliable. To this end reports from the participants in overseas news were actively encouraged. R.S., for example, contributed a factual account of the siege of Quebec written by 'a very intelligent Officer on the spot' and received the editors' printed '*thanks for his intelligence*' and the suggestion that they '*shall be happy in his future favours*' (*SJ*, 1 July 1776).

The Melksham riots were controversial local news presented by the young editors of a new paper who did little to disguise biases; the key events of American Independence took place far away, across the Atlantic for the most part, and were reconstructed on the pages of what had by then become a long-established weekly newspaper. The Collins brothers were at their most radical when the weavers rioted; Benjamin was look-ing to retire from the newspaper trade when the Declaration of Independ-ence was signed. Yet most of the news, local and foreign, was selected and reported in a measure that was designed to appeal to a differentiated Wessex market, and any number of stories—the battle of Cartagena, the

events of the 'Forty-Five, the Seven Years War, the Gordon Riots—
might serve to illustrate.

Occasionally other stories in the *Journal*, none of them so dramatic
as Melksham, invite a search for clues to ulterior motives. Collins and
most of the London book trade naturally were interested in preserving
the London booksellers' monopoly in copyright. That interest may have
underwritten an unrealistically optimistic interpretation of a Chancery
Court decision in 1770:

> Yesterday was heard in the Court of Chancery the cause which has been some
> years depending between Mr. Millar, late a bookseller in London, and Mr.
> Taylor, Bookseller at Berwick, for vending a pirated edition of Mr. Thomson's
> *Seasons*, when the Lords Commissioners of the Great Seal were pleased to
> decree, that Mr. Taylor should account to Mr. Millar's executors for all that he
> had sold, and farther to decree a perpetual injunction against Mr. Taylor. Thus
> the question about literary property is finally closed, which is a matter of great
> concern to all booksellers, who have given large sums of money to authors for
> their writings; and the booksellers in town and country will do well to take
> warning, *that they offened* [*sic*] *not by selling any pirated editions of books.*
>
> (*SJ*, 30 July 1770)

In fact the struggle continued for another four years until the decision in
another case, Donaldson *v*. Beckett, finally put an end to the perpetual
copyright the booksellers had hoped to maintain.[10] Was it purely by accident
that verses mourning the death of Prince Frederick ('Weep all ye inhabitants of the land')[11] were juxtaposed with the announcement that 'We
hear there will be a Jubilee Ball at Ranelagh the 16th of April next' (*SJ*,
25 March 1751)? Was there anything unusual behind stories such as that
of the robbery committed by a man wearing a 'Masquerade Nose' (*SJ*, 28
January 1751)? Even the story of a night-time raid on Benjamin Collins's
own cabbage patch and pigsty (*SJ*, 12 May 1766) might have been the
product of some personal animosity.

Besides ordinary news, the *Journal* frequently included essays from
other periodicals, as well as poetry ranging from two-line epigrams to the
annual New Year's Ode. Verse was a leading component of the *Salisbury
Journal* from at least 1730, when the final number of the first unsuccessful
Journal began with 'The Peaceful Subject' ('What care I how the King of

---

[10] A clear and accessible synopsis of the issue is Sir Frank Mackinnon's 'Notes on the
History of English Copyright', in *The Oxford Companion to English Literature*, 5th edn., ed.
Margaret Drabble (Oxford: Oxford University Press, 1985), 1113–25.

[11] Frederick died 20 Mar. 1751.

Spain'). Between 1736 and 1770 over 1,100 poems were printed in the paper. One cannot escape the impression that much of the verse in the *Journal* was there for the purely practical purpose of filling out the columns: verse might be composed in type and left standing until required, when it could be used to fit almost any hole in the news columns. There was less of it when hard news was abundant. Yet readers clearly tolerated poetry, read it, and even sent in their own contributions. Such major writers as Pope were well regarded by both editor and readers throughout Wessex. Pope's death was a distressing event that was itself an inspiration to other poets. A number of their works, some of it local, and some of it unfortunately signalling 'The gen'ral Triumph of the *Dunciad* fry' were reprinted in the *Salisbury Journal*, including one 'On Mr. *POPE*'S Death being mentioned in some News-Papers, without any Account of his Character, Works, Life, Age, or Circumstances of his last Illness' (*SJ*, 26 June 1744).[12]

> *WHEN some fat Burgess nurs'd in legal Stealth*
> *Resigns his worthless Soul and Sin-got wealth;*
> *The pompous Paragraph expands his Name,*
> *And Advertiser's hawk him one Day's Fame;*
> *But when from* BRITAIN, *all the Muses fled,*
> *Scarce half a Line inform'd us POPE was dead!*
> *Thus should Oxonin's City sink in Fire,*
> *And Trade and Science in one Blaze—expire,*
> *As well on Shops might dull Attention turn,*
> *And unregarded, the—Bodleian burn.*

Almost any controversial political measure inspired a flurry of mediocre verse in the newspapers, a fact George Crabbe deplored in *The News-Paper* (1785).

> A time like this, a busy, bustling time,
> Suits ill with writers, very ill with rhyme;
> Unheard we sing when party rage runs strong,
> And mightier madness checks the flowing song:
> Or should we force the peaceful Muse to wield
> Her feeble arms amid the furious field,
> Where party pens a wordy war maintain,
> Poor is her anger, and her friendship vain;
>
>   .   .   .   .

---

[12] Other commemorative poems appeared 5 June, 10 July, 17 July, 7, 21 Aug., 4 Sept., and 13 Nov. 1744.

> Or should we sing the subject of the day,
> To-morrow's wonder puffs our praise away.[13]

Even the first lines of poetry in the *Journal* betray their mediocrity: 'Hosier! with indignant sorrow' and 'From Cadiz to Mahon see Haddock goes' are poetical comments on Walpole's administration; 'Oft' Fourteenth Lewis took the field' describes the French King's cowardice; 'Jove said, let there be light—and, lo' is one on the window tax; and 'Since Wilkes is your alderman, pray change your name' on Wilkes's recent election to MP for Middlesex, are but a few examples.[14] The Bishop of Cloyne, George Berkeley's tar water was another issue that aroused public interest. An infusion of tar in cold water, it was promoted as a panacea in his widely read *Siris: A Chain of Philosophical Reflections concerning the Virtues of Tar Water* (1744).[15] The properties of tar water were debated in the *Journal* in verse as well as prose, including one poem that begins 'Infected sheep commence a war' (*SJ*, 18 September 1744). It might seem a startlingly timely piece to any modern reader who is concerned about BSE, the so-called mad cow disease, but in fact the poet is discussing here the revolt of a metaphorical flock against its metaphorical shepherd.

Verse sometimes even found its way into advertising. One early jingle praised Thomas Ryall's new-invented cork wig:

> Till now, nor Hair, nor Wool, or Feather,
> Could e'er stand Buff against all Weather;
> And unrelaxed, like this, resist
> Both Wind and Rain, and Snow and Mist. (*SJ*, 28 December 1760)

Although poetical words could not be found to describe Ryall's other product, a 'Powder-Spurting Machine', wigs were evidently rather lyrical devices. Another cork-wig maker, Joseph Leach in Romsey, was able to advise his customers that

> When Baldness or grey Hairs, the Fruits of Age,
> Attacks Mankind with irresistless Rage,
> Nature's Defects may here obtain Repairs,
> And youthful Bloom restor'd by artificial Hairs. (*SJ*, 16 May 1763)

---

[13] George Crabbe, *The News-Paper: A Poem*, lines 1–8, 15–16, in his *Complete Poetical Works*, ed. Norma Dalrymple-Champneys and Arthur Pollard (Oxford: Clarendon Press, 1988), i. 181.

[14] These lines appeared 29 July 1740, 19 Aug. 1740, 24 Apr. 1744, 16 Feb. 1747, 6 Feb. 1769 respectively.

[15] The work, a collection of Berkeley's essays on the subject, was given the title *Siris*, after the Ethiopian name for the river Nile, only with the second edn.

Occasionally the triteness of some verse was paid the compliment of a mildly witty rejoinder:

An EPITAPH,
In a Church-yard in Dorsetshire.

FOR me, deceased, weep not my Dear,
I am not dead, but sleepeth here:
Your time will come, prepare to die;
Wait but a-while, you'll come to I.

Answered by a Gentleman, on his marrying a Fortnight after,

I am not griev'd, my dearest Life,
Sleep on, I've got another Wife;
And therefore cannot come to Thee,
For I must go to Bed to She.   (*SJ*, 18 June 1753)

Local contributions to the poetical side of the *Salisbury Journal* reflect the enthusiasm of some readers. One whose signed verse was regularly published in the *Journal* was Henry Price of Poole. His contributions were serious ones for the most part, considering such issues as the Jacobite cause in 1745 ('Presumptuous youth!', *SJ*, 10 September 1745), and true patriotism (*SJ*, 31 October 1748). He also addressed a scold ('Loud thund'ring thro' the throat fierce Juno storms', *SJ*, 3 July 1749) and comforted Mr Jolliffe in verse after the loss of his wife. In this last Price managed to bring together a line from Pope's translation of the *Iliad* and an allusion to 'a very neat House' the widower was building (*SJ*, 22 August 1748).

Other poetry that can be associated with local authors reflected on the beauty of two young women in Newton Tony (*SJ*, 19 May 1746) and a recent turnpike meeting (*SJ*, 26 August 1765). '*A Gentleman of* SARUM' discussed his first attack of the gout:

AND why, Sir, surly GOUT this new abode?
Strange! thus to wander from a beaten Road!
Which wou'd have led you to your wonted place,
Where's fitter entertainment for your Grace,
Who'd think your Quality shou'd stoop so low,
To make this Paltry Visit to my Toe?
I hope, gruff Sir, your Stay will not be long,
For I protest if 'tis, you'll spoil my Song. . . .   (*SJ*, 28 August 1744)

The variety of poetical topics in the *Salisbury Journal*, like the straightforward news, suggests the range of interests and views of the local reading population. Essays, which regularly supplemented the news, add another dimension.

'WRITERS who furnish daily papers with essays, may be aptly compared to the present venders of Ward's medicines; they endeavour to dole out nostrums for the good of the public at a very cheap rate' (*SJ*, 24 October 1763). The same might equally be said of those who supplied the *weekly* papers to the country, that is the provincial editors who selected the essays literary, political, serious, and comic to include in their various journals. The *Reading Mercury* was quite explicit in its policy for prose in 1747:

Before the breaking out of the late unnatural Rebellion, this Paper was in high reputation for the many agreeable Extracts it contain'd, it is therefore thought proper (now Peace is again restor'd in our own Country) to revive those Extracts, which cannot but afford a rational entertainment to those who have not the opportunity of seeing the originals. The 'Gentleman's Magazine' for February has a very elegant collection of curious, and entertaining particulars; out of which I shall select a few for the rest. (*Reading Mercury*, 16 March 1747)[16]

Such contributions appeared regularly in the *Salisbury Journal* in those newsless times of peace, more often than not as the first item in the paper. Essays had entertainment value and were useful fillers. The positioning of essays is another reminder that page 1 of a newspaper served a different purpose in the eighteenth century (and indeed on into the nineteenth) than it does today. If the compositor set the outer forme (that is pages 1 and 4) first, which was common practice, then less timely items such as essays could be prepared for the first page well before the weekly deadline. Samuel Johnson's *Rambler* and *Idler* essays were occasionally included, as well as extracts from Sir John Hill's *Inspector* series in the *Daily Advertiser*; John Hawkesworth's *Adventurer* (to which Johnson sometimes contributed); the *World*, which was originally published by Robert Dodsley and had numerous contributors; George Colman and Bonnell Thornton's *Connoisseur*, and John Wilkes's notorious *North Briton*. They were usually published in separate series: for example, *Rambler* essays were regularly published in the *Journal* in 1751; essays from the *Inspector* and the *Adventurer* appeared in 1752; extracts from the *World* in 1753–6; the *Connoisseur* in 1754–5; the *Idler* in 1759; *Citizen of the World* in 1760; the *North Briton* later still, and so on.[17] Oliver Goldsmith's *Citizen of the World* made

---

[16] Quoted in K. G. Burton, *The Early Newspaper Press in Berkshire (1723–1855)* (Reading: published by the author, 1954).

[17] See Richard B. Schwartz's essays on the *Adventurer*, the *Idler*, and the *Rambler* in Alvin Sullivan (ed.), *British Literary Magazines: The Augustan Age and the Age of Johnson, 1698–1788* (Westport, Conn.: Greenwood Press, 1983), 8–11, 164–7, 283–7; Lance Bertelsen on the *Connoisseur*, ibid. 46–52; and Deborah Ayer Sitter and John Sitter on the *World*, ibid. 369–72.

its first appearance as a series of Letters from Lien Chi Altangi in the *Public Ledger* early in 1760, and was reprinted in the *Salisbury Journal*, among other newspapers, very soon after: the *Journal* series began on 31 March 1760. As some of the favoured authors, notably Samuel Johnson and Oliver Goldsmith, were ones in which Benjamin Collins had invested as part-copyright owner, it was in his commercial interest to promote them to local readers.

The epistolary form was favoured by the authors of other essays too. One, who signed himself Democritus, commented ironically on the modish life in his '*Serious Exhortation to Learn to* Whistle', proposing that bored young men might better turn their minds to a pastime more useful than University and the Grand Tour: 'If they could but whistle well, they might converse with a Black-bird, or a Thrush, almost upon an Equality; which is an Advantage they seldom enjoy in human Conversations' (*SJ*, 7 July 1746). Other contributions ranged from Latin verse to essays on agricultural methods and included a letter from Farmer Trueman's dog Towzer to his friend Ponto, regarding the new dog tax and proposing an alternative tax on those humans called Sad-Dogs, Lazy-Dogs, and Puppies (*SJ*, 28 January 1751). Its hospitality to such literary excursions are evidence of the paper's concern to attract as wide and diverse a Wessex readership as possible. But during more turbulent times, news always pre-empted entertainment, and when Britain was engaged in war, the first story in the *Journal* was usually official news from the *London Gazette*, or occasionally a military essay from another periodical such as the *Monitor*. The obligation to make room for real news was one that most newspaper editors took seriously—one might recall that Robert Raikes was taken to task for allowing his 'Country Common Sense' essays to take space from the news (*SJ*, 3 July 1738).[18]

It is impossible to gauge the extent to which eighteenth-century public opinion was moulded by the newspapers; indeed it is difficult to prove that public opinion was directed by the mass media at all, although many contemporaries believed this to be so. There are eighteenth-century anecdotes both about those who would believe almost anything that appeared in print, and those who remained sceptical of anything that purported to be news if it was published in a newspaper. John Toland, writing about 1717, had no doubt that newspapers could 'poyson the minds of the common people against his Majesty . . . vilify his Ministers, & disturb the

---

[18] Similarly the editor of the *Kentish Post* was criticized for his 'Kentish Spectator' in 1738 (G. A. Cranfield, *The Development of the Provincial Newspaper 1700–1760* (Oxford: Clarendon Press, 1962), 104).

public peace, to the scandal of all good Government'.[19] As we have seen, Johnson usefully demonstrated both sides when he paid for fictitious news to be inserted in the *Public Advertiser*—one of the points he wanted to make to Mrs Thrale's mother was that she should take a more critical view of what she found in the papers.[20] There was scepticism about the validity of printed periodical news almost as soon as it existed. Ben Jonson talked about the 'publish'd pamphlets of *Newes*, set out euery Saturday, but made all at home, & no syllable of truth in them: then which there cannot be a greater disease in nature, or a fouler scorne put vpon the times'.[21] And the first number of John Crouch's *Mercurius Democritus* was introduced with verse along the same lines:

> *Of Wonders great I here shall tell,*
> *More strange did ne'er come out*
> *In* Lil-lyes Progg. *nor* Mandivil,
> Diurnall *or the* SCOUT.
>
> *Their* Lies *are now grown too too stale,*
> *Alas the more's the pitty,*
> *They should commixt with* Yest *and* Ale
> *Besot both Town and Citie.*
>
> *Here are more noble* Bonses *fair*
> *That gives greater report,*
> *Then* Spy, *or French* Intelligencer,
> *Or* Poll. *that* Lyes *in Court.*
>
> *Perhaps you'l say these are but* Lies,
> *Why should I this deny,*
> Lies *are all* truths *ith'* Antipodes,
> *Read on, Ile tell you why.*[22]

Another approach to contents and readers is through a single subject as it was observed in the *Salisbury Journal* over fifty years. The treatment of women in a provincial newspaper may be considered in this respect. John Dunton's *Ladies Mercury* might have signalled a new awareness

---

[19] John Toland, 'Proposal for Regulating the News-Papers', BL Add. MS 4295, fo. 49ᵛ.

[20] Betty Rizzo, ' "Innocent Frauds": By Samuel Johnson', *Library*, 6th ser., 8 (1986), 249–64.

[21] *The Staple of Newes*, in *The Workes of Benjamin Jonson: The Second Volume* (London: printed for Richard Meighen, 1640), prologue, act iii.

[22] *Mercurius Democritus, or a True and Perfect Nocturnall, Communicating Wonderfull News out of the World in the Moon*, 1 (8 Apr. 1652), 1. See also Carolyn Nelson and Matthew Seccombe (comps.), *British Newspapers and Periodicals 1641–1700: A Short-Title Catalogue of Serials Printed in England, Scotland, Ireland, and British America* (New York: Modern Language Association, 1987), no. 307.

of women readers and contributors in 1693;[23] certainly it helped create a tradition of literary periodicals written for, and sometimes by, women that was carried on into the eighteenth century with such magazines as *Records of Love or Weekly Amusements for the Fair Sex* (1710), the *Free-thinker or Essays on Ignorance* (1718–19), and the *Female Spectator* (1744–6).[24] One might therefore expect to find related developments in the newspaper press, perhaps in a regular address to female readers, or in attention to women's topics. Nevertheless the non-commercial content of the *Salisbury Journal* saw little change over the course of its first fifty years: it remained directed towards an audience that was largely composed of men, although the editors now and then were happy to acknowledge that there were women among its readers and listeners. The *Journal* numbered far more men among its paying subscribers as a matter of course, and that shows in detailed coverage of political events, agricultural improvements, peace treaties, battles, and so on. The Uncle Tobys would have found material enough in the pages of the *Salisbury Journal* to support any military passion, from eyewitness accounts of battles to woodcut illustrations. At this time women were excluded from coffee-houses, where a great deal of newspaper-reading commonly took place, although they had other opportunities to read a paper in public. Thomas Benge Burr described both coffee-houses and bookshops as 'places where the social virtues reign triumphant over prejudice and prepossession', but he thought that the

bookseller's shop has indeed an advantage over the coffee-house, because there the ladies are admitted; and, like so many living stars, shine in the greatest splendor, while they evidence, that british beauties are no less superior to their sex throughout the world, in the inward ornament of the understanding, than they are universally allowed to be in the external graces of the body——.[25]

Attitude towards women in the *Salisbury Journal* was complicated. It could be described as a form of benevolent paternalism, often coloured with admiration for the extraordinary and unusual, or disapproval of the socially unacceptable. There was nothing remarkable about such a position. The story of Miss Polly Baker of Connecticut is one example: threatened

[23] Bertha-Monica Stearns, 'The First English Periodical for Women', *Modern Philology*, 28 (1930–1), 45–59, and Gilbert D. McEwen, *The Oracle of the Coffee House: John Dunton's Athenian Mercury* (San Marino, Calif.: Huntington Library, 1972), 103–4.

[24] See Deborah Ayer Sitter and John Sitter's essay on the *Female Spectator* in Sullivan (ed.), *British Literary Magazines*, 120–3.

[25] *The History of Tunbridge-Wells* (London: printed; sold by M. Hingeston; J. Dodsley; T. Caslon; and E. Baker, at Tunbridge-Wells, 1766), 126–8.

with prosecution for the fifth time for having children out of wedlock, she spoke before the Bench in her own defence. Her speech, supposedly reproduced in full in the *Journal*, was eloquent; on its own it could have been a spirited defence of unwed motherhood. An editorial preface informs the reader that Miss Baker did so avoid punishment, but she was 'rewarded' with marriage to one of her judges the following day (*SJ*, 27 April 1747). Of course the story of a defendant so utterly persuasive was in itself worth printing, but placing the outcome first (and it was a conclusion that would satisfy the most conventional reader) effectively defuses any radical content and Baker's story becomes the more acceptable one of a deserving woman finding a good husband.

Practical considerations played a natural part in the selection of news. The pressures of providing four pages of material to meet a weekly deadline often meant that provincial editors were easier about dealing in stereotypes. This was a practice discouraged by some readers, one of whom wrote to his editor condemning those frivolous reports of 'the Slips and Failings of the *Fair-Sex*, their being found in suspicious Places at unseasonable Hours, *Virgins* getting out of their Parents Houses and running away with their *humble Servants*, or the much more heinous Offences of the *Elopement of Wives*, and leaving their *Husbands* for the Sake of *Gallants*' (*SJ*, 19 June 1738): unless of course they are framed round 'with some proper Animadversion'. Prostitutes who made good (*SJ*, 8 July 1751), 'lucky' poor girls who married much older, wealthier men (*SJ*, 9 May 1737), extravagant wives (*SJ*, 6 March 1738), and wives sold by their husbands (*SJ*, 19 April 1756, 31 October 1763, 18 September 1775) were almost stock characters in the *Journal*. One of the wives, the one who was sold in 1756, 'was too lavish in bestowing invigorating medicines on her new Spouse, [and] he expired without satisfying her Curiosity and Inclinations', giving an unusual twist to the story that would have made it practically irresistible. It was common to comment on brides as vehicles for financial transfer—one young woman was described as 'a 30,000 pounder from Bath', a description that would have been interesting for the large sum involved (*SJ*, 17 October 1763). Great female bravery was always newsworthy, particularly in times of war, when stories of young women dressing up as soldiers or petitioning to join the militia were intended to surprise or shame the more timorous male reader into effective military action (*SJ*, 23 October 1758).

The news sections of the *Salisbury Journal* do not offer much in the way of a portrait of ordinary women, since generally only women who had done or been something quite out of the ordinary were reported. The exceptions were notices of births, deaths, and marriages, and the ever-marketable stories concerning the royalty or nobility of either sex. Ordinary women did not fight in the battles recorded in the *Journal*; they did not judge other citizens; they did not vote; nor did they represent the larger business concerns in Wessex. They were minority readers of the newspaper and were therefore infrequently addressed. In many ways the non-commercial content of the *Salisbury Journal* reflected the secondary status of women in the eighteenth century. It is telling that the *Humours of the Old Bailey* could be promoted in the middle of the century as 'A Collection of all the merry and diverting Trials for above these thirty Years; particularly for *Rapes* and *private Stealing*' (*SJ*, 17 October 1757). That women were active members of the community at the business level is more apparent in the commercial section of the *Journal* where women occasionally advertised inns, bookshops, schools, millinery shops, and so on.

Whether or not the papers moulded opinion or bred cynicism, it is clear that the newspaper was a *foundation* for public opinion. What made the newsletter and later the newspaper different from other printed sources such as books and pamphlets was that they were cheaper, more widely dispersed, and were issued on a regular, predictable basis. Moreover the papers became a common, shared source of information, probably more so in the provinces where a larger proportion of the population might have natural access to the same local weekly. On the other hand in London, with its many newspaper titles, it was less likely that any one presentation of the news would become common knowledge. One must not, however, underestimate the power of the spoken word in the eighteenth century: word of mouth, rumour, the announcements of the town crier, remained influential means of communicating the news too, particularly at the lower levels of society closer to an oral culture. One is reminded of this even in the pages of a printed newspaper. That account of the Salisbury Michaelmas Fair, with its two wild orators—the quack dentist loudly pulling teeth and his 'Scholard' colleague who argued about books—is a good example.[26] This noisy account, particularly of the illiterate bookseller, just manages to convey a sense of how the oral tradition worked alongside the literate. Yet such information could only be recalled from memory, and memory becomes arguably less sure, less practised in a literate culture. One could always return to the text of the newspaper for verification of at least one version of the news. That also applies, of

---

[26] *SJ*, 16 Oct. 1749.

course, to any historical enquiry into its role. The content of the newspapers themselves is the principal evidence for any study of the complex relationship of production, editorial policy, and the reader in eighteenth-century Wessex.

Editorial policy was an important influence on circulation and readership, taking in the selection of news, the balance of news and advertising, and the overall tone of the newspaper. The editor ultimately determined what made up the non-commercial element of his newspaper. He solicited intelligence from his correspondents and selected news from other periodical sources. On the few occasions when he made his own editorial views clear, his personal role in determining the character of the paper was most pronounced. By contrast, the interests of the readers themselves are more directly expressed in the *Journal*'s advertisements. These had their limits: they had to be paid for, so the poorer classes would have been less inclined to use them; the editor could reject items he thought were unsuitable, although the evidence suggests that payment often overrode editorial squeamishness; and lack of space sometimes meant that a notice had to be postponed or omitted. Nevertheless advertising is the component that best describes a provincial newspaper's unique local character, and most eloquently testifies to the extraordinarily varied concerns of its community.

6

The Commercial Context: Advertising in a Local Newspaper

SAMUEL JOHNSON may not have been the first to consider why newspaper proprietors found the interdependence of news and advertising so attractive, but his observations, as ever, are worth recording:

Genius is shewn only by invention. The man who first took advantage of the general curiosity that was excited by a siege or battle, to betray the readers of news into the knowledge of the shop where the best puffs and powder were to be sold, was undoubtedly a man of great sagacity, and profound skill in the nature of man. But when he had once shewn the way, it was easy to follow him; and every man now knows a ready method of informing the publick of all that he desires to buy or sell, whether his wares be material or intellectual; whether he makes cloaths, or teaches the mathematics; whether he be a tutor that wants a pupil, or a pupil that wants a tutor. (The *Idler*, no. 40)

The history of newspaper advertising, distinctive, but still within the history of the book and newspaper trade, goes back to the seventeenth century.

The first advertisement to appear in any English periodical evidently was a timely notice of a new-engraved map of Breda in one of Nathaniel Butter and Nicholas Bourne's periodicals in 1624.[1] It is printed on the last page of the periodical, set off from the text by a rule, and describes in its style and tone the periodical advertisement through most of the seventeenth century:

In the last printed Newes of September 11, I told you there could be no perfect description of the siege of Breda . . . since this, is come ouer a perfect description of the same, the substance whereof is formerly set downe in this Relation. I doe purpose likewise to cut the Map, wherein you may with the eye behold the siege,

---

[1] Butter and Bourne had referred earlier to a book they were about to publish in their *Continuation of Our Weekely Newes*, 21 Apr. 1623, but this notice is more in the way of news than advertisement (see Joseph Frank, *The Beginnings of the English Newspaper 1620–1660* (Cambridge, Mass.: Harvard University Press, 1961), 301 n. 54).

in a manner, as liuely as if you were an eye-witnesse: you may not expect this Map this six dayes.[2]

Notices in the eighteenth-century newspapers were descendants of such advertising, for the commercial orientation and tactics of the early period-ical publishers were of course passed down to newspaper editors through several generations. A brief reconstruction of how the techniques and biases of advertising were transformed from the seventeenth century to the eighteenth, from London to the provinces, from a limited to a broader, national market, provides a historical context in which the commercial content of one eighteenth-century provincial newspaper and the impact it may have had on Wessex commerce and life can be assessed.

Editors of the early news periodicals, such as Nathaniel Butter (STo:1516) and Nicholas Bourne (STo:0313) in 1624, were not slow to understand that periodicals might convey more than just the news and thereby provide an advantage beyond those derived from subscriptions and casual sales, but it was not until the middle of the century that advertising became a regular, substantial section of any London paper.[3] In fact some seventeenth-century papers continued to ignore the oppor-tunities advertising offered. From the appearance of the first English news periodicals in about 1620, through the newsbooks that began in the 1640s,[4] until the 1650s, the emphasis was unquestionably on news and ideas: most periodical advertising was limited to one or two trade notices, that is to the books, pamphlets, and medicines already sold by the peri-odicals proprietors and their book-trade colleagues.[5] Notices for lost ser-vants, horses, and relatives were in evidence by the mid-century, but these, too, were sometimes trade-related since newspaper printers often printed the handbills that were posted round town to advertise such misfortunes. In late May 1657 Marchamont Nedham's eight-page weekly the *Publick Adviser* began publishing. Connected with a number of com-mercial offices of 'Publick Advice' in London, the *Publick Adviser* carried

---

[2] *The Continuation of the Weekly Newes from Septem: the 11, to the 16. 1624* (London: printed for Nathaniell Butter and Nicholas Bourne, 1624).

[3] See R. B. Walker, 'Advertising in London Newspapers, 1650–1750', *Business History*, 16 (1973), 112–30.

[4] Joad Raymond has a useful introduction to the history of newsbooks in his *Making the News: An Anthology of the Newsbooks of Revolutionary England 1641–1660* (Moreton-in-Marsh: Windrush Press, 1993).

[5] There was a longstanding link between selling nostrums and selling books, based on their centralized production and national distribution (see John Feather, *A History of British Publishing* (London: Croom Helm, 1988), 118–19, and John Alden, 'Pills and Publishing: Some Notes on the English Book Trade, 1660–1715', *Library*, 5th ser., 7 (1952), 21–37).

only advertising. It was evidently discontinued in September of the same year it started,[6] but it was the first of its kind and the first periodical to advertise coffee and chocolate.[7]

In the papers that sold such notices the average number of advertisements per issue increased after the 1650s,[8] but they did not appear in large numbers and there was little diversification in their content until very late in the century. In this context the *London Gazette* was one of the most important periodicals, for it was one of the few periodicals that was published with any regularity. In 1688 the *Gazette* carried 695 advertisements, about a quarter of which (162) were for books and book-related items. It is really only in the 1690s that advertisements appeared in any variety—books, medicines, and lost and stolen notices remained in significant numbers, but now individuals outside the book trade were beginning to see the advantages of the newspaper as a uniquely wide-ranging advertising medium: the *London Gazette*, *Post-Boy*, and *Flying Post* all promoted lotteries, real estate, various auctions, and goods for sale in the last few years of the century. This pattern of trade-related advertising with an increasing proportion of more broadly directed notices was one that was to develop in the eighteenth century.

The relatively narrow focus that is characteristic of most seventeenth-century newspaper advertising can be explained in part by the limitations of the market: wages were lower than they would be in the eighteenth century; demand was relatively inflexible; luxury commodities went to a small, well-defined group;[9] other forms of advertising—handbills, word of mouth, town criers, shop signs—were evidently adequate to promote local goods and services; and the comparatively low numbers of paid notices make it clear that proprietors were yet to realize the full revenue-making potential of the newspaper advertisement. Another part of the explanation lies in how newspaper owners viewed their investments. Before Charles Spens and James Emmonson entered into a partnership with the printer William Bowyer, Emmonson wrote to Bowyer that within the

---

[6] Carolyn Nelson and Matthew Seccombe (comps.), *British Newspapers and Periodicals 1641–1700: a Short-Title Catalogue of Serials Printed in England, Scotland, Ireland, and British America* (New York: Modern Language Association, 1987), Serial 573. Nelson and Seccombe record a complete run of the nineteen numbers in the BL Thomason Collection.

[7] Frank, *Beginnings of the English Newspaper*, 258.

[8] The *Perfect Diurnall* averaged about six advertisements per no. in 1653; Muddiman's *Kingdom's Intelligencer* and *Mercurius Publicus* about five in 1662; L'Estrange's *Newes* and *Intelligencer* about seven in 1665 (Walker, 'Advertising', 113).

[9] Aspects discussed by Neil McKendrick, 'The Consumer Revolution of Eighteenth-Century England', in Neil McKendrick, John Brewer, and J. H. Plumb, *The Birth of a Consumer Society* (Bloomington: Indiana University Press, 1982), 9–33.

terms of the new partnership, Spens 'proposes to keep on what he has to do with the News Paper, which will not take up three Hours a Day, as it will be 50L. a year clear Money, and a constant Introduction to the Booksellers'.[10] Emmonson was writing in 1754, but there is evidence that successful newspapers were valued for much the same reasons even in the seventeenth century. That 'constant Introduction to the Booksellers' was particularly important, for the booksellers, reinforced by Government legislation, had superseded the printers to become the most influential element in the book trade during the seventeenth century:[11] as copyright owners, booksellers were the ones who employed the printers (including newspaper printers) to print their books and pamphlets, and the trade publishers to distribute them; they could be a dependable source of steady advertising revenue; and newspaper proprietors (frequently booksellers themselves) might find benefits in joining with their colleagues in the purchase of more expensive or riskier copyrights, or in setting up more efficient distribution systems. In London the booksellers joined together to set up newspapers in order 'to contract the Expense of advertising their own Books by Partnership in public Papers of their own Property and Management, where they might the most freely, commodiously, and cheaply insert their own Advertisments, and command those of the Town' to cite the oft-quoted John Henley.[12] In the provinces cut-price newspaper advertising was one means of establishing and reaffirming links with a powerful segment of the London book trade.

Developments in provincial newspaper advertising during the eighteenth century may be placed against an economic background that included a strong London periodical trade that had been operating since the early seventeenth century; London newspapers that were readily available —but expensive—in the country; a new freedom for printers to set up trade anywhere in the kingdom after the lapse of the Printing Act; a London-based book trade dominated by the copy-owning booksellers; newspaper advertisements that preferentially included a large proportion

[10] Bodl. MS Eng. Misc. C.141, fo. 121. Charles Knight, writing in the 19th cent., thought that an established newspaper gave its owner 'influence and connexion' among other things (*The Newspaper Stamp, and the Duty on Paper, Viewed in Relation to their Effects upon the Diffusion of Knowledge* (London: Charles Knight, 1836), 31).

[11] John Feather describes the booksellers' rise to dominance of the Stationers' Company, a process that began early in the 17th cent., in his *History of British Publishing*, 38–40; enlightening discussion of the 17th-cent. book trade and its divisions may be found in D. F. McKenzie, *The London Book Trade in the Later Seventeenth Century* (privately published Sandars Lectures, 1976) and in Michael Treadwell, 'London Trade Publishers, 1675–1750', *Library*, 6th ser., 4 (1982), 99–134.

[12] *The Hyp-Doctor*, no. 39 (25 Jan. 1732).

of book-trade notices, but were showing increasing evidence of a new consumer orientation; and a postal, commercial, and private network, long established but underdeveloped, to distribute London-printed books and newspapers to the major provincial towns. While the country newspaper was in itself innovative, it none the less worked within a traditional framework.

To describe these new developments in advertising for both English newspapers in general and the Wessex newspapers in particular, one might begin by looking at aspects related to the mechanics of the eighteenth-century newspaper advertisement—for example the income that advertisements could produce and the trend towards uniform rates. Contemporary assessments of the value of newspaper advertising further describe the changes that took place during the eighteenth century. Another development, one that overtook provincial and metropolitan papers alike, was the accelerating trend to advertise in the periodicals. With an unrestrained entrepreneurial spirit that seems to have been characteristically British (or, later, British colonial), editors began to fill the pages of their newspapers with more and more paid notices.[13] The sheer number of advertisements per issue was one of the more remarkable aspects of newspapers after the mid-eighteenth century. But of first importance to the proprietors was the fact that advertisements brought in a measurable financial return.

One newspaper at the end of the century, the *Reading Mercury*, went so far as to claim that 'The Profits of a newspaper arise *only* from Advertisements'.[14] Before the Act of 1712 advertisements were duty-free and 100 per cent of the fees charged could return to the newspaper to meet production and distribution costs, and what was left could be regarded as profit. A common seventeenth-century advertising fee was 6*d*., but that was by no means uniform: Samuel Pecke, for example, was able to ask 1*s*. per advertisement in his newsbook, the *Perfect Diurnall*, in mid-century (though he conceded to the book trade a lower rate of 6*d*.), later the *Publick Adviser* charged 5*s*. for four insertions, and the *London Gazette*'s charges were generally higher than those of its competitors. With the proliferation

---

[13] French newspapers of the same period were less commercial in content for example. Stephen Botein, Jack R. Censer, and Harriet Ritvo take a fruitful comparative approach in their consideration of 18th-cent. newspapers in 'The Periodical Press in Eighteenth-Century English and French Society: A Cross-Cultural Approach', *Comparative Studies in Society and History*, 23 (1981), 464–90.

[14] The view implies that production costs were met by subscription revenue (*Reading Mercury*, 10 July 1797; cited in K. G. Burton, *The Early Newspaper Press in Berkshire (1723–1855)* (Reading: published by the author, 1954), 45).

of newspapers in the eighteenth century and the Government's imposi-
tion of a tax in 1712 that left proprietors little room to manœuvre, there
was greater concern that rates be competitive. So in 1736 the Collins
brothers, like numerous other provincial proprietors, were charging 2s.
6d. for an advertisement 'if short', while the London papers were likely to
ask 2s. There is no documented scale of charges for the *Salisbury Journal*,
but the scale must have been similar to that of the *Reading Mercury*,
which K. G. Burton has deduced to be 6d. for each additional $\frac{1}{2}$ inch of
copy after 2 inches (the 2 inches corresponding to the basic 'short' advertisement),[15] or to that of the *Hampshire Chronicle*. In 1778 the *Chronicle's*
basic price was 4s. for any notice up to about 16 lines or 2 inches, with 6d.
charged for each additional $\frac{1}{2}$ inch.[16] Prices rose accordingly in 1757 when
the Government doubled the tax to 2s. per advertisement, and again in
1780 when 6d. was added.[17]

Further complicating any attempts to calculate the exact measure of
advertising profit for eighteenth-century newspaper owners was a possible reduction in rates for repeat advertisements.[18] That notices commonly appeared three times in the early *Salisbury Journal* lends substance
to this possibility, although repeats became much less frequent after the
higher prices in the late 1750s. On the other hand, the *Chronicle* does
not seem to have made concessions for multiple entries in the late 1770s.
J. Martin was charged 4s. each week for his advertisement of the season at 'Martin's rooms', which appeared twice. E. Bevan advertised
Venetian window blinds five times; his account was charged 4s. a week for
five weeks.[19] Another variable was the 'puff'. It is often impossible to say
whether a 'puff' (that is an advertisement lightly disguised as a story in
the news section of the paper) was a paid or free advertisement—and if
it *was* paid for, was this subtler appeal to the market a more expensive
one? No evidence has been discovered that additional charges were made
for preferential placing of straightforward advertisements in any mid-
eighteenth-century provincial newspaper, or even that any particular placing was thought to be especially desirable; this practice was not unknown
in London in the late eighteenth-century and was probably followed by

[15] Burton, *Early Newspaper Press in Berkshire*, 49.

[16] *Hampshire Chronicle* Account Books: Advertisements, entries for 18 May 1778, PRO,
E. 140/90.   [17] Acts of 30 Geo. II, c. 19 and 20 Geo. III, c. 28.

[18] James Raven suggests that some customers booked and paid for advertisements by the
quarter, at a discounted rate, or were offered a free advertisement after so many paid ones
('Serial Advertisement in 18th-Century Britain and Ireland', in Robin Myers and Michael
Harris (eds.), *Serials and Their Readers, 1620–1914* (Winchester: St Paul's Bibliographies,
1993), 103–22).   [19] *Hampshire Chronicle* Account Books: Advertisements.

the provincials then.[20] Rather the mechanics of production seem to have determined where advertisements appeared in the mid-century provincial papers: longer-standing notices for books and medicines most often appeared in the outer forme, on page 4, set early in the week along with page 1 containing the oldest news; more recent advertisements and news made up pages 2 and 3, in the inner forme. There are occasional notices suggesting a deadline for advertisers who want to be certain that their notices will find a place in next week's paper. Finally, proprietors of newspapers, both in the provinces and London, commonly offered their colleagues 'duty-only' advertising.[21] All these variables make it difficult to know precisely what returns partners had for their investment. In the case of the *Salisbury Journal* it might be roughly calculated that from an average 675 advertisements a year in the 1740s, Collins could have had a gross annual income of about £50 (that is 675 × 1*s*. 6*d*. after tax). Exact figures aside, it is clear that newspaper advertisements did bring in direct revenue. When subscription sales covered production costs, it was easy for proprietors to view advertising as the profitable side of the business.

Advertisements worked in other, less obvious ways, too. A big percentage of advertising space in the *Salisbury Journal* is taken up with the books, stationery, medicines, and services available at Collins's Printing-Office on the New Canal. These served the dual purpose of providing copy while promoting Collins's business. He probably acted as commissioned agent himself in other advertisements that directed the potential customer first to Mr Collins, something that was particularly important when it came to the promotion of the lucrative quack-medicine business. Then of course Collins could promote the advantages to the general public of advertising in the *Salisbury Journal*:

---

[20] Trusler reported of London papers in 1786 that 'Advertisements in the front of the morning papers are inserted, if not above 18 lines in length, for 5*s*. 6*d*. in other parts of the paper for 3*s*. 6*d*. In the evening papers the price is 4*s*. each time.' (John Trusler, *The London Adviser and Guide* (London: printed for the author, 1786), 126.)

[21] For example the partners on the *Grub Street Journal* agreed that 'an Advertisement sent by a Partner [will] be inserted if there be room, [the partner to] pay only one Shilling if under Twelve Lines . . . but if an Advertisement be order'd positively, then the Partner to pay the full Price' ('The Minute Books of the Partners in the *Grub Street Journal*', *Publishing History*, 4 (1978), 52). Favourable rates seemed to apply in the case of the *Hampshire Chronicle* partners' own advertisements too: e.g. John Earleworthy paid 4*s*. 6*d*. cash for a notice that ran to eighteen lines (5.2cm.) about a William Smith's flight from justice, while the entry directly below his is for a notice about inoculation at Southampton contributed by Thomas Baker, one of the partners. Baker's was twenty-three lines (6.5cm.), but he paid only 4*s*. on account (Account Books: Advertisements). The *Chronicle* partners' Articles of Agreement did not cover such allowances (see the Bills and Answers, PRO E. 112/1959/147).

THE impolicy and excessive cruelty, of imposing an additional tax upon news-papers, must be evident to every candid mind, when it is considered that the great variety of advertisements which make their daily appearance, is a proof of their utility to all ranks of people. The merchant, the artist, the mechanic, have all recourse to news-papers; commerce is extended, the liberal sciences promoted, and all mutual intercourse in the ordinary connections of trade maintained and supported very principally by news-papers; houses and lands are purchased and disposed of by means of news-papers; offenders against the laws of their country are apprehended and brought to justice, and the peace and welfare of individuals preserved, entirely by news-papers: The public offices of London, great companies, and other societies established for the public good, are severally connected with, and their stability or credit promoted by, news-papers. All public charities are under indispensible obligations to news-papers, but none more so than that estab-lishment for the relief of the King's troops serving in America; the 'Luxurious' news-papers having raised for that charity upwards of eighteen thousand pounds. (*SJ*, Extra, 6 May 1776)[22]

For advertisements to remain a dependable source of income, they had to be effective, but it is difficult to *prove* that any given notice accom-plished its purpose. It is clear that the newspaper was the medium re-quired for certain advertising campaigns, at least in the eighteenth century. Christopher Smart, for example, wrote to Robert Dodsley in 1746 with tactical instructions for advertising a second edition of his Latin version of Pope's *Ode* 'but for three days, & only in one paper each day. The price of 'em is two shillings a piece. I beg the favor the advertisement may be carefully copied from the title page'.[23] And when Benjamin Collins suggested to John Nourse, a colleague in London, that James Harris's books be advertised in the *Salisbury Journal*, it was because 'otherwise twill be known but to few in these Parts that they are publishd'—this despite the fact that the Harrises were a well-known local family.[24] Occa-sionally the *Journal* drew attention incidentally to its advertising suc-cesses: 'WHEREAS *John Rose*, alias *Thomas Jones*, alias *Thomas Davis*, for breaking open the Dwelling-House and Stable of *John James*, at the Ship at the *Devizes*, and Stealing a Horse, Saddle, Bridles, *&c.* as Advertis'd in our last, was in Consequence of the said Advertisement and Reward therein offered by the said *John James*, taken up, and committed to our

---

[22] These sentiments are not original to Collins, rather their London orientation ('daily appearance' of advertisements; references to the London establishment) betrays their origins. This is the sort of essay that would be incorporated by provincial editors.

[23] Christopher Smart to Robert Dodsley, 6 Aug. 1746, *The Correspondence of Robert Dodsley 1733–1764*, ed. James E. Tierney (Cambridge: Cambridge University Press, 1988), 100–1.

[24] Benjamin Collins to John Nourse, 2 Jan. 1766, *Salisbury Journal* Office, Salisbury.

County Gaol, on Wednesday the 12th Instant' (*SJ*, 17 April 1749). The main intention of the advertisement was purportedly to follow this success with another in finding the owner of the little black horse the thief had had with him when he was apprehended. In another example 'The Box of Lace, advertised in our last, is found; and the Persons who advertised for Servants are by that Means supplied, which is mention'd to prevent for the present any farther Applications' (*SJ*, 26 September 1757).

Or a customer might obliquely acknowledge the success of one advertisement by placing another, as did the unfortunate Edward Bath in 1748. He was 'taken up and carried before *Thomas Missing*, Esq; Justice of the Peace for the County of Hants' as a direct result of a reward 'offer'd in the *Salisbury Journal*' for his apprehension on suspicion of housebreaking. He used the same newspaper to broadcast to 'his Friends in particular, and the Publick in general, That he never was any ways concerned in such vile and unlawful Practices' (*SJ*, 19 December 1748). The printed word evidently carried a wider-ranging truth and weight than did the spoken in such a situation.

The newspaper advertisement also offered a unique and very public venue for what amounted to a dialogue, usually between antagonistic parties.[25] The impersonality of the medium combined with the vagaries of the libel laws to allow the participants certain freedoms in stating their cases; on the other hand, that these cases would be printed and widely circulated (and the vagaries of the libel laws figured here too) placed restrictions on how the notice might be worded. One could call someone else a 'notorious Rascal', but not, evidently, a 'poxy' one, at least not in print. These advertisements most commonly took the form of a simple apology for possibly libellous spoken remarks, where the printed word brought to a conclusion an oral disagreement. But sometimes a heated exchange might go on for weeks, as in the battle between two Salisbury dancing masters in 1760, after one embarrassed the other by calling on his rival's inexperienced students to perform, which they did—badly and publicly. Evidently the reading public viewed the newspaper advertisement as an effective and efficient means of conducting and concluding certain arguments.

Most of the evidence for the success of these notices is to be found in the newspapers themselves, when the editor mentions its proven efficacy or when a dialogue of claim and counterclaim is constructed, but a wider range of material can sometimes be brought to bear on the question, as

---

[25] C. Y. Ferdinand, 'Serial Conversations: The Dialogue of the Eighteenth-Century Provincial Newspaper', in *Compendious Conversations*, ed. Kevin L. Cope (Frankfurt am Main: Peter Lang, 1992), 116–28.

John Styles has demonstrated.[26] He has examined criminal depositions to see if advertisements for stolen horses were an effective detective measure, or if all the advertiser was buying was a deterrent for potential horse thieves. Styles found that printed notices, usually in the form of newspaper advertisements, 'played the principal role in establishing the charge against the accused' in almost one-third of the 'intelligible cases' he considered, the intelligible ones being those in which it was possible to identify the means of detection.[27] Personal pursuit was the most effective measure if the horse was not long gone, but the newspaper superseded this method after the horse had been missing for more than a few days. Records for Yorkshire, Northumberland, Cumberland, and Westmorland, and northern newspapers between 1760 and 1799 formed the basis of this study. But there is no reason to believe that criminal advertisements differed radically in their effectiveness in other parts of the country—Wessex victims were just as apt to use the newspaper as a means of transmitting details of their lost or stolen property and just as apt to expect the return of that property by means of a printed advertisement.

Newspaper advertisements were clearly on the increase in the eighteenth century for a number of reasons. Proprietors benefited from the revenue and so increasingly sought to promote them. In a curious way the trend was verified by the first Newspaper Stamp Act in 1712, which taxed both the newspaper and each advertisement that appeared in it. The Government seriously expected to earn revenue by imposing a duty on what was viewed as a popular commodity; there was an element of censorship to the tax too, but to install the complex machinery for delivery, collection, and return of stamped paper simply for restrictive purposes would have been counterproductive. For their part, the newspaper owners could also hope for the indirect economic advantages that might develop with stronger book-trade connections. And newspaper advertisements multiplied because consumers were persuaded that they were an effective means of commercial and personal communication.

Samuel Farley probably miscalculated the commercial possibilities in Wiltshire when he started up the *Salisbury Post Man* in 1715.[28] Insufficient advertising revenue may have contributed to the paper's failure. The second attempt to set up a Salisbury newspaper failed too, with number

---

[26] John Styles, 'Print and Policing: Crime Advertising in Eighteenth-Century Provincial England', in Douglas Hay and Francis Snyder (eds.), *Policing and Prosecution in Britain 1750–1850* (Oxford: Clarendon Press, 1989), 55–111.   [27] Ibid. 77.

[28] The only known copy of the *Salisbury Post Man* is of the first no. (27 Sept. 1715), which is in the present office of the *Salisbury Journal*. The *Post Man* continued until at least early 1716: Robert Benson and Henry Hatcher mention the existence of a No. 40 (1 Mar. 1716) in their *Old and New Sarum, or Salisbury* (London: Nichols, 1843), 509.

58 (6 July 1730). Clues to the first *Journal*'s lack of success may lie in the
ten advertisements placed in its last issue: three for books; two for real
estate; and one each for an apothecary (the printer Charles Hooten himself evidently), an assembly and concert, a dancing master, a runaway
servant, and a notice regarding a dispute. Ten is a respectable number,
and the variety gives some definition to the market in 1730 Salisbury, but
it is significant that the printer of the paper places one of the advertisements, and, more important, that the three book notices are local ones—
there is no sign that the proprietors had cultivated the advertising business
of London colleagues even after a year in operation. This may well have
been a factor in the paper's failure, along with the low subscription numbers implied in Hooten's farewell notice[29] and perhaps a lack of experience in the proprietors.[30]

When the *Salisbury Journal* resumed publication in 1736, it met with
success. While the times seemed to favour new papers in general (thirty
provincial papers were in business in 1736, six of them established that
year[31]), different combinations of circumstances made some eighteenth-
century provincial papers more successful than others. One factor that
frequently applied before the mid-century was simply the lack of competition—by 1736 at least some Wiltshire residents must have deplored
the absence of a local paper and welcomed the Collinses' second attempt
to establish one. Salisbury and its vicinity had the population to support
a newspaper, a fairly stable 6,500 to 6,700 inside the town limits during
the century. The greater population within the *Journal*'s catchment area
was a diverse one including those connected with the cathedral and close,
those concerned in local agriculture, and those involved with cloth manufacture. Salisbury itself, a regional administrative centre as well as cathedral and market town, falls into the numerous category of 'regional centre'
in Peter Borsay's urban hierarchy. His next tier up is 'provincial capital'
(the highest level of country town)—of these important cities all but one
had newspapers, often in competition, from early in the century, while
regional centres such as Salisbury were generally slower to take to the
periodical press.[32]

---

[29] 'This Paper not being encouraged according to Expectation, I shall from this time
decline it'.
[30] William Collins was 25 years old in 1730 and Benjamin, probably also his brother's
apprentice, was then only 15.
[31] R. M. Wiles, *Freshest Advices: Early Provincial Newspapers in England* (Columbus:
Ohio State University Press, 1965), Appendix B.
[32] Borsay's seven candidates for provincial capital in 1700 are Norwich, Bristol, Newcastle-
upon-Tyne, Exeter, York, Chester, and Shrewsbury, the last of which had no substantial

The initial number of the revived *Salisbury Journal* (27 November 1736) was not auspicious at first sight, for it had only one advertisement. But this was for William Salmon's *Builder's Guide*, 'Printed for *James Hodges* at the Lookinglass on *London Bridge*, and Sold by *W. Collins* at *Salisbury*, *J. Gould* Bookseller at *Dorchester*, Mr. *Cook* Bookseller at *Sherborne* and *J. Langford* Bookseller at *Warminster*.' Here were two indicators of the *Journal*'s future success: contacts with London and provincial booksellers, and a fledgling provincial distribution network.

A detailed study of the advertisements in this successful newspaper during the years of Benjamin Collins's management from 1736 contributes a great deal of evidence towards an understanding of the evolution in newspaper advertising and of the related changes in the mid-eighteenth-century provincial market. Eighteenth-century newspaper advertisements can be read and measured in various ways—for the *Salisbury Journal* nearly every notice that has appeared in the paper from its beginning up to the present can still be consulted. The 50,000 or so advertisements that appeared between 1736 and 1770 make up a large body of quantifiable information about the eighteenth-century provincial newspaper and its customers. Many of the advertisements—for example those for real property and movable goods—are represented by statistics here, but even those numbers can tell a good deal about selling and buying trends, and about contemporary perception of the overall utility of the newspaper for advertising. Other categories relating to literacy, the history of the book, and leisure activities are considered in greater detail; for example, in the course of this work every advertisement for schools of any sort has been transcribed into a database for reference, and any information that can help to describe the growth of the provincial book trade has been similarly recorded. In all, ten categories of advertisement have been considered: real property; straightforward notices for meetings, of crimes, &c.; medicines; leisure; movable goods; lost-and-found; services, including professional and transportation; employment; runaways; and book trade. These are all described first in broad statistical outline, and then in greater detail for several categories.

It is important to keep in mind that those other advertising media— the town criers, the shop signs, word of mouth, handbills—continued to operate in conjunction with the newspaper. Their complementary nature

newspaper until after 1760. While Borsay admits that his urban hierarchy is not a precise measure, it is a useful reference for comparison. See his *The English Urban Renaissance: Culture and Society in the Provincial Town 1660–1770* (Oxford: Clarendon Press, 1989), 4–11.

is demonstrated in a newspaper notice for the Painter's Complete Antidote and Grand Assistant that advises that 'A particular and full Account of this Preparation is printed in Hand-Bills, which will be distributed throughout the Kingdom' (*SJ*, 24 July 1758). Unfortunately their ephemerality—the crier's words transformed within each hearer's memory and then lost, the handbill replaced with a newer notice—makes them practically inaccessible and absolutely unquantifiable. It is now difficult to gauge with any accuracy their impact on contemporary consumers and their interaction with newspaper advertising, let alone their numbers, frequency, and range. In fact some of the little evidence we have for their effectiveness in the eighteenth century derives from the newspapers themselves.[33]

The rapid and sustained growth in the number of advertisements documented here is a measure both of the commercial health of the *Salisbury Journal* and of a developing consumerism. In 1737, the first complete year of the *Journal's* life, there were just over 200 advertisements, more than half of them for books. During the 1740s annual totals fluctuated between 550 and about 900, with advertisements for books ranging between 19 and 43 per cent. Benjamin Collins was at his most innovative during this first decade of his proprietorship, experimenting with the typography and placement of notices in his efforts to build up circulation, contacts, and advertising revenue. By 1752 there were over 1,000 advertisements carried in the *Journal* each year; nine years later, in 1761, there were over 2,000; in 1768 over 3,000. By 1770, the year Benjamin Collins turned over the management of the newspaper to George Sealy and John Alexander, there were nearly 3,400. This is an increase in the average number from four per week to nearly sixty-five. It is significant that newspaper advertising increased so dramatically while the population, at least in Salisbury itself, and probably in its area of circulation too, remained stable, although the few records available show a slight decrease in Salisbury population from the end of the seventeenth century to the mid-eighteenth. A new market for newspapers and the products they advertised was being created, not as a natural development of population growth—a factor in the nineteenth century—but from a reading and buying segment that was actually expanding. The idea of the provincial newspaper as an agent for stimulating and servicing the needs of an extended market had caught on—clearly its readers considered the

---

[33] The *Journal* occasionally mentioned an item's discovery after being cried about several towns, and the paper's printers frequently solicited printing jobs, including handbills.

Salisbury Journal an effective advertiser. At the same time the *Journal* was itself a window onto these very developments.

The most striking difference between the *Salisbury Journal* of the 1730s and of the 1760s is in the *number* of advertisements—from an annual average of 296 in the 1730s, to 675 in the 1740s, 1,350 in the 1750s, to nearly 2,500 in the 1760s, and to over 3,300 in 1770. By the middle of the century the newspaper had become a widely accepted method of promoting local businesses, which was good news for the newspaper proprietors who derived much of their profit from advertising. The newspaper also became the most effective medium for extending the market for services and products such as boarding schools, real estate, and books, as well as for publishing information on highly movable stolen goods. The new-created consumer lived anywhere within the broad reach of his country newspaper, for the paper's carrier also undertook to deliver the dyed silks, the hats, the serial books, the tea, the medicines, and the silver watches it advertised, as well as the notices for distant services and leisure events, plus the transport to get there.

Of the broad categories of advertisement now considered, all ten types are represented in the *Journal* by 1739, when the first employment advertisement appears; all show a gradual increase in numbers; and many reach relative stability in the 1740s. (1) The largest group of advertisements is for books and book-related material in the 1740s and 1750s, with an average of about 30 per cent of the total number; real estate takes the lead in the 1760s when books drop to about 18 per cent. (2) After 1740 real-estate notices make up about 25 per cent, with highs of 29 per cent in 1763 and 1764, and a low of 20 per cent in 1752. (3) Advertisements for quack medicines are popular in the *Journal*'s first decade, at 14 per cent. Medical notices proved convenient for the printer because they were so often published unaltered from week to week and the type could be left standing through all the reprints, but tiresome for the reader. From mid-century they account for well under 10 per cent of the total—a decrease that may have been an implicit acknowledgement of customer complaints.[34]

---

[34] No complaints of this sort are recorded in the *Salisbury Journal*—in fact the most frequently printed customer complaint in the *Journal* is that an advertisement or letter was omitted from an overfull number. However, at least one provincial editor incidentally recognized the problem when he defended one of his news items: 'supposing the Paragraph alluded to had been a Fiction, we are sanguine enough to hope that it would be more entertaining to our Readers than the whole Column stuffed up with Notices of Quack Medicines, Corn-Salve, Weal Registers, Nun's Drops, etc. etc. etc.' (*Liverpool Chronicle*, 17 Mar. 1758, quoted in Cranfield, *Development of the Provincial Newspaper 1700–1760* (Oxford: Clarendon Press, 1962), 222).

(4) Sale of movable goods by newspaper advertisement grows steadily, in numbers *and* proportion, averaging 9 per cent in the 1740s, about 16 per cent in the 1760s. (5) So too do notices of meetings, robberies, markets, and the like, which increase from an average 6 per cent in the 1740s to about 15 per cent later. (6) Lost-and-found notices remain about 4 per cent of the total through the mid-century. (7) Notices of fugitive husbands, wives, prisoners, and soldiers almost never make up more than 1 per cent. (8) Advertisements for jobs are relatively rare in the 1740s (some years of that decade saw none at all), averaging less than 0.5 per cent. In 1755 they amounted to 4 per cent, the average through the 1760s. (9) Leisure activities are promoted in an average 4 per cent of the advertisements throughout this period. (10) Advertisements for services average four per cent in the 1740s; in the 1750s the average doubles and remains at 8 per cent.

In a sense these general statistics rather obscure the developments in eighteenth-century provincial consumer habits, for, aside from the dramatic numerical growth they record, they tend to promote an idea of continuity or very gradual change: there was no exuberant increase in advertisements for leisure activities, which was, in fact, the category that showed the least proportional change; services averaged about 8 per cent through at least two decades; even for movable goods, which increased from 9 per cent in the 1740s to 16 per cent in the 1760s, the growth is fairly even. The differences that might be said to signal the changes are to be seen with more clarity in the composition of the individual categories themselves.[35]

Advertisements promoting services are a good example: the first professional service of any kind to be advertised in the *Salisbury Journal* was Philip Davies's new school in Blue Boar Row, Salisbury (5 September 1737, almost a year after the *Journal* began publishing again). The notice is brief and unsophisticated both in approach and typography, describing Mr Davies's credentials (he, like a number of other schoolmasters

---

[35] Categories that were recorded in additional detail as a basis for this study are medical advertisements, which include the name of each nostrum; those for leisure activities, which include the activity and location; lost-and-found, which include a description of the missing article; services, which include the type of service—educational advertisements were transcribed in full; employment advertisements, which are broken down by sex when possible; runaways, by type (husband, wife, etc.); and book-trade advertisements, which include details about the book advertised (price, format, method of publication, etc.), as well as a list of the book-dealers involved. A register of the Wessex book trade in the 18th cent. and a first-line index to the verse recorded in the *Salisbury Journal* are available in C. Y. Ferdinand, 'The *Salisbury Journal* 1729–1785: A Study of a Provincial Newspaper', D.Phil. thesis (Oxford University, 1990), apps. 1 and 2.

who looked for customers in the *Salisbury Journal*, had started out as assistant to the famous Mr Willis of Orchard School) and outlining the subjects taught, '*Writing, Arithmetick, Algebra, Geometry, Trigonometry* and other usefull Learning'. That the utility of learning is mentioned suggests a newspaper-reading market different from that for the seventeenth-century London papers—Philip Davies directs his notice to the gentleman or tradesman who would ensure his son's practical earning power. Other early advertisements for services are equally prosaic: the Golden Lyon in Axminster, the Crewkerne-to-London carrier, more schoolmasters, stallions to cover, a hearse 'fit to travel', farriers, and so on, with no remarkable changes until the late 1740s. Until then the market for services described in the *Salisbury Journal* was one with a utilitarian bias, taking in a growing literate class that was interested in the cheapest way to convey parcels from Crewkerne to London, or a good farrier, or a serviceable education.

The demand for more luxurious services and goods, the lower prices that came with greater production,[36] as well as the opportunity the local newspaper offered for more systematically promoting such enterprises, introduced new colour to the *Journal*'s growing advertising columns. In 1747 the first advertisements for made-to-order goods appeared, with notices for a whip-maker (11 May), a coat-maker (21 September), and a stay-maker (19 October). The following year more services were offered: brushmaking (18 January), coach painting (22 August), and watchmaking (14 November). The next twenty years saw advertisements for a whole range of services that traditionally had been offered (and not through newspapers either) only to the wealthier classes—architects, estate surveyors, milliners,[37] portrait painters, plumbers, decorative plasterers, gardeners, all invested in *Salisbury Journal* advertising. Many of them were careful to claim London credentials, such as William Biden, a stay-maker who made a point of going 'to London once a Year to have the newest Fashions' (*SJ*, 25 November 1754). This is not to say that any of these skilled services were new ones, rather that for the first time they were being offered to any reader of the *Salisbury Journal* who desired and could

---

[36] Schumpeter-Gilboy price indices, 1696–1823, indicate low consumers' and producers' goods prices from the 1730s, with consumer goods (other than cereals) rising in the 1770s. See Peter Mathias, *The First Industrial Nation: An Economic History of Britain 1700–1914*, 2nd edn. (London: Methuen, 1983), fig. 1 and table 6, pp. 63, 420.

[37] Collins might have taken a disingenuous line when he assigned one service to the field of millinery: 'The Advertisement of *Duet and Solo Love Toys*, &c. &c. *soon expected from Paris, and to be sold by* ——, is received, with the Contents: But as we are not Connoisseurs enough in Millenery Matters to comprehend its Meaning; must, before we insert it, beg the Favour of a Hint of the Design, whether serious or comic' (*SJ*, 9 Dec. 1765).

afford them. The newspaper was (and is) almost the ideal medium for reaching those who had not yet realized they required the services of, for example, an architect of garden grottoes. If commercialization meant the exploitation of a broader market, then luxury services, promoted through the wide-reaching medium of newspapers, were in the process of commercialization around Wessex from the late 1740s.

Education was another area to show the effects of market changes through the eighteenth century. Most of the notices in the *Journal* were for middle-class boarding schools and academies, probably because schools at either end of the scale tended not to advertise in the newspaper: local dame schools drew their recruits from the local population and the top-ranking grammar schools relied on their reputations. The number of educational advertisements in the *Journal* increased at an erratic pace from the 1740s to the 1760s, by when there were usually more than twenty each year. In all, about 200 teachers or schools in seventy-eight towns bought nearly 400 advertisements in the *Salisbury Journal* before 1770.[38] A good proportion of the advertisements were for schools that had just opened—evidence for the very existence of some of them, as well as further evidence that literacy was so assisted in the eighteenth-century provinces.[39] In the face of increasing competition educators became remarkably direct in their approach, outlining their curricula, describing accommodation, quoting competitive prices, emphasizing care of morals and behaviour, and noting past successes. Most of the advertisements were directed to those parents who were considering honouring one of these educators with 'the tender and important trust of their Children'. But occasionally the approach was to the adult who wanted to cultivate certain skills—for example Mr Edgcombe in Portsmouth usually instructed children for sea or land professions; but he also suggested that 'Any Person (that is versed in common Arithmetic, and will omit the projective Part) may be taught to keep an accurate Journal of a Ship's Run at Sea, in a very few Days' and that he could help gentlemen qualify as gunners in the Royal Navy (*SJ*, 29 August 1757). There was nothing revolutionary in the curricula offered—girls were generally taught reading, writing, and needlework; boys reading, writing, arithmetic, and often Latin, navigation, or bookkeeping; many boarding schools offered optional dancing and French language instruction to their children—but one anonymous 'experienc'd Accomptant

---

[38] The total includes repeat advertisements.
[39] Advertisements for country book clubs, reading rooms, lending libraries, and coffee-houses and inns that offered reading material also assist in an investigation of literacy in the provinces.

from LONDON' took the unusual step of directing the last paragraph of his notice to

Ladies that would amuse themselves with Business, and at the same Time be truly beneficial to their Families and Children, usefully qualify'd to transact their Husbands Affairs when absent, and consequently in case of Widowhood, be able to manage a Fortune, or carry on Trade, by learning any of the useful Branches of Business aforesaid, may prevent much Expence, and many Inconveniencies, that attend trusting to Servants or others. (*SJ*, 25 July 1748)

These 400 advertisements, with their cumulative detail, provide a fairly good measure of the educational options that increasingly became available to middle-class Wessex.

The leisure activities that could most effectively be promoted in a country newspaper were the major, increasingly commercial, events—horse races and the entertainments around them, annual musical festivals, the beginning of a series of assemblies, a travelling exhibition—the sort of thing that might attract a public audience from outlying areas. As country people came to have more disposable income, advertisements for out-of-town amusements (and the means of getting to them) increased. No one needed a newspaper to find out about the more ordinary, strictly local events, or even to find information on regular gatherings once the season had started (an assembly that routinely took place at the Vine in Salisbury on Wednesday evenings, say, would usually have only one or two advertisements at the commencement). And there were always private gatherings from which the public would have been excluded. This makes leisure advertising a less precise gauge of changes in the market. Still, it is useful to look in greater detail at what readers of the *Salisbury Journal* might do with their spare time. If they based their leisure plans on what they found in the newspaper, they would have had considerably more to choose from than had their seventeenth-century predecessors.

The coffee-house is one of the very few day-to-day pastimes to be advertised. John Childs's coffee-house in Winchester could provide

the Votes, King's Speech and Addresses, the Gazette, Daily Advertiser, General Evening-Post, Evening Advertiser and London Chronicle, Salisbury Journal, Monthly Magazines, Sessions Papers and Dying Speeches; the best Coffee, Tea, Chocolate and Capillair,[40] will be constantly provided, with all due and proper Attendance . . . The Room is conveniently fitted up large, light, and warm, and subject to no Annoyance whatever. (*SJ*, 28 March 1757)

[40] A drink based on a syrup extracted from maidenhair.

Francis Collins (Benjamin's brother) also ran a coffee-house, the Mitre in Silver Street, Salisbury, for a time. He provided maps to supplement the newspapers, and promised that 'a good Fire will be constantly found at Four o'Clock in the Afternoon, during the Winter Season' (*SJ*, 20 October 1755). A related pastime is to be found in the circulating library: Edward Easton's and Samuel Fancourt's libraries competed for customers in the advertising section of the *Salisbury Journal* in the 1730s and 1740s before Fancourt conceded defeat and moved his library to London.[41] Once a circulating library or reading room was established and known, its proprietor, like the organizer of a series of assemblies, had less need of the newspaper. Advertisements for musical instruments, billiard tables, and hunting dogs might also represent leisure possibilities. Otherwise most ordinary folk probably spent their extra time much as Thomas Turner records in his diary—reading, visiting neighbours, dancing, eating, and sometimes coming home drunk.[42]

Newspaper advertisements are better at documenting the occasional and annual or semi-annual events, although even then they sometimes give away other forms of advertisement: for example, advertisements for the Salisbury Races usually conclude with a note that there will be balls and assemblies 'as usual', demonstrating a continuing reliance on those other traditional means of advertising. There were always clusters of events advertised around race weeks (both in Salisbury and in the surrounding area), assize weeks, and, especially in Salisbury, the annual music festival. These inevitably included cock matches, which took place 'as usual' but at different venues advertised from year to year, and often took in various balls, assemblies, and ordinaries, as well as the odd wrestling, backsword, or single-stick match. The organizers used the newspaper to promote a broad cultural and entertainment programme that was designed to appeal to the gentry who might turn up (themselves an attraction at some of these events), to the middling classes with their increasing spending power, and even to the contestants who undertook to break so many heads to win the prize at single-stick.[43] Theatre was

---

[41] For further discussion of Fancourt's unusual career see Monte Little, *Samuel Fancourt, 1678–1768* (Trowbridge: Wiltshire Library & Museum Service, 1984).

[42] *The Diary of Thomas Turner, 1754–1765*, ed. David Vaisey (Oxford: Oxford University Press, 1984). There are other published contemporary diaries, but Turner's seems especially relevant—he was a book- and newspaper-reading man, a provincial grocer who used the newspaper to buy some of the goods he retailed.

[43] Looney proposes three divisions for leisure activity, which are loosely based on audience: first, 'short-term promotions [such as lectures, shows, performing animals], which tended to aim at a wide audience, were imported from outside the town and often timed to arrive when

another activity advertised seasonally, commonly as a 'puff' in the Salisbury news section. A growing interest in the theatre can be detected in the *Journal* from the 1750s in the greater number of advertisements as well as in increased news coverage.

Lower-class blood sports (if such activity can be called sport) such as cock throwing were never advertised in the *Salisbury Journal*; in fact, when they are mentioned at all in the news, it is with some distaste. Bull baiting, and the variant badger and stag baiting are advertised a number of times after 1752, but not at all before then. The gentler sport of cricket is noticed only a few times: in the light of its well-documented popularity then,[44] this omission must simply mean that times and locations of cricket matches were easily discovered by other forms of advertisement, and that its commercial potential was not so evident in the eighteenth century. There were also competitions, some of them annual, some occasional, for bell-ringers, florists, marksmen, and singers, who were usually required to subsidize the event by paying an entry fee.

The itinerant performers, lecturers, and showmen who stopped at Salisbury are probably best entertainment value for a twentieth-century audience: For sixpence one could view a 'curious little Four Wheel open CHAISE, with the Figure of a Man in it, drawn by a FLEA, which performs all the Offices of a large Chaise, as running of the Wheels, Locking, &c. and all together weighing but one Grain. It has been shown to the Royal Family, and several of the Nobility and Gentry, with great Approbation'. The flea-drawn chaise was part of an exhibition of miniatures, including a working pair of scissors wrapped in a fly's wing (*SJ*, 22 February 1743). An altogether surprising menagerie that included a rhinoceros, a 'surprising Buffalo', a lynx, a 'Man Tyger from Bengal, very surprising', and 'Two surprising Wolfs' toured the Wessex region in 1744 (*SJ*, 20 October 1744); a troupe of rope dancers and tumblers was at the Vine in Salisbury early the following year (*SJ*, 15 January 1745). Three 'surprizing Mathematical STATUES, lately arrived from Italy' spent a week there in 1742. One of them was 'a Merchant Grocer in his Shop, who, at the Word of Command, opens and shuts his Door himself, and brings Sugar, Tea, Coffee, and all sort of Spices'. A second represented 'a Country

---

the town was packed because of a fair, assize or race meeting'; second, 'amateur activities organized from within'; and third, the events organized by and for the 'resident elite' ('Cultural Life in the Provinces', 489–90). While this structure has not been imposed here, it might be useful to note that these events could fall within Looney's first and third categories.

[44] See e.g. David Rayvern Allen, *Early Books on Cricket* (London: Europa Publications, 1987).

Lass, with a Pidgeon upon her Head, holding a Glass in her Hand which she lifting up, makes to run out of the Pidgeon's Bill either Red or White Wine, at the Desire of the Spectators' (*SJ*, 4 May 1742). 'Mr. POWELL, The *CELEBRATED* FIRE-EATER' demonstrated his skills in 1753: His repertoire included eating burning charcoal 'as natural as Bread'; broiling beef in his mouth; and concocting a soup of rosin, pitch, bees wax, sealing wax, brimstone, allum, and lead, which he then apparently swallowed 'to the great Surprise of all Spectators' (*SJ*, 14 May 1753).

Trained animals, especially horses, bears, and birds, had long been popular entertainment in England.[45] The eighteenth century saw the debut of such improved performers as the Wonderful Learned Pig, Daniel Wildman's marching bees, and Le Chien Savant. Not to be outdone, the English produced their own

amazing learn'd ENGLISH DOG—This entertaining and sagacious Animal, reads, writes, and casts Accompts by Means of Typographical Cards, in the same Manner that a Printer composes; and by the same Method answers various Questions in Ovid's Metamorphoses, Geography, the Roman, English, and sacred History; knows the Greek Alphabet, reckons the Number of Persons present, sets down any Capital or Surname, solves Questions in the four Rules of Arithmetick, tells by looking on any common Watch of the Company what is the Hour and Minute, knows the Foreign as well as the English Coins; he likewise shews the impenetrable Secret, or tells any Person's Thoughts in Company, and distinguishes all Sorts of Colours. (*SJ*, 23 June 1755)

The 'impenetrable Secret' could in fact be penetrated with the purchase of a set of cards from the dog's proprietor after the performance.[46] Compared to the Chien Savant, this was 'a Dog superior in all his Accomplishments to any Thing of the Kind ever yet presented . . . a Dog really vers'd in the History of Nations, Empires, and Kingdoms' (evidently alluding to some deficiency in the French dog). One last performer, Mr Maddox, deserves mention: he worked on the slack wire, mimicked 'the German Flute with his Voice to Admiration', and was accompanied by Signora Catarina from Sadler's Wells who exhibited 'sundry and amazing Postures, never perform'd in England before' (*SJ*, 6 December 1756). He was evidently well received in Salisbury since he returned several times.

[45] See e.g. Richard D. Altick, *The Shows of London* (Cambridge, Mass.: Belknap Press, 1978).

[46] I am grateful to John Bidwell for revealing the secret, which is to be found in *The Impenetrable Secret Probably Invented by Horace Walpole: An Explanation of the Secret. With a Note on the Original by W. S. Lewis* (Windham, Conn.: privately printed for W. S. Lewis, 1939).

He was last there near the end of 1756, and we learn from the *Salisbury Journal* that he, along with the comedian Theophilis Cibber and the bookseller James Rudd, perished on the ship *Dublin* two years later when she went down in the Irish Sea (*SJ*, 27 November 1758). Such examples can be positively distracting and it should be stated that the *Journal* advertised a fairly well-balanced programme ranging from the popular to the cultural, from wrestling matches to Handel's oratorios. It should also be remembered that advertisements are self-selective, in that only those who could afford the 2s. 6d., could afford to advertise. By providing wider coverage of certain events, the *Salisbury Journal* played a somewhat prescriptive role, helping to give shape to the body of cultural and leisure activities available to those who read that newspaper.

The development of the provincial book trade is closely related to changes in consumption, particularly the consumption of reading material, for it was the distribution network developed by the booksellers and newspaper proprietors that systematically brought news, books, and other products to the farthest reaches of every county. The level of literacy in the eighteenth-century provinces is impossible to assess, but the obvious health of the local book and newspaper trade provides some measure of the phenomenon. Offering books in parts that anyone could afford and that were delivered without fail each week by the newsman surely influenced the development of reading. Their accessibility coupled with the invention of a relatively painless method of payment was intended to encourage a new class of reader. '*A Lover of Mankind*' wrote especially to praise the *Family Library*, one of those weekly part-books:

I can't therefore help recommending the said Books to all Sorts, Ranks, and Degrees of People, as what the *Great* may not be ashamed to peruse; neither is it needless to the *Poor*, who ought more particularly to seek for Attainments in *Knowledge*, Did People know the *Advantage* and *Satisfaction* they would reap ... they would not grudge this Two-pence per Week for *so rich a Treasure*.

... I am often moved with Pity to see my Brethren, the common Sort of People, nay Men well stricken in Years, so ruff and unpolished for Want of *Knowledge*, when they have Parts, if rightly cultivated, to make them appear like Men; and I think nothing more proper for so *necessary a Work*, as *this Book or Books* now publishing ... (*SJ*, 18 December 1752)

Promoting books in weekly, affordable sections, selling monthly magazines, and backing up these products with regular delivery fit naturally into the administration of a local weekly newspaper.

Minor country booksellers played a critical role in these developments, acting as paid agents, middlemen, and retailers for the big provincial booksellers and newspaper proprietors. Yet frequently the only surviving evidence of such activity is in newspaper advertising. A case in point is Newport, on the Isle of Wight, for which a fairly complete book-trade history can be constructed from advertisements in the *Journal*.

In 1705 John Dunton could write of one Mr Keblewhite, the Isle of Wight's earliest recorded bookseller, that he 'has a good trade, considering the place; but that is not his whole dependence, he has been twice Mayor of the town, and is not only rich, but a grave and discreet churchman'.[47] This Keblewhite seems to have been working in Newport from about 1684 to 1693. The 'place' was probably not much improved in the eighteenth century and F. A. Edwards, writing almost 200 years after Dunton, was unsuccessful in documenting any real book-trade activity on the island from Keblewhite until the 1790s.[48] To move the investigation closer to the present day, a computer-assisted search through the *Eighteenth-Century Short Title Catalogue* (which records books, of course, but also pamphlets and other ephemeral printing) is not much more revealing: only four items falling within the scope of this study were recorded with Newport in their imprints, three sermons and the sensational trial between James Annesley and the Earl of Anglesea.[49] They discover a total of three booksellers in Newport in the 1740s. Yet the advertisements in the *Salisbury Journal* provide evidence of at least seven booksellers active during those middle years, suggesting a book trade that was a continuing commercial presence throughout much of the century.

Benjamin Collins seems to have employed a bookselling agent on the Isle of Wight from 1740, after he had assumed full control of the *Salisbury Journal*. One incentive for establishing such an outlet was the potential market on the island for books and newspapers—Newport parish alone had a population of something like 3,000 during the mid-century;[50] in addition, Collins may have had family connections there. Thomas Geare is the first Isle of Wight bookseller to be recorded in the pages of the *Journal*. He may have moved to the island from Yeovil, for a 'T. Geare' was selling Squire's Elixir there in 1737; he may well have moved specifically to fill the post of off-shore agent for Benjamin Collins. At any rate, an advertisement of 26 August 1740 invites readers to subscribe through Benjamin Collins and Thomas Geare to the *Musical Entertainer*,

[47] John Dunton, *Life and Errors* (London: S. Malthus, 1705).
[48] F. A. Edwards, 'Early Hampshire Printers', *Papers and Proceedings of the Hampshire Field Club*, 2 (1891), 110–34.   [49] *ESTC* search, Sept. 1995.
[50] It was 3,585 in the 1801 census.

and in 1742 they are the two local booksellers for the fourth edition of the *London and Country Brewer*. It should be added, as a slight corrective, that Geare was also selling Bolton Simpson's Greek and Latin edition of Xenophon's *Memorials*, so it wasn't all wine and song on the Isle of Wight in those days. By March 1743, Thomas Geare was able to serve islanders from a 'Shop in *Newport*, near the BUGLE Inn, facing *St. James*'s Square, [where] Gentlemen may be supply'd with Books in all Languages and Faculties, whether printed at Home, or imported from Abroad. Together with all new Pamphlets, Maps and Prints; and every Thing in the Stationary Way at the lowest Price' (*SJ*, 1 March 1743). He also took in books 'to be Bound or Letter'd *firm* and *neat* . . . on the most reasonable Terms', and of course he sold quack medicines. Quite a reasonable provision for a country town in 1740. In June 1743 Geare is named in the *Journal*'s colophon as an agent for the first and only time; the following week he is replaced by Richard Baldwin, junior, about whom a good deal more is known.[51]

Numerous advertisements in the *Salisbury Journal* attest to the variety of books and pamphlets Baldwin helped market during his three-year term on the island—children's books such as *Pretty Book for Children* and *Little Pretty Pocket Book*, Conyers Harrison's *Impartial History of the Life and Reign of Queen Anne* in twenty-two parts, Bishop Berkeley's controversial *Siris*, Dr James's *Medicinal Dictionary*, Sarah Harrison's *House-Keeper's Pocket Book*, *The Universal Library of Trade and Commerce*, local sermons, and so on. Besides selling printed material, we find the industrious Baldwin advertising to buy any quantity of bees' wax (*SJ*, 14 August 1744); he sold 'All Sorts of Stamp Paper and Parchment, Blank Bonds, and all other Sorts of Blanks' (*SJ*, 27 August 1745), stationery of every variety, and, towards the end, Sterrop's True Spectacles: 'For the Conveniency of Persons at a Distance, they may be supplied, by sending their Age, either with the common Form, or the approved Sort, to fix on the Temples. He likewise sells the best and most curious Optical Instruments, as Telescopes, Microscopes, reflecting and common' as well as 'all Manner of Musical Instruments, as Violins, German, and common Flutes, &c. Also, the most curious painted Paper for Rooms' (*SJ*, 24 September 1745).

Baldwin's direct successor was Jonathan Moore, who replaced him in the *Journal*'s colophon, 24 November 1746. Persuading the islanders to buy books was possibly not an easy matter, and business difficulties may

---

[51] See C. Y. Ferdinand, 'Richard Baldwin Junior, Bookseller', *Studies in Bibliography*, 42 (1989), 254–64.

have been behind Jonathan Moore's move from the High Street 'to his own House in St. *James's Square*, the Sign of the Bible' (*SJ*, 25 January 1748). (While he does not seem to have been compelled to sell musical instruments and glasses, he did include bonnet paper among the stock listed at the time of the move.) In August 1749 Jonathan Moore opened a boarding school where he undertook to instruct in reading, writing, and arithmetic, in such a manner that 'Boys of a tolerable Genius' learned 'as much in one Year, as by ordinary Methods in Three', and were thereby 'more expeditiously [fitted] . . . for the public Grammar School, or Business, as their several Circumstances require' (*SJ*, 14 August 1749). He provided 'All Materials except Printed Books', which doubtless he was prepared to sell to his students and their parents. The relationship between eighteenth-century provincial booksellers and educators seems to have been an amicable and close one for the most part, and Jonathan Moore is only one *Salisbury Journal* example of the two combined in one man, not only taking advantage of the existing market, but actively creating a new market of readers and buyers. Jonathan Moore's career ended on the Isle of Wight when he died in 1753. He is not to be found in Plomer's *Dictionary of Printers and Booksellers* nor in McKenzie's *Apprentices*.

Neither is Simon Knight 'the Organist' who carried on the business at the Sign of the Bible in St James's Square in hopes that 'such Gentlemen, and others, as were Customers to the deceas'd, will continue their Favours to his Successor'. Like his predecessors, Knight was listed as the Isle of Wight outlet in numerous book advertisements; he also sold stationery goods, patent medicines, and those 'Paper Hangings for Rooms'. But he is the first to draw attention to his lending facilities: 'SIMON KNIGHT, BOOKSELLER and STATIONER . . . lends Books to read either by the single Book or Quarter' (*SJ*, 20 May 1753). And later, 'This is to acquaint all Readers, That Books in all faculties and Parts of Learning, likewise all New NOVELS, HISTORIES, VOYAGES, TRAVELS, &c. are *Lent to Read* by S. Knight, Bookseller in Newport . . . by whom all Kinds of Books are Sold at the lowest Prices, and all Sorts of Almanacks, Baldwin's Daily Journal, Ladies Pocket Book . . . Wholesale or retail' (*SJ*, 23 December 1754). So by mid-1753 at the latest, residents of Newport could borrow books for a small fee. Simon Knight also provided a bookbinding service. In spite of these innovations, Knight continued his bookselling business only until May 1756 when his stock in trade was advertised for sale (*SJ*, 31 May 1756).

Peter Milligan kept the bookshop and house in St James's Square for six years after this, though apparently not without difficulties: less than a year after his arrival, he gave notice that outstanding debts would be placed in an attorney's hands. 'Books, Pamphlets, Weekly Numbers, Monthly Magazines, and Stationary Wares, &c.' were provided as usual until Milligan's stock and household goods were dispersed in a four-day sale in July 1762.

It is useful to have a list of titles that Collins and his local agents believed they could sell from a Newport bookshop, of course, and to monitor trends in local book buying—the weekly delivery of the newspaper clearly encouraged the sale of books in weekly parts, for example. But the advertisements also provide some of the only evidence we have of the developing commercial structure of the provincial book trade: when another country bookseller of comparable standing to the Newport booksellers in the *Salisbury Journal*, William Pitt in Blandford, went out of business in 1749, his stock in trade was advertised for sale (*SJ*, 18 December 1749). His books amounted to about 350 volumes, hardly enough to support the usual provincial dealer's claim that any title published anywhere could be purchased locally at the same price as in London. What the provincial book advertisements suggest is that local booksellers stocked a basic collection made up of one or more copies of those titles actually advertised as available from named retailers. In the case of Thomas Geare and his successors to the Newport bookshop, out-of-stock books would have been ordered through Benjamin Collins in Salisbury, who in turn would have placed orders through his own agents in London. And the carriage from London to Salisbury to the Isle of Wight need not add to the price of a book, since the network of *Salisbury Journal* distributors and newsmen could be employed at no additional expense.

The book advertisements also provide some clues about the different levels of relationship a provincial newspaper proprietor/bookseller such as Benjamin Collins might establish with his country colleagues. During the mid-1740s, what seems to be a small consortium consisting of Benjamin Collins in Salisbury (always first named), Richard Baldwin in Newport, and Thomas Burrough in Devizes is suggested by the appearance of their three names together in advertisement after advertisement. Other provincial booksellers' names are listed, both in the book advertisements and in the colophon of the *Journal*, but they do not appear with the same regularity and they are not linked in the same way. This partnership was place-specific, rather than person-specific, for when Richard Baldwin went to London, Jonathan Moore replaces him in that section of the book-trade advertisements, and Simon Knight replaces Moore, and so on. The advertisements do not reveal what special arrangements Collins made with his partners on the Isle of Wight and in Devizes—perhaps a higher level of service, including centralized job printing, was involved; and the three could well have invested, as a consortium or provincial conger, in local books. On another level, numerous country booksellers acted as agents for Collins, taking in subscriptions and advertisements for the *Salisbury Journal*, serving as distribution points for the newspaper, and selling the products therein advertised. Finally, there was the network of distributors, carriers, newsmen, and hawkers, so often mentioned in the pages of local papers. The advertisements in the *Salisbury Journal* can tell us a good deal about just how books, other goods, and services were conveyed and marketed on the Isle of Wight and in almost any provincial town within the *Journal*'s range, starting with the fact that such services existed. The development of the provincial book trade was in effect the development of the mechanism for getting information and goods to the provincial consumer.

It is possible to draw some comparisons between what was happening in the newspaper trade in Wessex and in the rest of the provinces. Evidence that the provincial newspaper was employed more and more to circulate news and advertising is to be found in the growing number of titles and subscribers—that seems to be an undisputed national trend, well borne out by the *Salisbury Journal* in the eighteenth century. And more advertising was one general symptom of a growth in consumerism. J. Jefferson Looney's work on Yorkshire newspaper advertisements offers a few specific points of comparison where this study overlaps with his. Looney finds that newspaper advertising in York, a city he describes as one that attracted wealth, 'a traditional gentry gathering-spot', was somewhat different from newspaper advertising in Leeds, a city that created wealth. This is supported by detailed statistics compiled for sample years from the *York Courant* and the *Leeds Mercury*.[52] There are similar statistics for the *Salisbury Journal* for two of the sample years (1741 and 1760). The city of Salisbury itself probably attracted more wealth than it created, although within its catchment area there was a good deal of wealth creation (much of it far removed from the increasingly industrial way of Leeds). And indeed a comparison of statistics shows that advertising in Salisbury had more of an affinity with that in York, at least on a rudimentary level.

The year 1760 is especially telling for by then all three newspapers were

---

[52] Looney's representative years are 1741, 1760, 1784, and 1807. See 'Advertising and Society in England 1720–1820', Ph.D. diss. (Princeton University, 1983), esp. 'Appendix D. Types of Ad: A More Detailed Breakdown', 299–317.

well established ones: that year saw a large number of advertisements for books and other printed material in both the York and Salisbury papers (the *York Courant* had 541, the *Salisbury Journal* had 483), while the *Leeds Mercury* had only 88. York and Salisbury advertised more quack medicines (90 and 73 respectively to Leeds's 53); more movable goods for sale (170 and 221 to 29); more lost-and-found items (77 and 72 to 17); more educational establishments (11 and 20 to 0); more real estate (965 and 421 to 300); and more leisure activities (168 and 64 to 13). It was not simply that the *York Courant* and the *Salisbury Journal* carried more paid notices than the *Leeds Mercury*; the composition of the advertising columns seems to reflect other differences. The three newspapers had in common a high proportion of notices for real estate and books in 1760; but the *York Courant* had a staggering 335 advertisements for stallions to cover—Salisbury had 33, Leeds 8. York's importance as a northern centre for horse-racing is further reflected in the similar disproportions for advertisements of race meetings. Salisbury, like York, had a relatively high proportion of advertisements for such cultural activities as lectures, concerts, and assemblies in both 1741 and 1760. *Salisbury Journal* advertising, then, describes a market more like that of York than of Leeds, a Wessex market that was perhaps, as Looney suggests for York, readier to patronize 'commercialized leisure activity'.

In terms of the *Salisbury Journal* and the market it reached, there is something of a consumer revolution documented in its advertising columns: first, in the record numbers of advertisements; then in the overall greater diversity, most obvious in a comparison with the newspapers of the seventeenth century; and finally in the transitions that took place within each category of advertisement. Services that had been considered luxuries for any but the wealthy were advertised extensively round eighteenth-century Wessex; leisure activities were sold to a larger public audience; more and more goods were sold through the newspaper; the system for conveying these goods to customers became more sophisticated; educators pitched their appeals to a broader clientele; the change is noticeable even in the lost-and-founds, where lost anonymous working dogs or hunters with such names as Ranger and Smoaker are increasingly replaced with missing Violet, Gregory, Chloe, Fop, and (especially) Pompey. In almost every type of advertisement underlying economic change can be discerned: analysis of this one eighteenth-century newspaper describes a lively and changing market in and around Wiltshire.

Paid notices in different periodicals reflect their different regions, different catchment areas, as the example of the *Salisbury Journal* demonstrates.

Yet these trends in advertising in the eighteenth century have a broader, national context. More newspapers began to incorporate the word *Advertiser* into their titles. Studies of almost any newspaper of the period notice the rise in advertisements, and their variety. Investigations in numerous fields—history, education, medicine, clothing, crime, leisure, etc.—have drawn on eighteenth-century newspaper advertisements, further testimony to their various nature. One contemporary, who may have the last word on advertisements in the *Salisbury Journal*, was even moved to rhapsodize on their diversity and efficiency:

> If any gem'man wants a wife
> (A partner, as 'tis term'd, for life)
> An advertisement does the thing
> And quickly brings the pretty thing.
>
> If you want health, consult our pages,
> You shall be well, and live for ages;
> Our empirics, to get them bread,
> Do every thing—but raise the dead.
>
> Lands may be had, if they are wanted,
> Annuities of all sorts granted;
> Places, preferments, bought and sold;
> Houses to purchase, new and old.
> Ships, shops, of every shape and form,
> Carriages, horses, servants swarm;
> No matter whether good or bad,
> We tell you where they may be had.
> Our services you can't express,
> The good we do you hardly guess;
> There's not a want of human kind,
> But we a remedy can find.
> (Anonymous, *SJ*, 27 December 1784)[53]

[53] The *Salisbury Journal* was not the only newspaper to recognize the literary merit of the poem—it had appeared in the *Reading Mercury* for 20 Dec. 1784, and was probably picked up by other papers too. An earlier version of this chapter appeared in John Brewer and Roy Porter (eds.), *Consumption and the World of Goods* (London: Routledge, 193), 393–411.

Conclusion

SOME years ago James E. Tierney suggested that studies of individual provincial newspapers were needed to inform the larger history of the newspaper trade in England.[1] More recently Jeremy Black could make the similar observation that no one had yet built on Cranfield's and Wiles's broad studies of the provincial newspaper press.[2] This discussion of the eighteenth-century English newspaper trade, which starts from a close study of the *Salisbury Journal* and the *Hampshire Chronicle*, is intended as a contribution to that particular history.

Evidence accumulated from reading fifty years' production of the *Salisbury Journal* has provided, first, a basis for discussion of the place it held in the history not only of the newspaper trade but of the increasingly interdependent book trade. Editorial comment, imprints, and lists of news agencies compiled from the paper itself have helped to re-create the administrative structure of the paper. The account books of the *Hampshire Chronicle*, here used for the first time in such an investigation, have added significantly to the record, for not only are they among the very few eighteenth-century provincial newspaper account books known to have survived, but they offer information relevant to the *Salisbury Journal* and Benjamin Collins, who, not surprisingly, owned a controlling interest in the *Chronicle* for a time. It was to Collins's forceful direction at the managerial level that the *Journal* owed much of its success in the eighteenth century. He built up a sophisticated network of newsagents, distributors, carriers, and newsmen that incorporated elements of other longer-established communications systems (such as the metropolitan book-distribution system and local carriage networks). The same evidence more precisely describes the specific roles played by those newsagents and others who ensured that the *Salisbury Journal*, other local papers, and a whole range of commercial products got to their readers. And it offers a definition of the geography of Wessex readership.

---

[1] James E. Tierney, 'The Study of the Eighteenth-Century British Periodical: Problems and Progress', *Publications of the Bibliographical Society of America*, 69 (1975), 165–86.

[2] Jeremy Black, *The English Press in the Eighteenth Century* (Philadelphia: University of Pennsylvania Press, 1987), p. xiii.

Within the context of newspaper history the *Salisbury Journal* must be viewed as exceptionally successful: its proprietors, especially Benjamin Collins, demonstrated an ability to define and dominate a large catchment area. That Collins managed this in the face of regional competition is an indication of the market-place strategies that earned him a fortune over his lifetime. Readers clearly thought that Collins's newspaper was influential too, if the numbers of paid advertisements are any measure. The fact of the *Journal*'s continued circulation today may be another indication of the firm basis he made for it in identifying it with Wiltshire and the adjacent counties.

Wiles and Cranfield did a great deal to set the background of the provincial newspaper press in England in the first half of the eighteenth century, and what is now known of the Salisbury paper can be linked with their work, and that of newspaper historians such as Michael Harris and Jeremy Black. Studies of other provincial newspapers, each in its entirety, are still required, however, so that a broader foundation for comparison can be constructed.

There are implications in this study for areas of research outside newspaper- and book-trade history. What an established weekly paper meant for the average Wessex resident was regular and dependable access not only to a newspaper, but to a range of periodicals, books, medicines, and other goods and services. This suggests a much broader context for the study of individual country newspapers. Certainly the Wessex newspapers provide ample evidence for the wide availability of printed material in the country, the existence of numerous educational establishments, local interest in cultural events, and the marketability of political and military news, for example. And the evidence cannot be dismissed simply because much of it, in a country newspaper, was derived from other sources. Just as a twentieth-century editor can select news from different syndicated versions, so Benjamin Collins and his colleagues selected the material they would offer their readers from eighteenth-century syndicate-equivalents. Some advertisements, particularly those for books and medicines, were intended for a national audience and were reproduced in any number of London and provincial newspapers; many other services and goods, however, were advertised only locally or regionally and their advertisements were often unique to one paper. A particular combination of derived news and local reports and advertising marked different provincial newspapers. Investigation of individual country newspapers can, over the years, describe significant political, social, and cultural change.

Samuel Johnson defined *intelligence* as the 'commerce of information', 'notice', 'mutual communication', and the *intelligencer* as 'one who sends or conveys news . . . one who carries messages between parties'. Benjamin Collins was, among other things, an intelligencer, and the business of his newspapers was principally the commerce of information. Their history during the critical first fifty years of the newspaper develops our knowledge of eighteenth-century provincial life and commerce.

APPENDIX: WILLS

THE WILL OF BENJAMIN COLLINS[1]

This is the last Will and Testament of me Benjamin Collins of the City of New Sarum in the County of Wilts Gentleman made and published the twenty fifth day of March in the year of our Lord one thousand seven hundred and seventy eight in manner following that is to say In the first place it is my Will and desire to be buried in the Church Yard of St Edmund in the said City of New Sarum and not elsewhere and in such part thereof as my dear Wife Mary Collins shall think fit Also it is my Will and I do hereby direct that all my just debts be fully paid and discharged And I do hereby expressly charge all my Real and Personal ⌈and other⌉ Estate whatsoever and wheresoever with and to the payment thereof and Subject to the payment of my debts as aforesaid I give and bequeath unto my said Wife Mary Collins the Sum of Fifty Pounds to be paid her immediately on my decease and the further Sum of Five hundred Pounds to be paid her within twelve Months next after my decease Also I give bequeath and confirm unto my said Wife Mary Collins all her Rings Jewells and Paraphernalia whatsoever Also I give and bequeath unto my Brother Joseph Collins one clear Annuity or yearly Sum of five Pounds to commence from the day of my decease and be payable and paid by quarterly proportions for and during the term of his natural Life Also I give and bequeath unto my Brother Francis Collins the sum of fifty Pounds Also I give and bequeath unto my Mother in Law Mrs Jane Cooper my Sisters in Law Mrs Sarah Cooper and Mrs Jane Elderton my Cousin Mrs Ann Batt my Nieces Lydia Compton Margaret Towers Mary Tatlock Elizabeth Saunders Ann Evatt Lucy Poole and my Nephews the Reverend John Elderton and Joseph Elderton Junr to each and every of them five Guineas apiece for Mourning and unto my Nephew and Godson the Reverend Edward Cooper and to my Brothers in Law Mr John Cooper and Mr Joseph Elderton ten Guineas a piece for a Ring and Mourning Also I give devise and bequeath unto my Son William Collins all my Copyhold Estates at Milford near the City of New Sarum and my Leasehold Messuage and Garden there occupied by Edward Williams Blacksmith To hold to my said son William Collins his Heirs Executors administrators and Assigns for all my Term Estate and Interest respectively to come therein at the time of my decease Also I give devise and bequeath unto my son Benjamin Charles Collins my Freehold

[1] PRO PROB. 11/1127. In fact the will was contested, and was not proved until 18 Aug. 1810. A marginal note in the PRO copy reads: 'Proved at London 18th Aug 1810 before the Judge by the Oath of William Collins the Son and Surviving Executor he haveing retracted the Renunciation formerly made having been first duly sworn . . .'

Messuage or Dwellinghouse Shop Warehouses Printing Office and Premises with
the Apurtenances now in my own occupation situate on the New Canal in the
City of Sarum aforesaid together with all the Fixtures in the said Shop Printing
Office and Warehouses and all my Stock in the several Trades or Business of a
Printer Bookseller Bookbinder and Vender of Medicines and all the Implements
Utensils Tools and Materials in the said Printing and Bookbinding Business and
also the said several Trades and Businesses and all my Rights and Interest therein
now carried on by and in the Name of my Son Benjamin Charles Collins and
John Johnson for my Use and Benefit And likewise my Copyright or Right of
Printing Publishing and Vending the Salisbury Journal together with my Copyrights and Shares of Copyright of and in the following Books Viz my third share
of the Royal Battledore Royal Primmer Pretty Book for Children Pretty Book of
Pictures or the History of Tommy Trip Museum or Private Tutor for Masters
and Misses Royal Psalter Daily Journal or Gentlemans and Tradesmans compleat
Annual Pocket Book one eighth part of Fenning's Spelling Book and one third
part of the Compleat Letter Writer and my full Moiety or half part of my property in Cephalic Snuff now made and prepared by me and of the Patent for the
same To hold unto my said son Benjamin Charles Collins his Heirs Executors
Administrators and Assigns respectively as his and their own absolute and [*sic*]
property for ever subject nevertheless to and charged and chargeable with the
payment of a clear annuity of one hundred and five pounds to my dear Wife Mary
Collins which I do hereby give and bequeath to her to be paid to her yearly and
every year for and during the course of her natural Life by four equal quarterly
payments on the four following days of the year to wit Lady Day Midsummer
Michaelmas and Christmas and the first payment thereof to begin and be made on
such of the s^d. several Days as shall first and next happen after my decease which
said Annuity with the Legacies and Beneficial Interest by this my Will intended
for my said Wife is by me meant in Satisfaction of all claims which she may have
on my real or personal Estate by Settlement or otherwise or out of my Real or
Copyhold Estates as being my Widow Also I give devise and bequeath unto my
Daughter Elizabeth the Wife of the Reverend Barfoot Colton Clerk all my Estate
and Interest for the Lives of the said Elizabeth Colton and M^r. [space] Gardener
from and after the decease of M^{rs}. Barbara Gardener of and in a Leasehold Estate
at Purse Candle in the County of Dorset To hold to my said daughter Elizabeth
Colton her Executors Administrators and Assigns as and for her and their own
absolute Property Also I give and bequeath unto my Daughter Jane the wife of
George Leonard Staunton Esqr. my Annuity or yearly Sum of sixty seven pounds
and four Shillings Subject to the stipulated abatements on punctual payment
thereof charged on and payable out of the said Plantation Estates late of John
Missett Esqr deceased in the Island of Montserratt for the Life of the said Jane
Stanton [*sic*] my daughter To hold unto her my said daughter Jane Staunton and
her Assigns for all my Estate Term and Interest in and to the same also I give
devise and bequeath unto my daughter Sarah the wife of the Reverend Peter

Bellinger Brodie Clerk the immediate Income from my decease of the Rectory of Shilling Okeford in the county of Dorset of which I am now in possession for the Life of the Reverend M^r. [space] Moreau the Incumbent thereof To hold to my said Daughter Sarah Brodie her Executors Administrators and Assigns for all my Term and Interest therein during the Incumbency of the said M^r. Moreau and I give devise and bequeath unto my Executors and Trustees hereinafter named my Right and Interest of in and to the next Presentation to the said Rectory on the death or Cession of the said M^r. Moreau or other Avoidance thereof In Trust to present my Son in Law the said Peter Bellinger Brodie or such person as he his Executors or Administrators shall nominate or appoint thereto in order that he or such Person so nominated may be instituted and inducted into the same with the Rights Members and Appurtenances thereof Also I give devise and bequeath unto my said Wife Mary Collins all my Reversionary Estate and Interest for the Life of my Daughter Charlotte Collins after the decease of M^rs. [Bricke?] of in and to a certain Leasehold Estate at Foffant [i.e. Fovant] in the said County of Wilts held under the Earl of Pembroke Also I give devise and bequeath all my Manor and all other my Messuages Farms Lands Tenements Hereditaments and Estates Freehold Leasehold or otherwise and of what Tenure Nature or Kind soever the same may be within the Counties of Somerset Dorset Wilts Middlesex Surry or elsewhere within the Kingdom of Great Britain And all the Rest Residue of my Monies Mortgage and other Securities Goods Chattels and Real and Personal Estate whatsoever and wheresoever unto ~~my said Wife Mary Collins my said son William Collins my said Brother Francis Collins my said Son in Law the said Peter Bellinger Brodie and my said Brothers in Law John Cooper and Joseph Elderton their Heirs Executors Administrators and Assigns~~ [initials 'B.C' appear in margin against each line crossed out] In Trust nevertheless to sell and dispose of my said Manors Messuages Farms Lands Tenements and Hereditaments Leasehold and other Estates and the Residue of my said Real and Personal Estate such Price or Prices in such Parts by such Proportions at such time and times and in such manner as they in their discretion think adviseable for making the most thereof and in Trust after paying or reimbursing to themselves all such Costs Charges and Expences as they my said Trustees shall sustain or be put unto in the Execution of the Trusts hereby in them reposed that all my said Manors Messuages Farms Lands Tenements Hereditaments Leasehold and other Estates and all such the Residue of my Monies Securities Goods Chattels and Personal Estate or the Produce thereof and the Sum of three thousand seven hundred pounds in the whole by me advanced in portioning out my three married daughters and the amount in value of the foregoing specifick devises and Bequests to and for the Benefit of my said Wife and Sons and Daughters hereafter ascertained in value to be added to and thrown into Hotchpot therewith shall and may be considered and valued together and make and constitute one entire aggregate Stock or Fund and upon Trust to pay and divide the Produce and Amount thereof unto and amongst my said Wife Mary Collins and my said Sons and Daughters William Collins

Benjamin Charles Collins Elizabeth Colton Jane Stanton [*sic*] and Sarah Brodie respectively in such Proportions manner and form and so and in such manner as that my said Son William Collins together with and including the said Copyhold Estates at Milford aforesaid ⌈before devised⌉ to him which shall be valued to him and considered at the Sum of two thousand Pounds shall and may have and receive two full Eighth parts or shares thereof (the whole into eight equal parts or shares to be divided) and my said Son Benjamin Charles Collins together with and including my said Freehold dwelling house Shop Printing Office Warehouses Fixtures Stock Trades or Businesses Copyrights and Premisses before given and devised to him subject to my said Wife's Annuity which shall be valued to him and considered at the Sum of six thousand and five hundred Pounds shall and may have and receive two other full eight Parts or shares thereof (the whole into eight equal parts or shares to be divided) and my said daughter Elizabeth Colton (together with and including the Sum of twelve hundred and fifty Pounds by me already advanced to and for my said Daughter Elizabeth Colton by way of Fortune or Portion on her Marriage and the said Reversionary Interest in the said Estate at Purse Candle aforesaid before given to her which shall be valued to her and considered at the Sum of seven hundred Pounds) shall and may have and receive one full eighth Part or Share thereof (the whole into eight equal Parts or shares to be divided) and my said Daughter Jane Staunton (together with and including the ⌈like⌉ Sum of twelve hundred and fifty Pounds by me already advanced to or for my said daughter Jane Staunton by way of Fortune or Portion on her Marriage and the said annuity charged on the said Montserrat Estate for Life as aforesaid before given to her which shall be valued to her and considered at the Sum of four hundred and fifty Pounds) shall and may have and receive one other full eighth part or share thereof (the whole into eight ⌈equal⌉ parts or shares to be divided) and my said Daughter Sarah Brodie together with and including the Sum of twelve hundred Pounds by me already advanced to or for my said Daughter Sarah Brodie by way of Fortune or Portion on her Marriage and the immediate Income from my decease of the said Rectory of Shilling Okeford during the Incumbency of the said M[r]. Moreau before given to her my said Daughter Sarah Brodie and the next presentation to the said Rectory before devised to my said Trustees for the Benefit of her Husband the said Peter Bellinger Brodie both which shall be valued to her and considered at the Sum of fifteen hundred Pounds shall and may have and receive one other full eighth part or share thereof (the whole into eight equal parts or shares to be divided) and my said Wife together with and including only the said Reversionary Interest in the said Leasehold Estate at Foffant before given to my said Wife which shall be valued to her and considered at the Sum of two hundred and ten Pounds but in no wise to include the two Pecuniary Legacies of Fifty Pounds and Five hundred Pounds before given her which are respectively intended for her use and benefit independant of and over and above the share hereafter mentioned and not meant to be thrown into or make a part of the said aggregate Stock or Fund shall and may have and receive the remaining one full eighth part or share thereof (the whole into eight equal parts or shares to be divided) But it is my express and [*sic*] Will and Meaning and I do hereby direct that the several eighth Shares of my said three Daughters shall be payable and paid unto them in such shares and proportions at such time and times and in such manner as my said Trustees shall think fit and proper in their discretion and as Circumstances shall in Prudence point out and not otherwise yet nevertheless that Interest thereof shall be paid and payable for the Same as it shall from time to time arise provided and it is my Will that if my Daughter Jane Staunton shall not chuse to accept the said Annuity for her Life charged on the said Plantation Estate at Montserratt at the said Sum of four hundred and fifty Pounds for which she shall have one years time from my decease to consider and determine then and in such case she shall be paid and receive an equivalent for the same out of the Residue of my said Estate in lieu thereof And it is my Will and I do hereby declare that the said eighth part of my said Estate so given to my Wife shall be in her absolute Power and disposal as a Fund that she may thereby or thereout be enabled to make such provision either of the whole or any Part or Parts by way of Fortune or Portion during her Life time or by her last Will and Testament or other writing to take Effect before or after her decease for my said Daughter Charlotte Collins and in and by such Sum or Sums at such time or times and ⌈ in ⌉ such way and manner as she my said Wife shall think fit and proper and that my said Wife shall be at Liberty to lend the whole any Part of her said eighth Share on real Security or on Bond or Note to any Person or Persons whomsoever And that she shall not be Responsible for any Loss by means thereof or liable to account for the same or any part of the Interest thereof leaving it to her Judgement and Pleasure to maintain and educate my said daughter Charlotte thereout in such manner as she shall think Proper and I do hereby constitute and appoint my said Wife Mary Collins Guardian of my said daughter Charlotte Collins during her minority and in case of the death of my said Wife before my said daughter Charlotte shall attain her Age of twenty one years then such Person or Persons as my said Wife shall be [sc. by] her Will appoint or in default thereof the said John Cooper and Peter Bellinger Brodie shall be and I do hereby appoint them Guardians of my said daughter Charlotte during her minority Also it is my will and I hereby direct that my said Son William Collins shall be released from all debts Sum and Sums of Money whatsoever from him due and owing to me which I hereby give acquit him from and relinquish to him accordingly And it is my Will and I do hereby direct that my said Son William Collins shall for the term of six years next after my decease have a Right and be at Liberty to carry on the Business of a Banker in the Front of the House And also the Compting house on the New Canal where the same is now carried on and also to have the use of the Bed Chamber backwards looking into the Garden adjoining to the Library being severally parts of the said Freehold premises so devised to my said Son Benjamin Charles Collins ~~and my said Son William Collins paying the clear yearly Sum of ten Pounds by way of Rent for~~

~~[these Rooms] to my said Son Benjamin Collins~~ Provided further that if from unforeseen Circumstances the specifick provision considered and valued at the Sum of six thousand five hundred Pounds hereinbefore made for my said Son Benjamin Charles Collins in part of his two eighth Shares of the said aggregate Fund shall exceed two Parts in eight of the said Fund then it is my Will and I do hereby direct that he shall pay or allow thereout so much as will reduce each of his two shares in eight to an equality with each of the other eight shares And I do hereby further direct that my said Son Benjamin Charles Collins shall be considered as of full age if he shall not have attained thereto at the time of my decease and that all Arts and deeds by him done in Pursuance and by virtue of this my Will shall be binding as effectually as if he was actually of full age And likewise that my said Wife Mary Collins shall have Liberty to reside in the House upon the New Canal as long as she shall live rent free and also in the House at Milford whilst my said Son William Collins shall continue unmarried in the same manner as she has always done And I further direct that my Trustees and Executors hereinafter named shall receive all the debts due in the several Trades carried on for me by my said Son Benjamin Charles Collins and John Johnson as aforesaid and pay all those which be due from the same respectively and what shall remain after payment thereof shall make a part of my residuary Estate And I do hereby make and appoint my said Wife Mary Collins my said Sons William Collins and Benjamin Charles Collins my said Brother Francis Collins my said Son in Law Peter Bellinger Brodie and my said Brothers in Law John Cooper and Joseph Elderton joint executors in Trust of this my last Will and Testament hereby revoking all former Wills In Witness whereof I have hereunto set my hand and Seal the day and year first hereinbefore written, Ben^{jn}. Collins Signed sealed published and declared by the said Benjamin Collins the Testator as and for his last Will and Testament in the presence of us who have hereunto subscribed our names as witnesses thereto in the presence of the said Testator and of each other Edwd Wray Edward Joye Tho Chubb

By this Codicil I declare it to be my further Will and direct that if it shall so happen that my Son Benjamin Charles shall die under twenty one years of age the whole of his shares and beneficial Estate and Interest under my said Will shall go equally unto and amongst my then surviving Children their Heirs and Assigns And if my said daughter Charlotte shall die under the age of twenty one years the share of my said Wife in the aggregate Fund in my said Will mentioned shall go and be equally divided amongst my then surviving Children Dated the twenty fifth day of March 1778 Benjn. Collins Esq Signed sealed published and delivered by the said Benjamin Collins in the presence of Edwd. Wray Edward Joye Tho. Chubb

This is a Codicil to the last Will and Testament of Benjamin Collins of the City of New Sarum Banker and to be taken as part thereof that is to say whereas my Brother Francis Collins one of the Trustees and Executors in my said Will named lately departed this Life And whereas since the date and execution of my said Will and a short Codicil written at the foot thereof I am by Purchase or otherwise become seized possessed of interested in or intitled unto divers Messuages Lands Tenements and Hereditaments to me and my Heirs or otherwise Now I do by this present Codicil to my said last Will and Testament give and devise all such Messuages Lands Tenements Hereditaments and Premises as well in Possession as Reversion of whatsoever nature or Tenure and wherever lying and being unto the surviving Trustees in my last Will named their Heirs Executors Administrators and Assigns to and for the same Uses Intents and Purposes as all and singular my Manors Messuages Farms Lands Hereditaments and other Estates and Effects of what nature and kind soever whereof I was seized Possessed Interested in and intitled unto at the time of making and executing my last Will were and are therein and thereby given and devised And in all other respects I do hereby ratify and confirm my ⌈said⌉ last Will and Testament in Witness whereof I have to this present Codicil set my hand and seal this eighteenth day of February in the year of our Lord one thousand seven hundred and eighty one, Benjn. Collins Esqr Signed sealed published and declared by the said Benjamin Collins the Testator as and for a Codicil to his last Will and Testament in the presence of us Mary Collear Jos^h. Hillary Chris^r. Hallett Junr.

This is ⌈a⌉ **further Codicil** to my last Will and Testament and to be taken as part thereof that is to say I give and devise the Freehold Estate at Somersham in Huntingdonshire by me lately Purchased of Christopher Milburne Esqr. to the Trustees in my said Will named their Heirs and Assigns for ever to and for the same Uses Intents and Purposes as all other my Estates were and are thereby given and devised And again in all other Respects ratify and confirm the same Will and my former Codicil In Witness whereof I have hereunto set my hand and Seal the twenty eighth day of February one thousand seven hundred and eighty three Benjn. Collins Esq Signed sealed published and declared by the said Benjamin Collins the Testator in the presence of John Sanger Thos. Frampton Jos^h. Hillary

This is a Codicil to the last Will and Testament of me Benjamin Collins of the City of New Sarum Banker I hereby Confirm the several Legacies in my said Will contained which are capable of taking Effect and the devise to my Son William of my then Copyhold and Leasehold Estates at Milford with the benefit of the Life or Lives since added therein and to my son Benjamin Charles Collins of my Freehold on the Canal at Sarum and Fixtures and Stocks in Trade Implements Tools and Materials of the said Trades and Businesses and my Copyrights therein mentioned and of every kind Subject to the Payment of a clear Annuity of one hundred and fifty Pounds (instead of one hundred and five Pounds) to my Wife Mary Collins for her Life payable in the like manner and by the like proportions as the said Annuity of one hundred and five Pounds was thereby made payable and I revoke the Bequest to my daughter Staunton thereby made of an Annuity out of the Estates of John Missett Esqr. in Montseratt without prejudice to my said daughter Staunton in respect to the beneficial Interest she is otherwise entitled to share under my said Will and I give devise and bequeath the several Copyhold or other Estates at Milford by me purchased since the 25th. day of March 1779 being the date of my said Will and all Messuages Lands Tenements and Hereditaments Freehold or otherwise by me Purchased also since the date of the said Will or to which I am intitled in any other way of subsequent Acquisition and all other my Messuages Farms ⌈Manors⌉ Lands Tenements and Hereditaments and Estates Freehold Leasehold or otherwise in the Kingdom of Great Britain and all the Rest and Residue of my Monies Mortgages and other Securities Goods Chattels and Real and Personal Estate whatsoever and wheresoever instead of the Persons therein named as Trustees to my Wife Mary Collins Robert Cooper of Milford Street in the City of New Sarum Linendraper my Son Benjamin Charles Collins and Son in Law Peter Bellinger Brodie Clerk their Heirs Executors Administrators and Assigns In Trust and to and for the same Uses Intents and Purposes as are mentioned expressed and declared in and by my said Will of my Manors and Estates and Residue of my Real and Personal Estates thereby devised to such Persons therein named as Trustees save such variations as are herein aftermentioned Viz^t. the value of the Montserratt Annuity not be taken into the eighth share intended for my daughter Staunton the value of the Income of Shilling Okeford during M^r. Moreau's Incumbency and the next Presentation thereto to be considered at Twelve hundred Pounds instead of Fifteen hundred Pounds in the Eighth share intended for my daughter Brodie and nine hundred Pounds and Interest due from my Son William Collins on the Ballance of an amount under his hand for which I have his Bond which is lost or mislaid to be considered as part of the two Eighth Shares intended for my said Son William and save also that I do hereby give and bequeath an Annuity of One hundred Pounds per Ann^m payable by Lord Arundell for the Life of my s^d. Son William unto my said Son William Subject to the Payment of twenty five Pounds yearly thereout to my daughter Charlotte to her said and seperate use which shall be valued and considered Subject to such yearly Payment to my said daughter Charlotte at seven hundred and fifty Pounds of my said Son Williams two eighth Shares intended for him under the said Trust and as to the eighth Share thereby directed or intended for my said Wife for and notwithstanding any thing in my said Will expressed or implied to the contrary the same shall be considered as a Fund in her hands for such purposes as she shall think proper to apply the same either in her life time or after her decease by deed or Will either for the Benefit of my daughter Charlotte or any Child or Children of hers or otherwise in my Family trusting and confiding entirely in the discretion of my said Wife who shall be no ways questionable or accountable for the same or what she may can or shall do therewith or with any part thereof with or without deed or Will to any person whomsoever provided and it is my express Will and Meaning that if it shall unfortunately happen (which God forbid) that my Son William Collins who is now abroad beyond the Seas should die before me then and in that Case any all and every devise Bequest and Beneficial Interest made and intended to and for my Son William Collins under and by virtue of my Will and this Codicil or the Trusts thereof shall become vested in my said Trustees and added to the Bulk of my Estates Real and Personal devised to them In Trust as aforesaid And my said Trustees their Heirs Executors Administrators and Assigns shall stand seized and possessed of such Estates and Beneficial Interest so made and intended for my said Son William as to one Moiety thereof in Trust for my said Son Benjamin Charles Collins his Heirs Executors and Administrators and as to the other Moiety thereof In Trust for my said daughter Colton my said daughter Staunton my said daughter Brodie and my said Wife in Addition to their several Eighth parts intended in and by the said Will and this my Codicil In Witness whereof I have to this Codicil set my hand and seal the fifth day of June in the year of our Lord one thousand seven hundred and eighty four Benjn. Collins Esq—Signed sealed published and declared by the said Benjamin Collins the Testator as and for a Codicil to his last Will and Testament in the presence of us who have subscribed our names as Witnesses to the Execution thereof in the presence and at the request of the said Testator and also in the presence of each other Catharine Kimber Willm. Collier Jos^h. Elderton.

I do hereby make a further Codicil to my said Will by declaring that it is my express Wish and Meaning that the two eighth shares to my Son William and the one Eighth share to my daughter Colton are meant and intended to include all demands they may respectively have out of my Real or Personal Estate under and by virtue of any Settlement Contract Bond or Engagement by me made and entered into on my Marriage with their late Mother Edith Good and in firm Satisfaction thereof Witness my hand and Seal the same day and year—Benjn. Collins Esq—Signed sealed published and declared as a further Codicil, by the said Testator Benjn. Collins in our presence. Catharine Kimber William Collier, Jos^h. Elderton.

This Will was proved at London with five Codicils the first day of March in the year of our Lord one thousand seven hundred and eighty five[2] before the Right Worshipful Peter Calvert doctor of Laws Master Keeper or Commissary of the Prerogative Court of Canterbury lawfully constituted by the Oath of Benjamin Charles Collins Esquire the Son of the deceased and the Reverend Peter Bellinger Brodie Clerk two of the surviving Executors named in the said Will to whom Administration of all and singular the Goods Chattels and Credits of the said deceased was granted they having been first sworn by Commission duly to Administer Power reserved of making the like Grant to Mary Collins Widow the Relict William Collins Esquire the Son of the said deceased John Cooper and Joseph Elderton Esquires the other surviving Executors named in the said Will when they or either of them shall apply for the same.

---

[2] In fact Benjamin Collins's will was not finally proved until twenty-five years later, in 1810. See marginal note transcribed in n. 1 above.

THE WILL OF BENJAMIN CHARLES COLLINS[3]

This is the last Will and Testament of me Benjamin Charles Collins of Salisbury in the County of Wilts Esquire First I direct that all my just debts funeral Expences and the Charges of proving this my Will to be paid and discharged and from and after the payment thereof and Subject thereto and also Subject and Charged with the payment of the several Legacies and Sums hereafter given and bequeathed by me I give devise and bequeath unto my dear Mother Mary Collins my Brother in Law Sir George Staunton my Brother in Law the Reverend Peter Bellinger Brodie my Brother in Law the Reverend Barford Colton and my Brother William Collins all my Estate and Effects of what nature or kind soever and wheresoever both real and personal To have and to hold the same unto them their Heirs Executors Administrators and Assigns equally share and share alike as Tenants in Common and not as joint Tenants I give and bequeath unto Mary Elizabeth Goodenge calling herself Mary Castle now residing with me at No. 40 New Road in the Parish of Saint Mary le Bone in the County of Middlesex One Annuity or clear yearly Sum of One hundred pounds during the term of her natural Life payable Quarterly I give to William Tomlyn of Salisbury Banker the Sum of Five hundred pounds Also the like Sum of Five hundred pounds to Elias Hibbs of Monument yard London Wine Merchant I give to my uncle M[r]. John Cooper of Salisbury one Annuity or clear yearly Sum of One hundred pounds during the term of his natural Life payable half yearly I give Two hundred and fifty pounds apiece to Harriet Dennett and Frances Eliza Dennett the daughters of Jonathan Dennett of Leicester Place Gentleman I give to the Reverend Edward Cooper of Yetminster near Sherborne in Dorsetshire the Sum of Five hundred pounds I give Two hundred and fifty pounds and my Gold Watch to my Friend M[r]. Robert Dennett I give the Sum of One hundred pounds to Miss Sarah Greaves and the like and the like Sum of One hundred pounds to each of her Brothers William Greaves and Robert Greaves I give to Henry Stevens of Salisbury Gentleman the Sum of One hundred pounds I give to William Havers of Salisbury the Sum of One hundred pounds and the like Sum of One hundred pounds to John Dowding my Clerk I discharge John Luxford my Overseer from the payment of all Debts Claims and Demands which I have against him I also release and discharge Mr. Thomas Williams of Vere Street from the payment of all Debts Claims and Demands whatsoever due to me alone or jointly with any of my present or late Partners I also give and bequeath to my Cousin Frances Henrietta Elderton now or late of Salisbury the Sum of Five hundred pounds [And lastly I do hereby nominate constitute and appoint the said Sir George Staunton Townley Ward of Soho Square in the County of Middlesex Esquire the said Peter Bellinger Brodie and Barford Colton Executors of this my Will] hereby revoking and making void all former and other Wills by me at any time heretofore

---

[3] PRO PROB. 11/1478/368.

made and do declare this to be my last Will and Testament as Witness my Hand and Seal this nineteenth Day of August in the year of our Lord one thousand seven hundred and ninety six [signed:] Benjamin Chas. Collins Signed sealed published and declared by the said Testator Benjamin Charles Collins as and for his last Will and Testament in the sight and presence of us who have hereunto subscribed our Names as Witnesses at his request and in his sight and presence and the sight and presence of each thereto Cliff: Ashmore, James Moss, Matt^w. Thompson

I also direct that my Executors before named do immediately after my decease deliver up to the said M^r. Thomas Williams all and every Agreement entered into by him with M^r. William Bacon relating to the supplying of Medicines for the Shop in Oxford Street and which Agreement or Agreements has or have been assigned over to me in order that the same may be cancelled and put an end to I also give and bequeath unto John Sawyer now my Clerk employed in the Business carried on in Oxford Street the Sum of Five hundred pounds I also give and bequeath to John William Hucklebridge of Salisbury late my Clerk the Sum of Two hundred pounds [signed:] B:C: Collins—Cliff. Ashmore, James Moss Matt^w. Thompson

I Benjamin Charles Collins of Salisbury in the County of Wilts Esquire do publish and declare this present writing as and for a Codicil to my last Will and Testament dated the nineteenth day of August now last past Whereas in and by my said Will after Payment of my just debts funeral Expence and Legacies and Sums of Money therein mentioned I have given devised and bequeathed all the rest residue and remainder of my Estate and Effects of what nature or kind soever and wheresoever both real and personal unto my dear Mother Mary Collins my Brother in [*sic*] Sir George Staunton my Brother in Law the Reverend Peter Bellinger Brodie my Brother in Law the Reverend Barford Colton and my Brother William Collins To have and to hold the same unto them their Heirs Executors Administrators and Assigns equally between and amongst themselves and share alike as Tenants in Common and not as joint Tenants and I have also in and by my said Will appointed the said Peter Bellinger Brodie one of my Executors and I have likewise in and by my said Will given and bequeathed unto William Tomlyn of Salisbury Banker the Sum of Five hundred pounds and to the Reverend Edward Cooper of Yetminster near Sherborne in Dorsetshire the like sum of Five hundred pounds and to my Cousin Frances Henrietta Elderton then or late of Salisbury the Sum of Five hundred pounds Now I do hereby revoke and make void so much of my said Will as relates to or concerns the several Bequests therein contained to the said Peter Bellinger Brodie, William Tomlyn, Edward Cooper, Frances Henrietta Elderton and also the appointment of the said Peter Bellinger Brodie as such Executor as aforesaid and I do hereby give and bequeath unto Townley Ward one of the Executors named in my said Will the Sum of One hundred pounds and the like Sum of One hundred pounds to Mrs Ward Wife of the said Townley Ward and I the said Benjamin Charles Collins do hereby nominate and appoint Jonathan Dennett in my said Will named another Executor in my said Will and I do give and bequeath unto the said Jonathan Dennett the

Sum of One hundred pounds and to M^rs. Dennett Wife of the said Jonathan Dennett the like Sum of One hundred pounds and In Witness whereof I the said Benjamin Charles Collins have hereunto set my Hand and Seal this seventh day of November one thousand seven hundred and ninety six, Benjamin Charles Collins Signed sealed published and declared by the said Benjamin Charles Collins as and for a Codicil to be annexed to and taken as part of his last Will and Testament in the presence of us who at his request and in his presence and in the sight and presence of each other have subscribed our Names as Witnesses Cliff: Ashmore, Sam^ll. Sowther, James Brough, Clerks to Messrs. Ward Dennetts and Greaves of Covent Garden

Memorandum Friday April 21st. 1797 It was on the seventh day of July 1792 that I delivered by Letter the inclosed draft value seven hundred and sixty nine Pounds to my most able and faithful Sollicitor Townley Ward Esqr. as and for his own sole and entire use in gratefull yet humble Token of my Sense of the many and important Services rendered to me and to my Family during a long and most arduous executorship the same being in part a small portion only of my share of very large Sums wrested by his able Head from the hands of needy and artful Villains namely Maurice Lloyd, Viscount Newhaven and Gregory Bateman as also from Rogues of lesser Note all which services were done and rendered without Law and Litigation the more meritorious this and to the Estate of Benjamin Collins my Father deceased immensely advantageous for the experience of Time has shewn that had a Chancery Suit or even the usual delays of a nisi prius Court taken place a very great portion of the large Sums so recovered must have been lost All these three Swindlers being long since dead and the two last named died insolvent It was on this day the 21st. of April 1797 that my worthy and honorable Friend M^r. Ward returned to my hands this draft and as he was peremptory that I should take it I did so But I now give it herewith unto the hands of my esteemed Friend and Sollicitor Mr Robert Dennett by him to be placed herewith in my Last Will and Testament in his keeping and in case of my death by him to be delivered unto the hands of his Brother one of my Executors for the uses and Purposes of M^r. Ward or as he only shall direct and all this I declare to be a Codicil to my aforesaid Will Signed with my Name and sealed with my Seal this 21st. day of April 1797 Ben. Chas. Collins

[Copy of banker's draft inserted]

1801- Dec: 25 Christmas day This is a Codicil to my Will in the hands of Robert Dennett Esqr. Covent Garden London I owe not one Penny to my Fathers Estate in any way I owe not one Penny to all or any of my late partners in the Banking Business I give to Robert Dennett aforesaid to his Brother Jonathan and to his Partner William Greaves Esqr Three thousand five hundred pounds In Trust five hundred Pounds for Frances Eliza Dennett and the residue for Maria Castle (so called) at Mrs Butts Ladies School Great Marlbro Street Carnaby Market the said Maria to be a Ward of Chancery B. C. Collins.

2ᵈ. May 1808

Appeared Personally Gerard Selby of Lincolns Inn Fields in the County of Middlesex Gentleman and made Oath that on the 6ᵗʰ. day of February last he went down to the City of Salisbury for the purpose of being present at the examination of the papers of Benjamin Charles Collins late of Salisbury aforesaid Esquire deceased who died as this deponent has been informed and believes on the 24ᵗʰ. day of the Month of January last past and of selecting those of a Testamentary nature that on this deponents arriving at Salisbury a search was made by him and William Collins Esquire Samuel Emly Esquire John Luxford and John Dowding Gentlemen of Salisbury aforesaid and the said deceased's papers were carefully examined and on examining a Memorandum Book purporting to be the daily journal for the year 1801 containing different Memorandums of the said deceased was found by the said Samuel Emly locked up in the said deceaseds Bureau situate in the Dining Parlour in the presence of this deponent and of the said other persons that the said Book was immediately examined and on reading the same a Codicil was found therein written in a page of the said Book described Memorandums and Resolutions at the end of the year 1801 the said Codicil beginning thus 1801 Dec. . . . [verifying the authenticity of the codicils].

This Will was proved at London with four Codicils the sixth day of May in the year of our Lord one thousand eight hundred and eight before the worshipful George Ogilvie Doctor of Laws Surrogate of the Right Honourable Sir William . . .

THE WILL OF JAMES LINDEN[4]

I James Linden of the Town and County of Southampton, Schoolmaster being infirm in Body but of sound Mind and Memory do make and ordain this My last Will & Testament in manner and form following, that is to say First, I will & desire that all my Just Debts & funeral Expences may be paid & discharged And I herby direct my Executors herinafter named that they do, within one Year of my decease sell and dispose of My Dwelling House, Garden and other Premises situate in the High Street Southampton for the most Money that can be got for the same, but if any One of My children shall be inclined to become the Purchaser for and at the Sum of Sixteen Hundred Pounds, him, or her shall have the preference, the produce of which together with all Rents due or arising therefrom shall go and be applied to the several Uses following—viz to discharge the Mortgage on my aforesaid Dwelling House and the Interest due thereon, and the following Debts prior to my Failure, viz, to Arthur Atherley Esq. One hundred Seven Pounds nineteen Shillings, to the legal Representative of the late Rev. John Peverell Thirty Seven Pounds nineteen Shillings ten pence half-penny, and to the

---

[4] HRO 1806/A/56 (I am grateful to J. Ruthven for providing a transcription of the will).

legal Representative of the late Mary Gannaway of Portswood in the County of Southampton Forty five Pounds twelve Shillings four pence, if so much shall remain due to Them at the Time of my decease—And whereas My son in Law, Edward Hellyer, did, at my request, and to assist my Daughter Charlotte, sell out One hundred Pounds five per Cent Bank Stock, which Sum, arising from such Sale, he lent unto her husband A. Cunningham and took his Note for the same, Now my Mind and Will is that My Executors shall, out of the Proceeds of the Sale of My Estate, buy in and replace the said one hundred Pounds five per Cent Bank Stock agreeable to my written Promise in the hands of My said Son in Law Edward Hellyer bearing date the eighteenth of August one thousand Eight Hundred and Two, but no interest to be paid Thereon because it never was my intention to charge My Estate with any—And my Mind and Will farther is, that the Residue or remainder, after My Executors have replaced the said Stock and paid and discharged my Debts, Funeral Expences, Mortgage, Repairs &c as aforesaid, and taken to themselves Two Guineas each for Rings, shall be divided into Six equal parts or Shares, one Part I give unto my Daughter Rosamond, One Part I give unto My Daughter Elizabeth for her own Use and benefit and the remaining Two Parts I also give unto my said Daughter Elizabeth—in Trust—out of which as she may have advanced ⌈from time to time⌉ to My late Son Daniel, and also to Matthew Preston Husband of my late Daughter Dinah and the remaining Sum after such repayment of herself, to go towards helping and assisting my Grandchildren Charlotte Linden and Dinah and Georgiana Preston at the discretion of my said Daughter Elizabeth—I give unto my Daughter Elizabeth all my Household Furniture, Linen, Goods & Chattels Whatsoever, and it is my desire that she may remain in the House ⌈rent free⌉ until such time as the same is disposed of—I give unto My Grand Son William Sydney Smith Towning My pair of Globes, I give unto my Grandson Anthony James Linden My Watch, I give unto My Grandson William Henry Linden my wearing Apparel—And I hereby nominate and appoint My Son James and my worthy Friend William Taylor of Warwick Square in the Parish of Christchurch in the City of London Printers Agent, joint Executors of this my Will, and revoking all former Wills do declare this to be My last Will and Testament—In Witness whereof I have hereunto set my Hand & Seal this twenty Seventh day of July in the year of Our Lord One Thousand eight hundred and four.

Signed and sealed by the Testator James Linden
and declared to be his last Will and Testament
in the presence of Sarah Evens Richard Evens Edward Rogers

On the 23 day of June 1806 The within named Executor James Linden was duly sworn to administer And made Oath that the Goods, Chattels and [?] of the said Deceased did not at the time of his Death amount unto the sum of One Hundred Pounds as he believes Reserving the Right of William Taylor the other Executor . . .

BIBLIOGRAPHY

MANUSCRIPT SOURCES

Barclays Bank, London
  Gosling Bank Archives
Berkshire Record Office, Reading
  Faringdon Parish Registers, D/P53/1/1–2
Bodleian Library, Oxford
  Graham Pollard Papers, MS 280
  Nichols Letters, MS Eng. lett. C.355
  Ralph Griffiths Papers, MS Add. C.89
  Robert Gosling Account Book, MS Eng. Misc. C.296
British Library, London
  Hardwicke Papers (re: *Tonson* v. *Collins*), Add. MSS 36193, 36201, 36224
  John Toland Letters and Papers, Add. MS 4295
  Newcastle Papers, Add. MS 33054
  Public Advertiser Accounts, Add. MS 38169
  Upcott Papers, Add. MSS 38728–30
  William Strahan Papers, Add. MSS 48800, 48808
Dorset Record Office, Dorchester
  Shaftesbury Holy Trinity Parish Registers
Duke University, William R. Perkins Library, Durham, NC
  Sirs George Leonard and George Thomas Staunton Papers
Guildhall Library, London
  Land Tax Assessment Books, MS 11,316
  Royal Exchange Insurance Policies, MS 7253
  Sewer Rate Books, MS 2137
  St Martin Ludgate Parish Registers, MS 10,213–14
  Sun Fire Office Fire Policies, MS 11936
India Office Library, London
  Stock Ledgers, 1738–83, L/AG/14/5/8–21
Isle of Wight Record Office, Newport
  Lease, HG/2/151
  Feet of Fines, Hampshire
National Westminster Bank, London
  Dimsdale Bank Archives
Public Record Office, London
  Lawsuits:
    Collins v. *Brewman*, CH. 12/1254/11

Collins v. *Faden*, CH, 12/104/32
Wilkes v. *Collins*, Bills and Answers, E. 112/1959/147
—— Exhibits: *Hampshire Chronicle* Account Books, E. 140/90–1
Wills:
    Henry Baldwin, PROB. 11/1510/180
    Richard Baldwin, jun. (Administrations), PROB. 31/558/245
    Richard Baldwin, sen., PROB. 11/1027/6
    Robert Baldwin, PROB. 11/1542/116
    Sarah Chauklin, PROB. 11/980/286
    Benjamin Collins, PROB. 11/1127/120
    Benjamin Charles Collins, PROB. 11/1478/368
    Francis Collins, PROB. 11/1091/274–5
    Joseph Collins, PROB. 11/1206/321
    Mary Collins, PROB. 11/1477/168
    William Collins I, PROB. 11/632/243
    William Collins III, PROB. 11/1514/81
    Edward Easton, PROB. 11/805/314
Salisbury, Personal Collection of June Coates, Bell Inn
    Benjamin Collins's Leases of the Bell Inn, Salisbury
Salisbury Journal Office, Salisbury
    Letter, Benjamin Collins to John Nourse, 2 January 1766
Stationers' Hall, London
    Register of Copies, 1710–86
Wiltshire Record Office, Trowbridge
    Assignment, 88/9/20
    Leases and Releases, 130/39, 383/646, 911/1, and 1075/87
    Solicitor's Instructions Book, 761/1
    Parish Registers:
        Laverstock Parish, 1324/1
        St Edmund's Parish, 1901/3–4
        St Thomas's Parish, 1900/7
Yale University, Beinecke Library, New Haven, CT
    Staunton Papers (Osborn Files)

PRINTED SOURCES

ALBERT, WILLIAM, *The Turnpike Road System in England 1663–1840* (Cambridge: Cambridge University Press, 1972).
ALDEN, JOHN, 'Pills and Publishing: Some Notes on the English Book Trade, 1660–1715', *Library*, 5th ser., 7 (1952), 21–37.
[ALMON, JOHN], *Memoirs of a Late Eminent Bookseller* (London: no pub., 1790).
ANDREWS, ALEXANDER, *The History of British Journalism, from the Foundation of*

the Newspaper Press in England to the Repeal of the Stamp Act in 1855, 2 vols. (London: Richard Bentley, 1859).

ANDREWS, J., and DURY, A., *A Map of Wiltshire* (London: no pub., 1773).

ASPINALL, ARTHUR, *Politics and the Press, c. 1780–1850* (London: Home & Van Thal, 1949).

——— 'Statistical Accounts of the London Newspapers in the Eighteenth Century', *English Historical Review*, 63 (1948), 201–32.

ASQUITH, IVON, 'Advertising and the Press in the Late Eighteenth and Early Nineteenth Centuries: James Perry and *The Morning Chronicle* 1790–1821', *Historical Journal*, 18 (1975), 703–24.

ASTBURY, RAYMOND, 'The Renewal of the Licensing Act in 1693 and Its Lapse in 1695', *Library*, 5th ser., 38 (1978), 296–322.

AUSTIN, ROLAND, 'Robert Raikes the Elder & the "Gloucester Journal"', *Library*, 3rd ser., 6/21 (1915), 1–24; repr. (London: Alexander Moring Ltd., 1915).

Bailey's British Directory, or Merchant's and Trader's Useful Companion, 4 vols. (London: J. Andrews, 1784).

BAKER, T. H., *Notes on St. Martin's Church and Parish* (Salisbury: Bennett Bros. for Brown & Co., 1906).

BARKER, A. D., 'Edward Cave, Samuel Johnson and the *Gentleman's Magazine*', D.Phil. thesis (Oxford University, 1981).

BARKER, HANNAH JANE, 'Catering for Provincial Tastes: Newspapers, Readership and Profit in Late Eighteenth-Century England', *Historical Research*, 69/168 (1996), 42–61.

——— 'Press, Politics and Reform: 1779–1785', D.Phil. thesis (Oxford University, 1994).

BELANGER, TERRY, 'Booksellers' Sales of Copyright: Aspects of the London Book Trade, 1718–1768', Ph.D. diss. (Columbia University, 1970).

——— 'Booksellers' Trade Sales, 1718–1768', *Library*, 5th ser., 30 (1975), 281–302.

BENSON, ROBERT and HATCHER, HENRY, *Old and New Sarum, or Salisbury* (London: Nichols, 1843).

BENTLEY, G. E., JR., 'Copyright Documents in the George Robinson Archive: William Godwin and Others 1713–1820', *Studies in Bibliography*, 35 (1982), 67–110.

——— 'The Freaks of Learning: Learned Pigs, Musical Hares and the Romantics', *Colby Library Quarterly*, 18 (1982), 87–104.

BLACK, JEREMY, *The English Press in the Eighteenth Century* (Philadelphia: University of Pennsylvania Press, 1987).

——— 'Flying a Kite: The Political Impact of the Eighteenth-Century British Press', *Journal of Newspaper and Periodical History*, 1, 2 (1985), 12–19.

BLAGDEN, CYPRIAN, 'Booksellers' Trade Sales 1718–1768', *Library*, 5th ser., 5 (1951), 243–57.

BOND, DONOVAN H., and McLEOD, W. REYNOLDS (eds.) *Newsletters to Newspapers:*

Eighteenth-Century Journalism: Papers Presented at a Bicentennial Symposium at West Virginia University, Morgantown, West Virginia March 31–April 2, 1976 (Morgantown: West Virginia University, 1977).

BOND, RICHMOND P., *Growth and Change in the Early English Press,* University of Kansas Publications, Library Series, 35 (Lawrence: University of Kansas Libraries, 1969).

—— and MARJORIE N. BOND, 'The Minute Books of the *St. James's Chronicle*', *Studies in Bibliography,* 28 (1975), 17–40.

BOOTH, FRANK, *Robert Raikes of Gloucester* (Redhill, Surrey: National Christian Education Council, 1980).

BORSAY, PETER, *The English Urban Renaissance: Culture and Society in the Provincial Town, 1660–1770* (Oxford: Clarendon Press, 1989).

BOTEIN, STEPHEN, CENSER, JACK R., and RITVO, HARRIET, 'The Periodical Press in Eighteenth-Century English and French Society: A Cross-Cultural Approach', *Comparative Studies in Society and History,* 23 (1981), 464–90.

BOURNE, H. R. FOX, *English Newspapers: Chapters in the History of Journalism,* 2 vols. (London: Chatto & Windus, 1887).

BOYCE, GEORGE, CURRAN, JAMES, and WINGATE, PAULINE (eds.), *Newspaper History from the Seventeenth Century to the Present Day* (London: Constable, 1978).

BRACK, O M, Jr. (ed.), *Writers, Books, and Trade: An Eighteenth-Century Miscellany for William B. Todd* (New York: AMS Press, 1994).

BREWER, JOHN, 'Reconstructing the Reader: Prescriptions, Texts and Strategies in Anna Larpent's Reading', in James Raven, Helen Small, and Naomi Tadmor (eds.), *The Practice and Representation of Reading in England* (Cambridge: Cambridge University Press, 1996), 226–45.

—— and PORTER, ROY (eds.), *Consumption and the World of Goods* (London: Routledge, 1993).

BRODIE, SIR BENJAMIN COLLINS, *Autobiography of the Late Sir Benjamin C. Brodie, Bart.* (London: Longman, Green, Longman, Roberts, & Green, 1865).

BROWN, P. S., 'Medicines Advertised in Eighteenth-Century Bath Newspapers', *Medical History,* 20 (1976), 152–68.

—— 'The Venders of Medicines Advertised in Eighteenth-Century Bath Newspapers', *Medical History,* 19 (1975), 352–69.

BRUSHFIELD, T. N., 'Andrew Brice, and the Early Exeter Newspaper Press', *Transactions of the Devonshire Association,* 20 (1888), 163–214.

BURNETT, DAVID, *Salisbury: The History of an English Cathedral City* (Tisbury, Wilts.: Compton Press, n.d.).

BURR, THOMAS BENGE, *The History of Tunbridge-Wells* (London: printed and sold by M. Hingeston, J. Dodsley, T. Caslon, and E. Baker, Tunbridge Wells, 1766).

BURTON, K. G., *The Early Newspaper Press in Berkshire (1723–1855)* (Reading: pub. by the author, 1954).

CAMPBELL, R., *The London Tradesman. Being a Compendious View of All the Trades,*

Professions, Arts, Both Liberal and Mechanic, Now Practised in the Cities of London and Westminster (London: printed by T. Gardner, 1747).

CARPENTER, KENNETH E. (ed.), *Books and Society in History* (New York: Bowker, 1983).

The Case as It Now Stands, between the Clothiers, Weavers, and Other Manufacturers, with Regard to the Late Riot, in the County of Wilts. . . . By Philalethes (London: printed for the author, sold by T. Cooper, 1739).

CHALKLIN, C. W., *The Provincial Towns of Georgian England: A Study of the Building Process 1740–1820* (London: Edward Arnold, 1974).

CHANDLER, JOHN, *Endless Street: A History of Salisbury and Its People* (1983; repr. with corrs., Salisbury: Hobnob Press, 1987).

CHANDLER, JOHN H., and DAGNALL, H., *The Newspaper & Almanac Stamps of Great Britain & Ireland* (Saffron Walden, Essex: Great Britain Philatelic Society, 1981).

CHRISTIE, IAN R., 'British Newspapers in the Later Georgian Age', in *Myth and Reality in Late Eighteenth-Century British Politics and Other Papers* (London: Hutchinson, 1970).

CLARK, CHARLES E., *The Public Prints: The Newspaper in Anglo-American Culture, 1665–1740* (New York and Oxford: Oxford University Press, 1994).

COLLINS, A. S., *Authorship in the Days of Johnson, being a Study of the Relation between Author, Patron, Publisher and Public, 1726–1780* (London: Robert Holden & Co., 1927).

CORFIELD, P. J., *The Impact of English Towns 1700–1800* (Oxford: Oxford University Press, 1982).

CRABBE, GEORGE, *The News-Paper: A Poem*, in his *Complete Poetical Works*, i, ed. Norma Dalrymple-Champneys and Arthur Pollard (Oxford: Clarendon Press, 1988).

CRANE, R. S., and KAYE, F. B., with the assistance of M. E. Prior, 'A Census of British Newspapers and Periodicals, 1620–1800', *Studies in Philology*, 24 (1927), 1–205.

CRANFIELD, G. A., *The Development of the Provincial Newspaper 1700–1760* (Oxford: Clarendon Press, 1962).

—— *A Handlist of English Provincial Newspapers and Periodicals, 1700–1760*, Cambridge Bibliographical Society Monographs, 2 (Cambridge: Cambridge University Press, 1952).

—— 'A Handlist of English Provincial Newspapers and Periodicals, 1700–1760. Additions and Corrections', *Transactions of the Cambridge Bibliographical Society*, 2 (1956), 269–74.

DAHL, FOLKE, *A Bibliography of English Corantos and Periodical Newsbooks 1620–1642* (London: Bibliographical Society, 1952).

DALE, CHRISTABEL, *Wiltshire Apprentices and Their Masters 1710–1760*, Wiltshire Archaeological and Natural History Society, Records Branch, 17 (Devizes: Wiltshire Archaeological and Natural History Society, 1961).

DARLOW, T. H., and MOULE, H. F., *Historical Catalogue of Printed Editions of the English Bible 1525–1961*, rev. A. S. Herbert (London: British and Foreign Bible Society, 1968).

DAVIES, ROBERT, *A Memoir of the York Press, with Notices of Authors, Printers, and Stationers in the Sixteenth, Seventeenth, and Eighteenth Centuries* (Westminster: Nichols & Sons, 1868).

DEFOE, DANIEL, *A Tour thro' the Whole Island of Great Britain, Divided into Circuits or Journies*, 3 vols. (London: printed, and sold by G. Strahan; W. Mears; R. Francklin; S. Chapman; R. Stagg; and J. Graves, 1724–7).

DOBSON, HENRY AUSTIN, *Life of Goldsmith* (London: Walter Scott, 1888).

DODSLEY, ROBERT, *The Correspondence of Robert Dodsley 1733–1764*, ed. James E. Tierney (Cambridge: Cambridge University Press, 1988).

DOWNIE, J. A., *Robert Harley and the Press: Propaganda and Public Opinion in the Age of Swift and Defoe* (Cambridge: Cambridge University Press, 1979).

DUFF, E. GORDON, *A Century of the English Book Trade* (London: The Bibliographical Society, 1905).

DUNTON, JOHN, *Life and Errors* (London: S. Malthus, 1705).

EDWARDS, F. A., 'Early Hampshire Printers', *Papers and Proceedings of the Hampshire Field Club*, 2 (1891), 110–34.

—— 'A List of Hampshire Newspapers', in *The Hampshire Antiquary and Naturalist: Being the Local Notes and Queries . . . Reprinted from 'The Hampshire Independent'*, 2 vols. (Southampton: F. A. Edwards; London: Eliot Stock, 1891).

The Eighteenth-Century Short Title Catalogue, CD-ROM version (London: The British Library, 1992); on-line version available through the Research Libraries Information Network.

ELLIOT, BLANCHE B., *A History of English Advertising* (London: Business Publications in assoc. with B. T. Batsford, 1962).

ELLIS, KENNETH, *The Post Office in the Eighteenth Century: A Study in Administrative History* (London: Oxford University Press, 1958).

FEATHER, JOHN, *Book Prospectuses before 1801 in the John Johnson Collection: A Catalogue with Microfiches* (Oxford: OMP for the Bodleian Library, 1981).

—— 'From Censorship to Copyright: Aspects of the Government's Role in the English Book Trade 1695–1775', in Kenneth E. Carpenter (ed.) *Books, and Society in History: Papers of the Association of College and Research Libraries Rare Books and Manuscripts Preconference 24–28 June, 1980, Boston, Massachusetts* (New York and London: R. R. Bowker, 1983), 173–98.

—— *A History of British Publishing* (London: Croom Helm, 1988).

—— *The Provincial Book Trade in Eighteenth-Century England* (Cambridge: Cambridge University Press, 1985).

FERDINAND, C. Y., 'Benjamin Collins: A Salisbury Printer', in M. Crump and M. Harris (eds.), *Searching the Eighteenth Century* (London: British Library, 1983), 74–92.

FERDINAND, C.Y., 'Benjamin Collins, the *Salisbury Journal*, and the Provincial Book Trade', *Library*, 6th ser., 11 (1989), 116–38.

—— 'Distribution Networks for the Local Press in the Mid-Eighteenth Century', in Robin Myers and Michael Harris (eds.), *Spreading the Word: The Distribution Networks of Print* (Winchester: St Paul's Bibliographies, 1990), 131–49.

—— 'Richard Baldwin Junior, Bookseller', *Studies in Bibliography*, 42 (1989), 254–64.

—— 'The *Salisbury Journal* 1729–1785: A Study of a Provincial Newspaper' D.Phil. thesis (Oxford University, 1990).

—— 'Selling It to the Provinces: News and Commerce round Eighteenth-Century Salisbury', in John Brewer and Roy Porter (eds.), *Consumption and the World of Goods* (London: Routledge, 1993), 393–411.

—— 'Serial Conversations: The Dialogue of the Eighteenth-Century Provincial Newspaper', in Kevin L. Cope (ed.), *Compendious Conversations* (Frankfurt am Main: Peter Lang, 1992), 116–28.

FONTAINE, LAURENCE, *History of Pedlars in Europe*, tr. Vicki Whittaker (Oxford: Polity Press, 1996).

FOXON, D. F., *English Verse 1701–1750: A Catalogue of Separately Printed Poems with Notes on Contemporary Collected Editions*, 2 vols. (Cambridge: Cambridge University Press, 1975).

—— *Pope and the Early Eighteenth-Century Book Trade*, rev. and ed. James McLaverty (Oxford: Clarendon Press, 1991).

FRANK, JOSEPH, *The Beginnings of the English Newspaper 1620–1660* (Cambridge, Mass.: Harvard University Press, 1961).

GASKELL, PHILIP, *A New Introduction to Bibliography* (Oxford: Oxford University Press, 1972).

GENT, THOMAS, *The Life of Mr. Thomas Gent, Printer, of York. Written by Himself* (London: Thomas Thorpe, 1832).

GERHOLD, DORIAN, *Road Transport before the Railways* (Cambridge: Cambridge University Press, 1993).

GODDARD, EDWARD HUNGERFORD, *Wiltshire Bibliography: A Catalogue of Printed Books, Pamphlets, and Articles bearing on the History, Topography, and Natural History of the County* (Trowbridge: no pub., 1929).

GRANT, JAMES, *The Newspaper Press: Its Origin—Progress—and Present Position*, 3 vols. (London: Tinsley, 1871–2).

GREENWOOD, JEREMY, *Newspapers and the Post Office (1635–1834)*, Special Series Publication, 26 (Reigate: Postal History Society Publications, 1971).

HAIG, ROBERT L., The *Gazetteer 1735–1797: A Study in the Eighteenth-Century English Newspaper* (Carbondale, Ill.: Southern Illinois University Press, 1960).

HANDOVER, P. M., *A History of* The London Gazette *1665–1965* (London: HMSO, 1965).

—— *Printing in London from 1476 to Modern Times* (London: George Allen & Unwin, 1960).

—— *Red and Black: The Duty and Postage Stamps Impressed on Newspapers 1712–1870 and on 'The Times' or Its Postal Wrappers from 1785 to 1962* (London: Times, 1962).

HANSON, LAURENCE, *Government and the Press, 1695–1763* (London: Oxford University Press, 1936).

HARRIS, MICHAEL, 'The London Newspaper Press, 1725–1746', Ph.D. diss. (London University, 1973).

—— *London Newspapers in the Age of Walpole: A Study of the Origins of the Modern English Press* (London and Toronto: Associated University Presses, 1987).

—— 'The Management of the London Newspaper Press during the Eighteenth Century', *Publishing History*, 4 (1978), 95–112.

—— 'Newspaper Distribution during Queen Anne's Reign: Charles Delafaye and the Secretary of State's Office', in R. W. Hunt, I. G. Philip, and R. J. Roberts (eds.) *Studies in the Book Trade in Honour of Graham Pollard* (Oxford: Oxford Bibliographical Society, 1975).

—— 'Periodicals and the Book Trade', in Robin Myers and Michael Harris (eds.), *Development of the English Book Trade 1700–1899* (Oxford: Oxford Polytechnic Press, 1981).

—— 'The Structure, Ownership and Control of the Press, 1620–1780', in George Boyce, James Curran, and Pauline Wingate (eds.), *Newspaper History from the Seventeenth Century to the Present Day* (London: Constable, 1978).

—— 'Trials and Criminal Biographies: A Case Study in Distribution', in Robin Myers and Michael Harris (eds.), *Sale and Distribution of Books from 1700* (Oxford: Oxford Polytechnic Press, 1982).

—— and ALAN LEE (eds.), *The Press in English Society from the Seventeenth to the Nineteenth Centuries* (London: Associated University Presses, 1986).

HATCHER, HENRY, *The History of Modern Wiltshire: Old and New Sarum, or Salisbury* (London: S. & J. Bentley, Wilson, & Fley, 1843).

HEY, DAVID, *Packmen, Carriers, and Packhorse Roads: Trade and Communications in North Derbyshire and South Yorkshire* (Leicester: Leicester University Press, 1980).

The History of the Salisbury Infirmary Founded by Anthony Lord Feversham, A.D. 1766 (Salisbury: Salisbury Times Co., 1922).

HODGSON, NORMA, and BLAGDON, CYPRIAN, *The Notebook of Thomas Bennet and Henry Clements (1686–1719), with Some Aspects of Book Trade Practice*, Oxford Bibliographical Society Publications, NS 6 (Oxford: Oxford University Press, 1956).

HOLMES, TIMOTHY, *Sir Benjamin Collins Brodie* (London: T. Fisher Unwin, 1898).

HUDSON, DEREK, *British Journalists and Newspapers* (London: Collins, 1935).

HUNT, F. KNIGHT, *The Fourth Estate: Contributions towards a History of Newspapers, and of the Liberty of the Press*, 2 vols. (London: Bogue, 1850).

JANSSENS-KNORSCH, U., 'The Mutual Admiration Society—or Who Reads Whom in 18th-Century Journalism', in Hans Bots (ed.), *La Diffusion et la lecture des journaux de langue française sous l'Ancien Régime: Actes du Colloque International, Nimègue, 3–5 juin 1987* (Amsterdam and Maarssen: APA-Holland University Press, 1988), 21–9.

JONSON, BEN, *The Staple of Newes*, in *The Workes of Benjamin Jonson: The Second Volume* (London: printed for Richard Meighen, 1640).

KENT, ELIZABETH EATON, *Goldsmith and His Booksellers*, Cornell Studies in English, 20 (Ithaca, NY: Cornell University Press, 1933).

KERNAN, ALVIN, *Printing Technology, Letters & Samuel Johnson* (Princeton, NJ: Princeton University Press, 1987).

KNAPP, MARY E., 'Political and Local Verse in the Early Years of the *Salisbury Journal*, and a Poem "By a Country Curate", 1742', *The Hatcher Review* (October 1983), 260–7.

—— 'Reading *The Salisbury Journal*, 1736–99', *Yale University Library Gazette*, 56 (April 1982), 7–39.

KNIGHT, CHARLES, *The Old Printer and the Modern Press* (London: John Murray, 1854).

—— *The Newspaper Stamp, and the Duty on Paper, Viewed in Relation to their Effects upon the Diffusion of Knowledge* (London: Charles Knight, 1836).

—— *Passages of a Working Life during Half a Century: With a Prelude of Early Reminiscences*, 3 vols. (London: Bradbury & Evans, 1864–5).

—— *Shadows of the Old Booksellers* (London: Bell & Daldy, 1865).

LACKINGTON, JAMES, *Memoirs of the First Forty-Five Years of the Life of James Lackington, the Present Bookseller in Chiswell-Street, Moorfields, London* (London: printed for the author, 1792).

LANGFORD, PAUL, *A Polite and Commercial People: England 1727–1783* (Oxford: Clarendon Press, 1989).

LILLYWHITE, BRYANT, *London Coffee Houses: A Reference Book of Coffee Houses of the Seventeenth, Eighteenth, and Nineteenth Centuries* (London: George Allen & Unwin, 1963).

LITTLE, MONTE, *Samuel Fancourt 1678–1768: Pioneer Librarian*, Wiltshire Monographs, 3 (Trowbridge: Wiltshire Library and Museum Service, 1984).

LONSDALE, ROGER (ed.), *Eighteenth-Century Women Poets: An Oxford Anthology* (Oxford: Oxford University Press, 1989).

—— *The New Oxford Book of Eighteenth-Century Verse* (Oxford: Oxford University Press, 1984).

LOONEY, JOHN JEFFERSON, 'Advertising and Society in England 1720–1820: A Statistical Analysis of Yorkshire Newspaper Advertisements', Ph.D. diss. (Princeton University, 1983).

—— 'Cultural Life in the Provinces: Leeds and York, 1720–1820', in A. L. Beier, David Cannadine, and James W. Rosenheim (eds.), *The First Modern Society: Essays in English History in Honour of Lawrence Stone* (Cambridge: Cambridge University Press, 1989), 483–510.

McEwen, Gilbert D., *The Oracle of the Coffee House: John Dunton's* Athenian Mercury (San Marino, Calif.: Huntington Library, 1972).

McGuinness, Rosamund, 'Newspapers and Musical Life in 18th Century London: A Systematic Analysis', *Journal of Newspaper and Periodical History*, 1, 1 (1984), 29–36.

McKendrick, Neil, 'Josiah Wedgwood: An Eighteenth-Century Entrepreneur in Salesmanship and Marketing Techniques', *Economic History Review*, 2nd ser., 12 (1960), 408–33.

—— Brewer, John, and Plumb, J. H., *The Birth of a Consumer Society: The Commercialization of Eighteenth-Century England* (Bloomington: Indiana University Press, 1982).

McKenzie, D. F., 'Printers of the Mind: Some Notes on Bibliographical Theories and Printing-House Practices', *Studies in Bibliography*, 22 (1969), 1–77.

—— *Stationers' Company Apprentices 1641–1700*, Oxford Bibliographical Society Publications, ns 17 (Oxford: Oxford Bibliographical Society, 1974).

—— *Stationers' Company Apprentices 1701–1800*, Oxford Bibliographical Society Publications, ns 19 (Oxford: Oxford Bibliographical Society, 1978).

—— and John Ross, *A Ledger of Charles Ackers, Printer of* The London Magazine, Oxford Bibliographical Society Publication, ns 15 (Oxford: Oxford Bibliographical Society, 1968).

McKerrow, R. B., *A Dictionary of Printers and Booksellers in England, Scotland and Ireland, and of Foreign Printers of English Books 1557–1640* (London: The Bibliographical Society, 1910).

[Maclaurin, John, Lord Dreghorn], *Considerations on the Nature and Origin of Literary Property* (Edinburgh: printed by Alexander Donaldson, 1767).

Mann, Julia de L. (ed.), *Documents Illustrating the Wiltshire Textile Trades in the Eighteenth Century*, Wiltshire Archaeological and Natural History Society, Records Branch, 9 (Devizes: Wiltshire Archaeological and Natural History Society, 1964).

Mathias, Peter, *The First Industrial Nation: An Economic History of Britain 1700–1914*, 2nd edn. (London: Methuen, 1983).

Maxted, Ian, *The British Book Trades, 1710–1777: An Index of Masters and Apprentices Recorded in the Inland Revenue Registers at the Public Record Office, Kew* (Exeter: Ian Maxted, 1983).

—— *The British Book Trades, 1731–1806: A Checklist of Bankrupts*, Exeter Working Papers in British Book Trade History, 4 (Exeter: Ian Maxted, 1985).

—— *The British Book Trades, 1775–1787: An Index to Insurance Policies*, Exeter Working Papers in British Book Trade History, 8 (Exeter: Ian Maxted, 1992).

—— *The Devon Book Trades: A Biographical Dictionary* (Exeter: I. Maxted, 1991).

Merrill, John C., *The Élite Press: Great Newspapers of the World* (New York: Pitman, 1968).

Milford, Robert Theodore, and Sutherland, Donald Martell, *A Catalogue of English Newspapers and Periodicals in the Bodleian Library, 1622–1800* (Oxford: no pub., 1936).

MITCHELL, C. J., 'Women in the Eighteenth-Century Book Trades', in O M Brack, Jr. (ed.), *Writers, Books, and Trade: An Eighteenth-Century English Miscellany for William B. Todd* (New York: AMS Press, 1994), 25–75.

MITCHELL, CHARLES, *The Newspaper Press Directory . . . Entirely Revised for the Year 1857* (London: C. Mitchell, [1857]).

MOENS, WILLIAM J. C., *Hampshire Allegations for Marriage Licences Granted by the Bishop of Winchester 1689–1837* (London: Harleian Society, 1893).

MORISON, STANLEY, *The English Newspaper: Some Account of the Physical Development of Journals Printed in London between 1622 & the Present Day* (Cambridge: Cambridge University Press, 1932).

—— *Ichabod Dawks and His News-Letter, with an Account of the Dawks Family of Booksellers and Stationers, 1635–1731* (Cambridge: Cambridge University Press, 1931).

MUDDIMAN, J. G. [J. B. Williams], *The King's Journalist 1659–1689: Studies in the Reign of Charles II* (London: John Lane/Bodley Head, 1923).

MULLINS, SAM, ' "And Old Mrs. Ridout and All": A Study of Salisbury's County Carriers', *Wiltshire Folklife*, 2 (1978), 29–35.

NELSON, CAROLYN, and SECCOMBE, MATTHEW (comps.), *British Newspapers and Periodicals 1641–1700: A Short-Title Catalogue of Serials Printed in England, Scotland, Ireland, and British America* (New York: Modern Language Association, 1987).

NICHOLS, JOHN, *Literary Anecdotes of the Eighteenth Century*, 9 vols. (London: Nichols, 1812–15).

OLDFIELD, JOHN, *Printers, Booksellers and Libraries in Hampshire, 1750–1800*, Hampshire Papers, 3 (Winchester: Hampshire County Council, 1993).

O'MALLEY, THOMAS, 'Religion and the Newspaper Press, 1660–1685: A Study of the *London Gazette*', in Michael Harris and Alan Lee (eds.), *The Press in English Society from the Seventeenth to the Nineteenth Centuries* (London: Associated University Presses, 1986), 25–46.

PATTERSON, A. TEMPLE, *A History of Southampton 1700–1914*, i. *An Oligarchy in Decline 1700–1835* (Southampton: University Press, 1966).

PAWSON, ERIC, *Transport and Economy: The Turnpike Roads of Eighteenth-Century Britain* (London: Academic Press, 1979).

PIPER, ALFRED CECIL, 'The Book Trade in Winchester, 1549–1789: Extracts from the Local Records of the City', *Library*, 3rd ser., 7 (1916), 191–7.

—— 'The Early Printers and Booksellers of Winchester', *Library*, NS 1 (1920), 103–10.

PLOMER, H. R., *A Dictionary of the Printers and Booksellers Who Were at Work in England, Scotland, and Ireland from 1668 to 1725* (London: The Bibliographical Society, 1922).

—— *A Dictionary of the Printers and Booksellers Who Were at Work in England,*

Scotland and Ireland from 1726 to 1775 (London: The Bibliographical Society, 1932).

PLUMB, J. H., *The Commercialisation of Leisure in Eighteenth Century England* (Reading: University of Reading, 1974).

POLLARD, A. W., and REDGRAVE, G. R., *A Short-Title Catalogue of Books Printed in England, Scotland, & Ireland and of English Books Printed Abroad, 1475–1640*, iii. Katherine F. Pantzer, *A Printers' & Publishers' Index, Other Indexes & Appendices, Cumulative Addenda & Corrigenda*, with a Chronological Index by Philip R. Rider (London: The Bibliographical Society, 1991).

POLLARD, H. G., and GRAHAM, W., 'Periodical Publications', in F. W. Bateson (ed.), *The Cambridge Bibliography of English Literature* (Cambridge: Cambridge University Press, 1940), ii. 656–739.

POPKIN, JEREMY, 'The Élite Press in the French Revolution: The *Gazette de Leyde* and the *Gazette universelle*', in Harvey Chisick (ed.), *The Press in the French Revolution* (Oxford: The Voltaire Foundation, 1991), 85–98.

PORTER, ROY, 'English Society in the Eighteenth Century Revisited', in J. Black (ed.), *British Politics and Society from Walpole to Pitt* (London: Macmillan, 1990), 29–52.

—— *Health for Sale: Quackery in England 1660–1850* (Manchester: Manchester University Press, 1989).

PRESSER, RICHARD B., 'A List of Wiltshire Patentees', *Wiltshire Notes & Queries*, 1 (1893–5), 3–6.

PRESSNELL, L. S., and ORBELL, JOHN, *A Guide to Historical Records of British Banking* (New York: St Martin's Press, 1985).

—— *Country Banking in the Industrial Revolution* (Oxford: Clarendon Press, 1956).

PRICE, J. M., 'A Note on the Circulation of the London Press 1700–1714', *Bulletin of the Institute of Historical Research*, 31 (1958), 215–24.

PROBYN, CLIVE, *The Sociable Humanist: The Life and Works of James Harris 1709–1780* (Oxford: Clarendon Press, 1991).

RABICOFF, R., and McKITTERICK, D. J., 'John Nichols, William Bowyer, and Cambridge University Press in 1765', *Transactions of the Cambridge Bibliographical Society*, 6 (1976), 328–38.

RANSOME, MARY, *Wiltshire Returns to the Bishop's Visitation Queries 1783*, Wiltshire Record Society, 27 (Devizes: Wiltshire Record Society, 1972).

RAVEN, JAMES, *Judging New Wealth: Popular Publishing and Responses to Commerce in England, 1750–1800* (Oxford: Clarendon Press, 1992).

—— 'Marts and Early Newspapers in Britain and America', *Journal of Newspaper and Periodical History*, 1, 2 (1985), 2–8.

—— 'Print and Trade in Eighteenth-Century Britain', Thirlwall Essay, Cambridge, 1985.

—— 'Serial Advertisement in 18th-Century Britain and Ireland', in Robin Myers and Michael Harris (eds.), *Serials and Their Readers, 1620–1914* (Winchester: St Paul's Bibliographies, 1993), 103–22.

RAVEN, JAMES, SMALL, HELEN, and TADMOR, NAOMI (eds.), *The Practice and Representation of Reading in England* (Cambridge: Cambridge University Press, 1996).

RAYMOND, JOAD (ed.), *Making the News: An Anthology of the Newsbooks of Revolutionary England 1641–1660* (Moreton-in-Marsh: Windrush Press, 1993).

REA, ROBERT R., *The English Press in Politics 1760–1774* (Lincoln: University of Nebraska Press, 1963).

RICHARDSON, MRS HERBERT (NORAH), 'The Old English Newspaper', English Association Pamphlet 86 (Oxford: Oxford University Press, 1933).

—— 'Supplement to the *Salisbury and Winchester Journal*' (7 June 1929).

—— 'Wiltshire Newspapers—Past and Present. Part III. The Newspapers of South Wilts', *Wiltshire Archaeological & Natural History Magazine*, 40 (1919), 318–51.

—— 'Wiltshire Newspapers—Past and Present. Part III. (*Continued*.) The Newspapers of South Wilts', *Wiltshire Archaeological & Natural History Magazine*, 41 (1920), 53–69.

—— 'Wiltshire Newspapers—Past and Present. Part III. (*Continued*.) The Newspapers of South Wilts', *Wiltshire Archaeological & Natural History Magazine*, 43 (1925–7), 26–38.

RIZZO, BETTY, ' "Innocent Frands": By Samuel Johnson', *Library*, 6th ser., 8 (1986), 249–64.

ROSCOE, SIDNEY, *John Newbery and His Successors 1740–1814* (Wormley, Herts.: Five Owls Press, 1973).

The Salisbury Guide: Giving an Account of the Antiquities of Old Sarum, and of the Ancient and Present State of the New City of Sarum . . . (Salisbury: printed and sold by E. Easton; sold also by Robert Horsfield and J. White, London, 1769).

Salisbury Journal and Times Series: The Facts [Salisbury, 1989].

SAUSSURE, CÉSAR DE, *Lettre et Voyages de Mons' César de Saussure en Allemagne, en Hollande et en Angleterre, 1725–1729* (Lausanne: George Bridel; Paris: Fischbacher; Amsterdam: Feikema, Caarelsen, 1903).

SCHWARTZ, RICHARD B., *Daily Life in Johnson's London* (Madison: University of Wisconsin Press, 1983).

SHAABER, M. A., *Some Forerunners of the Newspaper in England 1476–1622* (1929; repr. New York: Octagon Books, 1966).

SIEBERT, FREDRICK SEATON, *Freedom of the Press in England, 1476–1776: The Rise and Decline of Government Controls* (Urbana: University of Illinois Press, 1952).

SMITH, ALBERT H., *The Printing and Publication of Early Editions of the Novels of Tobias George Smollett*, 3 vols., Ph.D. diss. (London University, 1975).

SMITH, DAVID NICHOL, 'The Newspaper', in Turberville, A. S. (ed.), *Johnson's England* (1933; repr. Oxford: Clarendon Press, 1952), ii. 331–67.

SNYDER, HENRY L., 'The Circulation of Newspapers in the Reign of Queen Anne', *Library*, 5th ser., 23 (1968), 206–35.

—— 'Newsletters in England, 1689–1715: With Special Reference to John Dyer— A Byway in the History of England', in Donovan H. Bond and W. Reynolds

McLeod (eds.), *Newsletters to Newspapers: Eighteenth-Century Journalism* (Morgantown: West Virginia University Press, 1977), 3–19.

SPECK, WILLIAM, 'Politics and the Press', in Michael Harris and Alan Lee (eds.), *The Press in English Society from the Seventeenth to Nineteenth Centuries* (London: Associated University Presses, 1986), 47–63.

—— *Society and Literature in England (1700–1760)* (Dublin: Gill & Macmillan, 1983).

SPECTOR, ROBERT DONALD, *English Literary Periodicals and the Climate of Opinion during the Seven Years' War* (The Hague: Mouton & Co., 1966).

SPUFFORD, MARGARET, *Small Books and Pleasant Histories: Popular Fiction and Its Readership in Seventeenth-Century England* (Cambridge: Cambridge University Press, 1981).

STAUNTON, GEORGE THOMAS, *Memoirs of the Life & Family of the Late Sir George Leonard Staunton, Bart.* (Havant: Henry Skelton [for private circulation], 1823).

STEARNS, BERTHA-MONICA, 'The First English Periodical for Women', *Modern Philology*, 28 (1930–1), 45–59.

STYLES, JOHN, 'Print and Policing: Crime Advertising in Eighteenth-Century Provincial England', in Douglas Hay and Francis Snyder (eds.), *Policing and Prosecution in Britain 1750–1850* (Oxford: Clarendon Press, 1989), 55–111.

SULLIVAN, ALVIN (ed.), *British Literary Magazines: The Augustan Age and the Age of Johnson, 1698–1788* (Westport, Conn.: Greenwood Press, 1983).

SUTHERLAND, JAMES, 'The Circulation of Newspapers and Literary Periodicals, 1700–1730', *Library*, 4th ser., 15 (1934), 110–24.

—— *The Restoration Newspaper and Its Development* (Cambridge: Cambridge University Press, 1986).

TALBOT, WILLIAM, 'Collins of Salisbury', *Publishers' Circular and Booksellers' Record* (27 May 1933), 575.

TIERNEY, JAMES E., 'The Study of the Eighteenth-Century British Periodical: Problems and Progress', *Publications of the Bibliographical Society of America*, 69 (1975), 165–86.

TIMPERLEY, C. H., *A Dictionary of Printers and Printing, with the Progress of Literature, Ancient and Modern; Bibliographical Illustrations, etc. etc.* (London: H. Johnson, 1839).

TREADWELL, MICHAEL, 'Lists of Master Printers: The Size of the London Printing Trade, 1637–1723', in Robin Myers and Michael Harris (eds.), *Aspects of Printing from 1600* (Oxford: Oxford Polytechnic Press, 1987), 141–70.

—— 'London Trade Publishers 1675–1750', *Library*, 6th ser., 4 (1982), 99–134.

TRUSLER, JOHN, *The London Adviser and Guide: Containing Every Instruction and Information Useful and Necessary to Persons Living in London, and Coming to Reside There* (London: printed for the author, 1786; 2nd edn., 1790).

TUER, ANDREW, *History of the Hornbook* (London: Leadenhall Press, 1897).

TURBERVILLE, A. S., *Johnson's England: An Account of the Life & Manners of His Age* (1933; repr. Oxford: Clarendon Press, 1952).

TURNER, ERNEST S., *The Shocking History of Advertising* (New York: E. P. Dutton, 1953).

TURNER, MICHAEL L. (ed.), 'The Minute Book of the Partners in the *Grub Street Journal*', *Publishing History*, 4 (1978), 49–94.

TURNER, THOMAS, *The Diary of Thomas Turner, 1754–1765*, ed. David Vaisey (Oxford: Oxford University Press, 1984).

The Universal British Directory of Trade and Commerce, i, comp. Peter Barfoot and John Wilkes (London: C. Stalker; Brideoake & Fell, 1790).

Victoria County Histories:

VCH Berkshire, ii, ed. P. H. Ditchfield and William Page (London: Constable, 1907).

VCH Dorset, ii, ed. William Page (London: Constable, 1908).

VCH Gloucester, ii, ed. William Page (London: Constable, 1907).

VCH Hampshire and the Isle of Wight, v, ed. William Page (London: Constable, 1912).

VCH Somerset, ii, ed. William Page (London: Constable, 1911).

VCH Wiltshire, iv, ed. Elizabeth Crittall (London: Oxford University Press for the Institute for Historical Research, 1959).

WALKER, R. B., 'Advertising in London Newspapers, 1650–1750', *Business History*, 16 (1973), 112–30.

—— 'The Newspaper Press in the Reign of William III', *Historical Journal*, 17 (1974), 691–709.

WATT, TESSA, *Cheap Print and Popular Piety 1550–1640* (Cambridge: Cambridge University Press, 1991).

WEED, KATHERINE K., and BOND, RICHMOND P., *Studies of British Newspapers and Periodicals from Their Beginning to 1800*, *Studies in Philology*, extra ser. 2 (Chapel Hill: University of North Carolina Press, 1946).

WELSH, CHARLES, *A Bookseller of the Last Century: Being Some Account of the Life of John Newbery, and of the Books He Published, with a Notice of the Later Newberys* (London: Griffith, Farran, Okeden & Welsh; New York: E. P. Dutton, 1885).

WERKMEISTER, LUCYLE, *The London Daily Press 1772–1792* (Lincoln: University of Nebraska Press, 1963).

WILES, R. M., *Freshest Advices: Early Provincial Newspapers in England* (Columbus: Ohio State University Press, 1965).

—— 'Further Additions and Corrections to G. A. Cranfield's *Handlist of English Provincial Newspapers and Periodicals 1700–1760*', *Transactions of the Cambridge Bibliographical Society*, 2 (1958), 385–9.

—— 'Periodical Publications', in George Watson (ed.), *New Cambridge Bibliography of English Literature* (Cambridge: Cambridge University Press, 1971), ii. 1257–1390.

—— 'The Relish for Reading in Provincial England Two Centuries Ago', in Paul J. Korshin (ed.), *The Widening Circle: Essays on the Circulation of Literature in*

Eighteenth-Century Europe (Philadelphia: University of Pennsylvania Press, 1976), 85–115.

——— *Serial Publication in England before 1750* (Cambridge: Cambridge University Press, 1957).

WOODFORDE, JAMES, *The Diary of a Country Parson: The Reverend James Woodforde, 1758–[1802]*, ed. John Beresford, 5 vols. (London: Humphrey Milford, Oxford University Press, 1924–31).

WORDSWORTH, CHRISTOPHER, 'The Journal of a Wiltshire Curate, 1766 and Leaves from the Journal of the Poor Wiltshire Vicar of Cricklade in 1764–5 (Composed by Zschokke, about 1800–25)', *Wiltshire Archaeological Magazine*, 34 (1905–6), 361–73.

WRIGLEY, E. A., and SCHOFIELD, R. S., *The Population History of England 1541–1871* (Cambridge: Cambridge University Press, 1989).

YOUNG, ARTHUR, *A Six Weekes Tour, through the Southern Counties of England and Wales* (London: printed for W. Nicoll, 1768).

INDEX

Index